Fromm

Prague and the Best of the Czech Republic

by John Mastrini, Alan Crosby, and Dan Levine

Assisted by Hana Mastrini

Macmillan • USA

ABOUT THE AUTHORS

John Mastrini, who wrote Chapters 1, 6, and 7, is a former television news anchor from the United States who arrived in Prague soon after the 1989 revolution and decided to stay. He has worked in Prague as a journalist and media consultant.

Alan Crosby, who wrote Chapters 10, 11, and 12, has lived and worked as a journalist in Prague for the past six years.

Dan Levine, who updated chapters 3, 4, 5, 8, and 9, has contributed to *Europe From $50 a Day* and is the co-author of *Frommer's Walking Tours: London.* He lives in Santa Barbara, California.

Special thanks to **Hana Příhodová Mastrini,** a native of Karlovy Vary who moved to Prague in 1987 and is a veteran of the 1989 Velvet Revolution, for her help in researching and writing the Prague material in this edition.

MACMILLAN TRAVEL

A Simon & Schuster Macmillan Company
1633 Broadway
New York, NY 10019

Find us online at **http://www.mgr.com/travel** or
on America Online at **Keyword: Frommer's**

ISBN: 0-02-860903-4
ISSN: 1086-220X

Editor: Robin Michaelson
Design by Michele Laseau
Digital Cartography by Ortelius Design and John Decamillis
Maps copyright © by Simon & Schuster, Inc.

SPECIAL SALES

Bulk purchases (10+ copies) of Frommer's travel guides are available to corporations at special discounts. The Special Sales Department can produce custom editions to be used as premiums and/or for sales promotion to suit individual needs. Existing editions can be produced with custom cover imprints such as corporate logos. For more information write to: Special Sales, Simon & Schuster, 1633 Broadway, New York, NY 10019.

Manufactured in the United States of America

Contents

7 Strolling Around Prague 136

by John Mastrini

8 Prague Shopping 155

by Dan Levine

9 Prague After Dark 166

by Dan Levine

List of Maps

AN INVITATION TO THE READER

In researching this book, we discovered many wonderful places—hotels, restaurants, shops, and more. We're sure you'll find others. Please tell us about them, so we can share the information with your fellow travelers in upcoming editions. If you were disappointed with a recommendation, we'd love to know that, too. Please write to:

Frommer's Prague & the Best of the Czech Republic, 1st Edition
Macmillan Travel
1633 Broadway
New York, NY 10019

AN ADDITIONAL NOTE

Please be advised that travel information is subject to change at any time—and this is especially true of prices. We therefore suggest that you write or call ahead for confirmation when making your travel plans. The authors, editors, and publisher cannot be held responsible for the experiences of readers while traveling. Your safety is important to us, however, so we encourage you to stay alert and be aware of your surroundings. Keep a close eye on cameras, purses, and wallets, all favorite targets of thieves and pickpockets.

WHAT THE SYMBOLS MEAN

✪ **Frommer's Favorites**

Hotels, restaurants, attractions, and entertainment you should not miss.

$ **Super-Special Values**

Hotels and restaurants that offer great value for your money.

The following abbreviations are used for credit cards:

AE	American Express	EU	Eurocard
CB	Carte Blanche	JCB	Japan Credit Bank
DC	Diners Club	MC	MasterCard
DISC	Discover	V	Visa
ER	enRoute		

Introducing Prague, the City of Spires

by John Mastrini

Seen from high atop Vyšehrad, the 10-centuries-old battlement at the south end of the city, ancient Prague (*Praha* in Czech) hugs the rolling hills that rise from the river Vltava. Silhouetted steeples stacked upon onion domes jump up and pierce the sky. From this angle, the "City of a Thousand Spires" is awe-inspiring; you're looking at a nearly pristine view of a thousand years of history.

But if you look more carefully at the buildings, you'll notice that Prague's classical heart has been infected by faceless socialist architecture, the physical remains of four decades of Communist leadership. And if you look even more closely, you'll see that the grime on the decaying masterpieces is being cleaned up and the facades of many forgettable architectural follies are being etched away. A postrevolution renaissance mixed with a rush of real estate speculation is changing the city's face yet again.

Prague's sinuous brick paths have felt the hooves of king's horses, the jackboots of Hitler's armies, the heaving wheels of Soviet tanks, and the shuffling steps of students in passive revolt. Today the streets are jammed with an army of friendly invaders from across the planet. Visitors are looking for memories to take home, while entrepreneurs are searching for profit.

The combination of Prague's turbulent past with its promising future gives the city an eclectic energy. For the romantic, historian, or news junkie, Prague is a perfect end-of-millennium European destination. Another chapter in the city's triumphant yet tragic history is unfolding, as Praguers reconstruct their city after the fall of Communist rule.

The years following the 1989 bloodless citizens' revolt known as the "Velvet Revolution," one of the flurry of revolutions ending Communist rule in Eastern Europe, have been a boon to Prague tourism. The city sees itself as the westernmost of the former East Bloc capitals, both on the map and in the mind. Praguers wince when anyone uses the term "Eastern Europe" in describing their home.

In summer, visitors inundate the city and change its character, much like the way New Orleans is changed during Mardi Gras. To feel the true Czech character of the city, try coming here off-season. You'll also find more space to move in the outlying towns of the Czech Republic, making for not only an interesting but more relaxing holiday. Bohemia and Moravia are dotted with beautiful castles and spa towns that can be reached easily.

Prague's rebirth has not come without labor pains—inflated prices, traffic jams (albeit with new Western cars), people jams, and the constant pounding of construction crews. Yet these inconveniences are overlooked by citizens buoyed by a sense of confidence that came with the dollars, marks, and shillings carried by the flood of new visitors who arrived in Prague and said: "I didn't know all this was here . . ."

1 Frommer's Favorite Experiences in Prague & the Czech Republic

- **A Stroll across Charles Bridge at Dawn or Dusk:** The silhouettes of the statues lining the six-centuries-old crown jewel of Czech heritage hover like ghosts in the still of the sunrise skyline. Early in the morning you can stroll across the bridge without encountering the crowds that will be there by midday. At dusk, the statues are the same, but the odd light play makes the bridge and the city completely different than in the morning.
- **A Late Night Romp on Charles Bridge:** "Peace, Love, and Spare Change" describes the scene, as musicians, street performers, and flower people come out late at night to become one with the bridge.
- **Your Own Procession down the Royal Route:** The downhill jaunt from Prague Castle, through Malá Strana (Lesser Town), across Charles Bridge to Old Town Square is a day in itself. The trip recalls the route taken by the carriages of the Bohemian Kings; today it's lined with quirky galleries, shops, and cafes.
- **A Moment with the Children of Terezín:** On display at the Ceremonial Hall of the Old Jewish Cemetery are sketches drawn by children held at the Terezín concentration camp. These drawings are a moving lesson in the Nazi occupation of Bohemia and Moravia.
- **Getting Lost in Old Town:** Every week a new cafe nook or gallery cranny seems to pop up along the narrow winding streets of Staré Město (Old Town). Prague is best discovered by those who easily get lost on foot, and Old Town's impossible-to-navigate streets are made for it.
- **A Wander around the Practice Halls:** During hotter weather, many windows of rehearsal rooms scattered throughout Staré Město (Old Town) and Malá Strana (Lesser Town) are open. Lucky wanderers may stumble upon a free concert amid the ancient alleys.
- **An Afternoon in the Letná Beer Garden:** Nice weather also sends Czechs in search of open air and affordable beer. The tree-covered Letná Chateau (Letenský Zámeček) garden on the Letná plain is a hidden treasure that serves up a local favorite brew from Velké Popovice called "Kozel" (Goat) and a great city view.
- **Beer and Oom Pah Pah at U Fleků:** A more raucous and touristy beer experience can be found at the U Fleků beer hall in New Town. You can wash down traditional Czech dishes with U Fleků's own dark home brew, accompanied by traditional drinking music.
- **A Slow Boat down the Vltava:** Many of the city's most striking architectural landmarks can be seen from the low angle and low stress vantage point of a row boat you pilot yourself. At night, you can rent a dinghy with lanterns for a romantic ride.
- **A Faster Boat down the Vltava:** For those not willing to test their navigational skills or rowing strength, large tour boats offer similar floating views of the city, many with meals. Be sure to check the direction of your voyage so it flows past the castles and palaces.

The Czech & Slovak Republics

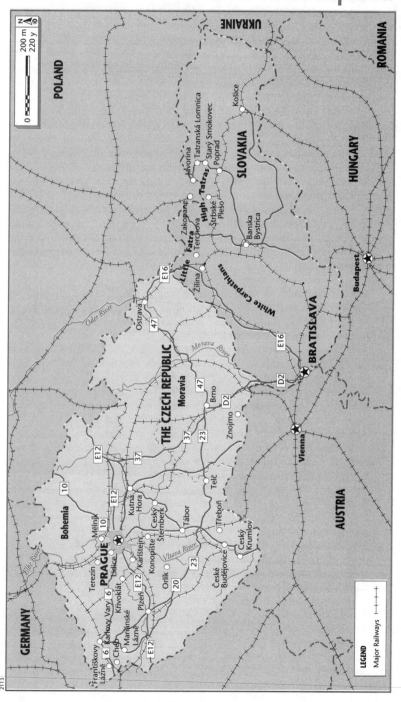

LEGEND

Major Railways

- **A Visit to a Large Communist-era Housing Estate:** Anyone wondering how most latter-day Praguers live should see these mammoth housing blocks called *paneláky*. The size astounds and piques the debate over form versus function, living versus surviving.
- **"The Wall":** The sizable American population in Prague has given rise to a shrine to the Gods of Junk Food in one corner of the K-Mart (yes, that K-Mart) on Národní Třída. The most unlikely fare (never before seen in this part of the world) forms the altar in the arteriosclerosis temple simply known as "The Wall." It's great if you've been on the road a while and crave a kitschy taste of home.
- **"Odysseus" at Laterna Magika:** This avant-garde multimedia rock musical tells the story of the fabled Greek traveler in a shockingly creative way without the need for translation. If it's playing when you are in town, and you are not easily offended by nudity, don't miss it.
- **A Picnic on Vyšehrad:** Of all the parks where you could picnic in Prague, the citadel above the Vltava that guards the south end of the old city is the most calm and interesting spot. Its more remote location means less tourist traffic, and the gardens, city panoramas, and the national cemetery provide pleasant walks and poignant history.
- **A Trip to Karlštejn Castle:** A 30-minute train ride south puts you in the most visited Czech landmark outside of Prague, built by King Charles IV (Karel IV in Czech— the namesake of Charles Bridge) in the 14th century to protect the crown jewels of the Holy Roman Empire. This Romanesque hilltop bastion fills the image of the castles of medieval lore.
- **"4-D" Jumping at Orlík:** After exploring Orlík Castle and taking a relaxing stroll through the castle gardens, you can jump into the fourth-dimension, in a variation of bungee jumping. It's quite a quick pick-me-up.
- **A Festive Beer Hall in České Budějovice:** Forget touristy remakes. Masné Krámy's spirit conjures up the feel of an 18th-century Czech pub, and the brew is as fresh as the bread.
- **New Year's Eve in Český Krumlov:** At midnight, the Plaštovy bridge at the castle overlooking the town turns into mini-United Nations, as revellers from all over gather to watch and light fireworks, see who can uncork the champagne the fastest, and just plain celebrate.
- **Relaxation in Třeboň:** If you're looking for a small Czech town not overrun with tourists, travel to Třeboň. This serene place, surrounded by forests and ponds, is a diamond in the rough, a walled city that time, war, and disaster have failed to destroy.
- **A Walk through the Šatov Wine Cellar:** Some of the finest Moravian wine is produced here, and at this wine cellar, you'll find more than the local product. The cellar's walls are carved and painted in intricate detail with scenes from Prague Castle and Snow White.

2 The City Today

The spaghetti strands of interwoven alleys that wind through Prague's Old Town have become so inundated with visitors during the high season that they now resemble an intricate network of scurrying ants looking for the next palace to devour. This town was not built for tourists.

Impressions

"Your struggle to preserve what you have inherited, and to reintegrate it into the values and character of the society you are rebuilding, is a struggle you must win, or there will not be much hope for any of us."

Britain's Prince Charles in a speech to Prague's leaders, May 1991

Although its current leaders are trying desperately to make Prague more visitor friendly, there's little they can do about the problem that is also one of the city's key attractions—those all-too-cozy honed-brick streets. But as you squeeze through to catch your first glimpse of Old Town Square (try taking the backstreets to avoid the heavy crowds), you'll suddenly find out why it's worth the push. Nowhere will you see such a unique and well-preserved panorama of baroque and Renaissance houses standing in crooked order with the ominous belfries of Týn Church eerily hovering in judgment.

Prague was spared the ravages of World War II, suffering only one brief accidental raid by American bombers who confused Prague for Dresden. Regardless of the furious development and reconstruction popping up all over the city, the classical monuments stand stoically through it all. Prague Castle's reflection in the Vltava or the mellow nighttime glow of the lanterns around the 18th-century Estates Theater (Stavovské Divadlo) give the city a Mozart-really-was-here feel. But the landmarks that make Prague a living postcard only form a picturesque backdrop for the social dramas that are playing out yet again.

The years spent under Soviet and Communist domination smothered much of Prague's psyche, but the sparks of inventiveness were never snuffed out. Prague's first attempt at regaining its lost spirit came in 1968 in the pro-democracy movement known as the "Prague Spring," which was abruptly put down in a Soviet-led invasion in August of that year. Many say the bloodless 1989 student-led uprising over Communism, dubbed by journalists as the "Velvet Revolution," carried out what was hoped for in 1968.

The city in the mid-1990s is now at ease with its new democracy and is enmeshed in its new capitalism. The castles and cathedrals that draw most visitors are now surrounded by entrepreneurs trying to make back the bucks (or *koruny*) denied them under Communism. And they are trying to make money as quickly as possible. For example, a bottle of water that costs just 15 Kč (55¢) in most shops can cost 50 Kč ($1.85) or more when purchased from a cart in the main tourist areas. Supply and demand has caught on.

Developers are making the most of new opportunities as well. The pounding of jackhammers and the tinny hollow thump of scaffolding being raised and lowered incessantly are now the sounds most familiarly mixed with the bells and whir of Prague's streetcars. Luckily, most of the city's great architecture has been left alone. But there's hardly a corner you'll turn where cobblestones haven't been dug up or sidewalks torn out. And multi-colored advertising now covers some of the city's classical facades.

Prague is a city rebuilding its face and its spirit, trying to keep up with the massive new flood of cars and visitors, and getting used to the pros and cons of its renewed affluence.

AT THE CROSSROADS OF EUROPE Prague lies in the epicenter of Bohemia, which borders Germany to the north and west and Austria to the south. Slovakia to the east—which joined with the Czechs at the end of the Austro-Hungarian Empire in 1918 to form the Republic of Czechoslovakia—split with their Slavic neighbors in 1993 to form independent Czech and Slovak Republics in what came to be known as "The Velvet Divorce" (see below).

About 10.4 million people inhabit the Czech lands of Bohemia and Moravia, with about 1.2 million living in the dozen districts that make up the Prague metropolitan area. Less than 30,000 people live in the classical quarters of the city most frequented by tourists, and that number is bound to drop as many buildings are bought and remodeled to satisfy the need for quality office space.

Most Praguers actually live in the satellite Communist-built housing estates that ring the city. In the high summer tourist season, visitors will double the number of locals in most main areas in the city center, taking away much of the city's indiginous character.

THE CZECH LANGUAGE   Bohemia, through good times and bad, has been under a strong Germanic influence, and throughout a great deal of its history, German was the practiced language of the power elite. The Czech language, however, stems from the Slavic family, which includes Polish, Russian, Slovak, and others, although many Czech words are altered from German. Czech uses a Latin alphabet with some letters topped by a small hat called a *háček* to denote Slavic phonic combinations like "sh" *š*, "ch" *č*, and everyone's favorite "rzh" *ř*. Slovak differs slightly from Czech, but Czechs and Slovaks easily understand each other's language.

English, however, has become the post-revolutionary foreign tongue of choice for most Czech movers and shakers, although little is spoken outside the capital. Outside Prague, it's rare to find someone who speaks English fluently, so be patient, expect to be misunderstood, and cultivate a sense of humor. Many new words in the Czech vocabulary derive from business English—like *marketink, manažer* (manager), *bondy* (bonds)—or pop culture, like *bingo* and *rokenrol* (rock 'n' roll).

3 A Look at the Past

Dateline

- 300 B.C. Celtic people, the Boii, settle in the area of today's Czech Republic, giving it the name Bohemia.
- A.D. 450 Huns and other Eastern peoples arrive in Bohemia.
- 870 Bohemia becomes part of Holy Roman Empire. Castle constructed in Hradčany.
- 973 Bishopric founded in Prague.
- 1158 First stone bridge spans the Vltava.
- 1234 Staré Město (Old Town) founded, the first of Prague's historic five towns.

continues

ROAMING CELTS AND THE NEW BOHEMIANS   A Celtic tribe, the Boii, first settled three hundred years before Christ in the land around the Vltava River, which forms the heart of present-day Czech territory. The Latin term Bohemia (Land of the Boii) became etched in history.

The Marcomanni, a Germanic tribe, drove out the Boii around 100 B.C., only to be pushed out by the Huns by A.D. 450. The Huns, in turn, were expelled by a Turkic tribe, the Avars, about a century later.

Near the turn of the sixth century, Slavs crossed the Carpathian Mountains into Europe, and the westernmost of the Slavic tribes tried to set up a kingdom in Bohemia. The farming Slavs often fell prey to the nomadic Avars, but in 624 they united under a Franconian merchant named Samo to begin expelling the Avars from Central Europe.

CYRIL AND METHODIUS IN THE MORAVIAN EMPIRE

Throughout the ninth century the Slavs around the River Morava consolidated their power. Mojmír I declared the foundation of the Great Moravian Empire—a kingdom that eventually encompassed Bohemia, Slovakia, and parts of modern Poland and Hungary—in a Christian order still outside the boundaries of the Holy Roman Empire.

In 863 the Greek brothers Cyril and Methodius arrived in Moravia to preach the Eastern Christian rite to a people who did not understand them. They created a new language mixing Slavic with a separate script, which came to be known as Cyrillic. When Methodius died in 885, the Moravian rulers re-established the Latin liturgy, although followers of Cyril and Methodius continued to preach their faith in missions to the East. Ultimately the Slavonic rite took hold in Kiev and Russia where the Cyrillic alphabet is still used, while western Slavs kept the Latin script and followed Rome.

The Great Moravian Empire only lasted about a century—until the Magyar invasion of 896—and not until the 20th century would the Czechs and Slovaks unite under a single government. After the invasion, the Slavs living east of the River Morava swore allegiance to the Magyars, while the Czechs, who lived west of the river, fell under the authority of the Holy Roman Empire.

BOHEMIA LOOKS TO THE WEST

Bořivoj, the first king of the now separate Czech lands of Bohemia and Moravia, built Prague's first royal palace at the end of the ninth century on the site of the present-day Prague Castle on Hradčany hill. In 973 a bishopric was established in Prague, answering to the archbishopric of Mainz. Thus, before the end of the first millennium, the German influence in Bohemia was firmly established.

The kings who followed Bořivoj in the Přemyslid dynasty ruled over Bohemia for more than 300 years, during which time Prague became a major commercial area along Central Europe's trade routes. In the 12th century, two fortified castles were already built at Vyšehrad and Hradčany, and a wooden plank bridge stood near where the stone Charles Bridge spans the Vltava today. Václavské náměstí (Wenceslas Square) was a small horse market, and the city's 3,500 residents rarely lived to see their 45th birthday. In 1234, Staré Město (Old

- **1257** Malá Strana (Lesser Town) established by German colonists.
- **1306** Přemyslid dynasty ends following the death of teenage Václav III, who has leaves no heir.
- **1344** Prague bishopric raised to an archbishopric.
- **1346** Charles IV becomes king and Holy Roman Emperor, as Prague's Golden Age begins.
- **1403** Jan Hus becomes rector of the University of Prague, and launches a crusade for religious reform.
- **1415** Hus burned at the stake by German Catholics, and decades of religious warfare begin.
- **1419** Roman Catholic councilors thrown from the windows of New Town Hall in the First Defenestration.
- **1434** Radical Hussites, called Taborites, defeated in the Battle of Lipany, ending religious warfare.
- **1526** Roman Catholic Habsburgs gain control of Bohemia.
- **1584** Prague made seat of the imperial court of Rudolf II.
- **1618** Second Defenestration helps ignite Thirty Years' War, entrenching Habsburg rule.
- **1648** Praguers defend the city against invading Sweden—the last military action of the Thirty Years' War.
- **1784** Prague's four towns united.
- **1818** National Museum founded.
- **1848** Industrial Revolution begins in Prague, drawing people from countryside and fueling Czech national revival.

continues

- **1875** Horse-drawn trams operate on Prague's streets.
- **1881** National Theater completed during wave of Czech push for statehood against Austro-Hungarian rule.
- **1883** Franz Kafka is born in Staré Město.
- **1918** Czechoslovakia founded at the end of World War I after the fall of the Austro-Hungarian Empire. Independence leader Tomáš G. Masaryk becomes first president.
- **1921** Prague's boundaries expand to encompass neighboring villages and settlements.
- **1938** Leaders of Germany, Great Britain, Italy, and France meet to award Czech border territories (The Sudetenland) in the Munich Agreement, an attempt to appease Hitler.
- **1939** Hitler absorbs the rest of the Czech lands as a German protectorate; puppet Slovak Republic established.
- **1940s** In World War II more than 130,000 Czechs are murdered, including more then 80,000 Jews.
- **1942** Nazi protectorate leader Reinhard Heydrich assassinated in Prague by soldiers trained in England. Hitler retaliates with the mass murder and destruction of the nearby village of Lidice.
- **1945** American army liberates western Bohemia, Soviet army liberates Prague; 2.5 million Germans expelled, their property expropriated under decrees of returning President Edvard Beneš.
- **1946** Communist leader Klement Gottwald appointed prime minister after his party wins 38% of vote.

continues

Town), the first of Prague's historic five towns, was founded.

Encouraged by Bohemia's rulers, who guaranteed German civic rights to western settlers, Germans established entire towns around Prague, including Malá Strana (Lesser Town), which was founded between the castle and Staré Město in 1257. The Přemyslid dynasty of the Czechs ended with the death of teenage Václav III in 1306, who had no heirs. After much debate, the throne was offered to John of Luxembourg, husband of Václav III's younger sister, who spent little time in Bohemia. It would be John's first-born son who would leave the most lasting marks on Prague.

CHARLES IV BUILDS PRAGUE'S FIRST GOLDEN AGE   Charles IV (Karel IV), christened first as Václav, took the throne when his father died while fighting in France in 1346. Educated among French royalty and fluent in four languages (but not Czech), Charles almost single-handedly ushered in Prague's first golden age (the second began in the late 16th century).

Even before his reign, Charles wanted to make Prague a glorious city (he eventually learned to speak Czech). In 1344, Charles had won an archbishopric for Prague independent of Mainz, and when he became king of Bohemia, Charles also became, by election, Holy Roman Emperor.

During the next 30 years of his reign, Charles transformed Prague into the bustling capital of the Holy Roman Empire and one of the most important cities in Europe, with some of the most glorious architecture of its day. Charles commissioned St. Vitus Cathedral's construction at Prague Castle as well as the bridge that would eventually bear his name. He was most proud of founding the University of Prague in 1348, the first higher education institution in Central Europe, which is now known as Charles University. In 1378, Charles died of natural causes; he was 62 years old.

JAN HUS & THE PROTESTANT REFORMATION   While Charles IV's reign was the most heralded of the Bohemian kings, the short-lived reign of his son Václav IV was marked by serious social upheaval, a devastating plague, and the emergence of turbulent religious dissent.

Reformist priest Jan Hus drew large crowds to Prague's Bethlehem Chapel preaching against what he considered the corrupt tendencies of Prague's bishopric. Hus became widely popular among Czech nationals who rallied behind his crusade against the German-dominated religious and political establishment. Excommunicated in 1412, and charged with heresy two years later, Hus was burned at the stake on July 6, 1415 in Konstanz (Constance), Germany, an event that sparked widespread riots and, ultimately, civil war.

THE HUSSITE WARS The hostilities began simply enough. Rioting Hussites threw several Roman Catholic councilors to their deaths from the windows of Prague's New Town Hall (Novoměstská radnice) in 1419, a deed popularly known as the First Defenestration. It didn't take long for the Pope to declare a crusade against the Czech heretics. The conflict widened into a class struggle, and by 1420 several major battles had been fought between the peasant Hussites and the Catholic crusaders, who were supported by the nobility. A schism split the Hussites when a more moderate faction, known as the Utraquists, signed a 1433 peace agreement with Rome at the Council of Basel. Still the more radical Taborites continued to fight, until they were decisively defeated at the Battle of Lipany.

HABSBURG RULE In the period that followed, the nobility of Bohemia began to concentrate its power, forming fiefdoms called the Estates. In 1526, the nobles elected Archduke Ferdinand king of Bohemia. This marks the beginning of Roman Catholic Habsburg rule, which continued until World War I. Emperor Rudolf II ascended to the throne in 1576 and presided over what was to become known as Prague's second golden age. Rudolf re-established Prague as the seat of the Habsburg empire. He invited the great astronomers Johannes Kepler and Tycho de Brahe to Prague, and endowed the city's museums with some of the best art in Europe. The Rudolfinum, which was recently restored and houses the Czech Philharmonic, pays tribute to Rudolf's opulence.

Conflicts between the Catholic Habsburgs and Bohemia's growing Protestant nobility came to a head on May 23, 1618, when two Catholic governors were thrown out of the windows of Prague Castle, in the Second Defenestration. This event marked the start of a series of complex political and religious conflicts known as the Thirty Years' War, during which Bohemia was a battleground for Roman Catholic and Protestant armies. After a Swedish army was defeated on Charles Bridge by

- **1948** Communists seize power amid cabinet crisis.
- **1950s** Top Jewish Communists executed in purge as Stalinism reaches its peak. Giant statue of Stalin unveiled on Letná plain overlooking Prague.
- **1968** Alexander Dubček becomes General Secretary of the Communist Party and launches "Prague Spring" reforms; in August, Soviet-led Warsaw Pact troops invade and occupy Czechoslovakia.
- **1977** Czech dissidents form Charter 77 to protest suppression of human rights.
- **1989** Student-led anti-government protests erupt into revolution; Communist government resigns; Parliament nominates playwright Václav Havel as president.
- **1990** Free elections held; Havel's Civic Forum captures 170 of 300 parliamentary seats.
- **1991** Country begins massive program of privatizing shares in thousands of companies by distributing coupons that could be exchanged for stock.
- **1992** Havel resigns saying he doesn't want to preside over the division of Czechoslovakia.
- **1993** Czechoslovakia splits into independent Czech and Slovak states—"The Velvet Divorce"—in mutual agreement of cabinets. Havel accepts new five-year term as president of the independent Czech Republic. Country given first investment-grade rating of any post-Communist country by U.S. bond agencies.
- **1994** Czech Republic applies to join the OECD, the organization of the world's

continues

- 25 richest countries. Confirmation expected by 1996.
- 1995 Soldiers begin training in NATO's Partnership for Peace program setting stage for hoped-for membership. The cabinet drafts application for full European Union membership, saying it expects to get in by 2000.
- 1996 Parliamentary general elections scheduled for June.

a local force that included Prague's Jews and students, the Thirty Years' War came to an end with the Peace of Westphalia. The Catholics won a decisive victory, and the focus of empire shifted back to Vienna. Fresh waves of immigrants practically turned Prague and other towns into German cities. By the end of the 18th century, the Czech language was on the verge of dying out.

THE CZECH REVIVAL   In the 19th century, the Industrial Revolution drew Czechs from the countryside into Prague, where a Czech national revival began.

As the industrial economy grew, Prague's Czech population increased in number and power, overtaking the Germans. In 1868, the Czech people threw open the doors to the gilded symbol of their revival, the neo-Renaissance National Theater (Národní divadlo), with the bold proclamation *"Národ Sobě"* ("the Nation to Itself") inscribed over the proscenium of the stage. That was further augmented by the massive National Museum building (Národní muzeum), completed in 1890 at the top of Wenceslas Square and packed with exhibits proclaiming the rich history and culture of the Czech people.

As the new century emerged, Prague was on the cusp of the art nouveau wave sweeping Europe, and the Moravian Alfons Mucha's sensuous painting of Sarah Bernhardt set the standard in Paris.

MASARYK AND THE FOUNDING OF CZECHOSLOVAKIA   As Czech political parties continued to call for more autonomy from Vienna, Archduke Ferdinand, the Austrian prince and proprietor of the Konopiště manor south of Prague, was assassinated in Sarajevo, setting off World War I. Meanwhile, a 65-year-old philosophy professor named Tomáš Masaryk seized the opportunity during the war to tour Europe and the United States speaking in favor of creating a combined Czech and Slovak nation state. He was supported by a Slovak scientist, Milan Štefánik.

As the German and Austrian armies wore down in 1918, the concept of "Czechoslovakia" gained international support. U.S. President Woodrow Wilson joined Masaryk on October 18, 1918, in Washington, D.C., as Masaryk proclaimed the independence of the Czechoslovak state in the so-called "Washington Declaration." On October 28, 1918, the sovereign Republic of Czechoslovakia was founded in Prague. Masaryk returned to Prague in December after being elected Czechoslovakia's first president in absentia.

THE RISE AND FALL OF THE FIRST REPUBLIC   The 1920s ushered in an exceptional but brief period of freedom and prosperity in Prague. Czechoslovakia, its industrial strength intact after the war, was one of the ten strongest economies in the world. Prague's capitalists shined their spats and lived the Jazz Age on a par with New York's industrial barons. Palatial art nouveau villas graced the fashionable Bubeneč and Hanspaulka districts, where smart parties were held nonstop.

The depression of the 1930s gradually spread to Prague, drawing sharper lines between the classes and nationalities throughout the country. As ethnic Germans in Czech border regions found a champion in new German Chancellor Adolph Hitler in 1933, their calls to unify under the Third Reich grew louder.

In 1938, Britain's Neville Chamberlain and France's Edouard Daladier, seeking to avoid conflict with the increasingly belligerent Germans, met Hitler and Italy's Benito Mussolini in Munich. Their agreement to cede the Bohemian areas, which Germans called the Sudetenland, to Hitler on September 30 marked one of the darkest days in Czech history.

Chamberlain returned to London and told a cheering crowd that he had achieved "peace in our time." But within a year, Hitler and the Nazis absorbed the rest of the Czech lands, and installed a puppet government in Slovakia. Soon Europe was again at war.

WORLD WAR II During the next six years, more than 130,000 Czechs were systematically murdered, including more than 80,000 Jews. Hitler sought to preserve much of Prague and its Jewish ghetto as part of his planned museum of the extinct race.

The Nazi concentration camp at Terezín, about 30 miles northwest of Prague, became a way station for many Czech Jews on their way to death camps at Auschwitz and Buchenwald. Thousands died of starvation and disease at Terezín although the Nazis used it as a "show" camp for Red Cross investigators.

Meanwhile, the Czechoslovak government in exile, led by Masaryk's successor Edvard Beneš, tried to organize resistance from friendly territory in London. One initiative of resistance occurred in May 1942 when two Czechoslovak paratroopers, in a mission called "Anthropoid," attempted to assassinate Hitler's lead man in Prague, Reich Protector Reinhard Heydrich. Setting a charge at an intersection north of Prague, the soldiers stopped Heydrich's limousine and opened fire, seriously wounding him. He later died.

Soon after, Hitler retaliated by ordering the total liquidation of a nearby Czech village, Lidice, where 192 men were shot dead and more than 300 women and children were sent to concentration camps. Every building in the town was bulldozed to the ground.

The soldiers, Jozef Gabčík, and Jan Kubiš, were eventually hunted down by Nazi police and trapped in the Cyril and Methodius church on Ječná street near the Vltava. They reportedly committed suicide, shooting themselves, to avoid capture. The debate still rages whether "Anthropoid" brought anything but more terror to occupied Bohemia.

THE WAR ENDS, COMMUNISM BEGINS The final act of World War II in Europe played out where the Nazis started it, in Bohemia. As American troops liberated the western part of the country, General George Patton was told to hold his troops at Plzeň and wait for the Soviet army to sweep through Prague because of the Allied Powers agreement made at Yalta months before. Soviet soldiers and Czech civilians liberated Prague on May 9, 1945, a day after the Germans had signed their capitulation.

On his return from exile in England, President Edvard Beneš ordered the expulsion of 2.5 million Germans from Czechoslovakia and the confiscation of all their property. (Many Sudeten Germans are still seeking compensation for the property today, complicating post-Communist relations between Bonn and Prague.) Meanwhile, the postwar Czech government, exhausted and bewildered by fascism, nationalized 60% of the country's industries, and many looked to Soviet-style Communism as a new model. Elections were held in 1946, and Communist leader Klement Gottwald became prime minister after his party won about one third of the vote.

Through a series of cabinet maneuvers, Communists seized full control of the government in 1948, and Beneš was ousted. Little dissent was tolerated, and a series of show trials began, purging hundreds of perceived threats to Stalinist Communist authority. Another wave of political refugees fled the country. The sterile, faceless style of centrally planned Communist architecture began seeping into classical Prague.

PRAGUE SPRING   In January 1968 Alexander Dubček, a career Slovak Communist, became First Secretary of the Czechoslovak Communist Party. He began to build a new kind of Communism that he called "socialism with a human face." His program of political, economic, and social reform (while still seeking to maintain one-party rule) blossomed into a brief intellectual and artistic renaissance known as the "Prague Spring."

Increasingly nervous about what seemed to them as a loss of party control, Communist hard-liners in Prague and other East European capitals conspired with the Soviet Union to remove Dubček and the government. On Wednesday morning, August 21, 1968, Praguers awoke to the rumble of tanks and 200,000 invading Warsaw Pact soldiers claiming "fraternal assistance." Believing they would be welcomed as liberators, these soldiers from the Soviet Union, Poland, East Germany, Bulgaria, and Hungary were bewildered when angry Czechs confronted them with rocks and flaming torches. The Communist grip tightened, however, and Prague fell deeper into the Soviet sphere of influence. Another wave of political refugees fled the country. The following January, a university student named Jan Palach walked onto Wenceslas Square and in a lonely protest to Soviet occupation doused himself with gasoline and set himself on fire. He died in the hospital days later. The Soviet soldiers stayed for more than two decades during the gray period the Communists called "normalization."

CHARTER 77   In 1976, during the worst of "normalization," the Communist government arrested a popular underground rock band called the *Plastic People of the Universe* on charges of disturbing the peace. This motivated a group of Prague's most prominent artists, writers, and intellectuals, led by playwright Václav Havel, to establish Charter 77, a human-rights advocacy group formed to pressure the government—then the most repressive in Europe—into observing the principles of the Helsinki Accords. In the years that followed, Havel, the group's perceived leader, was constantly monitored by the secret police, the StB, and was put under house arrest and jailed several times for threatening public order.

4   The Velvet Revolution & Beyond

Just after the Berlin Wall fell, thousands of students set out on a chilly candlelight march on November 17, 1989. As part of their nonviolent campaign, they held signs simply asking for a dialogue with the government. Against police warnings, the students marched from the southern citadel at Vyšehrad and turned up the wide National boulevard, Národní Třída, where they soon met columns of helmeted riot police. Holding fingers in peace signs and chanting "our hands are free," the bravest 500 or so students sat down at the feet of the surrounding police. After an excruciating standoff, the police moved in, squeezing the group against buildings and wildly beating the young men and women with their clubs.

Although nobody was killed and the official Communist-run media played the story as the quiet, justified end to the whims of student radicals, clandestine video tapes and accounts of the incident blanketed the country. By the next day, Praguers began organizing their outrage. Havel and his artistic allies seized the moment and called a meeting of intellectuals at the Laterna Magika theater on Národní, where they planned more nonviolent protests. Students and theaters went on strike, and hundreds of thousands of Praguers began pouring into Wenceslas Square, chanting for the end of Communist rule. Within days of the student protest, factory workers and citizens in towns throughout the country joined in a general strike. In Wenceslas Square, the protesters jingled their keys, a signal to the Politburo that it was time to go. On November 24, General Secretary Miloš Jakeš resigned, and by the end of year, the Communist government fell. By New Year's Eve, Havel, joined by Dubček, gave his first speech as president of a free Czechoslovakia. Because hardly any blood was spilled, the nonviolent coup d'etat earned the name the "Velvet Revolution."

ECONOMIC & POLITICAL CHANGES   In June 1990, the first free elections in 44 years gave power to Civic Forum, the movement led by Havel. But it would be another Václav, this one named Klaus, who launched the country on its hyperspeed course of economic reform. First as federal finance minister and then as Czech prime minister, Klaus, an economist, helped form a right-wing off-shoot of Civic Forum called the Civic Democratic Party (ODS). The ODS won the 1992 elections on a program of massive privatization. First, thousands of small businesses, such as fruit shops, shoe shops, flower shops, and restaurants, were auctioned off for a song. By the end of 1994, shares in some 1,800 large companies were privatized by giving citizens, for a nominal fee, government coupons that could be exchanged for stock or fund shares. In less than five years, private companies churned out 80% of the Czech economy (growing at a robust 4% rate in 1995). Privatization, however, did little to bring in new capital or reorganize management at larger companies. As a result, the country has begun to swing into a major trade deficit as Czechs buy up Western goods and equipment with their new wealth and ignore domestic suppliers.

While voices of discontent have grown louder as socioeconomic divisions have widened, the Czech reforms have been the most politically stable of any in the former East Bloc. Klaus and his center-right government, however, appeared to be facing a stiff challenge by the opposition Social Democrats in elections scheduled for June 1996. Meanwhile, the successors to the Communist party have had little success returning to government the way they have in Poland and Hungary.

While Prague has been the engine for political and economic transformation, cities and towns in the Czech Republic have caught the fever of capitalism. The second city, Brno, has become a thriving center for trade shows, and trappings of tourism are appearing in the most prominent castle villages and spa towns.

Czech politicians have moved quickly to prove to the world that the country belongs in the league of industrialized nations. In December 1995, the Czech Republic became the 26th member—and the first former communist member—of the Organization for Economic Cooperation and Development (OECD), the Paris-based club of advanced economies.

THE VELVET DIVORCE   During 1992, leaders of the Czech and Slovak republics peacefully agreed to split into separate states. The Slovaks wanted to get out of

Impressions

"In an atmosphere of decency, creativity, tolerance, and quiet resolution, we shall bear far more easily the trials we have yet to experience, and resolve all the large problems we must face."

—Czech President Václav Havel in a New Year's address to the nation,
January 1, 1992

From Prisoner to President: Václav Havel

His personal crusade for morality in politics has made him a most unlikely world leader.

Born in 1936 to a wealthy building developer, Václav Havel was on the wrong side of Communism's bourgeois divide and therefore was not allowed a top education. His interest in theater grew from his first stint as a set boy and led to the staging of his first plays at Prague's Theater on the Balustrade (Divadlo na Zábradlí). His play *The Garden Party* was widely acclaimed. He became the dissident playwright from the place he would later call "Absurdistan." After Havel publicly criticized the Soviet invasion and Communist policies, his plays and essays were banned.

In 1977, he helped draft Charter 77, a manifesto urging the government to respect human rights and decency. He was under almost constant surveillance by the secret police, the StB, first put under house arrest and then put in prison on numerous occasions for his views. Havel's philosophical writings about life under repression during the period— especially his essay "The Power of the Powerless"— became world-renowned for their insight into the dark gray world behind the Iron Curtain.

Soon after Havel helped lead the citizen's movement Civic Forum that ousted the Communist government in 1989, he told a joint session of U.S. Congress in Washington, D.C. why he accepted the offer to become president of Czechoslovakia. "Intellectuals cannot go on forever avoiding their share of responsibility for the world and hiding their distaste for politics under an alleged need to be independent," he said.

Virtually overnight, Havel had moved from the prison dungeon to the presidential throne, although he chose to live in his modest apartment on the river even when he could have lived in Prague Castle. (He has since bought and now lives in a stylish villa in the smart part of town.) Havel, however, has not dirtied his hands much in the rough and tumble of post-revolution politics, instead using his mostly ceremonial post to act as the country's moral balancing wheel, warning against the possible excesses of the new freedoms.

"From the West we have learned to live in a soulless world of stupid advertisements and even more stupid sitcoms and we are allowing them to drain our lives and our spirits," he told the nation in a speech marking the fifth anniversary of the Velvet Revolution.

Havel has been nominated for the Nobel Peace Prize every year since the Velvet Revolution but has yet to win it. Still, he has received a global vault full of medals and commendations, including the prestigious Roosevelt Four-Freedoms Medal, the Philadelphia Freedom Medal, France's *Grande Croix de la Légion d' Honneur*, and India's Indira Gandhi Prize. An unabashed fan of rock music artists, Havel has kept close company with Frank Zappa, Lou Reed, Pink Floyd, Bob Dylan, and Joan Baez, and he even once held up runway traffic at an Australian airport so he could have a conversation on the tarmac with Mick Jagger and the Rolling Stones.

the shadow of Prague (Slovak nationalists had been calling for that since 1918), and the Czech government was happy to get rid of the expected financial burdens of Slovakia's slower reconstruction. The amicable "Velvet Divorce" was final on January 1, 1993, with common property split on a 2-to-1 ratio, without lawyers taking anything—yet. They still are arguing over gold reserves, trade payment accounts, and bank ownership, just like a real divorce.

Slovakia has since seen its share of political turbulence. The government of Vladimír Mečiar was ousted in a parliamentary vote of no confidence in March 1994, after a very public battle with President Michal Kováč over the direction of economic and political reforms. But Mečiar, a populist-nationalist, was re-elected in October 1994, and formed a coalition government in a peculiar pact with a leftist workers' party and an ultra-nationalist right-wing party.

Headlines out of the capital, Bratislava, have again been filled with verbal vollies between Mečiar and Kováč. While economic growth has begun to pick up, foreign investors have been wary about sinking their money into Slovakia until the political picture becomes clearer.

While many Czech and Slovaks still lament the end of Czechoslovakia, many observers believe that the split allowed both countries to work out their own problems and begin to thrive.

CRIME AND RACISM   Throughout Eastern Europe, overt racism appears to be an unwelcome by-product of revolution. The demise of iron-fisted Communist control over the Czech lands, combined with a more competitive economy, has resulted in the public expression of long-held racist sentiments. Romanies (Gypsies) and Jews have been the targets of most attacks. The government has stepped up efforts to weed out and crack down on these racist groups after several violent incidents. It is unclear whether these hate crimes are occurring more or are just being more openly reported; regardless, the racist groups are becoming more visible and vocal.

With police carrying a smaller stick, crime has risen sharply, as pickpockets and car thieves take advantage of Prague's new prosperity. Violent crime, while rising, is still well under American levels, and Prague's streets and parks are safer than those in most large Western cities.

5 The Spoils of Revolution: Capitalism & Culture

Prague has once again become a well-heeled business center in the heart of Central Europe. Both nostalgic Czechs and successful Czechs say that it is capitalism, not communism, that comes most naturally to citizens. But what's happening to Prague's classical soul as capitalism seeps in?

THE FIRST REPUBLIC LIVES ON   If you talk to a Praguer long enough, the conversation will often turn into a lecture about how the country had the world's sixth-richest economy, per capita, between the World Wars. Communism, a Praguer will say, was just a detour. The between-wars period, lovingly called the "First Republic," recalls a time when democracy and capitalism thrived here, and Prague's bistros and dance halls were filled with dandies and flappers swinging the night away.

The "First Republic" motif has been revived in many clubs and restaurants, and shades of this style can be seen in Czech editions of top Western fashion magazines. Swing music has become popular again; crooner Ondřej Havelka has taken his place on the pop hit parade.

KEEPING UP WITH THE NOVAKS—THE "*NOVO-BOHATÝ*"   Since the Velvet Revolution, Praguers have been obsessed with style. Many people rushed out to buy the flashiest Mercedes or BMW they could find with the quick money gained from the restitution of Communist-seized property. The Czech edition of *Playboy* magazine became the handbook for the *novo-bohatý* (nouveau riche), with step-by-step instructions on how to see and be seen at the city's most opulent balls.

While the average annual income per person is still less than $4,000, the trappings of conspicuous consumption are evident throughout Prague, from the designer boutiques in the city center to the newly developed luxury suburbs with split-level ranch executive homes and tailored lawns. Women's fashion has had the most stunning evolution in the past five years; the blur of loud polyester minidresses that used

The American Invasion

After the Velvet Revolution, Czechs sought the antithesis of Communism—namely anything that could be called "Western." And Westerners became quite curious about life on the other side of the raised Iron Curtain, and excited to find a new market.

So post-revolutionary Prague quickly came to know a once-rare species in this part of the world: the American. An estimated 30,000 live here either legally or illegally. Many are twentysomethings who heard that the inevitable job hunt could be postponed in a place where free love, cheap beer, and bad poetry were the order of the day. Some claimed it was their chance to get a taste of the 1960s that their parents had always talked about.

But Prague did not replicate the Left Bank of Paris in the 1920s or San Francisco's Haight-Ashbury in the 1960s, according to veterans of both eras. Instead, Prague offered an environment charged with the first feel of freedom on people's skin after years of repression. Yet today's Western consumer habits make being "Bohemian" in Bohemia somewhat ironic. "There's no bathtub," or "I can't find any iceberg lettuce," complain the sandalled masses, yearning to drink beer and "get away" from life in the United States.

With the American invasion came the inevitable array of shops and services for those who really did not want to wander that far from home. At the spot on Národni Třida (National Boulevard) where the Velvet Revolution began, the U.S. discount retailer K-Mart bought out an old Communist state department store known as the *Maj*. The store, K-Mart's first in Europe, featured its famous half-off "Blue Light Special" sales (the flashing *Modré Svetlo* in Czech). Deep in the bowels of K-Mart, shelf upon shelf of peanut butter, microwave popcorn, nacho cheese tortilla chips, and fudge brownie mix called faithful junkfood expatriates to prayer. But the future of this "Junkfood War" is unclear. In spring 1996, the British retailer Tesco bought the store from K-Mart. Those who still crave canned chili are pleading with Tesco to let the wall stand.

At one point, three weekly newspapers and a daily were battling for the English-language audience, as were two magazines, a radio station, and several theater productions. Sports bars, taco bars, and New York and Chicago-style pizzerias have opened—even a surf shop (odd in a country with no coastline, but those who know say surfing is merely a state of mind). At this writing, however, rising rents and beer prices, coupled with a lack of jobs with Western-level pay, are starting to push many young Americans back home—or perhaps these young Americans are assimilating better and don't stick out as much anymore.

But while many Czechs welcomed the "Americány" soon after the Velvet Revolution, they are now using the pejorative moniker "Amíci" more frequently. Perhaps familiarity does breed contempt. The English-language daily newspaper and one weekly paper, plus the radio station, have died a quiet death, and most Americans who arrive in Prague today sport tailored suits and wingtips instead of plaid flannel shirts and sandals. Still, American pop culture—and accents—have made a lasting mark on post-Communist Bohemia.

to be seen on Prague's streets are now a chic sampling of the latest looks from Europe's catwalks.

GOING WEST POLITICALLY   While Praguers tend to look Westward and insist that they never belonged in the Soviet Bloc, the average Czech has been ambivalent about the government's rapid push to join the European Union and the NATO security alliance. According to opinion polls, a majority of Czechs are not interested in being in either institution. That is understandable after a long history of living under various foreign spheres of influence. Still, the government presses on with membership plans, expecting to be enrolled in both groups by the end of the century.

WHERE TO FIND A TRUE BOHEMIAN   In the evening, a typical, real Bohemian can be found playing cards with friends at the neighborhood *pivnice* (beer hall), or debating at a nearby *kavárna* (cafe). Most likely, though, the characteristic Czech will be parked in front of the television, as the country maintains one of the highest per capita nightly viewing audiences in Europe. Not that there's a lot to choose from—only three nationwide channels exist with a fourth on the way. But TV Nova—a venture launched by New York cosmetics heir Ronald Lauder's company—attracts around 70% of the country's population with its nightly mix of dubbed American action films, sitcoms (*M*A*S*H* is most popular), and tabloid-esque news shows.

Even pop culture reading materials have overwhelmed the classics since the Velvet Revolution, with scandal sheets surging in newspaper sales, and pulp fiction romances ruling the booksellers.

WHAT CZECHS BELIEVE   In contrast to neighboring Poland, Hungary, and former partner Slovakia, the Czech Republic is not a deeply religious country. Although Prague was once the seat of the Holy Roman Empire and churches lace the city, less than 20% of contemporary Czechs say they believe in God, and around 10% say they are religious. One opinion poll showed that more Czechs believe in UFOs than believe in God.

Czechs may not be religious, but they are often very superstitious. One piece of their folk wisdom is similar to Groundhog Day in the United States. If it rains on the day of Medard (June 8), Czechs plan to carry an umbrella another 40 consecutive days. Czechs also believe that having a baby carriage in the house before a child is born is extremely bad luck for your expected child's future. Czechs will do almost anything to keep a carriage out of a pregnant mother's home.

Each day on the calendar corresponds to one or more of the Czech first names, and it is customary to present a gift to close friends and colleagues on their *svátek* (name day)—it's like having two birthdays a year.

AVANT-GARDE   Prague's avant-garde community used to thrive in secret while mocking Communism, but now has to face the realities of capitalism, such as rising rents and stiffening competition. Many of the most inventive artists have had to find more mainstream work to survive. But if you look hard enough, you still might find an exhibition, a dance recital, or an experimental performance that is surprising, shocking, and satisfying. *The Prague Post*, the English-language weekly, usually serves as a good source for finding these events.

TODAY'S CHALLENGES   The city now faces a host of problems that didn't occur under Communism rule. Taxi drivers, who were once strictly licensed under the old regime and formed a small and exclusive club, have become one of the mayor's biggest headaches. Reports that these new entrepreneurs have been gouging tourists have grown exponentially with the number of drivers and visitors. Even prostitutes, who were kept behind closed doors in the old days, now display their wares on convent steps.

The city's leaders have tried to keep a lid on anything obscuring the best sights, including a tornado of billboards. They are also searching for a way to curb the traffic rambling through the ancient streets. Although the eyesores keep popping up, the traffic keeps getting worse, and the finicky phones wear you down . . . those spires still stand above it all.

6 Famous Czechs

Princess Libuše (pre-ninth century)   Fabled mother of Bohemia. Legend holds that the clairvoyant Libuše, the daughter of Bohemian philosopher Krok, stood on a cliff on Vyšehrad Hill looking over the Vltava and conjured that on this land a great city would stand. She and Prince Přemysl Orač declared the first Bohemian state, launching the period known as the Přemyslid Dynasty that lasted from the 10th through the 12th centuries.

St. Wenceslas (Svatý Václav) (circa 907–935)   Patron saint of Bohemia. Prince Wenceslas was executed at the site of the present-day city of Stará Boleslav—on the orders of his younger brother Boleslav, who then took over the Bohemian throne. A popular cult arose proclaiming the affable and learned prince Wenceslas as the perpetual spiritual ruler of all Czech people. The horse market, the traditional meeting place of Prague, was the scene of a brief thrust of Czech nationalism against the Austrian Empire in 1848, when people named the place Wenceslas Square (Václavské náměstí). A statue at the top of the square, depicting the horse-mounted warrior, was erected in 1912.

Charles IV (Karel IV) (1316–78)   Bohemian king, Holy Roman Emperor, and chief patron of Prague. Born to John of Luxembourg and Eliška, the sister of the last Přemyslid king, Charles, originally christened as Václav, was reared as John's successor; John had taken over the Bohemian crown in 1310. Charles was educated in the royal court in Paris and spent much of his adolescence observing rulers in Luxembourg and Tuscany. Charles ascended to the throne in 1346, and during his reign he made Prague the seat of the Holy Roman Empire, and one of Europe's most advanced cities. He also inspired several key sites through the country, including Prague's university (Universita Karlova), stone bridge (Karlův most), largest New Town park (Karlovo náměstí), and the spa town of Karlvy Vary.

Master Jan Hus (1369 or 1370–1415)   Religious reformer, university lecturer, and Czech nationalist symbol. Upset with what he thought was the misuse of power by Rome and the German clergy in Prague, Hus questioned the authority of the pope and called for the formation of a Bohemian National Church. From his stronghold at Bethleham Chapel in Old Town, he advocated that the powerful clergy cede their property and influence to more of the people. In 1414, he was summoned to explain his views before the Ecclesiastic Council at Konstanz in Germany, but was arrested on his arrival. He was burned at the stake as a heretic on July 6, 1415, a day considered the precursor to the Hussite Wars, and now commemorated as a Czech national holiday. His church lives on today in the faith called The Czech Brethren.

Kilian Ignac Dienzenhofer (1689–1751)   High baroque architect and builder. He and his son, Kryštof, were responsible for some of the most striking Czech church designs, including the Church of St. Nicholas in Lesser Town, the Church of St. Nicholas in Old Town, and the Church of St. John of Nepomuk on Hradčany.

Bedřich Smetana (1824–84)   Nationalist composer. After studying piano and musical theory in Prague, Smetana became one of Bohemia's most revered composers, famous for his fierce nationalism. His *Vltava* movement in the symphony

Má Vlast (My Country) is performed the opening night of the Prague Spring music festival; it is also used as a score in Western movies and TV commercials. His opera *The Bartered Bride* takes a jaunty look at Czech farm life.

Josef Zítek (1832–1909)   Neo-Renaissance architect, and professor of technology. The most revered of Czech building designers, he was responsible for the National Theater, the Rudolfinum concert hall, and the grand spa Colonnade in Karlovy Vary.

Antonín Dvořák (1841–1904)   Neo-romantic composer and head of Prague Conservatory. Dvořák is best-known for his symphony, *From the New World,* which was inspired by a lengthy tour of the United States. His opera about a girl trapped in a water world, *Rusalka,* remains a Czech favorite; it became a popular film in Europe, starring Slovak actress Magda Vašáryová.

Franz Kafka (1883–1924)   Writer. Author of the depressing but universally read novel *The Trial,* Kafka was a German-Jewish Praguer who, for much of his life, worked in relative obscurity as a sad Prague insurance clerk. In works such as *Metamorphosis, The Castle,* and *Amerika,* Kafka described surreal and suffocating worlds of confusion. Now many people use the adjective "Kafka-esque" to mean living in hell. Anyone who tries to apply for anything at a state office here will know that Kafka's world lives on in Prague.

Tomáš G. Masaryk (1850–1937)   Philosopher, professor, Czechoslovakia's first president. Educated in Vienna and Leipzig, Masaryk spent decades advocating Czech statehood. In 1915, Masaryk made a landmark speech in Geneva calling for the end of the Habsburg monarchy. He traveled to Washington and received the backing of President Woodrow Wilson at the end of World War I for a sovereign republic of Czechs and Slovaks, which was founded in October 1918. During his nearly 17 years as president, Masaryk played the stoic grandfather of the new republic. He resigned for health reasons in 1935 and died less than two years later.

Klement Gottwald (1896–1953)   Communist leader. He was named prime minister after his Communist party won the highest vote count in the first postwar election in 1946. By February 1948, he had organized the complete communist takeover of the government and eventually forced out President Edvard Beneš. When he became president in June 1948, the name of his home town Zlín was changed to Gottwaldov (it changed backed to Zlín after the 1989 revolution). He was abhorred for his role in the 1950s show trials that purged hundreds.

Alexander Dubček (1921–92)   Government leader. Although he's not a Czech, Dubček is a key figure in the history of Prague and the country. A Slovak Communist, Dubček became the First Secretary of the Communist Party in January 1968, presiding over the Prague Spring reforms. After he was ousted in the Soviet-led invasion in August 1968, Dubček faded from view, only later to stand with Havel to declare the end of hard-line communist rule in 1989. He returned to become Speaker of Parliament after the Velvet Revolution, but was killed in a car accident on a wet highway outside of Prague in 1992.

Václav Havel (1936–)   Playwright, dissident, president. Absurdist playwright in the 1960s, Havel became a leading figure in the pro-democracy movement Charter 77, and the country's first president following the Velvet Revolution. See the "From Prisoner to President" box (page 14).

   Three of the most famous Czechs in the world today are now Americans: The academy award-winning film director **Miloš Forman**, and the two tennis superstars **Ivan Lendl,** and **Martina Navrátilová.** The noted author of *The Unbearable Lightness of Being,* **Milan Kundera** now is a French citizen (see "Books" below). All four left Czechoslovakia during the darkest days of "normalization" in the 1970s and 1980s.

7 Architecture 101

Look up. That's the most straightforward advice a visitor to Prague can receive. The city's majestic mix of medieval, renaissance, and contemporary architecture shares one fairly universal element—the most elegant and well-appointed facades and fixtures are not to be found at eye level, or even street level, but on top floors and roofs. Hundreds of buildings are decorated with intricately carved cornices or ornamental balconies and friezes depicting mythical, religious, or heroic figures.

The grime of Prague pollution has been gradually and delicately stripped away, and each restored building reveals some previously hidden detail. What's interesting, though, is how visitors react to the grime. When tourists visit Paris or Venice and see dirty, crumbling buildings, they consider them quaint. When they see the same old, dirty, crumbling buildings in Prague, however, they point to the failure of Communism. But that's not entirely fair— if you look at photos of Prague taken in 1900, you'll also see dirty and crumbling buildings.

The city's earliest extant architectural forms are Romanesque, and date from 1100 to 1250. The long Gothic period followed, spanning about 1250 to 1530. You'll find many Gothic buildings in Staré Mésto. Plus Prague Castle's most visible superstructure, St. Vitus Cathedral, is a Gothic masterpiece—that is, its older east-facing half (the cathedral's western sections exemplify Renaissance and neo-Gothic styles). From 1500 to the early 1600s, the Italian Renaissance style prevailed; on building exteriors, you can still see *sgraffito,* pictures made by cutting away layers of colored plaster.

Many of Prague's best-known structures are baroque and rococo, in the high Austrian style inspired by the Habsburgs of the 17th and 18th centuries. Instead of trying to satisfy some ideal form of beauty, baroque artists tried to satisfy the direct, emotional needs of people. In baroque churches, columns direct your eye upward to God and forward to the altar; but the flowing lines and ornate decorations force your eye to stop along the way, as if you were being diverted by this world on your way to the next. The baroque church was meant to be God's castle.

Some of the city's most flamboyant buildings are art nouveau, a style popular from about 1900 to 1918. The art nouveau movement that swept across Europe developed with the continent's ongoing Industrial Revolution. Innovative building materials— primarily steel and glass—opened endless possibilities for artistic flourishes and embellishments. Architects abandoned traditional stone structures, built in a pseudo-historical style, for ones made for their aesthetics. This style is characterized by rich, curvaceous ornamentation; these frills raise form to as important a status as function.

Several intriguing cubist designs from that era have also been hailed for their ingenuity. Cubism, an angular artistic movement that originated with the paintings of Pablo Picasso and Georges Braque in Paris in 1906, was confined to painting and sculpture in France and most of Europe. As an architectural style, cubism is exclusive to Bohemia.

The late 20th century has played havoc on Prague's architecture. Communists were partial to functional designs with no character. Their buildings shed all decorative details and were built solely according to the function of the structure. Today, the city's most unappealing structures are these functional, socialist designs. No visitor should leave Prague before taking the metro out to Prosek to see the thousands of Communist-era flats, called "rabbit huts" even by their occupants.

These prefabricated apartment buildings, or *paneláks,* were built during the Communist era. Created partly out of socialist dogma and partly out of economic necessity, paneláks were named after the concrete slabs used to build them. Ugly, cheap, and unimaginatively designed, the apartment buildings are surrounded by a featureless world, seemingly numb to all that is aesthetic. Exteriors were made of plain, unadorned cement and hallways were lined with linoleum. The same room, balcony, and window design was stamped out over and over.

But panelák living was not always viewed as a scourge. Unlike the larger, older apartments, paneláks had modern plumbing and heating, and were once considered the politically correct way to live. They're also amazingly cheap. Rent and utility costs still only amount to about 1,000 Kčs ($37) per month, although price deregulation is just beginning. These behemoths now house half of Prague's residents.

Two major post-Communist projects have already triggered a new debate among the progressives and the traditionalists. The Myslbek shopping and office complex on Na Příkopě near Wenceslas Square is the business district's first attempt at blending the new with the old in a functional yet elegant way. And the so-called "Dancing Building" on the embankment at the Rašínovo nábřeží has conservative tongues wagging. Its design strays from the 19th-century Empire classical houses that line the river next to it, but in a most peculiar way. Controversial U.S. architect Frank Gehry, who designed the American Center in Paris, and new wave Yugoslav designer Vlado Milunic have created a building that ironically pays tribute to the most classic of dancing pairs: Fred Astaire and Ginger Rogers. The Prague headquarters of a Dutch insurance company depicts Fred and Ginger intertwined in a dip above the Vltava. See "For the Architecture Buff" in Chapter 6 for a discussion of Prague's important architectural sights.

8 *Není Pivo Jako Pivo:* There's No Beer Like Beer

While Czechs on the whole are not very religious people, there is still one thing that elicits a piety unseen in many orthodox countries—*pivo,* or beer. This golden nectar has inspired some of the country's most popular fiction and films, poetry and prayers. One Czech proverb states: "Wherever beer is brewed, all is well. Whenever beer is drunk, life is good."

For many Czechs, the corner beer hall (*hospoda*) functions as a social and cultural center. The regulars in these smoke-encrusted airless caves drink beer as lifeblood and seem ill at ease when a foreigner takes their favorite table or disrupts their daily routine. Fortunately for those wanting to sample the rich, aromatic, and powerful taste of Czech lagers without ingesting waves of nicotine, dozens of more ventilated pubs and restaurants have emerged since the Velvet Revolution. Unfortunately, the suds in these places often cost five to ten times more than those in the hospoda.

While always informal, Czech pubs observe their own unwritten code of etiquette:

- Large tables are usually shared with strangers.
- When sitting, you should first ask "*Je tu volno?*" ("Is this place taken?"). If not, put a cardboard coaster down in front of you to show you want a beer.
- Don't wave for a waiter, it will only delay the process when he or she sees you.
- When the waiter does finally arrive and sees the coaster in front of you, simply nod or hold up fingers for the number of beers you want between you and your companions.

"When You Say Bud . . ."

The world's largest brewer, Anheuser Busch, and its tiny Czech competitor have agreed to let the foam settle in their battle over the use of the brand name Budweiser.

The Czech state-owned brewery, Budějovický Budvar, continues to block Busch from selling its flagship brand, Budweiser, in key markets in Europe, mainly Germany and Austria. Meanwhile the Czech version of the brew—the roots of which span centuries when České Budějovice was known by its German name, Budweis (hence the German adjective Budweiser)—cannot be sold in North America.

Both brewers have staked their claim to the Budweiser trademark using legal and historical arguments.

Busch established the name Budweiser in the United States when German immigrants founded their St. Louis family brewery in the latter part of last century, while the Czechs claim they had been using the name long before Columbus discovered the New World, even though they did not legally register it in Europe until 1911. The trademark row has been woven into the debate about how the Czech government should privatize the Budvar brewery. Several politicians and commentators have called Budvar part of the "Czech Family Silver," saying it should be beyond foreign intervention.

But in January 1994, the Czech government awarded Busch the exclusive right to negotiate for a minority stake in Budvar as part of the privatization of the brewery, which claims to have its roots when beer-making in Budweis was licensed by Bohemian King Otakar II in 1256. Busch has used its exclusive position to launch a public relations campaign—the likes of which had not been seen in a country still shaking off 40 years of communism—to convince Czechs that their intentions are earnest. Busch has opened a representative office in České Budějovice as well as a cultural center that provides free English courses to citizens and management advice to budding entrepreneurs. Busch's newspaper ads tout the possibilities of future cooperation.

Many Czechs are not convinced that a partnership with their big American friend would lead to better things. There is a widespread fear in Czech bars that the Americans would change Budvar's distinctively heavy Czech flavor for a lighter style more popular in the U.S. Commented one Budvar regular: "I tasted the American Budweiser once. It's something wet, but it's not beer."

- If there is a choice, it usually is between size—*malé* (pronounced "mah-lay") is small, *velké* (pronounced "vel-kay") is large—or type— *světlé* is light (pronounced svyet-lay), *černé* is dark (pronounced cher-nay).
- The waiter will pencil marks on a white slip of paper that remains on your table.
- If your waiter ever comes back for a second round, order enough for the rest of your stay and ask to pay. When he or she returns, say *"zaplatíme"* ("we'll pay") . . . you might not see your waiter for a long time.

According to brewing industry studies, Czechs drink more beer per capita than any people in the world. The average Czech downs 320 pints of brew each year; the average American drinks about 190 pints a year. Of course a Czech hospoda regular will drink the year's average for a family of six.

Czechs have brewed beer since the ninth century, but the golden lager known around the world as Pilsner beer was born in 1842 in the western Bohemian town of Plzeň (Pilsen in German). Until that time, all beer or ale carried a murky, dull body, but the Pilsner method kept the brew bright and golden, and has been copied throughout the world ever since. The key, beer experts say, is the exceptionally light and crisp hops grown on vines in the western Bohemian region of Žatec. Breweries emerged in every major Czech and Moravian district, and the best of the lot now ship their suds to Prague and around the world.

Czech beer comes in various degrees of concentration, usually marked on the label or menu. This does not indicate the amount of alcohol, although the higher degree does carry a higher alcohol content. The standard premium 12° brew contains about five percent alcohol, although each label varies. If you want something a little lighter on the head, try a 10°, with 3.5% to 4% alcohol.

The never-ending debate over which Czech beer is best rages on, but here are the top contenders, all readily available in Prague (each pub or restaurant usually will flaunt which is their choice on the front of the building):

GAMBRINUS   The best-selling domestic label, direct from the Pilsner Breweries, smooth and solid, not too bitter.

PILSNER URQUELL   The more familiar, sharper tasting brother of Gambrinus, mostly packaged for export.

BUDVAR   The original "Budweiser," a semisweet lager that hails from České Budějovice, a town also known by its German name, Budweis. The clash with the U.S. Anheuser Busch over the duplicate trademark was still brewing at this writing, but there is nothing similar about the taste.

STAROPRAMEN   The flagship label from Prague's home brewery holds its own, and is easiest to find.

KOZEL   A favorite with the American expatriate community, with its distinctive namesake goat on the label. Its nonbitter but spicy taste is the antithesis of most American brews. Light beer this is not.

Several widely believed Czech superstitions are connected with drinking beer. One says that you should never, ever pour a different kind of beer in a mug holding the remnants of another brew. Bad luck is sure to follow. Another says that the toast— usually "*na zdraví*" ("to your health")—is negated if anyone fails to clink their mug with any of the others at your table and then slam the mug on the table before taking the first chug.

9 Czech Cuisine

PLACES TO EAT

VINÁRNA   Beyond the basic Czech food in the smoky hospoda, you usually can get a more rounded meal in a wine bar known as a *vinárna*. Traditionally, the vinárna was an establishment without food that specialized in wine from a particular vineyard. Later, the role of the vinárna changed, and it became a restaurant reserved for special occasions. When eating in a vinárna, always ask about special wines.

RESTAURACE   Since many a hospoda and vinárna double as eateries, the term *restaurace* (restaurant) has become a sort of rubric under which several kinds of establishments converge. When it comes to food, the distinctions between hospoda and vinárna have blurred.

PIVNICE   No food, beyond potato chips and other salties, is served here usually. The pivnice has one main purpose: it serves as a place to drink massive quantities of beer.

CUKRÁRNA   A small cafe serving coffee, tea, and pastries, the cukrárna began as a kind of specialist bakery ("cukr" means sugar).

KAVÁRNA   The Czech kavárna, or coffee bar, is a mainstay of Czech life. At these usually simple places, patrons can idle with a newspaper and linger over a cup of espresso or cappuccino; many kavárnas offer hot menu items now. Most also serve pressed or filter coffee, but five years ago it was rare to find any place that offered anything but so-called "*turek*" (Turkish) coffee—hot water poured over coffee grounds— which was often a chewy experience.

VEPŘO-KNEDLO-ZELO: PORK-DUMPLINGS-CABBAGE

The true Czech dining experience can be summed up in three words: *Vepřo-Knedlo-Zelo*—Pork-Dumplings-Cabbage. Forget the endive, sprouts, and tofu as Czech menus are packed with meat, meat, and more meat. When prepared with care and imagination, the standard Czech fare can be hearty and satisfying, although it should be ingested at a point in the day when a short nap can follow to aid the digestive process. But it's getting easier to eat light, as restaurants serving foreign cuisines and salad bars respond to the demands of visitors.

The most common Czech meal is roast pork with boiled cabbage and dumplings (*vepřová pečeně se zelím a knedlíky*). Dumplings, or *knedlíky*, come in several varieties. Made of potato or bread and boiled, they are typically sliced flat. Dessert dumplings (*ovocné*)— stuffed with strawberries or apricots, sponging up melted butter, and topped with powdered sugar—are about the heaviest thing one might ever eat. Take a deep breath and try them anyway; they're hedonistically tasty, and one plate could fill up your whole dinner party.

Duck, chicken, and trout are also popular menu items, as is potato soup (*bramborová polévka*), another important staple. Another heavy but recommended Czech dish is *Svíčková na Smetaně*, a sliced roasted sirloin in a cream sauce that, when prepared properly, should take two days to make. The sirloin is baked with carrots, greens, and herbs, and the drippings and vegetables are then puréed with cream and left to sit overnight. Bread dumplings drink up the sauce and provide a bed for the sirloin in another can't-move-when-you're-done dinner. A sour cranberry chutney called *brusinky* is usually served on the side to help cut through the sauce.

BEYOND BEER

You'll find some other liquid treasures beyond beer in the Czech Republic.

BECHEROVKA   Born in the spa town Karlovy Vary (the original Carlsbad in German) in 1807, the herb liqueur Becherovka became a fabled cure for stomach ailments. Dr. Jan Becher developed the drink to complement the medicinal mineral waters that drew cure-seekers to Karlovy Vary from all over the world. Becherovka is made from a secret recipe of 42 herbs—only two people supposedly know the recipe. There are 12 sources emanating from underground providing the bubbling mineral water to Karlovy Vary, but locals call Becherovka "The 13th Source." (See Chapter 11 for coverage of Karlovy Vary and its hot springs.)

WINE   Although Czech wines are relatively unknown abroad, the country has a long history of wine making. Most wine is produced in southern Moravia, where both reds and whites are winning wider reputations. Happily for visitors, the relative obscurity of Czech wines translates into low prices. In stores, very drinkable bottles can be bought for $1.50 to $2; top vintages cost about $20. Prices triple in restaurants. The most notable white wines are Mopr, Rýnský Ryzlink, Rulandské, and Tramín.

The best reds are Frankovka, Rulandské, and Vavřinecké. (See Chapter 12 for coverage of Moravia.)

WATER   No one says that Prague's water is particularly tasty, but there's lots of debate as to whether water from the tap is safe to drink. Many people claim that Prague's water supply is plagued with numerous unmentionables—some even radioactive, although local water officials say it is perfectly potable. So, while Prague tap water may harm you in the long run, personal experience proves that the city's water is free from things that will ruin your trip.

10   Recommended Films, Books & Recordings

FILMS

While Czech literature and music have carved their places in classical culture, the country's films and their directors have collected the widest praise in the second half of this century. Cunning, melancholy views of Bohemian life (before the Soviets moved in for a few decades) were captured by some of the finest filmmakers in the era known as "The Czech New Wave" of the 1960s. The directors Jiří Menzel and Miloš Forman were in the vanguard. An easy-to-find example of this period's work (with English subtitles) is Menzel's Oscar-award winning *Closely Watched Trains*, which takes a snapshot of the odd routine at a rural Czech rail station.

Forman made his splash in the film world with a quirky look at one night in the life of a town trying to have fun in spite of itself. *The Fireman's Ball* shows Forman's true mastery as he captures the essence of being stone bored in a gray world, yet makes it strangely intriguing. Of course, this movie was made before Forman emigrated to the big budgets of Hollywood and first shocked Americans with *Hair*. He then directed the Oscar-winning *One Flew over the Cuckoo's Nest*. For *Amadeus*, Forman sought authenticity, so he received special permission from the Communists to return to Prague, and while filming, he brought back to life the original Estates' Theatre (Stavovské Divadlo), where Mozart first performed.

Czech-based directors after the New Wave mostly disappeared from view, but one stunningly brave film was made in 1970, just as the repressive post-invasion period known as "normalization" began its long, cold freeze of talent. In *The Ear* (*Ucho*) director Karel Kachyňa presents the anguished story of a man trapped in an apartment wired for sound, subject to the Communists leaders' obsession and paranoia with Moscow. That *The Ear* was made in the political environment of the time was astounding. That it was quickly banned was not. Fortunately, local television has dusted off copies from the archives, and it has begun playing to arthouse audiences again.

Czech filmmaking has a long tradition, as the Prague studios in the Barrandov hills churned out glossy pre-Communist romantic comedies and period pieces rivaling the output of Paris, Berlin, and even Hollywood at the time.

A few Czech films have made their mark after the Velvet Revolution. The father-and-son team of Zdeněk and Jan Svěrák was nominated for the 1992 Best Foreign Film Oscar for *Elementary School* (*Obecná škola*). Jan directed and his father starred in the story of golden reflections about Czech boyhood following World War II. Prague has been a popular location of late for shooting major motion pictures, in spite of itself. *Immortal Beloved*, the story of Beethoven, made use of Prague's timeless streets and palaces. *Swing Kids* told the story of restless youth who fought against losing their identity to Hitler's brownshirts in Berlin, but only Prague's streets could provide a convincing setting. And *Mission Impossible*—the movie—drew Tom Cruise and company to shoot the shoot-em-up action flick with an ancient central European backdrop.

The film about Prague probably most familiar to contemporary audiences is *The Unbearable Lightness of Being,* based on a book by the émigré author Milan Kundera. Set in the days surrounding the Soviet invasion, the story draws on the psychology of three Praguers who can't escape their personal obsessions, while the political world outside collapses around them. Real Praguers find the film disturbing, some because it hits home, others because they say it portrays a Western stereotype of life in their city.

BOOKS

Any discussion of Czech literature with visiting foreigners usually begins with Milan Kundera. Nobody has made the contemporary Czech experience more accessible to foreign readers. Rightly or wrongly—and this theme starts arguments among Czechs who stayed—Kundera creates a visceral, personal sense of the world he chose to leave. In *The Unbearable Lightness of Being* the anguish over escaping the Soviet-occupied Prague he loves tears the libidinous protagonist Dr. Tomáš in the same way the love for his wife and the lust for his lover does. More Czech post-normalization angst can be found in *The Book of Laughter and Forgetting* and *Laughable Loves.* Kundera's biting satire of Stalinist purges in the 1950s, *The Joke,* however, is regarded by Czech critics as his best work. In reality, the author left Prague behind for Paris in 1975, and he has not returned since, even after the revolution. He has begun, as of late, to write his original manuscripts in French instead of Czech.

Iva Pekařková, one of the few top female Czech novelists whose works are translated into English, draws on her experiences as a Bohemian hitchhiker, refugee camp inmate, and New York City cabby. Her first novel, translated as *Truck Stop Rainbows,* was written at age 23.

Arnošt Lustig, a survivor of Czechoslovakia's Nazi-era Terezín concentration camp and author of many works, including *Street of Lost Brothers,* shared the 1991 Publishers Weekly Award for best literary work with John Updike and Norman Mailer. In mid-1995 he took over as the editor-in-chief of the Czech edition of *Playboy* magazine.

Ivan Klíma, also a survivor of Terezín, is another of the best-known contemporary Czech novelists. His best work, translated as *Judge on Trial* (Vintage), is about a judge who struggles with a death sentence for a guilty prisoner.

Jaroslav Hašek wrote the Czech harbinger to *Forrest Gump* in *The Good Soldier Švejk* (Viking Penguin), a post-World War I satire about a simpleton soldier who wreaks havoc in the Austro-Hungarian army during the war.

Bohumil Hrabal is the author of the Czech everyman. He has had two internationally acclaimed hits: *Closely Watched Trains* (Viking Penguin) upon which the Menzel film was based, and *I Served the King of England* (Vintage). When President Bill Clinton visited Prague in early 1994, he asked to have a beer with Hrabal in one of the aging author's favorite haunts, the pub U Zlatého Tygra (At the Golden Tiger) in Old Town. Clinton may have gotten more than he bargained for, as the gruff but lovable Hrabal, who turned 80 that year, launched into his views of the world.

No Czech reading list would be complete without reference to Franz Kafka, Prague's most famous novelist. *The Collected Novels of Franz Kafka* (Schocken), which includes *The Castle* and *The Trial,* binds most of the writer's claustrophobic works into a single volume.

If it's contemporary philosophy you want, there is, of course, the philosopher president. Václav Havel's heralded dissident essay "The Power of the Powerless" explained how the lethargic masses were allowing their complacency with communism to sap their souls. His "Letters to Olga," written to his wife while in prison in the 1980s, takes you into his cell and his view of a moral world. Available are two solid English-translated compilations of his dissident writings: *Living in Truth* and *Open Letters*. *Disturbing the Peace* is an autobiographical meditation on childhood, the events of 1968, and Havel's involvement with Charter 77. His first recollections about entering politics are in "Summer Meditations," a long essay written during a vacation.

While he hasn't had much time to write since becoming president, Havel says his speeches given around the world each continue a dialogue about morality in politics. Read together in the anthology of his presidential speeches, *Toward a Civil Society*, it is clear that Havel has not stopped being the dissident. The difference now is that his target is corruption in politics and society, including in democracies.

Heda Margolis Kovlay's *Prague Farewell* (Viking Penguin) is the heartfelt autobiography of a woman who was confined to concentration camps during World War II, and then married a Communist Party hack who was executed in 1952. The book recounts the widespread feelings of fear and paranoia that prevailed during the Stalinist era.

Dubček and Czechoslovakia 1918–1990 (Simon & Schuster), by William Shawcross, is one of the best biographies of the most famous figure of the 1968 Prague Spring. It also discusses Dubček's role in the 1989 Velvet Revolution.

RECORDINGS

Nineteenth-century Czech composers Bedřich Smetana and Antonín Dvořák are the country's most important musical figures. Smetana, composer of the operas *The Bartered Bride* and *The Kiss*, is considered the father of modern Czech music. Dvořák, known for the symphony *From the New World*, is one of the few truly world-class Czech composers. Lesser-known, highly respected 20th-century classical composers include Leoš Janáček (*The House of the Dead* and *The Cunning Little Vixen*) and Bohuslav Martinů (*Thunderbolt*).

The Czech recording companies have put together volumes of standard classics played by talented Czech orchestras; these recordings are available for a song at many record shops around town.

In the contemporary bins, the folksy rock group Žlutý pes (Yellow Dog) have become de facto post-revolutionary pop historians. The group's balding Dylan-esque lead singer, Ondřej Hejma (who has a day job as a correspondent for an American news agency) has landed two number-one hits, "Sametová" and "Náruživá," both taking Czech thirty-somethings back to the old days.

For a truly eclectic Czech mix that combines blues and reggae with driving rock and horns, try Laura and Her Tigers (Laura a její tygři). Even if you don't understand the lyrics, the band's unique sound is easy to appreciate.

2

Planning a Trip to Prague

While visitor services in Prague have improved greatly in the last few years, the city is still not the most tourist-friendly place. Careful pretrip planning will both save you money and enrich your Czech experience. This chapter is designed to help you plan your trip, save time, and get the most out of your Prague stay.

1 Visitor Information & Entry Requirements

VISITOR INFORMATION

Despite heavy lobbying by some government officials who understand the importance of tourism to the nascent Czech economy, Parliament has not yet been able to properly fund a state-run tourist bureau. A few meager brochures are distributed from a small window at Prague's Ruzyně Airport, but it's a far cry from most Western convention and visitors bureaus. **Čedok,** the former Communist government's official travel arm, now operates as a commercial travel agency, dispensing literature detailing only the hotels and tours that they offer. If you ask for information, you're likely to receive little more than a city map and a glossy brochure of expensive all inclusive tours. Contact Čedok in the United States at 10 E. 40th St., New York, NY 10016 (☎ **212/689-9720**). In Britain, contact Čedok at 49 Southwark St., London SE1 1RU (☎ **0171/ 378-6009**).

For a comprehensive list of information sources in Prague, see "Visitor Information" in Chapter 3.

ENTRY REQUIREMENTS

DOCUMENTS American and British citizens do not need visas for stays under 30 days. Canadians, Australians, New Zealanders, and Irish citizens must obtain tourist visas before entering the Czech Republic.

The easiest way to legally extend your stay in the country is to take a short trip (even of a few hours) to a neighboring country like Slovakia, and get your passport restamped on your return journey into the Czech Republic (usually done only upon request). Many expat Americans and Brits don't even bother to make this journey, although they successfully claim they did to any immigration official who might ask. Health certificates are not required for travel to the Czech Republic.

If you have special needs or questions about entry requirements, contact the Czech Embassy in the **United States,** 3900 Linean Ave. NW, Washington, DC 20008 (☎ 202/363-6308). In **Canada,** contact the Consulate General of the Czech Republic, 1305 Pine Ave., West Montreal, Quebec, H3G IB2 (☎ 514/849-4495). In **Great Britain,** contact the Czech Embassy, 26 Kensington Palace Gardens, London W8 4QY (☎ 0171/727-4918).

CUSTOMS   Czech customs laws are quite lax and poorly enforced. "Reasonable amounts" remains the de facto rule. Officially, the allowances for importing duty-free goods into the Czech Republic are 200 cigarettes (or 250 grams of tobacco), one liter of alcohol (or two liters of wine), and 50 grams of perfume (or $^1/_4$ liter of toilet water). Most items brought into the Czech Republic for personal use during a visit are not liable to import duty. Gifts are taxable if the quantity and value are not in keeping with the "reasonable needs" of the recipient. You may import (and export) any amount of foreign currency, but only 5,000 Czech crowns. Live animals, plants, produce, coffee, and tea may not be imported.

2 Money

CURRENCY   The basic unit of Czech currency is the *koruna* (plural, *koruny*), or crown, abbreviated *Kč*, which, at this writing is worth about $0.037 in U.S. dollars. U.S. $1 buys 27 Kč; U.K. £1 buys 41 Kč.

Each crown is divided into 100 *haléřů*, or hellers. To make budgeting easier, prices quoted in this book are accompanied by their U.S. dollar equivalents. Although the Czech crown has been fairly stable against major world currencies, rates can change drastically, especially considering how dynamic the Czech economy is.

CHANGING MONEY   Although the Czech crown does not "float" freely against the world's convertible currencies, the easing of export laws has all but erased black-market exchange. Never exchange money on the street. Street rates vary just a hair from official ones, and stories abound about tourists who have exchanged large sums illegally, only to discover they'd bought invalid Czechoslovak notes or Polish zloty. Check for a silver line on one side of every bank note you accept.

The money-changing business is a profitable growth industry in Prague, and hundreds of shops take advantage of this easy way to make money. In general, competition has kept commissions low, but beware of unspoken "fees" and "hidden" extra charges that are levied at some rip-off exchange shops. Many exchange bureaus advertise great rates, but their commissions (which usually remain unposted) can reach a whopping ten percent. **Chequepoint,** one of the ugliest offenders, maintains offices in the city's most heavily touristed areas and keeps long hours—sometimes all night—but their business practices are seriously deceptive.

Banks are the best places to convert cash into crowns; there's usually a 1% to 3% commission charge. **Komerčni Banka,** Na příkopě 33, Prague 1 (☎ 2402 1111), is the country's biggest bank with branches seemingly everywhere. They're usually open Monday to Friday from 8am to noon, and 1 to 5pm. **Živnostenská Banka**, Na přííkopž 20, Prague 1 (☎ 2412 1111), is Prague's most beautiful bank, and is open Monday to Friday from 9am to 5pm.

TRAVELER'S CHECKS   Those with traveler's checks will do best at **American Express** and **Thomas Cook Travel Services** offices, where rates are competitive, and checks are changed commission-free. Traveler's checks can also be changed at banks,

The Crown, the Dollar, and the Pound Sterling

At this writing U.S. $1 equaled approximately 27 Kč (or 1 Kč = 3.7¢), and this was the rate of exchange used to calculate the dollar values given in this book (rounded to the nearest nickel). At the same time, U.K. £1 equaled about 41 Kč.

Note that the rates given here fluctuate from time to time and may not be the same when you travel to the Czech Republic. Therefore this table should be used only as a guide.

Kč	U.S.$	U.K.£	Kč	U.S.$	U.K.£
1	0.037	0.024	150	5.55	3.60
5	0.18	0.12	200	7.40	4.80
10	0.37	0.24	250	9.25	6.00
15	0.55	0.36	500	18.50	12.00
20	0.74	0.48	750	27.77	18.00
25	0.93	0.60	1,000	37.00	24.00
30	1.11	0.72	1,250	46.30	30.00
35	1.30	0.84	1,500	55.55	36.00
40	1.48	0.96	1,750	64.80	42.00
45	1.67	1.08	2,000	74.07	48.00
50	1.85	1.20	2,250	83.33	54.00
75	2.77	1.80	2,500	92.60	60.00
100	3.70	2.40	2,750	101.85	66.00

The Czech Republic issued new currency in August 1993, and all notes and coins bearing earlier dates became invalid. There are now seven banknotes and nine coins. Notes, each of which bears a forgery-resistant silver strip and a prominent watermark, are issued in 20, 50, 100, 200, 500, 1,000, and 5,000 crown denominations. Coins are valued at 10, 20, and 50 hellers and 1, 2, 5, 10, 20, and 50 crowns.

but they are not accepted at many of the city's private money-change shops. Note that traveler's checks are usually not accepted at shops, restaurants, hotels, theaters, and attractions. Some restaurants and hotels—specially the fancier ones—will exchange foreign-currency traveler's checks, but their rates will routinely be worse than bank rates.

GETTING CASH WHILE YOU'RE THERE Automatic Teller Machines (ATMs) are popping up all over Prague. More than 100 cash machines connected to the worldwide Cirrus network are now on-line, dispensing crowns and communicating in English. Most American banks will give you a good exchange rate, and charge just $1 per transaction. Because locals rarely use the ATMs, there is hardly ever a line. Many of these machines can also accept VISA cards (if you have a personal identification number). Centrally located machines are in Old Town, at the corner of 28 Října and Perlová (near Wenceslas Square); in Malá Strana, on Mostecká (just past Charles Bridge); and in the Hilton Atrium Hotel.

CREDIT CARDS American Express, MasterCard, and VISA are widely accepted in central Prague, but shopkeepers outside the city center still seem mystified by plastic. I've found that paying with plastic can be quite economical. The credit-card

What Things Cost in Prague	U.S $
Taxi from Ruzyně Airport to center city	14.00
Metro, tram, or public bus to anywhere in Prague	0.22
Local telephone call	0.08
Double room at Hotel Pařiž (expensive)	229.00
Double room at Hotel Harmony (moderate)	123.60
Double room at Hotel Evropa (inexpensive)	68.80
Lunch for one at La Provance (moderate)	10.00
Lunch for one at most pubs (inexpensive)	4.00
Dinner for one without wine at Parnas (expensive)	26.00
Dinner for one without wine at Restaurant Adria (moderate)	14.00
Dinner for one without wine at Hogo Fogo (inexpensive)	5.00
Half liter of beer	0.80
Coca-Cola in a restaurant	1.20
Cup of coffee	0.80
Roll of ASA 100 film, 36 exposures	7.50
Admission to the National Museum	1.30
Movie ticket	1.12 and up
National Theater ticket	2.80–22.00

companies bill at a favorable rate of exchange, and save you money by eliminating commissions. Cash advances on your MasterCard can be obtained from Komerční Banka, Na příkopě 33, Prague 1 (☎ 2402 1111).

3 When to Go

Spring is the most famous season in Prague, and one might easily believe it's because of the weather. Without a doubt, this is the best season to visit. Hotels are not yet fully booked and restaurants can be chosen without reservations.

In the summer, many Praguers head for the hills and their country cottages in southern Bohemia or the northern Krkonoše mountains. Prague is left for hoards of tourists who crush each other in Old Town Square and across Charles Bridge. You'll pay inflated prices for everything from beer to hotel rooms. The cultural seasons are in full swing, but seats are few, so you should secure tickets to musical and theatrical events immediately upon your arrival.

Autumn is beautiful, but like the summer, is a time when Prague is packed with visitors, including hundreds of Scandinavian school groups. October is usually the best month, as the skies are bluest, and the city hungrily grasps the last few warm days.

The best thing that can be said about the winter is that this off season promises lower rates and fewer crowds. Winters in Prague, however, can be downright dangerous—not because of the cold, but because of air pollution. Although the air is becoming cleaner, pollution still regularly exceeds the standards set by the World Health Organization. During such days, pollution-emitting heating plants are forced to reduce output and inner-city traffic restrictions are implemented, creating a logistical nightmare. Under city law, when specified pollution levels are reached, only private cars with catalytic converters or vehicles for persons with disabilities are allowed into the city center. Health officials warn senior citizens, children, and pregnant women to stay inside and keep the windows and doors closed.

THE CLIMATE   The Czech Republic has a temperate climate. The average temperature in summer is about 63° Fahrenheit. In winter, the temperature hovers around the freezing mark for the entire season. During the average January, it's sunny and clear only 50 hours for the entire month. During February, you can look forward to a total of 72 hours of cloudlessness. Pollution tends to keep snow from snowing in Prague, although surrounding areas may get several inches. The highest rainfall is in July, the lowest in February.

Prague's Average Daytime Temperature and Monthly Rainfall

	Jan	Feb	Mar	Apr	May	Jun	Jul	Aug	Sep	Oct	Nov	Dec
Temp° F	27	29	37	46	55	61	64	63	57	47	38	31
Rain (in.)	1.7	0.9	1.5	1.5	1.8	2.2	2.3	2.1	1.5	1.7	1.6	1.9

HOLIDAYS   Official holidays in the Czech Republic are observed on January 1 (New Year's Day); Easter Monday; May 1 (Labor Day); May 8 (Liberation Day, from Fascism); July 5 (Introduction of Christianity); July 6 (Death of Jan Hus); October 28 (Foundation of the Republic); December 24–25 (Christmas); and December 26 (St. Stephen's Day).

On these holidays, most business and shops (including food shops) are closed, and buses and trams run on Sunday schedules.

PRAGUE CALENDAR OF EVENTS

January

- **Anniversary of Jan Palach's Death.** Jan Palach, a 21-year-old student of philosophy, set fire to himself on January 19, 1969, as a protest against the Soviet invasion of Czechoslovakia. Palach became one of the most powerful symbols of Czech resistance. His death is commemorated annually at both the Memorial to the Victims of Communism on Wenceslas Square and at Olšany Cemetery where he is buried.

March

- **Prague City of Music Festival.** Contemporary and classical concerts are performed around town throughout the month. Contact Čedok, 10 E. 40th St., New York, NY 10016 (☎ 212/689-9720), or most any information/travel agency in Prague (see "Visitor Information" in Chapter 3) for schedule information.

April

- **Miss Czech Republic Competition.** Beauty contests, which the Communists had banned, have come to the Czech Republic with a vengeance. This annual parade of pillow-lipped beauties, held in mid-April, is popular nationwide. The 1996 edition is planned for the western Czech city of Plzeň (see Chapter 11). For tickets and information, call Prague-based Art Production K at 02/2491-5199.
- **Witches' Night.** Although it may still be extremely cold on April 30, this annual celebration marks the end of winter and the birth of spring. Huge bonfires are lit throughout the country, and an effigy of an old hag is often thrown on the flames. The largest fire in Prague is usually burned atop Petřin Hill.

May

☻ **Prague Spring Festival.** The city's largest music festival is a three-week-long series of classical music and dance performances that begins on the anniversary of Bedřich Smetana's death. Opening night is usually marked by a performance of Smetana's Symphonic poem *Má Vlast* (*My Country*). The country's top performers usually participate in the festival, which runs from May 12 to June 2. Tickets for concerts range from 250 to 2,000 Kč ($9.25 to $74), and are available in advance (beginning in November) from Hellichova 18, Prague 1 (☎ 02/2451 0422).

• **Prague International Book Fair.** Top Czech writers mingle with their international counterparts at this combination trade show/cultural event held in mid-May. The public is invited to attend readings and special literary events. For tickets and information, contact the Prague Information Service's InfoCentrum (☎ 187 in Prague or 02/264 022 outside of Prague).

• **Karlovy Vary Beer Olympiad.** This prestigious beer festival, sponsored by the nation's top breweries in mid-May, features endless tastings and dozens of "events," including drinking contests and relay races. About 20,000 people are expected to attend. For information call 017/322 9572.

• **Marlboro Rock-In.** The best annual rock music festival in Prague is held each year in the stunning Lucerna ballroom on Wenceslas Square sometime in late May. A kind of battle of the bands, the Rock-In attracts the country's best amateur musicians. For tickets, contact Lucerna, Štěpánská 31, Prague 1 (☎ 02/2421 2003).

June

• **AghaRTA Jazz Festival.** Sponsored by the club of the same name, the annual AghaRTA Jazz Festival celebrates an art form that the Communists vigorously suppressed. Performances are held both indoors and out in mid-June. For information and tickets contact AghaRTA Jazz Centrum (☎ 02/2421 2914).

• **Slavnost pětilisté ruže** (Festival of the Five-Petalled Rose). Held each year at the summer solstice, the festival gives residents of Český Krumlov the excuse to dress up in Renaissance costume and parade through the streets. Afterward, the streets become a stage with plays, chess games with people dressed as pieces, music, and more. For information, contact the town's Information Centrum (☎/fax 0337/5670).

July

☻ **Karlovy Vary International Film Festival.** Held the beginning of July every even year, this long-running festival crowns the best Czech and foreign films. For information call the Prague Information Service's InfoCentrum (☎ 187 in Prague or 02/264 022 outside of Prague).

• **National Harley Davidson Rally.** In mid-July, thousands of local and foreign hog-owners and wannabes converge on Prague's Strahov Stadium (Olympijská, Prague 6) for a motorcycle love fest made lively with live rock and country music. For information call the Czech Motorcycle Federation (☎ 0204/90 93 91).

• **Táborská Setkání** (Tábor Meeting). In mid-August, representatives from towns worldwide named after Mount Tábor congregate for some medieval fun—parades, music, and jousting—in Tábor. The four-day event even re-enacts the historical battle of Tábor, with brilliantly colored warriors fighting each other "to the death." For information contact Infocentrum města Tábor (☎/fax 0361/254 658).

August
- **Chopin Festival.** The spa town of Mariánské Lázně honors one of its frequent visitors, Chopin, with an annual festival held in late August. Concerts and recitals are held throughout the town. For information or tickets, contact Infocentrum KaSS, Dum Chopin, Hlavní 47, 353 01, Mariánské Lázně (☎ 0165/2427, fax 0165/5892).

September
- **Prague Autumn International Music Festival.** The festival, usually held during the first two weeks of September, features local orchestras and international soloists performing traditional and new works. Most concerts are performed at the Rudolfinum. Tickets can be bought in advance through the Festival Office, Sekaninova 26, Prague 2, Czech Republic (fax 02/242-7564 or 02/692-7650).

October
- **Mozart in Prague.** Prague's love affair with Mozart reaches its frenzied zenith with this city-wide, month-long celebration of the composer's works. Concerts are held in venues throughout Prague. For information contact Studio Forum Praha (☎ 02/643 7560).

November
- **Anniversary of the Velvet Revolution.** A demonstration held on Wenceslas Square on November 17, 1989 was the catalyst for a chain of events that eventually brought down the Communist government. The anniversary is not a party, but a solemn wreath-laying at the memorials on Wenceslas Square and Národní street (near number 20), where demonstrating students clashed with police.

December
- **Christmas** is a festive time in Prague. The "Good Bishop," the Czech equivalent of Santa Claus, dressed in a white priest's costume, distributes sweets to well-behaved children, and coal and potatoes to poorly behaved ones. Just before the holiday, large barrels of carp are brought into the city, and this traditional Christmas-dinner fish is sold throughout Staré Město.
- **A Christmas Market** in Old Town Square usually runs from mid-November through December. Holiday trinkets are sold at wooden stalls. Look for glass angel figurines, small porcelain bells, and other tree trimmers.

4 Health & Insurance

VACCINATIONS   Unless you are arriving from an area known to be suffering from an epidemic, no inoculations or vaccinations are required to enter the Czech Republic. Be sure to carry a doctor's prescription for any medication or controlled substance you require. It's best to bring all the medication you will need on your trip, however, since obtaining the same medicines in the Czech Republic may prove difficult.

INSURANCE   Most travel agents sell low-cost health, theft, and trip-cancellation insurance to clients. Compare these rates and services with those offered by local banks as well as by your personal insurance carrier. Flight insurance, against damages suffered in the event of a plane crash, is also available from self-service counters at most major airports. Some credit-card companies also offer free, automatic travel-accident insurance (up to $100,000) when you purchase travel tickets with their cards.

If you fall ill in Prague and wish the services of an English-language doctor, you will probably be required to pay up front for services rendered. Doctors and hospitals can be expensive, so although it is not required of travelers, health insurance is highly recommended. Check to see if you are covered in foreign countries by your insurance carrier before you purchase additional protection.

In addition to medical insurance, you can also protect your travel investment by insuring against lost or damaged baggage and trip cancellation or interruption. These coverages are often combined into a single comprehensive plan and sold by travel agents or credit-card issuers.

SAFETY   Crime is rising in the Czech Republic. Citizens are reporting a record number of burglaries and sexual assaults, and some visitors have been targeted. The best strategy against violent and nonviolent crime is to use common sense. Women should avoid walking alone late at night on dark streets, through parks, and around Wenceslas Square—one of the main areas for prostitution. All visitors should be watchful of pickpockets in the most highly touristed areas, especially on Charles Bridge, in Old Town Square, and in front of the main train station. Be especially wary in crowded buses, trams, and trains. Don't keep your wallet in a back pocket, and don't flash a lot of cash.

5 Tips for Travelers with Special Needs

FOR TRAVELERS WITH DISABILITIES   The Czechs have made little effort to accommodate the needs of disabled citizens. There are few elevators or ramps for those using wheelchairs, no beeping crosswalks for the people who are blind or visually impaired, and no TTD telephones for those with hearing impairments. The Olga Havel Foundation and other charities are lobbying for improved facilities for disabled citizens and are beginning to make some headway.

In the cobblestone streets of downtown Prague, wheelchairs are almost unknown. Only a few hotels (like the Renaissance Hotel) offer barrier-free accommodations. Most stores, public transportation, theaters, and restaurants are inaccessible to wheelchair users. The following metro stations are accessible to wheelchair-bound travelers: Florenc, Hlavní nádraží, Pankrác, Roztyly, Chodov, Karlovo náměstí, Skalka, and Nádraží Holešovice.

For the most part, Prague's theaters, nightclubs, and attractions do not offer discounts to people with disabilities. There are exceptions, however, so always ask before paying full price.

FOR GAY & LESBIAN TRAVELERS   During the Communist regime, homosexuality was met with official silence and popular ignorance. However, that same government also managed to instill in Czechs a genuine live-and-let-live attitude. Open hostility towards homosexuals is almost unknown, and gay-bashing is unheard of. Since November 1989, many gays have "come out," and the most prevalent Czech attitude seems to be indifference. Gay sex is legal in the Czech Republic (the age of consent is 15), and Parliament is considering a partnership law allowing same-sex marriages.

The Czech Republic's **Association of Organizations of Homosexual Citizens** (SOHO) was founded in 1991 as an umbrella organization uniting several smaller gay organizations. The organization's leaders have even met with President Václav Havel to discuss gay rights issues.

Several bars and nightclubs in Prague cater exclusively to the gay community and are listed in Chapter 9. The best information on happenings for gay visitors can be found in *SOHO Review*, a monthly magazine listing activities and events for gays throughout the Czech Republic. The magazine is in Czech, but does run some English-language information and personal ads. This and other gay-oriented publications are available at Wenceslas Square newsstands, and from most of the gay bars listed in Chapter 9.

Every once in a while, women-only events occur in Prague and are advertised or written about in one of the city's two English-language newspapers. Check the listings for the most up-to-date happenings.

FOR SENIORS   Seniors are accorded very few discounts in Prague. Because Communist equality meant that seniors as a group were no worse off financially than younger persons, Czechs have little experience offering special discounts to retirees. Older travelers should always ask if there's a senior discount, especially at hotels and shops. You might receive an unexpected markdown.

Older travelers are particularly encouraged to purchase travel insurance. When making airline reservations, ask about a senior discount (usually 10%), but also ask if there is a cheaper promotional fare.

FOR FAMILIES   Because facilities are not as good as those in most American and western European cities, Prague is not the easiest place to travel with kids. Only strollers with large wheels will be able to negotiate the cobblestone streets of Old Town and Malá Strana, but once through the door, baby carriages are welcome almost everywhere. While you should pack any medicines or special foods that your children need, you'll find baby food, diapers, and other children's needs readily available in food stores around town.

Older children will enjoy some sightseeing opportunities and special activities that Prague offers. See "Especially for Kids" in Chapter 6 for complete information.

Please note that all children, even infants, are required to have a passport.

FOR STUDENTS   Students in the Czech Republic regularly enjoy discounts on travel, theater, and museum tickets. The **International Student Identity Card (ISIC)** is the most readily accepted proof of student status, and is available from most university travel agents and from the **Council on International Educational Exchange,** 205 E. 42nd St., New York, NY 10017 (☎ 212/661-1450). To be eligible for the card, you must be enrolled in a degree program. The application must include proof of student status via an official letter from the school registrar or high school principal, a $16 registration fee, and one passport-size photo.

Prague's hostels are not only some of the cheapest places to stay, but they are also great for meeting other student travelers. You don't have to be a card-carrying member of the International Youth Hostel Federation (IYHF) to lodge at any of them, since none are affiliated with that organization.

Charles University is Prague's most prestigious postsecondary school. Although many of its associated colleges are spread throughout the city, the areas just north and east of Charles Bridge contain most of the university's main buildings. Like many urban schools, this university does not really have a campus, but the pubs and public squares of the neighborhood serve as student hangouts. Since Charles University is largely a commuter school, central Prague lacks the verve and bustle of a college community.

If you want to make some music or do some magic for money, you can do so legally anywhere in the city. If you want to sell something, beware that city authorities have recently been requiring permits to hawk on Charles Bridge.

6 Getting There

BY PLANE
THE MAJOR AIRLINES

About two dozen international airlines offer regularly scheduled service into Prague's Ruzyně Airport. **Delta** (☎ 800/221-1212), the principal U.S. carrier making the trip, connects via Frankfurt, Germany, with gateways at Atlanta, Cincinnati, Los Angeles, New York, Orlando, San Francisco, and Washington, D.C. **ČSA Czech Airlines** (☎ 800/223-2365), the national carrier of the Czech Republic, flies to Prague from New York, Chicago, Los Angeles, and Montreal. **Lufthansa** (☎ 800/645-3880) is quickly becoming the most dominant carrier in central Europe, offering more flights to Prague from America than any other airline. The carrier also operates nonsmoking flights New York and San Francisco to their Frankfurt hub.

Following are other major carriers serving the Czech Republic, along with their U.S. toll-free telephone numbers: **Air France** (☎ 800/237-2747); **Alitalia** (☎ 800/223-5730); **Austrian Airlines** (☎ 800/843-0002); **British Airways** (☎ 800/247-9297); **KLM Royal Dutch Airlines** (☎ 800/777-5553); **SAS** (☎ 800/221-2350); and **Swissair** (☎ 800/221-4750).

AIRLINE OFFICES IN PRAGUE   For information on flight arrivals and departures, or to make reservations or changes, contact the following airlines at their Prague city offices: **Air France,** Václavské nám. 10, Praha 1 (☎ 2/2422 7164); **Alitalia,** Revoluční 5, Praha 1 (☎ 2/2481 0079); **Austrian Airlines,** Revoluční 15, Praha 1 (☎ 2/231 3378 or 2/231 1872); **British Airways,** Staroměstské nám. 10, Praha 1 (☎ 2/232 9020 or 232 9040); **ČSA Czech Airlines,** Revoluční 1 (☎ 2/2421 0132); **Delta,** Národní 32, Praha 1 (☎ 2/2423 9309, 2423 2258, 268 521); **KLM** Royal Dutch Airlines, Václavské nám. 37, Praha 1 (☎ 2/2422 8678); **Lufthansa,** Pařížská 28, Praha 1 (☎ 2/2481 1007); **SAS,** Rytířská 13, Praha 1 (☎ 2/2421 4749); and **Swissair,** Pařížská 11, Praha 1 (☎ 2/2481 2111).

FINDING THE BEST AIRFARE

Airlines observe three pricing seasons to Prague: low (during winter), high (during summer), and shoulder (during spring and fall) At presstime, the lowest published round-trip summer fare from New York was $768; from Chicago, $798; and from Los Angeles, $898. During winter, the lowest published fare from New York was $548; from Chicago, $598; and from Los Angeles, $658.

Business-class seats can cost more than twice the price of coach. Expect to pay about $2,800 from New York, $2,900 from Chicago, and over $3,000 from Los Angeles. Czech Airlines often has good deals in business class that are a lot cheaper than Delta and other Western carriers. Meals, however, are the same in all of ČSA's classes, and are nothing to write home about. Unrestricted fares are the most expensive, but may still be less than a business-class seat.

Most airlines offer only a handful of expensive first-class seats on Prague flights. The published first-class airfare from New York is about $5,500; from Chicago, about $5,800; and from Los Angeles about $6,000. Before buying, see if your airline offers a first-class upgrade with a full-fare business-class ticket.

DISCOUNTED AIRFARES   **Consolidators,** or **bucket shops,** sell tickets on major scheduled carriers at deeply discounted rates—often 20% to 30% lower. For example, in winter from New York, you can buy bucket-shop tickets to Prague on well-known international airlines for as little as $198 each way; the prices rise to about $550 in summer. Remember, however, that it's very difficult to return these tickets and many restrictions apply.

The lowest-priced bucket shops are typically local operations with low profiles and overheads. Look for their advertisements in the travel or classified section of your newspaper. Nationally advertised consolidators are usually not as competitive as smaller local operations, but they have toll-free telephone numbers and are easily accessible. Such consolidators include **Travac,** 989 Sixth Ave., New York, NY 10018 (☎ 212/563-3303 or 800/TRAV-800).

Charter operators mostly sell seats through travel agents. One reliable company is **Council Charter,** 205 E. 42nd St., New York, NY 10017 (☎ 212/661-0311 or 800/800-8222). Look for round-trip fares from New York as low as $550 (mid-winter) and $700 (summer). Before deciding to take a charter, check the restrictions on the ticket. If you decide on a charter flight, seriously consider purchasing cancellation insurance.

You can also travel to Europe as a **courier.** Companies transporting time-sensitive materials, such as documents for banks and insurance firms, regularly hire couriers. All you have to do is give up your checked-baggage allowance and make do with carry-on. Expect to meet a courier service representative at the airport before departure to get the manifest of the checked items. Upon arrival, you deliver the baggage-claim tag to a waiting agent. One drawback, besides restricted baggage, is that you have to travel alone. You might contact **Now Voyager, Inc.,** 74 Varick St., Suite 307, New York, NY 10013 (☎ 212/431-1616 from 10am to 6pm daily). Prices change all the time, from low to very low. Flights are booked on a round-trip basis exclusively, though there is often nothing to carry on the way home.

INTRA-EUROPEAN FLIGHTS   If you're flying to Prague from Europe, fares are generally high. However, some airlines offer special promotions as well as 7- and 14-day advance-purchase fares. For instance, British Airways recently offered a $268 round-trip fare from London to Prague with 14-day advance purchase. Unlike domestic air travel in the U.S., lower-priced airfares are available throughout Europe on charter flights rather than regularly scheduled ones. Look in local newspapers or visit a European travel agent to find out about them. **Trailfinders** (☎ 071/937-5400), which sells discounted fares to Prague on a variety of airlines, is a highly recommended company. You may also want to check out the bucket shops in London's Earl's Court neighborhood. For your own protection, make sure that the company you deal with is a member of the IATA, ABTA, or ATOL.

Prague's Airport

Prague's **Ruzyně Airport** (☎ **02/36 78 14** or **02/36 77 60**), located 12 miles west of the city center, is now in the throes of a long-overdue major expansion. For the moment, the airport remains pleasingly small and terrifically convenient, making transit to and from Prague a relative breeze. Although the airport lacks conveniences that are common in other international gateways (such as duty-free shopping, left-luggage, and postal facilities), there is a bank for changing money (usually open 7am to 11pm), several car-rental offices (see "Getting Around by Car," below), and telephones that work.

GETTING DOWNTOWN   You can make your way from airport to hotel by taxi, airport shuttle bus, or city bus.

Taxis are plentiful, and line up in front of the airport. Unfortunately, the cars that line up directly outside the airport's main exit are crooks that all belong to the same mafia gang. (See "Getting Around," below for details.) If you do let one of these drivers convince you to use his services, negotiate the fare in advance. Expect to pay somewhere between 350 and 450 Kč ($13 and $17). Shrewd travelers might be able to get an honest ride from one of the few brave drivers that wait in their Škodas and Ladas just to the right of the airport's main exit, around the corner from the mafia taxi stand. Smile at the driver, point to the dishonest cabs, roll your eyes and say "mafia." The honest driver will know exactly what you're talking about. An honest cab ride should cost no more than 250 Kč ($9.25) to Václavské náměstí (Wenceslas Square). Travel time is about 20 minutes. If you want to save money, find other travelers to share the expense of a taxi.

ČSA, the Czech and Slovak national airline, operates an **airport shuttle bus** to and from their office in downtown Prague. The bus leaves the airport every 30 minutes from 7:30am to 7:30pm, and stops at the Dejvická metro station before continuing to a ČSA office in Old Town near the corner of Revoluční and Čásnovka, about five blocks from náměstí Republiky metro station. The shuttle costs 15 Kč (55¢) to Dejvická and 30 Kč ($1.11) to Old Town. Travel time to Old Town is about 30 minutes.

Even cheaper is **city bus 119,** which delivers passengers from the airport's main exit to Dejvická metro station (and visa versa). The bus costs only 6 Kč (22¢), but makes many stops along the way. Travel time is about 40 minutes.

BY TRAIN

European train fares are lower than those in the United States—Czech tickets are particularly inexpensive. Because European countries are relatively compact, it often takes less time to travel from one city center to another by train than by plane.

Direct trains to Prague depart daily from Paris (via Frankfurt) and from Berlin (via Dresden). The former takes 10 hours and costs about $300 in first class and $200 in second class; the latter takes 5 hours and 20 minutes and costs 1,117 Kč, ($41.30) each way.

The train from London to Prague costs about $350 or £215 in first class, or $250 or £150 in second class. The difference between the classes is relatively small, a matter of one or two inches of padding on the seats, and slightly more legroom. For information on routes and seat availability, visit the **International Rail Centre** in London's Victoria Station (☎ 071/834-2345). You can purchase rail tickets to Prague from any "international" ticket window in Victoria Station. And if you need some help planning your rail trip, visit **Wasteels, Ltd.** (☎ 071/834-7066), located opposite Victoria Station's platform 2.

Trains connect Prague and Vienna five times daily; the 5¹/₂ hour trip costs 716 Kč ($26.50) each way. Trains connect Prague and Budapest six times daily; the nearly 8-hour trip costs 1,250 Kč ($46.25). Trains connect Prague and Warsaw two times daily; the 9 hour trip costs 753 Kč ($28) each way.

You can also reach Prague from Munich or Frankfurt. The former runs three times daily, and the 7 hour trip costs 1,415 Kč ($52) each way. The latter runs two times daily, and the 7¹/₂ hour trip costs 2,044 Kč ($75) each way.

For more information on traveling on České dráhy (Czech Railways), see Chapter 10.

The **European East Pass** is good for first class unlimited rail access in Austria, the Czech Republic, Hungary, Poland, and Slovakia. You must purchase the pass from a travel agent or Rail Europe before you leave for Europe. A pass for any five days of unlimited train travel in a 15-day period costs $185 for adults, $93 for children ages 4 to 11. A pass for any 10 days of unlimited train travel in a one month period costs $299 for adults, $150 for children ages 4 to 11.

Also available is the **Czech Flexipass,** good for rail travel within the Czech Republic. It costs $69 for five days of travel within a 15-day period. However, it's twice as expensive as buying tickets yourself.

Following is a list of European rail passes, along with 1996 prices. *Note:* These passes are *not* valid in the Czech Republic.

Eurailpass: 15 days, $522; 21 days, $678; one month, $838; two months, $1,148; three months, $1,468. First class only, with access to many ferries, steamers, and buses free or at a discount.

Eurail Saverpass: For two or more people traveling together October through March, or for three people traveling together April through September: 15 days, $452 per person. First class only; same privileges as Eurailpass.

Eurail Flexipass: any 10 days within two months, $616; any 15 days within two months, $812. First class only; same privileges as Eurailpass. EDS: Note that's there's no more pass for 5 days of travel within two months.

Eurail Youthpass: 15 days, $418; one month, $598; two months, $798. For travelers under 26 years of age. Second class only; same privileges as Eurailpass.

Children under 12 travel for half fare, and under 4 for free, when with a parent holding a Eurailpass, Eurail Saverpass, and Eurail Flexipass.

Any of the passes mentioned above can be purchased from Rail Europe; call 800/4-EURAIL for tickets, information, or brochures.

Many rail passes are available in the U.K. for travel in Britain and Europe. Unfortunately, one of the most widely used of these passes, the InterRail card, is not valid for travel in the Czech Republic. Passengers under age 26 with lots of holiday time sometimes opt for a EuroYouth ticket, which allows unlimited stopovers en route between London and the Czech border, after which it costs the equivalent of £10 to £20 to reach Prague.

PRAGUE'S TRAIN STATIONS

Passengers traveling to Prague by train typically pull into one of two centrally located train stations: Hlavní Nádraží (Main Station) or Nádraží Holešovice (Holesovice Station). Both are on Line C of the metro system and offer a number of visitor services, including money exchange, a post office, and a luggage-storage area. At both terminals you'll find **AVE Ltd.** (☎ 2/2422 3521 or 2/2422 3226), an accommodations agency that arranges beds in hostels as well as rooms in hotels and apartments. They're open daily from 6am to 11pm. If you've arrived without room reservations, this agency is definitely worth a visit.

Hlavní Nádraží, Wilsonova třída, Praha 2 (☎ 02/24-21-76-54), is both the grander and more popular of Prague's two primary train stations. It's also seedier. Built in 1909, this beautiful, four-story art nouveau structure was certainly one of the city's most beloved architectural gems, before it was connected to a functionalist-style dispatch hall in the mid-1970s. From the train platform, you'll walk down a flight of stairs and through a tunnel before arriving in the station's ground-level main hall, which contains ticket windows, a marginally useful **Prague Information Service** office that sells city maps and dispenses information (sometimes inaccurate), and filthy restrooms. The station's basement holds a left-luggage counter, which is open 24 hours and charges 20 Kč (74¢) per bag per day. Though cheaper, the nearby lockers are not secure and should be avoided. Public-showering facilities are also located beneath the station's main hall. They are surprisingly clean and a good place to freshen up. The showers cost just 30 Kč ($1.11) and are open Monday through

Eastern Europe Rail Map

Friday from 6am to 8pm, Saturday from 7am to 7pm, and Sunday from 8am to 4pm. On the station's second floor you'll find the train information office (marked by a lowercase "i"), open daily 6am to 10pm. On the top floor is a tattered restaurant that I recommend only to the most famished traveler.

The train station is a 5-minute stroll to the "top" end of Václavské náměstí and 15 minutes by foot to Staroměstské náměstí. Metro line C connects the station to the rest of the city. Metro trains depart from the lower level, and tickets, which cost 6 Kč (22¢), are available from the newsstand near the metro entrance. Taxis line up just outside the station, and are plentiful enough throughout the day and night.

Nádraží Holešovice (☎ 02/2461 5865), Prague's second train station, is usually the terminus for trains from Berlin and other points north. Although it is not as centrally located as the main station, its more manageable size and location at the end of metro line C make it almost as convenient.

Prague contains two smaller rail stations. **Masaryk Station,** Hybernská ulice (☎ 02/2422 4200), is primarily for travelers arriving on trains originating from other Bohemian cities or from Brno or Bratislava. Situated about 10 minutes by foot from the main train station, Masaryk is located near Staré Město, just a stone's throw from náměstí Republiky metro station. **Smíchov Station,** Nádraží ulice (☎ 02/2461 5086), is the terminus for commuter trains from western and southern Bohemia, though an occasional international train pulls in here too. The station contains a 24-hour baggage check and is serviced by metro line B.

BY BUS

Throughout Europe, bus transportation is usually less expensive than rail travel and covers a more extensive area. European buses generally outshine U.S. counterparts. In the Czech Republic, buses cost significantly less than trains, and often offer more direct routes to the places you want to visit. **Europabus,** c/o DER Tours/German Rail, 11933 Wilshire Blvd., Los Angeles, CA 90025 (☎ 310/479-4140 or 800/782-2424), provides information on regular coach service. **Cosmos,** a British operator, specializes in economical bus tours of Europe that can be booked through travel agents in the U.S. It will match single travelers who want to share a room to avoid paying a supplement.

If you're coming from London, **Eurolines,** 52 Grosvenor Gardens, London SW1 W OAU (☎ 071/730-0202), runs regular bus service from London to Prague costing about £95 for a round-trip. Coaches are equipped with toilets and reclining seats, and trips take about 30 hours. By law, drivers are required to stop at regular intervals for rest and refreshment.

A daily bus connection between Prague and Vienna takes 4 hours and 15 minutes and costs 860 Kč ($32). Buses connect Prague and Budapest two times weekly. The 8 hour 15-minute trip costs 770 Kč ($28.50) each way. There is no bus service between Prague and Warsaw.

From Germany, buses connect Prague and Munich four times weekly. The 7 hour 20 minute trip costs 1,000 ($37) each way. Buses run between Prague and Frankfurt five times weekly. The 9 hour and 45 minute trip costs 1,780 Kč ($66) each way. The 6 hour trip between Prague and Berlin costs 1,150 Kč ($43) each way.

Fares on Czech buses are typically half those of trains. Reservations should be made as far in advance as possible. See Chapter 10 for more information on traveling by bus from Prague to destinations in the Czech Republic.

PRAGUE'S BUS STATION

The **Central Bus Station—Florenc,** Křižíkova 5, Praha 8 (☎ 02/2421 1060), is located a few blocks north of the main railroad station. Most local and long-distance buses arrive at this terminal, situated just beside the Florenc metro station, on both metro lines B and C. Florenc station is relatively small, and doesn't have many tourist services.

Kingscourt Express, Antala Staška 60 (☎ 02/6121 1668), operates the most popular scheduled bus service between London and Prague, which stops in Prague just across the street from the Florenc station. The nearly 21-hour trip runs three times weekly and costs 2,250 Kč ($83) each way.

Even smaller bus depots are located at **Želivského** (metro line A), **Smíchovské nádraží** (metro line B), and **Nádraží Holešovice** (metro line C).

BY CAR

You definitely do not need to rent a car to explore Prague. But if you want to see the countryside, driving can be a fun way to travel. In addition, a car will lend added mobility to find a budget hotel or a comfortable spot to camp. You'll find driving directions to the destinations listed in Chapters 10 through 12.

Travelers approaching Prague from the west drive through Nürnberg, Germany, before entering the Czech Republic at the Waidhaus/Rozvadov border crossing. Drivers from the northwest motor through Chemnitz (formerly Karl-Marx-Stadt), Germany, before entering the Czech Republic at the Reitzenhain/Pohraniční border crossing. From the south, Linz, Austria, is a gateway to the Czech Republic, and from the east, Zilina, Slovakia, is a gateway.

See "Getting Around" in Chapter 3 for information on car-rental firms.

Driving distances are: from Vienna, 350 km; from Warsaw, 750 km; from Munich, 450 km; and from Berlin, 380 km.

BY FERRY, SEACAT, OR CHUNNEL FOR BRITISH TRAVELERS

If you're traveling from England and don't want to fly, there are several options for getting to continental Europe. If you want to drive, **P & O Ferries** (☎ 081/575-8555 or 0304/203-388) is one of the U.K.'s largest drive-on ferryboat operators, carrying cars, passengers, and freight. The company offers daily crossings of the English Channel from Dover to Calais, France, and from Folkestone to Zeebrugge, Belgium. **Brittany Ferries** (☎ 0752/221-321), P & O's largest competitor, offers regular ferry service from Portsmouth to Saint-Malo and Caen, in France.

Another way to cross the channel is by SeaCat (a form of high-speed motorized catamaran), which cuts your journey time from the U.K. to the Continent. A SeaCat trip can be a fun adventure, especially for first-timers and children, as the vessel is technically "flying" above the surface of the water. A SeaCat crossing from Folkestone to Boulogne, France, is longer in miles but more timesaving to passengers than the Dover to Calais route used by conventional ferryboats. For reservations and information, call **HoverSpeed** at 0304/240-241.

You can also go via the Channel Tunnel. The "Chunnel" runs between Folkestone and Calais, France. Travel time under the water between England and France is a brief 30 minutes. Train passengers can use the tunnel on direct routes to Paris from London's Waterloo Station. If you opt to take a car with you, you'll drive it into a railway compartment in preparation for the crossing, and drive it away from the rail yard once you reach France. For up-to-the-minute information, call **Brit Rail** at 071/928-5100.

PACKAGE TOURS

Several tour operators offer escorted and independent tours to Prague and the Czech Republic and are described below. However, using this book, you can put together your own independent itinerary for about a third less in cost.

Most airlines listed above offer both escorted tours and on-your-own packages. For example, **Delta Air Lines Dream Vacations** (☎ 800/872-7786) offers 5-night airfare and hotel packages departing from New York/Newark starting at $1059 in the spring and fall, and from $1259 in the summer. But if you can find round-trip airfare (from New York/Newark) for $750 or less, you won't be saving any money on Delta's tours. Likewise, the half-dozen add-ons, including walking tours, river cruises, and airport transfers, can all be easily purchased yourself for less money, once you arrive in Prague.

Czech tour operators include **Čedok,** 10 E. 40th St., Suite 1902, New York, NY 10016 (☎ 212/689-9720), the largest tour company in the Czech Republic that offers the most options in the most cities, including Prague, Karlovy Vary, Plzeň, Česky Krumlov, and Telč. During summer, their most comprehensive 7-day land package starts at $850 per person, based on double occupancy. Čedok's lowest-priced Prague-only package costs $150 per person for two nights at the hotel Atlantic. Again, you can do it yourself for less.

Isram World of Travel, 630 Third Ave., New York, NY 10017 (☎ 800/223-7460 or 212/661-1193) offers packages to many Eastern European cities that let you pick which cities you want to visit. They will arrange hotels, sightseeing tours, and airport/train station transfers. Their Prague package starts at $282 per person, based on double occupancy. If you want to stay in the center of the city, however, upgrade to the hotel Adria, which costs $367 per person.

Jewish Heritage Tours, 220 71st St., Suite 211, Miami Beach, FL 33141 (☎ 800/323-2219 or 305/861-0080), offers both group and independent tours of Prague, including several itineraries that combine a visit to the Czech capital with tours of Vienna, Budapest, Krakow, and Warsaw. A three-night independent Prague stay includes accommodations, airport transfers, sightseeing tours of both general and Jewish interest, and a visit to Terezin. Their land-only packages cost from $459 per person, based on double occupancy.

General Tours, 53 Summer St., Keene NH 03431 (☎ 800/221-2216) also offers escorted and independent tours to Prague.

Getting To Know Prague 3

by Dan Levine

This chapter will give you the basics you need to orient yourself in Prague. It will introduce you to Prague's neighborhoods, explain how the city is laid out, tell you how to get around, and more.

1 Orientation

VISITOR INFORMATION

Despite tourism's terrific importance to the Czech economy, the country's politicians haven't yet gotten around to properly funding an official visitor agency. For the moment, prospective visitors to Prague are largely on their own when it comes to collecting accurate travel information. One of the best strategies for obtaining accurate English-language information is to approach a concierge at a major hotel. You don't have to mention that you're not sleeping upstairs.

The *Prague Post*, the city's weekly English-language newspaper, publishes a "Summer in the City" supplement aimed at tourists. It's included with every edition from mid-June to mid-September. The monthly English-language magazine *Velvet* also includes some visitor information. Both publications are available from most news agents in Old Town.

Čedok, located at Na příkopě 18 and at Václavské náměstí 24, Prague 1 (☎ 02/2419 7111), once the country's official state-owned visitors bureau, is now just a traditional semiprivate travel agency. Like others in town, it prefers selling tickets and tours to dispensing free information. The company also books rail tickets and accepts major credit cards. The offices are open Monday to Friday from 8:30am to 5pm, and Saturday from 8:30am to 12:30pm.

Prague Information Service, Na příkopě 20, Prague 1 (☎ 187 in Prague or 02/264 022), located between Václavské náměstí and náměstí Republiky, is the city's second-largest tourist office, offering brochures on upcoming cultural events as well as tickets to sightseeing tours and concerts. In the summer, the PIS office is usually open Monday through Friday from 9am to 7pm, and on Saturday and Sunday from 9am to 5pm. In the winter, hours are slightly shorter and the office is closed on Sundays. A second PIS office is located inside the main railway station.

Prague at a Glance

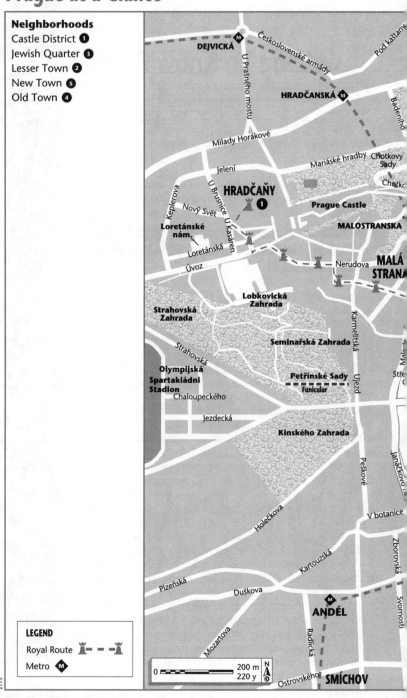

Neighborhoods
Castle District ❶
Jewish Quarter ❸
Lesser Town ❷
New Town ❺
Old Town ❹

DEJVICKÁ Ⓜ
Československé armády
Pod kaštany
U Prašného mostu
HRADČANSKÁ Ⓜ
Badeniho
Milady Horákové
Jelení
Mariánské hradby Chotkovy Sady
Keplerova
Nový Svět
U Brusnice
U Kasáren
HRADČANY ❶
Prague Castle
Chotk
Loretánské nám.
Loretánská
MALOSTRANSKA
Úvoz
Nerudova
MALÁ STRANA
Lobkovická Zahrada
Kamelitská
Strahovská Zahrada
Strahovská
Seminařská Zahrada
Ujezd
Stře
Olympijská Spartakiádní Stadion
Chaloupeckého
Petřínské Sady
Funicular
Jezdecká
Kinského Zahrada
Janáčkovo
Peškové
Holečkova
V botanice
Zborovská
Kartouzská
Plzeňská
Duškova
ANDÉL Ⓜ
Svornosti
Mozartova
Radlická
Ostrovského
SMÍCHOV

LEGEND
Royal Route ♜ - - - ♜
Metro Ⓜ

0 ___ 200 m / 220 y   N↑

46

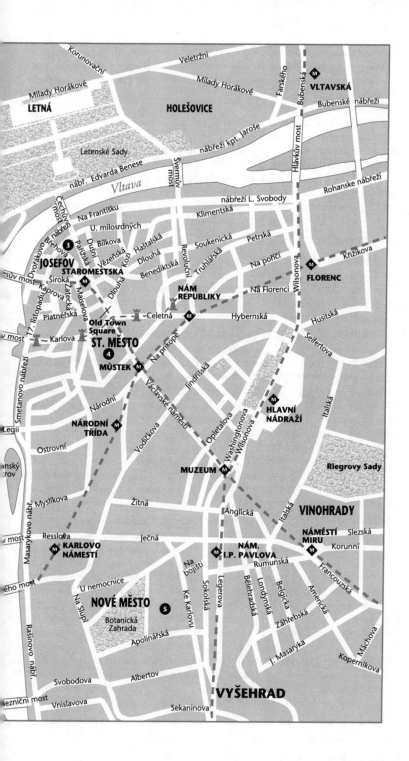

Literally dozens of other tour-and-ticket sellers disguised as information agencies are located throughout Prague's tourist center. While all are primarily interested in sales, most are also willing to answer simple questions. Many can also help you find accommodations.

When entering Prague via Ruzyně Airport, you might try your luck for information at the Tourist Information window, located by the main exit. They might even give you a city map, if they have one. The office is usually open daily from 9am to 6pm. Those arriving via train, into either of Prague's two primary stations, will find the greatest success obtaining information from **AVE Ltd.** (☎ 02/2422 3226 or 02/2422 3521), an accommodations agency that also distributes a limited amount of printed information. It is open daily from 6am to 11pm.

For information about travel by train, visit the train information window (marked with a lowercase "i") in the main train station (Hlavní Nádraží).

CITY LAYOUT

The Vltava (Moldau) River bisects Prague. Staré Město (Old Town) and Nové Město (New Town) are located on the east (or right) side of the river, while Hradčany (Castle District) and Malá Strana (Lesser Town) are situated on the river's west (or left) bank. Vinohrady, a gentrifying residential area located east of New Town, is becoming increasingly popular with visitors as well.

MAIN BRIDGES, SQUARES & STREETS   Bridges and squares are Prague's most prominent landmarks. Charles Bridge, the oldest and most famous of the 15 that span the Vltava, is right in the middle of the city. Staroměstské náměstí (Old Town Square), a few winding blocks east of Charles Bridge, is, appropriately enough, the center of Staré Město. Several important streets radiate from this hub, including fashionable Pařížská to the northwest, historic Celetná to the east, and Melantrichova, which connects to Václavské náměstí (Wenceslas Square) to the southeast. Karlova connects the square and bridge and can be a real zoo; it's better to stick to side streets and reorient yourself when you get to the river.

On the west side of Charles Bridge is Mosteká, a three-block-long thoroughfare that runs into Malostranské náměstí, Malá Strana's main square. Hradčany, the Castle District, sits atop a hill just northwest of the square, while a second hill, Petřín, is located just southwest of the square.

FINDING AN ADDRESS   At one time or another you'll probably get lost in Prague. To the chagrin of visitors and postal workers alike, the city's tangle of streets follows no discernible pattern. There are a few consoling factors, however. One is excellent street signing; signs are usually posted on the sides of buildings. The other is dependable house signing, with numbers that usually increase as one moves away from the Vltava. Note that on signs and literature in Prague, as well as in this book, street names always precede the numbers. Also, in contemporary Czech signage, the word for street (ulice) is either abbreviated to ul. or simply omitted altogether—Pařížská ulice, for instance, is best known as Pařížská. Třída (avenue) and náměstí (square) are also routinely abbreviated to tř. and nám., respectively.

Greater Prague is divided into 10 postal districts, each encompassing from 2 to 22 neighborhoods. While the postal districts are too large to effectively help you locate a particular restaurant or hotel, district numbers are routinely included in addresses, and are therefore listed below with their corresponding neighborhoods.

Prague 1   Hradčany, Malá Strana, Staré Město, Josefov, northern Nové Město.

Prague 2   Southern Nové Město, Vyšehrad, western Vinohrady.

Prague 3   Eastern Vinohrady Žižkov.

Prague 4   Nusle, Michle, Podolí, Braník, Krč, Chodov, Háje, Hodkovičvky, Lhotka, Kunratice, Šeberov, Újezd, Modřany, Libuš, Komořany, Cholupice, Točná, Písnice.

Prague 5   Smíchov, Motol, Košíře, Radlice, Jinonice, Stodůlky, Zličín, Sobín, Hlubočepy, Malá Chuchle, Slivenec, Holyné, Řeporyje, Velká Chuchle, Lochkov, Zadní Kopanina, Lahovice, Radotín, Zbraslav, Lipence.

Prague 6   Western Bubeneč, Dejvice, Vodovice, Střešovice, Břevnov, Veleslavín, Liboc, Ruzyně, Řepy Nůbušice, Lysolaje, Sedlec, Suchdol.

Prague 7   Eastern Bubeneč, Holešovice, Troja.

Prague 8   Karlín, Libeň, Kobylisy, western Střížkov, Bohnice, Čimice, Dáblice, Dolní Chabry, Březiněves.

Prague 9   Vysočany, Hloubětín, Hrdlořezy, Kyje, Hostavice, Černý most, Prosek, eastern Střížkov, Letňany, Kbely, Satalice, Dolní Počernice, Horní Počernice, Klánovice, Běchovice, Koloděhe, Újezd and Lesy.

Prague 10   Vršovice, Strašnice, Malešice, Štěrboholy, Dubeč, Hájek, Královice, Uhříněves, Dolní and Horní Měcholupy, Záběhlice, Hostivař, Petrovice, Křeslice, Pitkovice, Benice, Kolovraty, Lipany, Nedvězí.

STREET MAPS   A Prague street map is essential, especially if you want to venture off the main tourist streets without getting too lost. Bookstores, souvenir shops, and many sidewalk news agents sell local maps. Expect to pay about 50 Kč ($1.85). For an in-depth look at Prague's web of streets, buy a comprehensive accordion-style foldout map, available for about 100 Kč ($3.70). The many competing brands are more or less qualitatively equivalent. Velký Autoatlas produces the best maps for exploring roads outside of Prague; these exhaustive street guides cover the country's maze of back roads. Make sure it's an edition published after 1992.

NEIGHBORHOODS IN BRIEF

The invisible lines that divide local communities were drawn up long ago. Prague was originally developed as four adjacent, self-governing boroughs, plus a walled Jewish ghetto. Central Prague's neighborhoods have maintained their individual identities along with their medieval street plans.

Staré Město (Old Town)   Staré Město was established in 1234 as a result of Prague's growing importance on central European trade routes. Its ancient streets, most of which meander haphazardly around Staroměstské náměstí (Old Town Square), are still the city's biggest tourist draw. Many of Prague's most important buildings and churches are located here, as are many of the city's best shops, restaurants, and theaters. You'll likely spend most of your time exploring this beautiful neighborhood.

Old Town is relatively compact, bordered by the Vltava river on the north and west, and the streets Revoluční and Národní on the east and south. You can wander safely here, without having to worry about straying into an unsafe area. If you do get confused by the cobblestoned streets, don't cross any bridges, or any streets containing tram lines. You'll stumble upon some of the world's most beautiful baroque buildings and find some wonderful little restaurants, shops, bars, cafes, and pubs. For some direction, see "Walking Tour 3" in Chapter 7.

Josefov   Prague's celebrated Jewish ghetto, located entirely within Staré Město, was once surrounded by a wall, before it was almost all destroyed to make way for more modern 19th-century structures. The Old New Synagogue is situated in the geographical center of Josefov, and the surrounding streets are wonderful for strolling.

Prague is considered one of Europe's great historic Jewish cities, and exploring this remarkable area will make clear why. See Walking Tour 4" in Chapter 7.

Nové Město (New Town)   Draped like a crescent around Staré Město, Nové Město (New Town) is home to Václavské náměstí (Wenceslas Square), the National Theater, and many of the city's business-oriented buildings. When it was founded by Emperor Charles IV in 1348, Nové Město was the largest wholly planned municipal development in Europe. The street layout remains largely unchanged since the 14th century, but most of Nové Město's structures were razed in the late 19th century and replaced with the offices and apartment buildings that stand today.

Although New Town would be the toast of almost any other city, in Prague it takes a back seat to the more pretty and ornate districts of Old Town and Mála Strana. If you venture beyond Wenceslas Square, you'll find some good restaurants, interesting shops, and a work-a-day city that feels almost absent in the more touristed areas. Single women especially should be particularly careful at night around Wenceslas Square and nearby Perlová street; both areas are populated with pimps and prostitutes.

Malá Strana (Lesser Town)   Prague's "Lesser Town" was founded in 1257 by German settlers who were enticed here by the region's Přemyslid rulers. Nestled between Prague Castle and the Vltava River, Malá Strana is relatively compact. Its winding lanes are some of the city's prettiest, especially those surrounding Kampa Park, situated along the river just south of Charles Bridge. Many embassies are located here, as are old palaces and gardens that once belonged to the city's richest families. You'll want to get lost in its busy tangle of tiny streets. See "Walking Tour 1" in Chapter 7.

Hradčany   Literally "Castle District," this part of central Prague contains little more than the castle itself. Situated on a hilltop above Malá Strana, Hradčany has historically been the center of government, a tradition that continues to the current day. It's well worth spending a day in this district, exploring the castle, the Loreto, and the Strahov Monastery. If you arrive in the summer, you will, no doubt, have to battle with hoards of tourists, but Hradčany is worth visiting under any circumstances. Hearty travelers can walk up a steep hill to the district from Mála Strana, below. Better still, take tram 22 up and walk down, via Nerudova street, or through the gardens of Petřín.

Vinohrady   Once planted with the king's vineyards, leafy Vinohrady has developed into one of Prague's nicest residential neighborhoods. The beautiful apartments here are mostly bright and airy, built with large rooms and high ceilings. Since the Velvet Revolution, Vinohrady is gentrifying faster than any other part of Prague. Wealthier inhabitants have attracted many new shops and restaurants. Plus it's easy to get to the city center from here on Metro Line A.

2 Getting Around

BY PUBLIC TRANSPORTATION

Prague's public transportation network is both vast and efficient—one of the few sound Communist-era legacies. In central Prague, metro (subway) stations abound. Above ground, trams and buses traverse the city in all directions, and are so punctual that you can practically set your watch by them.

The city's metros, trams, and buses all share the same price structure and ticketing system. As of this writing, a one-ride ticket on all forms of transportation costs 6 Kč (22¢) each for adults and 3 Kč (11¢) for children ages 10 to 16. Rides are free for those under age 10 and over age 70. The same tickets are valid on the city's

Prague Metro

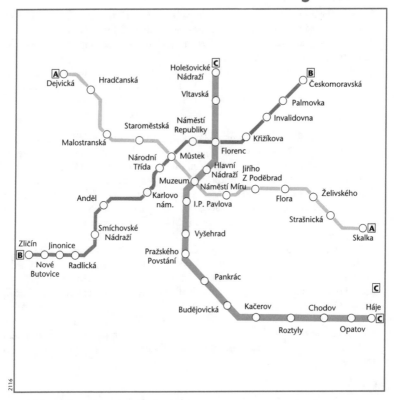

entire public transportation system each good for one ride (except for transfers within the metro system). Tickets can be purchased from orange coin-operated machines in metro stations or at most newsstands marked "Tabak" or "Trafika."

Hold on to your validated ticket throughout your ride—you'll need it to prove you've paid if a ticket collector asks you. If you're caught without a valid ticket, you'll be asked to pay a 200 Kč ($7.40) fine on the spot.

You can buy a one-day ticket good for unlimited rides for 50 Kč ($1.85), a two-day pass for 85 Kč ($3.15), a three-day pass for 110 Kč ($4.07), a four-day pass for 135 Kč ($5), and a five-day pass for 170 Kč ($6.30). If you're planning on staying for two or more weeks, it makes economical sense to buy a monthly pass for 320 Kč ($11.85). These can be purchased at the "DP" windows at any metro station. After the first week of the month, passes are only available at the Dopravní podnik (transport department) office on Na bojišti, near the I.P. Pavlova metro station, where you must purchase the photo ID for a monthly pass.

Note that in mid-1996 the city plans to go to a new payment system, where an adult ticket would cost 10 Kč (37¢) but would be valid for all forms of public transportation for one hour, with unlimited transfers within the hour after the ticket has been validated.

BY METRO (SUBWAY)

The Prague metro opened in 1974, and its trains are smooth, fast, and efficient. They operate daily from about 5am to midnight, and run every two to six minutes or so. Three lines—called A, B, and C—intersect with each other at various points around the city. The most convenient central Prague stations are Můstek, located at the foot of Václavské náměstí (Wenceslas Square); Staroměstská, for Staroměstské náměstí (Old Town Square) and Charles Bridge; and Malostranská, serving Malá Strana and Hradčany (Castle District).

Validate your ticket by inserting it into the date-stamping machine before descending on the escalator to the train platform. Tickets are then valid for one hour, but cannot be used to transfer to trams or buses.

BY TRAM

Even if you usually shy away from public transportation in foreign cities, use Prague's trams. The city's 22 electric streetcar lines run practically everywhere, they run regularly, and they're actually a lot of fun. You can never get too lost, because no matter how far from the city center you travel, there's always another tram with the same number traveling back to where you started. Trams, like trains, automatically make every stop. Schedules are posted at each stop, and trams are usually on time. The tram network is coordinated with the metro; an "M" on the tram schedule means that the stop is at a metro station.

✪ The most popular tram, number 22 (dubbed "the tourist tram" or "the pick-pocket express"), runs past top sights like the National Theater and Prague Castle. Tram routes are marked on most maps. In the winter, when the temperature routinely hovers around freezing, the individually heated seats on the trams are some of the warmest chairs in town.

Immediately after boarding, stamp your ticket in the machine on the tram. Face the side of the ticket with the numbers toward you, slide it into the ticket box, and pull the black lever forward. Note that new electronic time-validation boxes are in the process of being installed.

BY BUS

As with trams, bus riders must purchase tickets in advance, from either a newsstand or a metro station machine, and validate them upon boarding. Regular bus service stops at midnight, after which selected routes run reduced schedules (usually only once per hour).

BY FUNICULAR

The funicular, a kind of cable car on a track, dashes up and down Petřín Hill every 10 minutes or so from 9:15am to 8:45pm. The incline tram only makes two stops—one of which is at Nebozízek Restaurant in the middle of the hill (see Chapter 5, "Prague Dining")—and requires the same ticket as other means of public transport. The funicular departs from a small house in the park just above the middle of Újezd in Malá Strana.

BY CAR

My advice is simple: If you're staying in central Prague, don't drive. Fraught with adventure, driving in the city center is only for those with nerves of steel. There are a maze of narrow streets, pedestrian-only thoroughfares, one-way roads, and a plethora of restrictions designed to discourage driving.

If you are staying on the outskirts of the city, and need a car for trips into the countryside, that's another matter entirely. Driving around the Czech Republic is relatively straightforward. The country's major roadways radiate from Prague like spokes on a wheel, so touring the country is easy if you make Prague your base. The Brno motorway is the only highway in the country; the other "major" roads are all two-lane roads.

Roads for the most part are narrow and in need of repair. Add to this crazy Czech drivers—you may want to take the train. However, the main highways are in good shape, so whenever possible, stick to major roads, especially at night. If you have car trouble, major highways have some emergency telephones where you can call for assistance. There's also the **UAMK,** a 24-hour-a-day motor assistance club, which can provide service for a fee. They drive bright yellow pickup trucks and can be summoned on the main highways by using the SOS emergency telephones located at the side of the road about every kilometer or so. If you're not near an emergency telephone or are on a road that does not have them, you can contact UAMK at ☎ **123** or ☎ **0123** outside of major towns.

Foreign drivers are required to have an international drivers' license and proof of international insurance (a green card that is issued with rental cars). Czech police are infamous for stopping cars with foreign plates, and the "fines" they exact are often negotiable. If you're stopped, expect to pay 500 Kč ($18.50), the typical bribe. Those caught by the police should ask for some type of receipt (*účet* in Czech; pronounced oo-chet); this can help cut down on overpayment.

RENTALS   The big American car-rental firms are the most expensive. Rates vary, but expect to pay about 2,125 Kč ($79) per day and 10,375 Kčs ($384) per week, including unlimited milage, for a Škoda Favorit or similar tin can. Expect a standard-shift vehicle unless you specifically ask for an automatic.

Europcar/InterRent, Pařížská 28, Prague 1 (☎ 02/2481 0515 or 02/2481 1290), is open daily from 8am to 8pm. A second Europcar office is located at Ruzyně Airport, and is open daily from 8am to 10pm. Other large companies are **Hertz,** Karlovo nám. 28, Prague 2 (☎ 02/29 62 37 or 02/29 01 22); **Budget,** at Ruzyně Airport (☎ 02/316 52 14) and in the Hotel Inter-Continental, nám. Curieových, Prague 1 (☎ 02/231 95 95); and **Avis,** E. Krásnohorské 9, Prague 1 (☎ 02/231 55 15).

Local Czech car-rental companies sometimes offer lower rates than the big international firms. Check prices with **Prague Car Rent,** Opletalova 33, Prague 1 (☎ 02/2422 9848); and **SeccoCar,** Přístavní 39, Prague 7 (☎ 02/684 34 03).

Bohemia Travel Service, Výstaviště Praha, Prague 7 (☎ 02/2010 3625) rents Mercedes, Jaguar, and Lincoln limousines by the hour for trips in Prague, and all around the Czech Republic. Rates are 1,500 Kč ($55.50) per hour. The office is open 24 hours.

Car rates can be negotiable. Try to obtain the best possible deal with the rental company by asking about special discounts. Special deals are sometimes offered for keeping the car longer, for unlimited mileage (or at least getting some miles thrown in free), or for a bigger car at a lower price. You can usually get some sort of discount for a company or association affiliation. Check before you leave home and take a member-identification card with you.

Since extras can send prices into the stratosphere, find out all the charges you are likely to incur from the car-rental company; besides the daily or weekly rental charge, consider a mileage charge, insurance, the cost of fuel, and tax on the total rental bill (22 percent in Prague). In addition, you may be paying for parking along the way. If you already have collision coverage on your own automobile insurance, you're most likely covered when you are behind the wheel of a rental car; check with your insurance carrier. If you decide on European insurance, be sure it doesn't come with a $1,000 deductible.

A collision-damage waiver (CDW) costs a hefty $7 to $13 per day. Some credit-card companies, including American Express, automatically insure cardholders against collision damage at no additional charge when they rent a car using their card.

GASOLINE   Not only are rentals pricey, but gasoline in the Czech Republic costs much more than Americans are accustomed to paying—about $3.50 per gallon, and filling stations can be difficult to find. Gas stations open 24 hours in center city are located in Prague 3 on Olšanská; in Prague 4 on Újezd; and in Prague 7 on Argentinská. Over the past few years, the number of gas stations in the Czech Republic has skyrocketed. It's no longer difficult to find an open pump, and many stations now have mini-markets as well. As a rule, however, it's wise to fill up when your tank drops to the quarter-tank mark. If you're leaving the country, fill up near the border since the price of gas in Austria and Germany is much higher.

PARKING   Finding a parking spot in Prague can sometimes be more of a challenge than driving in this maze of a city. Fines for illegal parking can be stiff, but worse are "Denver Boots," which immobilize cars until a fine is paid. If you find your car booted, you must pay a several-hundred-crown fine at police headquarters, Kongresová 2, Prague 4 (metro: Vyšehrad), the large building just south of the Forum Hotel, then return to your car and wait for the clamp removers.

SPECIAL DRIVING RULES   Seat belts are required, you may not legally make a right turn when a traffic light is red, and automobiles must stop when a pedestrian steps into a crosswalk. On major highways, the speed limit is 110 kilometers-per-hour.

The yellow diamond road sign denotes the right-of-way at an unregulated intersection. When approaching an intersection, always make sure who has the right of way since it can change several times within blocks on the same street.

BY BICYCLE

Although there are no bike lanes and smooth streets are unheard of, Prague is a particularly wonderful city to bike in. Vehicular traffic is limited in the city center, where small winding streets seem especially suited to two-wheeled vehicles. Surprisingly, few people take advantage of this opportunity; cyclists are largely limited to the few foreigners who have imported their own bikes. The city's ubiquitous cobblestones make mountain bikes the natural choice for cyclists. Unfortunately, the two shops that rented them have recently closed. Check the English-language newspaper *Prague Post* or the magazine *Velvet* for information on or advertisements by bicycle rental companies. Hopefully one will spring up soon.

BY TAXI

Taxis can be hailed in the streets or found in front of train stations, large hotels, and popular tourist attractions. ***But be warned:*** The great majority of cab drivers routinely rip off unsuspecting tourists. Taxi horror stories abound. You will likely see a Christmas tree-shaped "odor-eater" or other ornament hanging in front of the taxi meter. Ask the driver to remove it so you can see the meter.

When entering a taxi, sit in the front seat next to the driver. The meter should start no higher than 10 Kč (37¢). When riding within the city center, the meter should then climb at a rate of 12 Kč (44¢) per kilometer. You will see two numbers on the taxi meter. The one on the left that keeps climbing is the fare. The one on the right will read either 1, 2, 3, or 4. The higher the number, the faster the meter runs. If the rate window doesn't read 1, you're getting ripped off. You still might be getting ripped off, as some drivers have rigged their meters to show 1, but run at a higher rate. Keep your eye on the meter, as drivers will often start the trip with the meter on 1, then raise the number stealthfully while shifting gears. Be prepared to tell the driver to stop if you spot cheating. Writing down the cab's license number is a good way to persuade drivers to charge you the correct fare. If the driver tells you that his is a special taxi, he's lying. The driver is also lying if he says that your trip is out of the center where rate 1 applies.

If you phone for a taxi, chances are pretty good that you'll be charged the official rate, as your trip is logged in an office and is a matter of public record. So if you know that you are going to need a taxi, phone in advance to find an honest ride. Reputable taxi companies with English-speaking dispatchers include **AAA Taxi** (☎ 02/34 24 10 or 3399); **RONY Taxi** (☎ 02/692-1958 or 02/43 04 03); and the unfortunately-named **ProfiTaxi** (☎ 02/6104 5555 or 02/6104 5550).

A final warning: Only the foolish hail cabs in Václavské náměstí, Malostranské náměstí, or at the foot of Charles Bridge, as these areas attract thieving mafia drivers—the worst offenders.

If you suspect a driver of cheating while the ride is in progress, you can either tell him to stop and then get out without paying, or wait until you're at your destination before you argue about it. At least then you're where you want to be. Unfortunately, no governmental body oversees taxis in Prague, so your only recourse is the police—and they are likely to answer you with blank stares or shrugs, maybe even a chuckle or two.

FAST FACTS: Prague

Airport   See "Getting There" in Chapter 2.

American Express   For travel arrangements, traveler's checks, currency exchange, and other member services, visit the city's sole American Express office, located at Václavské nám. (Wenceslas Square) 56, Prague 1 (☎ **02/2421 9992;** fax 02/2422 7708). It's open Monday through Friday from 9am to 6pm, and Saturday from 9am to 3pm. The office sometimes closes for lunch from 1:30 to 2pm. To report lost or stolen Amex cards, call 2/2421-9978.

Area Code   The area code in Prague is 02. If you are dialing Prague from outside of the Czech Republic, drop the 0. To call Prague direct from the United States, dial 011 (international code), 42 (the Czech Republic country code), 2 (Prague's area code, without the "0" prefix), and the six-, seven-, or eight-digit local telephone number.

Babysitters   If your hotel can't recommend a sitter, phone **Affordable Luxuries,** Štepanská 15, Prague 1 (☎ **02/2166 1319** or **02/2166 1266**), an American-owned company that provides various child-minding services. Make reservations far in advance. The fee is 180 Kč ($6.66) per hour.

Bookstores   The largest English-language bookshops in Prague are **The Globe,** Janovského 14, Prague 7 (☎ **02/6671 2610**); **Bohemian Ventures,** nám. Jana Palacha 2, Prague 1 (☎ **02/231-9516**); and **U knihomola,** Mánesova 79, Prague 2 (☎ **02/627-7770**). See Chapter 8 for complete information.

Business Hours   Most **banks** are open Monday through Friday from 9:30am to 3:30pm. Some also open Saturday from 9:30 until noon. Business **offices** are generally open Monday through Friday from 8am until 4pm. **Pubs** are usually open daily 11am to midnight. Most **restaurants** open for lunch from noon to 3pm and for dinner from 6 to 11pm. Only a few stay open later; see "Late-Night Bites" in Chapter 9. **Stores** are typically open Monday through Friday from 10am to 6pm, and 10am to 1pm on Saturday, but those in the tourist center keep longer hours and open on Sunday as well. *Note:* Some small food shops that keep long hours charge up to 20 percent more for all their goods after 8pm or so.

Camera Repair   Jan Pazdera, Vodíčkova 28, pasáž ABC, Prague 1 (☎ **02/2421-6197**), can fix all types of cameras. If they can't, maybe they can interest you in a new or used one. Open 10am to 6pm Monday through Friday, 10am to 1pm Saturday.

Car Rentals   See "Getting Around" earlier in this chapter.

Climate   See "When to Go" in Chapter 2.

Currency   See "Money" in Chapter 2.

Currency Exchange   Banks generally offer the best exchange rates, but **American Express** is competitive and does not charge commission for cashing traveler's checks, regardless of the issuer. Don't hesitate to use a credit card; I have found that card exchange rates are regularly to my advantage. There is one American Express office in Prague (see above).

Komerční Banka has three Prague 1 locations: Na příkopě 28, Na příkopě 3-5, and Václavské nám. 42. The exchange offices are open Monday through Friday from 8am to 5pm.

Živnostenská Banka has two Prague 1 locations: Na příkopě 20 (exchange office only open Monday to Friday from 10am to 9pm, Saturday from 3pm to 7pm) and Celetná 3 (open daily 9am to 9pm).

Čekobanka Chequepoint keeps the longest hours, but offers the worst exchange rates. Central Prague locations include Října 13 and Staroměstské nám. 21. (both open 24 hours); Staroměstské nám. 27 (open daily 8am to 11:30pm); and Václavské nám. 1 (open daily 8am to 11pm).

See "Money" in Chapter 2 for more information.

Customs   See "Visitor Information & Entry Requirements" in Chapter 2.

Doctors and Dentists   If you need a physician or dentist, and your condition is not life-threatening, visit the **First Medical Clinic of Prague Ltd.,** Vyšehradská 35, Prague 2 (☎ **02/29 22 86**). The clinic provides 24-hour emergency health care as well as EKGs, diagnostics, ophthalmology, house calls, and referrals to specialists. Normal walk-in hours are Monday to Saturday from 7am to 8pm. **Health Care Unlimited,** Revoluční 19, Prague 1 (☎ **02/231 1838**), is another safe bet for 24-hour medical and dental services. Examinations cost about 1,000 Kč ($40).

For **emergency medical aid** call the **Foreigners' Medical Clinic,** Na Homolce Hospital, Prague 5 (☎ **02/5292 2146** or **5292 2191**).

Documents Required   See "Visitor Information & Entry Requirements" in Chapter 2.

Driving Rules   See "Getting Around," earlier in this chapter.

Drugstores   See "Pharmacies," below.

Electricity   Czech appliances operate on 220 volts, and plug into two-pronged outlets that differ from those in America and in Great Britain. Appliances designed for the U.S. or U.K. markets must use an adapter and transformer. Do not attempt to plug an American appliance directly into a European electrical outlet without a transformer; you will ruin your appliance and possibly start a fire.

Embassies   The **U.S. Embassy,** Tržiště 15, Prague 1 (☎ **02/2451 0847**), is open Monday through Friday from 8am to 11:30am and 2:30pm to 4pm. The **Canadian Embassy,** Mickiewiczova 6, Prague 6 (☎ **02/2431 1108**), is open Monday through Friday from 8:30am to noon and 2 to 4pm. The **British Embassy,**

Thunovská 14, Prague 1 (☎ 02/2451 0439), is open Monday through Friday from 9am to noon. Call for an appointment at the **Australian Honorary Consul,** Na Ořechovce 38, Prague 6 (☎ 02/2431 0743).

Emergencies Prague's police and fire services can be reached by dialing **158** from any phone. To call an ambulance, dial **155.**

Eyeglass Repair A number of spectacle shops are located on Na příkopě and Václavské náměstí. The best place for repairs is **Lumia Optic,** Skořepka 1, Prague 1. (☎ 02/2421 9915). Simple repairs are usually free, even if you didn't buy your frames here.

Holidays See "When to Go" in Chapter 2.

Hospitals Particularly welcoming to foreigners is **University Hospital Motol,** V úvalu 84 (Motol), Prague 5 (☎ 02/2443 111). Their English-speaking doctors can also make house calls. See "Doctors & Dentists" above for additional information. In an emergency, dial **155** for an ambulance.

Hotlines There are no English-language help lines in the Czech Republic. Check the *Prague Post* or *Velvet* for support groups.

Information See "Visitor Information" earlier in this chapter.

Language The Lonely Planet series publishes a particularly good phrase book covering Czech and other Eastern European languages.

Laundry and Dry Cleaning **Laundry Kings,** Dejvická 16, Prague 6 (☎ 02/312 3743) was the first American-style coin-operated self-service laundromat in Prague. Washes cost 100 to 150 Kč ($3.70 to $5.55) per load, depending on how much drying power you need. An attendant can do your wash for 50 Kč ($1.85) additional, but the service takes at least 24 hours. From Hradčanská metro station, take the "Prague Dejvice" exit and turn left. Laundry Kings is open seven days a week 6am to 10pm.

Prague Laundromat, Korunni 14, Prague 2 (☎ 25 55 41) offers dry cleaning services, as well as laundry, and charges about the same as Laundry Kings. Located two blocks from the Náměstí Míru metro station, it's open daily from 8am to 8pm.

Affordable Luxuries, Štepanská 15, Prague 1 (☎ 02/2166 1319 or 02/2166 1266), will pick up your laundry and dry cleaning and return it to your hotel within 48 hours. The charge is 160 Kč ($5.90) per 6 kilogram load (13.2 lb.). Dry cleaning is 60 Kč ($2.22) per shirt, and 85 Kč ($3.15) per trouser. Prices include delivery.

Liquor Laws There is no minimum drinking age in the Czech Republic. Alcohol can legally be sold at any hour, and pubs and clubs can stay open 24 hours.

Lost Property If you lose something in Prague, it's probably gone for good, but optimists might try visiting the city's **Lost Property Office,** Karoliny Světlé 5 Bolzanova 5 (☎ 02/2423 5085).

Luggage Storage and Lockers The **Ruzyně Airport Luggage Storage Office** never closes, and charges 60 Kč ($2.22) per item, per day. Left-luggage offices are also available at the main train stations, **Hlavní Nádraží** and **Nádraží Holešovice.** Both charge 20 Kč (74¢) per bag, per day, and both are technically open 24 hours, but if your train is departing late at night, check to make sure someone will be around. Luggage lockers are available in all of Prague's train stations, but they are not secure and should be avoided.

Finally, you can often leave luggage at a fancy, well-located hotel even if you are not a guest. At an average cost of 50 Kč ($1.85) per item, your bags can stay at the **Hotel Paříz.**

Mail   Post offices are plentiful and are normally open Monday through Friday from 9am to 5pm and on Saturday from 9am to noon. At presstime, the post office was negotiating a postage hike, so check with your hotel for current rates. Mail boxes are orange, and are usually attached to the sides of buildings. If you are sending mail overseas, make sure it's marked "Par Avion" so it doesn't go by surface. If you mail your letters at a post office, the clerk will add this stamp for you. Mail can take up to 10 days to reach its destination.

The **Main Post Office (Hlavní pošta)**, Jindřišská 14, Prague 1, 110 00 (☎ 02/ 2422 8856), just a few steps from Václavské náměstí, is open 24 hours. You can receive mail here, marked "Poste Restante," and addressed to you, care of this post office. If you carry an American Express Card or Amex traveler's checks, you would be wiser to receive mail care of **American Express,** Václavské nám. (Wenceslas Square) 56, Prague 1 (☎ 02/2421 9992; fax 02/2422 7708).

Maps   See "City Layout" earlier in this chapter.

Money   See "Money" in Chapter 2.

Newspapers and Magazines   The 1995 failure of *Prognosis*, Prague's first English-language newspaper, left the weekly *Prague Post* with a virtual monopoly. Published each Wednesday, the paper is a quick read that usually offers a couple of interesting features, along with skimpy listings of sightseeing and entertainment happenings. The upstart magazine *Velvet*, a glossy American-owned monthly, is giving the Post a run for its money with beefier listings and a hipper attitude. Both publications are available from newsstands throughout Old Town.

Přehled, a monthly listings booklet, is an excellent Czech-language publication with information on theaters, galleries, concerts, clubs, films, and events around town. It costs 20 Kč (74¢), and is not difficult for non-Czechs to understand.

Newsstands are located inside most every metro station, and good-sized, international magazine shops are located in major hotels and on most busy shopping streets.

Pharmacies   The most centrally located 24-hour pharmacy (lékárna) is located at Na příkopě 7 (☎ 02/2421 0229).

Police   In an emergency, dial **158.**

Post Office   See "Mail" above for more information.

Radio   More than a dozen private stations compete with publicly owned Radiožural (94.6 FM) and Radio Praha (92.6 FM; 639 KHz AM). Radio BONTON (99.7 FM) is a light rock station that gives Czech bands lots of airplay. Radio Kiss (98 FM) is an Irish-owned station with a strict pop-oriented playlist. Radio 1 (91.9 FM) is one of Europe's best rock music stations, playing a world-class assortment of contemporary dance and trance music, mixed with some grunge and novelty songs. Radio Free Europe (1287 KHz AM) is an American-funded news-oriented station that's headquartered in Prague's Communist-era Parliament building. English-language World News can be heard on the BBC World Service (101.1 FM).

Restrooms   You'll find plenty of public restrooms in Prague. Toilets are located in every metro station, and are staffed by cleaning personnel who usually charge users 2 Kč (7¢) and dispense to each a precious few sheets of toilet paper. Restaurants and pubs around all the major tourist sights are usually kind to nonpatrons who wish to use their facilities. Around the castle and elsewhere, public toilets are clearly marked with the letters WC. For comfort and cleanliness, my first pick for restrooms are the lobby-level lavatories in Prague's better-known hotels.

Safety   In Prague's center, one never has to worry about straying into a "bad" neighborhood, but common-sense precautions should always be taken. Be aware of your immediate surroundings. Women especially, might not feel comfortable walking alone at night around Wenceslas Square—one of the main areas for prostitution. All visitors should be watchful of pickpockets in the most highly touristed areas, especially on Charles Bridge, in Old Town Square, and in front of the main train station. Be especially wary in crowded buses, trams, and trains. Don't keep your wallet in a back pocket, and don't flash a lot of cash. Riding the metro or trams at night feels just as safe as during the day.

Taxes   A 22% value-added tax (VAT) applies to most goods and services. It is usually included in the ticketed price of most items, rather than being tacked on at the register. Most restaurants also include VAT in the prices stated on their menus. If they don't, that fact should be stated somewhere on the menu.

Taxis   See "Getting Around" earlier in this chapter.

Telephone and Fax   There are two kinds of **pay phones** in normal use. The first accepts coins, while the other operates exclusively with a Phonecard, available from post offices and newsagents in denominations ranging from 50 to 500 Kč ($1.85 to $18.50). The minimum cost of a local call is 2 Kč (7¢). You can deposit several coins at a time, but telephones don't make change, so unless you are calling long distance, use 2 Kč coins exclusively. Phonecard telephones automatically deduct the price of your call from the card. Cards are especially handy if you want to call abroad, as you don't have to continuously chuck in the change.

Dial tones are continual high-pitched beeps that sound something like busy signals in America. After dialing a number from a pay phone, you might hear a series of very quick beeps that tell you the line is being connected. Busy signals sound similar to dial tones.

Long-distance phone charges are higher in the Czech Republic than they are in the United States. In addition, hotels usually add their own surcharge, sometimes as hefty as 100 to 200 percent, which you may be unaware of until you are presented with the bill.

Even if you are not calling person-to-person, collect calls are charged at that high rate, making them pricey too. Charging a long-distance call to your telephone calling card is often the most economical way to phone home.

A fast, convenient way to call the United States from Europe is via USA Direct. This service bypasses the foreign operator and automatically links you to an AT&T operator in America. The access number in the Czech Republic is 0042 000 101. The same service is also offered via MCI; dial 0042 000 112.

Telephone books are printed in two editions: white pages contain alphabetical lists of telephone owners, and yellow pages list businesses according to trade. The yellow pages include an English-language index in back.

You can send faxes from the main post office (Hlavní pošta), Jindřišská 14, Prague 1. The fax office is open 24 hours, and charges 25 Kč (93¢) per page, plus the price of the phone call. The best place to receive faxes is the American Express office (Fax 2422 7708).

Television   There are four broadcast television stations in Prague. ČT1 and ČT2 (channels 1 and 2) are government-run stations featuring low-budget programming that includes live classical music broadcasts and news. Nova (channel 3) is a private station featuring popular American sitcoms, sensational newscasts, and Western movies. Premiéra (channel 4) is a private regional station quickly expanding to become a nationwide station. All four stations are off the air sometime between midnight and 2am. A wireless cable system operates in some parts of the country with a capacity of 16 channels, including Eurosport, MTV, the Children's Channel, and a movie channel. Many hotels already receive international programming via satellite.

Time Zone   Prague time is the same as most of continental Europe, one hour ahead of Britain's Greenwich mean time, and six hours ahead of U.S. eastern time. Clocks here spring forward and fall backward for daylight saving time, but the semiannual rituals follow a slightly different schedule than in the U.S. (about three weeks earlier).

Tipping   Rules for tipping are not as strict in the Czech Republic as they are in the United States. At most restaurants and pubs, locals just round the bill up to the nearest few crowns. When you are presented with good service at tablecloth places, a 10 percent tip is proper. Washroom and cloakroom attendants usually demand a couple of crowns, and porters in airports and rail stations usually receive 10 to 20 Kč (37¢ to 74¢) per bag. Taxi drivers should get about 10%, unless they've already ripped you off, in which case they should only get a good tongue lashing. Check restaurant menus to see if service is included before leaving a tip.

Transit Information   **Čedok,** located at Na príkopě 18 and at Václavské náměstí 24, Prague 1 (☎ 02/2419 7111), is your best bet for coherent English-language information on city transportation.

Prague Accommodations 4

by Dan Levine

Large international hotel chains have secured some of Prague's most important properties. In 1995, Hilton took over the Atrium Hotel, the city's largest, and Renaissance has put its name on a large new hotel in New Town. Many major hotels in Prague are Austrian-owned and managed, including the Grand Hotel Bohemia, Diplomat, Savoy, Moráň, and the Palace. Several of these hotels and many others are nearly brand new, having been built or opened since 1990. Czech hoteliers have lost ground in this rush and are no longer dominant in their own capital.

For reasons of supply and demand, Prague's hotels are relatively expensive, even when compared to major Western cities. Some experts believe that the situation is finally changing; as competition stiffens, quality is rising and prices are falling. Indeed, in the last year, room rates in the capital's priciest hotels have dropped slightly, though none can be considered a bargain. However, service might not match prices in many hotels; desk staff can be surly and unhelpful, as if they haven't learned that in a post-Communist world they have to earn their salaries and compete.

Hotels in the Czech Republic have received a lot of press recently due to the widespread practice of two-tier pricing—a policy of charging natives less than foreigners for the same goods and services. Czech government agencies have given their blessing to this practice, and other members of the government have called it a fair way to manage an economy in transition. For visitors who pay higher prices than residents, two-tier pricing smacks of discrimination. Like everything else, hotel prices are governed by supply and demand. If you show up at a hotel and think that rooms are going empty, you can always negotiate the price before committing to it.

Visitors can stay in five distinct areas of Prague. Old Town and Mála Strana are the two most desirable locations, both smack-dab in the center of everything and surrounded by some of the most beautiful buildings in the world. Unfortunately, this real estate is pricey, and staying here usually means spending up to $400 per night for the privilege. Because New Town is not quite as charming and has many more hotel rooms, prices here are generally lower than they are in those hotels located on quaint cobblestone streets. Most hotels in New Town are located around Wenceslas Square, a charmless, slightly seedy area that has little going for it, except location. In

Hradčany, the area surrounding Prague Castle, the situation is exactly reversed; this pretty neighborhood has everything going for it, except location. Because there is no convenient metro station servicing the area, staying in Hradčany means taking plenty of taxis and trams. Finally, many accommodations are situated on the outskirts of the center. But for the most part, these places, generally short on both charm and location, are only recommendable to those who want to save money.

Anywhere in Prague or the Czech Republic you have the option of staying in hotels on the main square. It's a lovely sight but be prepared for serious noise, particularly on weekends. Light sleepers may prefer to trade the view for a good night's sleep.

PENSIONS   Don't think that if you want a comfortable place to stay, your only option is a hotel. The best pensions are friendlier, more comfortable, more tasteful, and more sophisticated than all but the very top hotels—and cost half as much. We've listed the best pensions in Prague in this chapter, and those throughout the Czech Republic in Chapters 11 and 12.

If you'd like to try a pension or private apartment, an enterprising woman named Viviane Klima can arrange for top-flight accommodations in the city's diplomatic or historic neighborhoods, especially by Prague Castle. The prices vary according to her categories: "C" is one double room for $53 per night; "B" is two rooms for $67 per night; "B-deluxe" is three bedrooms for $75 per night; and "A" is an apartment with living rooms for $88 per night. All come with showers and other amenities can be negotiated. She can be reached at 22 Cukrovarnicka St., 162 00 Prague 6 (☎ 02/2431-1361; fax 02/2431-1359).

ROOMS IN PRIVATE APARTMENTS   You also have the option of renting a room in a private apartment—these are a traveler's best defense against Prague's sky-high hotel rates. Although few of these apartments are located right in the city center, most are within walking distance of a subway, tram, or bus stop. If you arrive in Prague by train, chances are you'll be approached by grandmothers offering their spare bedrooms. Several agencies carry listings and make reservations for visitors who want to stay in private apartments. The best are listed below.

ACCOMMODATIONS AGENCIES   Dozens of companies operating room-finding services have opened in the past few years; you'll see their outlets throughout Prague's Staré Město. These companies rent rooms as well as entire apartments. Expect to pay somewhere between 500 and 1,000 Kč ($18.50–$37) for a double room, and 1,500 to 6,000 Kč ($55.50–$222) for an apartment for two.

Rates depend on both size and location. Some large rental agencies include Prague Accommodation Service, Haštalské nám., Prague 1 (☎ 02/231 02 02; fax 02/2481 0603); Top Tour, Rybná 3, Prague 1 (☎ 02/232 1077; fax 02/2481 1400); Ave Ltd., Hlavní Nádraží and Nádraží Holešovice (☎ 02/2422 3226 or 02/2422 3521; fax 02/549 743 or 542 239); and Čedok, Na příkopě 18 (☎ 02/2419 7111; fax 02/232 1656).

LISTINGS   Hotels are listed below first by location, then by price, according to the following guide: **Very Expensive**—more than 6,500 Kč ($240); **Expensive**—3,900–6,500 Kč ($144–$240); **Moderate**—2,900–3,900 Kč ($107–$144); **Inexpensive**—less than 2,900 Kč ($107). Rates reflect the price for a double or twin room and include Prague's 22% value-added tax (VAT).

Good news is that breakfast is usually included in rates. Breakfast is usually a continental-style affair, consisting of bread and pastries with jam and butter, coffee and tea. Some hotels also offer sliced ham and cheese.

It's always a good idea to inquire about telephone charges before you dial. In Prague hotels, long-distance calls are often billed with a significant mark-up.

1 Best Bets

- **Best Historic Hotel:** Built at the beginning of this century, the **Hotel Evropa** (☎ 02/2422 8117) is one of world's finest examples of art nouveau architecture. Although it's a visual delight both inside and out, the quality of the guest rooms can't match the intrinsic beauty of the building.

- **Best for Business Travelers:** A very central location and big chain-hotel service combine to make the **Hotel Inter-Continental Prague** (☎ 02/2488 1111) the most useful hotel for business travelers. An excellent business center is open daily until 10pm, and a fax machine can be installed in your room or suite at no additional charge.

- **Best for a Romantic Getaway:** Prague's top hotel, the **Savoy** (☎ 02/2430 2122), makes guests feel special. Located within walking distance to Prague Castle, this expensive gem features opulent guest rooms and attentive service in a refined atmosphere that shuns groups.

- **Best Trendy Hotel:** Prague has no trendy hotels, but the **Palace** (☎ 02/2409 3111) still reigns as the one with the most cache. Tell any Praguer that you're staying here, and you won't have to do anything else to impress him or her.

- **Best Lobby for Pretending That You're Rich:** The beautifully restored art nouveau **Hotel Paříž** (☎ 02/2422 2151) has an extremely pretty lobby that's not fancy; rather it's just beautiful in an Old World way that reflects both style and elegance. Sit down in the adjacent lobby bar, order a glass of champagne, and tell the waiter to hold all your calls.

- **Best for Families:** If you are visiting Prague with your family in tow, you should certainly consider renting a **private apartment** (see above). Both larger and cheaper than most hotel rooms, apartments provide your children with lots of space, and come with kitchens so you can fix meals anytime.

- **Best Moderately Priced Hotel:** Clean, modern, comfortable, and close to public transportation, the **Hotel Diplomat** (☎ 02/2439 4111) has a lot going for it. At about $100 per night, including breakfast, this first-class hotel represents one of the best buys in Prague.

- **Best B&B:** Although the **Pension Větrník** (☎ 02/351 9622) is located far from the city center, this family-run pension is one of the friendliest places in Prague. Its historical windmill architecture and pleasant surroundings make this bed-and-breakfast worth the trip.

- **Best Service:** When phoning even Prague's most expensive hotels, receptionists don't always answer promptly, and sometimes even ask you to call back in a few minutes. Not so at the **Prague Renaissance Hotel** (☎ 02/2481 0396), where an excellently trained staff realizes that the customer comes first and doesn't pass problems onto other employees. Austrian-managed and service-oriented, this hotel can be counted on when you need to get things done.

- **Best Location:** If price is not your concern, choose a corner room at the **Grand Hotel Bohemia** (☎ 02/232 3417). It has a perfect location on a quiet Old Town corner one block from náměstí Republiky and close to Old Town Square.

- **Best Health Club:** The newest hotel health club in town at the **Hotel Inter-Continental Prague** (☎ 02/2488 1111) is also the best. The beautifully designed club has five stationary bikes, two StairMaster-like Airsteppers, an excellent circuit of weight machines, an equally extensive set of free weights, and one of the few treadmills in town. The club is also very clean.

Prague Accommodations

Anna Hotel 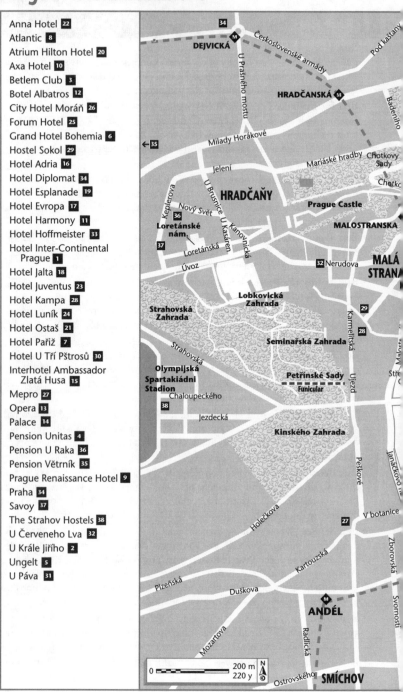22
Atlantic 8
Atrium Hilton Hotel 20
Axa Hotel 10
Betlem Club 3
Botel Albatros 12
City Hotel Moráň 26
Forum Hotel 25
Grand Hotel Bohemia 6
Hostel Sokol 29
Hotel Adria 16
Hotel Diplomat 34
Hotel Esplanade 19
Hotel Evropa 17
Hotel Harmony 11
Hotel Hoffmeister 33
Hotel Inter-Continental
  Prague 1
Hotel Jalta 18
Hotel Juventus 23
Hotel Kampa 28
Hotel Luník 24
Hotel Ostaš 21
Hotel Pařiž 7
Hotel U Tří Pštrosů 30
Interhotel Ambassador
  Zlatá Husa 15
Mepro 27
Opera 13
Palace 14
Pension Unitas 4
Pension U Raka 36
Pension Větrník 35
Prague Renaissance Hotel 9
Praha 34
Savoy 37
The Strahov Hostels 38
U Červeneho Lva 32
U Krále Jiřího 2
Ungelt 5
U Páva 31

2117

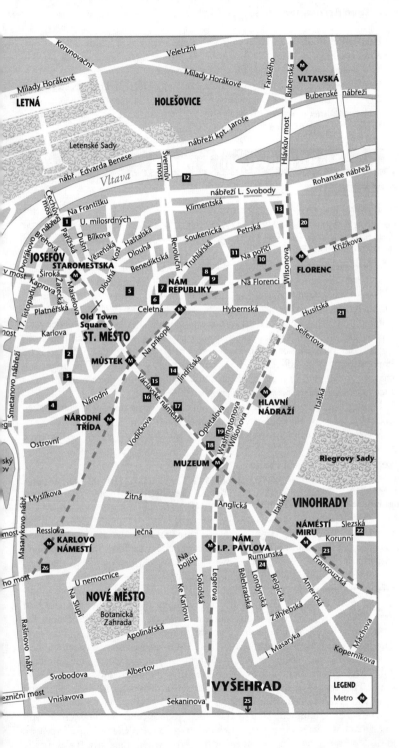

LETNÁ

Korunovační

Milady Horákové

Veletržní

Milady Horákové

Farského

Bubenská

VLTAVSKÁ

Bubenské nábřeži

HOLEŠOVICE

Letenské Sady

nábřeži kpt. Jaroše

Švermův most

Hlávkův most

nábř. Edvarda Beneše

Vltava

12

Rohanske nábřeži

nábřeží L. Svobody

Na Františku

Klimentská

13

Čechúv most

Dvořákovo nábřeži

Břehová

Pařížská

Na Frantíšku

U. milosrdných

1

Dušní

Bílkova

Hašťalská

Soukenická

Petrská

20

Vězeňská

Kozí

Dlouhá

Revoluční

Truhlářská

Na poříčí

11

10

Křižíkova

JOSEFOV

STAROMESTSKA

Široká

Zátecká

Maiselova

Benediktská

8

Na Florenci

FLORENC

17. listopadu

v most

Kaprova

Dlouhá

NÁM
REPUBLIKY

9

Wilsonova

Platnéřská

5

7

Husitská

21

nost

Karlova

Celetná

Hybernská

Seifertova

Old Town
Square

ST. MĚSTO

Na příkope

2

MŮSTEK

14

Jindřišská

Italská

3

Václavské náměstí

15

Smetanovo nábřeži

4

Národní

16

17

Opletalova

HLAVNÍ
NÁDRAŽÍ

gii

NÁRODNÍ
TŘÍDA

Vodičkova

Washingtonova

Wilsonova

19

Riegrovy Sady

Ostrovní

18

Myslíkova

Žitná

MUZEUM

Anglická

VINOHRADY

Italská

most

Resslova

Ječná

NÁMĚSTÍ
MIRU

Slezská

22

KARLOVO
NÁMĚSTÍ

NÁM.
I.P. PAVLOVA

Korunni

23

ho most

26

Na
bojišti

Rumunská

Legerova

24

Francouzská

U nemocnice

Ke Karlovu

Sokolská

Londýnská

Belgická

Americká

Máchova

NOVÉ MĚSTO

Na Slupi

Botanická
Zahrada

Bělehradská

Záhřebská

Rašínovo nábř.

Apolinářská

J. Masaryka

Kopernikova

ezniční most

Svobodova

Albertov

Vnislavova

Sekaninova

VYŠEHRAD

25

LEGEND

Metro **M**

65

- **Best Hotel Pool:** In addition to boasting the second-best health club in town, **Axa Hotel** (☎ 02/2481 2580) also has one of the city's largest indoor pools—a 25 meter, six-laner designed for serious swimmers.
- **Best Views:** Located in Mála Strana, the charming **Hotel U Tří Pštrosu** (☎ 02/2451 0779) offers some of the city's finest Old World views over the city's red rooftops. Corner rooms at this small hotel are best, providing views of both Charles Bridge and Prague Castle from adjacent windows.

2 Staré Město (Old Town) & Josefov

VERY EXPENSIVE

Grand Hotel Bohemia

Královdorska 4, Prague 1. ☎ **02/232 3417.** Fax 02/232 9545. 78 rms, 8 suites. A/C MINIBAR TV TEL. 6,700–9,000 Kč ($248–$333) double; from 10,000 Kč ($370) suite. AE, DC, MC, V. Metro: náměstí Republiky.

The first question to ask is whether this hotel is worth more than $300 per night. By general European standards, it isn't. But Grand Hotel Bohemia is as tasteful, sophisticated, and comfortable as any hotel in town—and if you don't care about being overcharged, it's certainly the place to stay. Opened in 1994, the wonderfully restored property is a beautiful art nouveau-style hotel. The hotel is decorated with muted earth tones both inside and out, evidence of its conservative orientation towards business travelers on expense accounts. The extravagant gilded public areas are impressive and quite different from the contemporary guest rooms. The bright and cheerful accommodations are not large, but are fitted with business-oriented extras such as trouser presses, fax, and answering machines.

Dining/Entertainment: The unspectacular hotel restaurant should only be used as a matter of convenience. There's also a small cafe.

Services: 24-hour room service, concierge, laundry, massage, business services, money exchange.

Hotel Inter-Continental Prague

nám. Curieovych 5, Prague 1. ☎ **02/2488 1111.** Fax 02/2481 1216. 365 rms, 27 suites. A/C MINIBAR TV TEL. 8,200–10,300 Kč ($304–$381) double; from 16,500 Kč ($611) suite. Rates include buffet breakfast. Children under 10 stay free in parents' room. AE, DC, MC, V. Metro: Staroměstská.

Opened in 1974, the Inter-Continental was once Prague's most important hotel and the only place in town with Western-style hospitality. It's hard to blame the building's ugly exterior on the Communist regime; 1970s architecture was unsightly the world over. Until 1993, the hotel's inside never reached world-class standards either, but pressure from capitalist competition provoked the hotel to undergo a serious multi-million dollar mending. The dark Dickensian lobby and drab guest quarters have been replaced by a comfortable but colorless lobby and fully remodeled rooms that are up to the standards of the chain's other international properties. None of the standard guest rooms are particularly large, though they are well dressed in top business style, with medium-quality wood-and-cloth furniture, good closets, and computer ports. Marble baths contain hair dryers, magnifying mirrors, and massage shower heads. The hotel's L-shaped suites are slightly larger than standard guest rooms and come with king-size beds, bidets, and fax machines.

Dining/Entertainment: Zlatá Praha, the top-floor continental restaurant with wraparound windows, offers terrific views of Prague's spires and rooftops. Expensive meals are lively renditions of Bohemian and continental standards. It's especially worth dining here during one of the regular gastronomic festivals, when a prominent guest chef is cooking. The less-formal lobby brasserie serves three meals daily. A separate cafe is open all day for light snacks and drinks; it's a pleasant place to relax. During the summer there is a snack bar on the patio in front of the hotel.

Services: 24-hour room service, concierge, laundry, massage, hairdresser, money exchange.

Facilities: State-of-the-art health club, Jacuzzi, sauna, business center, gift shop, newsstand, flower shop.

EXPENSIVE

✪ Hotel Paříž

U Obecního domu 1, Prague 1. ☎ **02/2422 2151.** Fax 02/2422 5475. 96 rms, 4 suites. TV TEL. 6,200–6,900 Kč ($230–$256) double; from 9,600 Kč ($356) suite. Rates include breakfast. AE, CB, DC, MC, V. Metro: náměstí Republiky.

Although the Paříž is one of the best hotels in Prague, it still doesn't compare to grand-luxe hotels in most Western cities. The building itself, located adjacent to the magnificent Municipal House (Obecní dům), is a neo-Gothic historical landmark, packed with plenty of eye-catching art nouveau elements. Acquired by the Brandejs family in 1923, this grand hotel was one of the city's most venerated, until it was seized by the Communists in 1948. Returned to the family in September 1992, the Paříž underwent a $1.3 million renovation that, unfortunately, didn't increase the size of any of the rooms. Every guest room is different and, although amenities can vary slightly, all are handsomely decorated, have tall ceilings, and are outfitted with contemporary mahogany furnishings, firm beds, soft couches, and wood and brass fittings. Baths feature gooseneck sinks and handheld showers. The higher-priced rooms, located on the top (fifth) floor, have minibars, safes, and hair dryers in the bathrooms. Guests and gawkers will want to tour the hotel's public areas, which feature perfectly restored art nouveau wrought-iron railings and unique deco lighting.

Dining/Entertainment: The restaurant Sarah Bernhardt features a beautiful dining room, but style outweighs substance. A better bet is to have a predinner drink in the equally classy lobby-level Café de Paris, and ask the concierge to make meal reservations for you elsewhere.

Services: 24-hour room service, concierge, laundry, business services, money exchange.

Ungelt

Štupartská 1, Prague 1. ☎ **02/2481 1330.** Fax 02/231 9505. 10 suites. TV TEL. 5,740 Kč ($213) one-bedroom suite; 7,200 Kč ($267) two-bedroom suite. AE, V. Metro: Staroměstská or line B to náměstí Republiky.

You can't find a more centrally located hotel in all of Prague. Nestled in a small backstreet just east of Staroměstské náměstí, the three-story Ungelt is a hidden gem, with the potential to be one of the most attractive finds in Europe. The building itself oozes with old-world charm, and contains 10 one- and two-bedroom suites, which can sleep two and four persons, respectively. Unfortunately, the hotel suffers from poor service and worse interior design. Each unit contains a living room, a full kitchen, and a handheld shower in the bath. Bedrooms, which are meagerly dressed with Communist-era beds and couches, are enlivened with antique dressers, Bohemian glass chandeliers, and other nice objects. Wall art is practically unknown. The Ungelt's three best rooms have magnificent, hand-painted wood ceilings, but the recent arrival of two late-closing bars across the street has made these rooms less attractive. Ask for a room in the back, don't expect much in the way of service, and this hotel becomes a terrific springboard for your explorations of Prague.

Dining/Entertainment: There's only a small bar, with terrace seating in summer. **Services:** Laundry.

MODERATE

Betlem Club

Betlémské nám. 9, Prague 1. ☎ **02/2421 6872.** Fax 02/2421 8054. 22 rms. MINIBAR TV TEL. 3,000 Kč ($111) double. Rates include breakfast. No credit cards. Metro: Národní třída.

The location is fantastic—just opposite Old Town's Bethlehem Chapel, where 15th-century Protestant crusader Jan Hus preached to the masses. Several restaurants and bars are on this relatively quiet square, and Charles Bridge, Wenceslas Square, and Old Town Square are all within easy walking distance. Betlem Club feels more like a private pension than a central city hotel. Most rooms are small, and none are pleasant enough for extended lounging. About half are decorated in typical Czech 1970s style, while others are more contemporary with black lacquer furnishings. Breakfast is served each morning in a vaulted medieval cellar.

INEXPENSIVE

Pension Unitas

Bartolomějská 9, Prague 1. ☎ **02/232 7700.** Fax 232 7709. 34 rms (none with bath). 1,200 Kč ($44) double. No credit cards. Metro: Staroměstská.

Owned by the Sisters of Mercy (the nuns, not the rock band), this ascetically decorated hotel is just about as plain a place as you can find. With a fantastic location in the middle of Old Town, the hotel was occupied by the Czech Secret Police in the 1950s, when it was turned into a prison. Cells in the basement once held political prisoners, including Václav Havel. You too can stay in the President's Cell—P6—though conditions don't seem to have improved much since Havel's imprisonment. It's cheerier upstairs, where rooms are bright but basic. Smoking and drinking are banned, and there's a 1am curfew.

⊛ U Krále Jiřího

Liliová 10, Prague 1. ☎ **02/2422 2013.** Fax 02/2422 1983. 8 rms. 1,800–2,000 Kč ($67–$74) double. Rates include breakfast. AE, V. Metro: Staroměstská.

You can't get more central than this unusual pension, offering eight attic rooms above two popular Old Town bars. Characterized by odd shapes and sloping beamed ceilings, rooms here are awkward at worst and charming at best. Although there are few cars out front, those who wish to go to sleep before 2am (when the bars close) should request a room in back. Except for beds, desks, and chairs, accommodations are devoid of decoration, and facilities and services are almost nonexistent.

3 Nové Město (New Town)

VERY EXPENSIVE

Hotel Esplanade

Washingtonova 19, Prague 1. ☎ **02/2421 3696.** Fax 02/2422 9306. 58 rms, 6 suites. TV TEL. 6,890 Kč ($255) double; from 7,390 Kč ($274) suite. AE, MC, V. Metro: Hlavní nádraží.

Physically, the Esplanade has all the makings of a top luxury hotel. Palatial on the outside and elegant within, the building is graced with a plethora of exquisite embellishments that include rich woods and Oriental rugs throughout. The mansion was constructed in 1927 for an Italian insurance company that maintained offices there. Two years later, the building and all its contents were purchased by hoteliers who preserved the unusual Italian decor. A Bacchus-inspired bas-relief over the hotel's front entrance is complemented by interior decorations that include Murano glass chandeliers and an abundance of quality art.

As with most older hotels, each guest room is different. Most are decorated in a tasteful Louis XVI style, and contain minibars, king-size beds, and large baths with amenities that include built-in hair dryers. Suite 101 is particularly special; it's outrageously Old World, with hand-carved tables and bed, museum-quality chairs, glass chandeliers, and busy wall coverings and carpeting that add to the charming clutter. Not all rooms and suites are as recommendable, however; in fact most are rather plain, with functional 1970s-style furniture. If you have the option, the best strategy for staying here is to wait until you can see your room before committing.

The hotel is located steps from the main railway station, and just a few blocks from Václavské náměstí.

Dining/Entertainment: The comfortable lobby-level cafe/lounge is decorated with castle-sized original oil paintings and marble floors. The adjacent Esplanade Restaurant serves a continental menu—with main dishes averaging 200 Kč ($7.40)—in a stunning dining room that seems as if it was built just for its spectacular multicolored glass chandelier.

Services: Room service from 6am to 4am, concierge, laundry, money exchange.

✪ Palace

Panská 12, Prague 1. ☎ **02/2409 3111.** Fax 02/2422 1240. 125 rms, 17 suites. A/C MINIBAR TV TEL. 8,900 Kč ($330) double; from 11,050 Kč ($409) suite. AE, DC, MC, V. Metro: Můstek.

One of the finest (and most expensive) hotels in town, the Palace is a stylish luxury hotel set in a beautifully restored art nouveau palace. Guests enter through an impressive front door flanked by imposing sconce-wielding statues. An ornate lobby continues the flamboyant theme, with comfortable sitting areas surrounded by rich woods and gold leaf. Although rooms are still considered small by American standards, these are some of the largest luxury accommodations in Prague. Painted the colors of rubies and emeralds, guest rooms contain all the requisite amenities, as well as white marble baths. The hotel's Lady Queen Rooms, which are priced the same as doubles, are washed in pink and contain oversized dressing tables. Only rivaled by the Savoy for comfort, the Palace beats the competition in terms of location, situated only a block from Wenceslas Square and Old Town.

Dining/Entertainment: While the hotel's single "serious" restaurant is nothing to write home about, its small ground-floor buffet contains the city's greenest salad bar, making it popular with locals. There's also a lobby bar.

Services: 24-hour room service, concierge, laundry, business services, money exchange.

EXPENSIVE

Atrium Hilton Hotel

Pobřežní 1, Prague 8. ☎ **02/2484 1111.** Fax 02/2481 1973. 788 rms, 20 suites. A/C MINIBAR TV TEL. 6,250 Kč ($231) double; from 7,490 Kč ($277) suite. AE, CB, DC, MC, V. Metro: Florenc.

One of Prague's most successful examples of modern functionalist architecture, the glass-and-steel cube-shaped Atrium Hilton is as imposing as it is huge. True to its name, the entire hotel is built around an enormous glass-topped atrium, dominated by glass elevators and an oversized, distinctly Communist-era steel chandelier. Thankfully, guest rooms are quite a bit more intimate than the chilly common areas. Most are identical to one another, making this hotel perfect for large tour groups and conventioneers, who are often around. While guest rooms are not large and far from fancy, they are of a relatively high standard—good enough for U.S. President Bill Clinton, who stayed here in 1994. The hotel's location, just outside of center city, is not ideal, but taxis and public transportation are plentiful, and hearty travelers can walk to náměstí Republiky in about 15 minutes.

Dining/Entertainment: The lobby-level Atrium Restaurant, serving breakfast, lunch, and dinner, is the largest of the hotel's six eateries. It's also one of the best places in town for an American-style breakfast. The other restaurants, specializing in a variety of cuisines, are less impressive. There's also a lobby bar and a subterranean nightclub offering variety shows and musical entertainment.

Services: 24-hour room service, concierge, laundry, massage, hairdresser, money exchange.

Facilities: Indoor swimming pool, small gym, tennis courts, sauna, putting greens, business center, gift shop, casino.

City Hotel Moráň

Na Moráni 15, Prague 2. ☎ **02/2491 5208.** Fax 02/29 75 33. 57 rms. MINIBAR TV TEL. 4,000–6,000 Kč ($148–$222) double. AE, MC, DC, V. Metro: Karlovo náměstí.

Built in the 19th century, this recently restored lime green hotel is far from fancy, but, for style and comfort, it ranks as one of the best in its price range. The inviting public areas are well-lit and welcoming, if a bit overdecorated with tasteless frills that only detract from the building's own intrinsic charm. Conversely, the design of the guest rooms bends too far in the opposite direction; each room feels terribly underdressed. Top-floor rooms are best, and those facing north enjoy a good view of Prague Castle. A distinct dearth of services keeps the business crowd at bay, though small groups are mainstays in summer. The hotel is located about a 20-minute walk from Old Town Square, just outside of the main tourist center. There's a small restaurant and bar on the premises.

Services: Laundry, money exchange.

Hotel Adria

Václavské náměstí 26, Prague 1. ☎ **02/2421 6543** or 2421 9274. Fax 02/2421 1025. 58 rms, 7 suites. MINIBAR TV TEL. 4,930 Kč ($183) double; from 5,950 Kč ($220) suite. Rates include breakfast. AE, DC, MC, V. Metro: Můstek.

Many of Prague's newly privatized hotels have skimped on guest rooms, preferring to spend the bulk of their renovation money on lobbies and exteriors. Adria is no exception. The sliding glass front door on the hotel's storybook 19th-century yellow-and-white exterior opens into a thoroughly contemporary brass and glass lobby. Guests file past a stylish espresso bar to the reception desk, and reach their rooms by elevator. Although this recommendable hotel could theoretically be located in any European capital, several idiosyncracies that are particularly Czech remind you of your locale. Wall art is scarce, there's always loud music playing in the lobby, service is a bit sluggish, and there are some comical design flaws—like exposed pipes beneath hung ceilings. The small and modern guest rooms are not fancy. Twins contain two single-size beds in a particularly narrow room. Odd-numbered rooms—most of which are doubles—are the same price, but larger. Like other guest rooms, these have budget Euro-style built-in furnishings. Bathrooms are clean and neat, and have wall-mounted hair dryers.

Dining/Entertainment: Breakfast is served in the contemporary Neptune Café. The Triton Club restaurant, in a unique quartz rock-encrusted cave, is worth a look. Dine here for overpriced Czech specialities and continental cuisine that's nothing more than par for the course.

Services: Room service, concierge, laundry, business services, money exchange.
Facilities: Small exercise room, sauna.

Hotel Jalta

Václavské náměstí 45, Prague 1. ☎ **02/2422 9133.** Fax 02/2421 3866. 87 rms, 10 suites. MINIBAR TV TEL. 6,000 Kč ($222) double; from 8,500 Kč ($315) suite. Rates include breakfast. AE, DC, MC, V. Metro: Můstek.

A top-to-bottom gutting and rebuilding has transformed the ancient marble Jalta into a very comfortable but characterless hotel. Part Japanese-owned, Jalta benefits from contemporary styling and respectable furnishings that make this the best hotel on Václavské náměstí.

What the guest rooms lack in warmth they make up for with high ceilings and good amenities like card-lock doors, taro bathrobes, built-in hair dryers, and large mirrors. Not all rooms in this seven-story hotel are created equal, however. Accommodations facing Václavské náměstí are brightest (and noisiest), and have small balconies overlooking the street. And five of the hotel's double rooms are significantly larger than the others, but rent for the same price. Beware of single rooms, which are furnished with a single-size bed.

Dining/Entertainment: In addition to a ground-floor restaurant with excellent sidewalk seating, the hotel contains a bar and nightclub.

Services: Room service, concierge, laundry, money exchange.
Facilities: Casino.

Interhotel Ambassador Zlatá Husa

Václavské náměstí 5–7, Prague 1. ☎ **02/2419 3111.** Fax 02/2423 0620. 155 rms, 17 suites. TV TEL. 4,700–5,900 Kč ($174–$219) double; from 7,400 Kč ($274) suite. Children under 6 stay free in parents' room. Rates include breakfast. AE, CB, DC, MC, V. Metro: Můstek.

One of the grandes dames of Václavské náměstí, the art nouveau Ambassador was opened in 1900, when the square was the most important place in town. Wenceslas Square has tarnished significantly since its heyday—prostitutes and neon proliferate—but a Václavské náměstí address is still notable. The lobby, which seems too small and sedate for such an imposing hotel, welcomes guests with wood paneling, Oriental runners, and 1970s-style leatherette chairs. Above are six floors of medium-size rooms that, although renovated after the Velvet Revolution, feel quite antique. The rooms have high ceilings and furnishings that tend toward faux Louis XVI and marble-topped desks. The single-size beds that furnish most twins leave much to be desired. Bathrooms are marble and some have whirlpools, others just have a stand-up shower. It all sounds pretty nice, but it could be nicer if the building's extra-wide hallways were filled with art, flowers, and antiques. Instead, most of the hotel contains cheap fixtures and little else to entertain the eye.

Dining/Entertainment: Full of nooks and crannies, the sprawling hotel contains many hidden surprises, including a dozen restaurants and bars and a topless nightclub. The Francouzská Restaurant, serving mediocre French cuisine, is one of Prague's most beautiful dining rooms. Surrounded by stained-glass windows, patrons eat from gold-embossed dishes and sit on velvet-covered chairs beneath exquisite ceramic ceilings. Staroprazska Rychta, the hotel's tribute to Prague beer halls, is located in the hotel's cellar. Follow the accordion music. Buffet breakfasts are served in Coffeehouse Pasaze, and lunches are available from a grill restaurant and a snack bar. Znojemská Vinárna and the smaller Vinárna Kecskemet are two wine bars that specialize in vintages from Moravia. In the summer, the best place to sit is at the sidewalk cafe, which offers some of the best people-watching in the city.

Services: 24-hour room service, concierge, laundry, massage, currency exchange.
Facilities: Casino, gift shop.

Prague Renaissance Hotel

V Celnici 7, Prague 1. ☎ **02/2481 0396.** Fax 02/2182 2200. 309 rms, 14 suites. A/C MINIBAR TV TEL. 5,900 Kč ($218) double; from 10,500 Kč ($389) suite. Children under 16 stay free in parents' room. Rates include breakfast. AE, CB, DC, MC, V. Metro: náměstí Republiky.

The Prague Renaissance, a marble monolith completed in 1993, is a top European-style business hotel with well-designed standardized rooms and unusually responsive management. A conventioneer's delight, the hotel's 300-plus guest rooms are almost all identically dressed, and feature good closets and lighting. "Standard" rooms are a bit on the small side, but thoughtfully outfitted with blond wood built-in desks and original prints. "King" rooms offer a bit more space, but are usually priced the same as standard doubles. Corner rooms (ending in numbers 18 and 19) are larger still, but don't offer the quiet of those in the rear. Rooms on the eighth and ninth floors have windows embedded in slanted ceilings, and for reasons of novelty are most recommendable. Suites on the top floor are exceptionally spacious, and have walk-in closets and sizable bathrooms. Baths in all rooms are equipped with hair dryers, telephones, and a small toiletry package. Specially designed rooms that are wheelchair-accessible are also available.

Dining/Entertainment: Breakfast and lunch are served in the Pavilion, a high-quality buffet-style eatery. The Potomac, an American restaurant, is smaller and brighter, offering fish and meat main dishes ranging from about 350 Kč to 450 Kč ($13 to $16). The bar is open until 2am.

Services: Room service, concierge, laundry, massage, money exchange.
Facilities: Indoor swimming pool, small exercise room, business center, gift shop.

MODERATE

ⓢ Atlantic

Na poříčí 9, Prague 1. ☎ **02/2481 1084.** Fax 02/2481 2378. 60 rms, 1 suite. TV TEL. 3,400 Kč ($126) double; 3,950 Kč ($146) suite. AE, MC, V. Metro: náměstí Republiky.

Originally built in 1845 and named The English Court, this hotel catered to society's elite until it fell into disrepair around 1900. Rebuilt in 1935, the five-story Atlantic never reclaimed its past prestige. Instead, the hotel has become one of the best moderately priced properties, situated just minutes from náměstí Republiky. It would be a mistake to expect too much from this place, which completed its last makeover just months before the Communist regime fell in November 1989. But these ample-sized rooms are functional and simply furnished. A pleasant wood-paneled restaurant and lounge is located just behind the lobby. The hotel offers laundry, dry cleaning, theater booking, and other concierge services.

✪ Hotel Harmony

Na poříčí 31, Prague 1. ☎ **02/232 0016** or **232 0720.** Fax 02/231 0009. 54 rms, 6 suites. TEL. 3,341 Kč ($124) double; from 3,541 Kč ($131) suite. A 12% discount available for guests staying more than one night. Rates include breakfast. AE, MC, V. Metro: náměstí Republiky or Florenc.

Completely overhauled in 1992, the Harmony is easily the nicest hotel in its price range. Contemporary design and post-Communist furnishings translate into a sparkling white hotel, inside and out. Double rooms, with two single beds pushed together as one, make up the bulk of the hotel's seven floors. Standard-issue hotel furnishings mean a blond wood desk and chair, a single small print on an oversized white wall, and miniature table lamps that look like toys. You probably wouldn't have chosen the Smurf blue carpeting for your own home, and it doesn't look that great here either. Suites are substantially larger and a bit nicer. Many have huge windows, and all come with minibars, stand-alone closets, larger beds, and good-sized baths. Don't expect frilly bath accessories, however. You'll get enough towels to dry the two of you, and a small bar of soap.

There are two restaurants on the ground floor, and the reception desk becomes the concierge desk when you need concert tickets or tour reservations.

INEXPENSIVE

Axa Hotel

Na poříčí 40, Prague 1. ☎ **02/2481 2580.** Fax 02/232 2172. 127 rms (100 with bath), 5 suites. TEL. 1,000 Kč ($37) double without bath, 2,500 Kč ($93) double with bath; from 2,000 Kč ($74) suite. Free for children under 6. Rates include continental breakfast. MC, V. Metro: náměstí Republiky or Florenc.

Built in 1932, and completely overhauled in 1992, Axa has all the hallmarks of a typical Prague hotel. It is rather drab on the outside, and sterile within. The lobby and rooms are rather plain—white and functional, and almost devoid of decoration. Frills are few, and so are towels. Beds are "Eastern European Specials"—thin mattresses on pullout-sofalike beds. In addition to a simple bathroom that lacks counter space for toiletries, most guest rooms contain a narrow closet, a table, two chairs, and a television. In most any other city, Axa would be overpriced. So why do I recommend this hotel and so many others like it? Because there's just no other choice.

On the positive side, Axa occupies a good location, close to náměstí Republiky, and the small front desk provides all the hotel's services, including check-in, concierge, money exchange, and even a newsstand. Plus the hotel has one of the best health clubs in town, containing a six-lane indoor lap pool, a sauna and solarium, and an enormous mirrored weight room with some 20 exercise machines and thousands of pounds of free weights.

Botel Albatros

nábřeží Ludvika Svobody, Prague 1. ☎ **02/2481 0541.** Fax 02/2481 1214. 80 rms, 4 suites. TEL. 2,546 Kč ($94) double; from 4,509 Kč ($167) suite. Rates include continental breakfast. AE, MC, V. Tram: 5, 14, 26, or 53.

Located at the end of Revoluční on the River Vltava, the permanently moored blue-and-white Albatros is a converted hotel boat, or "botel." It's no *Queen Mary*. Rooms are predictably cramped; each is just large enough to accommodate two single beds and the tiny table that separates them. At the near end of the berth is a diminutive closet and a miniature bathroom, both with no counter space. Each room has a radio, but no TV. Suites, located toward the back of the boat, are bright exceptions to these otherwise restricted accommodations. Particularly light, each enjoys wraparound windows and room enough to swing a cat. Although there is a small restaurant on the boat, guests will have more fun on the lively bar barge docked just behind the Albatros.

Hotel Evropa

Václavské náměstí 25, Prague 1. ☎ **02/2422 8117.** Fax 02/2422 4544. 104 rms (50 with bath), 3 suites. 1,860 Kč ($69) double without bath, 2,800 Kč ($104) double with bath; from 3,260 Kč ($121) suite. Rates include continental breakfast. AE, MC, V. Metro: Můstek.

Erected in 1889, and rebuilt in the art nouveau style during 1903–5, the Evropa remains one of the most magnificent turn-of-the-century structures in Prague. The fantastic, statue-topped facade is a festival for the eyes, beautifully painted and wrapped with hand-sculpted wrought-iron railings. Seats on the outdoor terrace of the hotel's ground-floor cafe are some of the city's most coveted—for style and people-watching, not food or service.

The public areas on the hotel's first and second floors are equally impressive, painted yellow and gold, and furnished with busy Louis XVI items. Unfortunately, rooms are adequate at best, and shabby at worst. Accommodations vary widely. The best rooms are the front-facing doubles, a half-dozen of which have balconies overlooking Václavské náměstí. These are relatively large and have high ceilings. Furnishings are limited to the essentials, however: beds and a table. Bathrooms are equally uninspired, have few towels, and contain handheld showers and aging tubs. The worst rooms are windowless, bathless, charmless boxes tucked way in the back of the hotel.

There's no trick to getting a good room here; luck is the only mitigator. Reservations are accepted by fax. Even if you choose not to check-in here, the hotel is definitely worth checking out.

Opera

Těšnov 13, Prague 1. ☎ **02/231 5609** or 231 5735. Fax 02/231 1477. 58 rms (12 with bath). 1,600 Kč ($59) double without bath, 1,800 Kč ($67) double with bath. Prices decrease by 10% Oct–Apr. Rates include breakfast. AE, MC, V. Metro: Florenc.

Like so many hotels in Prague, one approaches the stately Opera with great hopes. And like so many hotels in Prague, one is disappointed to discover that the interior lacks even a shred of the facade's charm. Popular with German tour groups, the hotel provides the most basic accommodations and services. Budget-style pine furnishings are set off by grotesque orange curtains. Guest rooms without private baths are outfitted with sinks, and all rooms have small original etchings on the walls.

The Opera is recommendable for being inexpensive and relatively clean compared to others in the neighborhood. The hotel offers laundry and dry-cleaning service, and contains a restaurant and snack bar on the ground floor.

4 Malá Strana

VERY EXPENSIVE

✪ Hotel Hoffmeister

Pod Bruskou 9, Prague 1. ☎ **02/2451 1015** or 2451 0381. Fax 02/53 09 59. 42 rms, 4 suites. TV TEL. 6,800–7,800 Kč ($252–$289) double; from 8,900 Kč ($330) suite. Rates include breakfast. AE, MC, V. Metro: Malostranská.

A small, independently owned hotel opened in 1993, Hotel Hoffmeister is one of the most welcome new arrivals in a city where $200 often buys little more than a thin bed in a nondescript room. Owned by the son of Adolph Hoffmeister, a respected artist and former diplomat, the hotel is one of the few in Prague assembled from the ground up with an emphasis on creativity and style.

The pink exterior of the three-story hotel resembles a Bohemian alpine cottage, although a corner of the building's first story is cut away and replaced with a glass-brick wall and a contemporary statue-cum-column. Inside, real Western-style beds have bright print covers that actually match the other high-quality furnishings and window treatments in the rooms. Details have not been overlooked here. Entry is via card lock, and there are good closets, well-placed wall sconces and lamp lighting, sparkling showers, hair dryers, and pants presses. Rooms are without a view, but guests can swing open all the oversized windows.

The hotel's best rooms—only slightly more expensive than the basic ones—are significantly larger. A circular staircase in the bi-level Presidential Suite connects a bright office with a cozy bedroom. There's a fax machine, and a bathroom with double sinks and large Jacuzzi tub.

Paintings and prints by Hoffmeister the elder adorn most every wall in the hotel, though unfortunately none are original. To view the real thing, guests must visit the small lobby, where Hoffmeister's line drawings of friends like Salvador Dalí, George Bernard Shaw, and John Steinbeck are on display.

Dining/Entertainment: Ada, a pretty French restaurant and cafe, serves an exceptional 500 Kč ($18.50) fixed-price menu for dinner.

Services: 24-hour room service, concierge, laundry, money exchange.

EXPENSIVE

U Červeného Lva

Nerudova 41, Prague 1. ☎ **02/537 239** or 538 192. Fax 02/538 193. 4 double rooms, 3 suites. MINIBAR TV TEL. 4,800 Kč ($178) double, from 5,900 Kč ($218) suite. Rates include breakfast. Metro: Malostranská.

The publisher of Frommer's stayed in three places when he visited Prague in August 1995, and "The House at the Red Lion" was his favorite. This recently restored pension is expensive, but costs less than the big hotels. It's also more of an "experience," with a very sophisticated and friendly atmosphere. The spacious rooms are decorated in soft, natural fabrics. Suites have a double bed in the bedroom and two twin beds in the living room. This historical burgher house, which dates back to the 15th century, is located on the Royal Route, near the entrance to Prague Castle.

Dining/Entertainment: There's a ground floor restaurant, with wood beam ceilings from the Renaissance period. In the basement preserved Gothic rooms house a wine restaurant and a bar.

Hotel U Tří Pštrosů

Dražického náměstí 12, Prague 1. ☎ **02/2451 0779.** Fax 02/2451 0783. 18 rms, 3 suites. TV TEL. 4,500–5,500 Kč ($167–$204) double; from 6,000 Kč ($222) suite. Rates include breakfast. AE, MC, V. Metro: Malostranská.

If you believe a hotel's most important features to be central location and old-world charm, then you can stay nowhere but U Tří Pštrosů. Sitting at the Malá Strana-side of Charles Bridge, this squat, five-story gem is right in the heart of the hustle, with street musicians and sidewalk sellers so close you can almost reach out and touch them without getting out of bed. As for charm, the hotel traces its roots back hundreds of years, when it was owned by a supplier of ostrich feathers. Later the building became one of the first coffeehouses in Bohemia. Rebuilt and reconstructed several times over the centuries, the hotel reopened in 1992, having preserved its painted wooden Renaissance ceilings and smattering of antique furnishings. Double rooms are well sized, fitted with green carpets, decent closets, and rolltop writing desks with inlaid woods. Unfortunately, the same cannot be said for the hotel's single rooms, which are small indeed, and contain a single-size bed. Suites are the hotel's most spectacular accommodations. These corner accommodations offer views of Charles Bridge and Prague Castle, seen over the city's red rooftops.

The small inn is run more like a casual bed-and-breakfast than a professional hotel, and some details— ranging from poor telephone placement to lack of services— have been overlooked. Still, if you don't mind the noise that being right in the heart of it all engenders, U Tří Pštrosů is one of my top hotel picks in Prague.

Dining/Entertainment: The hotel's recommendable ground-floor restaurant serves Bohemian specialties in sparkling new vaulted dining rooms that are supposed to look centuries old. It's open to the public daily for lunch from noon to 3pm, and for dinner from 6 to 11pm.

Services: Money exchange.

🅘 Family-Friendly Accommodations

Hotel Inter-Continental Prague *(see p. 66)* With plenty of services and restaurants, and near many of Prague's primary sights, the Inter-Continental makes it easier to travel with kids in tow.

Forum Hotel *(see p. 78)* The only Prague hotel with its own bowling alley, the comfortable Forum also gets high marks for its swimming pool, shops, and services.

Private Apartment *(see p. 62)* Your best bet may be to rent an apartment for your family. In addition to experiencing life like Praguers, you'll have more room, and access to a kitchen allowing you to prepare snacks and meals anytime for your children.

U Páva

U lužického semináře 22, Prague 1. ☎ **02/2451 0922** or 53 22 51. Fax 02/53 33 79. 11 rms. A/C MINIBAR TV TEL. 4,000–5,000 Kč ($148–$185) double. AE, DC, MC, V. Metro: Malostranská.

Although U Páva is not as distinctive as its high prices would suggest, this pension hotel distinguishes itself as the best in Malá Strana. Low-key and quiet, this very intimate hotel has a family-run atmosphere that's only thwarted by a small smattering of benefits including room service and an in-house bar. Rooms are comfortable, but hardly plush enough to put this relatively simple property into the "boutique" category of hotels. Wood-beamed ceilings preside over busy fabrics that are unfortunately neither classical nor contemporary. One pays for location here, smack-dab in the historical center, across from the city's prettiest gardens, and close to all manner of public transportation. Despite a modest amount of street noise, the best rooms are in the front of the house, where guests are treated to unobstructed views of Prague Castle.

Dining/Entertainment: The restaurant and bar on the ground floor is popular with tourists only.

Services: Room service, overnight laundry, money exchange.

MODERATE

Hotel Kampa

Všehrdova 16, (Malá Strana) Prague 1. ☎ **02/2451 0409**. Fax 02/2451 0377. 85 rms. TEL. 3,100 Kč ($115) double. Rates include breakfast. AE, MC, V. Metro: Malostranská.

Located on one of the cutest, quietest, and best-located streets in Prague, Hotel Kampa occupies what was once an armory, built at the beginning of the 17th century. Although it was renovated in 1992, the rehab was directed by a very modest decorator. Rooms are incredibly simple, and probably will not be acceptable to first-class travelers. Singles are furnished with just a single-size bed and a stand-alone wardrobe. There is no decoration on most walls, and bathrooms are compact. Doubles are larger and marginally nicer. Like singles, they are without TVs, but are outfitted with small clock radios. Try to reserve a double furnished with an extra bed, as these are the largest rooms. You can request a room with a view of the river or the park. A restaurant on the premises serves lunch and dinner, but the smartest guests dine elsewhere.

5 Hradčany

VERY EXPENSIVE

✪ Savoy

Keplerova 6, Prague 1. ☎ **02/2430 2122.** Fax 02/2430 2128. 61 rms, 6 suites. A/C MINIBAR TV TEL. 8,700 Kč ($322) double, from 10,900 Kč ($404) suite. AE, DC, MC, V. Tram: 22.

Opened in 1994, the Savoy is widely considered to be Prague's best hotel. Located on a moderately busy street three blocks from Prague Castle, the hotel's location is not ideal. But once inside, the hotel is hard to top. Opulent even by Western standards, the hotel's dressy public areas lead into equally well-decorated guest rooms, outfitted with every convenience one would expect from a top hotel. Rooms have all the requisite fittings, including firm oversize beds, marble baths, safes, and fax machines.

Dining/Entertainment: The lobby bar is an intimate place for an afternoon cocktail.

Services: 24-hour room service, concierge, laundry, massage, hairdresser, business services, money exchange.

Facilities: Small fitness room.

EXPENSIVE

Pension U Raka

Černínská 10, Prague 1. ☎ **02/35 14 53.** Fax 02/35 30 74. 6 rms. 4,200 Kč ($156) double; 6,900 Kč ($256) apartment. AE, MC, V. Tram: 22.

The Nový Svět district, a lovely cobblestoned section of town behind Prague Castle, is a pretty, residential neighborhood marked by quiet winding streets and charming houses. Pension U Raka, a small chalet-style home located within hearing range of the Loreto's bells, offers a half-dozen cozy rooms with raw wood walls and rug-topped pine floors. Their single "apartment" contains a fireplace and a private Japanese-style garden; it's popular with honeymooners. This modern pension feels very sophisticated, and the staff speaks good English. It's an easy 10-minute walk to the castle and Strahov Monastery, and another 10-minute walk downhill puts you in the center of Malá Strana. In any other city, U Raka would be considered overpriced. Because it's in tourist-heavy Prague, however, reservations for this modest hotel must be secured up to one month in advance—more during the summer months.

Services: Money exchange.

6 Vinohrady

MODERATE

Anna Hotel

Budečská 17, Prague 2. ☎ /Fax **02/254 163.** 23 rms. TV. 3,000 Kč ($111) double. No credit cards. Metro: náměstí Míru.

The neighborhood of Vinohrady, located behind the immense National Museum on Wenceslas Square, was once planted with the king's vineyards. Today this area is a good-looking working-class neighborhood that's largely unknown to tourists. Anna Hotel is located here, about 15 minutes' walk from Old Town. The hotel is spartan and clean, with few decorations and bright white bathrooms. The nearby restaurants and pubs are as authentic Czech as you can get—at prices that most tourists in Old Town only dream of. There's a restaurant and bar in the lobby, and parking nearby.

INEXPENSIVE

Hotel Juventus
Blanická 10, Prague 2. ☎ **02/25 51 51.** Fax 02/25 51 53. 20 rms (none with bath). 1,650 Kč ($61) double. Rates include breakfast. No credit cards. Metro: náměstí Míru.

Just about as basic a place as you can find in central Prague, the Juventus is typical of hotels in the $50-a-day range (per double) in the rest of Europe. Rooms are sparsely furnished—no telephones, TVs, or even clocks—but have high ceilings and a writing desk. A few small paintings on the walls constitute the decorations. No rooms have private baths, but all have sinks with cold and (sporadically) hot running water. At this writing, management is considering adding showers to all rooms, an improvement that would likely raise rates. I hope they also renovate the shabby lobby bar, in which patrons must strain to hear one another over the ever-trumpeting TV.

Hotel Luník
Londýnská 50, Prague 2. ☎ **02/25 27 01.** Fax 02/25 66 17. 35 rms. 2,200 Kč ($81) double. Rates include continental breakfast. No credit cards. Metro: náměstí Míru.

Behind Luník's faux off-white stucco front, which brandishes beautiful wooden windows, is a hotel so modest you'd think you were in a hostel. A small elevator takes guests up to 31 identical twin rooms and four single rooms that have matching wooden beds and closets. And that's all—no chairs, no desks, no lamps, nothing. The only redeeming features of the hotel's complete gutting and rebuilding in 1992 are showers that are pleasantly tiled from floor to ceiling, and full-length mirrors. Some rooms have telephones.

7 Elsewhere in Prague

EXPENSIVE

✪ Forum Hotel
Kongresová 1, Prague 4. ☎ **02/6119 1111** or 02/6126 1673. Fax 02/42 06 84. 531 rms, 10 suites. A/C MINIBAR TV TEL. 6,360 Kč ($236) double; from 10,000 Kč ($370) suite. Rates include breakfast. AE, DC, MC, V. Metro: Vyšehrad.

The Forum is something of a Czech anomaly. Located in "Prague Manhattan," a cluster of buildings about seven miles from the center city, the 24-story hotel is a self-contained mini-city, complete with restaurants, pubs, shops, a fitness center, and even a bowling alley. Staying here is as close to staying home as you can get.

Completed in 1988, this insulated and American-style hotel is one of the city's best managed, run by a division of the Inter-Continental Hotels Corporation. There are plenty of staffers, a dedicated concierge, and 24-hour room service. Rooms are not quite up to international standards, but they are luxurious for Prague, containing "real" Western-style beds, good lighting, and thoughtful decoration. All have satellite television and nice bathrooms with built-in hair dryers.

Although the city center is not within walking distance from the hotel, taxis are plentiful, and Vyšehrad metro station is just steps away.

Dining/Entertainment: Harmonie Restaurant, serving continental lunches and dinners daily, is the hotel's top eatery. The Czech Restaurant is open for all-day dining, and Café Praha serves pastry, ice cream, and gourmet coffee. There is a typical Czech beer pub, a large lobby bar, and a nightclub, where dance discs spin until about 1am.

Services: 24-hour room service, concierge, laundry, massage, hairdresser, money exchange.

Facilities: Indoor swimming pool, small but functional fitness center, squash court, bowling alley, business center, shops.

Praha

Sušická 20, Prague 6. ☎ **02/2434 1111.** Fax 02/2431 1218. 124 rms, 7 suites. A/C MINIBAR TV TEL. 5,000 Kč ($185) double. AE, DC. Metro: Dejvická.

Recommended for those who want to see how the Communists envisioned paradise, hotel Praha shocks with its massive size and 1970s showplace decor that includes brown leather couches illuminated by enormous globe lamps. Constructed for the Party elite, most rooms were routinely reserved for high-ranking officials, visiting dignitaries and dictators like Ceausescu and Castro. Though the very casual furnishings are laughable by Western standards, this hotel is the finest pre-revolution property in the city. What the Praha does have over the more contemporary competition are some of the city's largest guest rooms, private balconies, and magnificent views of the city center from those rooms facing south and west. Although accommodations in this time capsule don't come cheaply, the hotel boasts some of the best facilities in town, offers easy parking, and is close enough to the metro and the city center to make it a convenient place to stay.

Dining/Entertainment: There's a decent Czech restaurant, and a bar that stays open late.

Services: 24-hour room service, concierge, laundry, hairdresser, business services, money exchange.

Facilities: Swimming pool, sauna, bowling alley, volley ball courts.

INEXPENSIVE

⊛ Hotel Diplomat

Evropská 15, Prague 6. ☎ **02/2439 4111.** Fax 02/2439 4215. 363 rms, 5 studios, 12 suites. A/C MINIBAR TV TEL. 2,700 Kč ($100) double; 4,500 Kč ($167) studio; from 4,500 Kč ($167) suite. Rates include breakfast. Children under 6 stay free in parents' room. AE, CB, DC, MC, V. Metro: Dejvická.

Hotel Diplomat is one of the most popular places to stay in Prague. Constructed in 1990 to an uninspired cubist design, the hotel was built with prefabricated guest rooms that were imported wholesale, making each almost identical to the next. The small rooms have built-in beds and bureaus, alcoves instead of closets, and a shortage of towels that reflects poorly on their generosity of spirit. That said, at about $100 per night, including breakfast, the first-class Diplomat represents one of Prague's best buys. Its location, just outside the city center, is not ideal, but a metro station across the street makes getting around a breeze. Operated by an Austrian management team, the nine-story hotel gets praise for efficiency. There's a dedicated concierge, and a full-service business center. Studios are larger than standard rooms, and both earn marks for having clock radios and hair dryers. Suites come with pants presses, minibars, balconies, and larger baths outfitted with hair dryers and bidets. The hotel has several decent restaurants, as well as an exercise room with a sauna and whirlpool. There's 24-hour room service, and laundry and dry-cleaning services.

Hotel Ostaš

Orebitská 8, Prague 3. ☎ /Fax **02/627 9386** or 02/627 9418. 30 rms, 2 suites. TEL. 2,720 Kč ($101) double; from 4,600 Kč ($170) suite. Rates include breakfast. No credit cards. Tram: Lines 133, 168, or 207.

Known primarily to German tour groups, the extremely basic Ostaš is nothing to write home about, and just barely good enough to find inclusion here. Rooms are ascetically styled, with little more than beds and bureaus. And although the hotel was completely remodeled in 1992, furnishings and lighting are strictly functional, only suites have televisions, and guests cannot obtain an outside line directly from their bedside phones. Rack rates here are stiff even by Prague standards. If you decide to stay here, hard bargaining is in order.

Mepro

Viktora Huga 3, Prague 5. ☎ **02/52 12 50.** Fax 02/52 73 43. 26 rms. TV TEL. 2,450 Kč ($91) double. MC, V. Metro: Anděl.

Mepro is not a hotel one raves about. It's a basic hostelry in a working-class neighborhood that is strictly functionalist in both performance and design. Prices are high for such nondescription, but Mepro does have its pluses. The Smíchov neighborhood is pure Czech, and interesting to explore. The Vltava is nearby, Malá Strana is within hiking distance, and Old Town is a mere three metro stops away. There's a roof terrace up top and a charming wine cellar below, with prices that city center tourists can only dream of.

Pension Větrník

U Větrníku 40, Prague 6. ☎ **02/351 9622.** Fax 02/36 14 06. 6 rms. TV TEL. 2,000 Kč ($74) double. Rates include breakfast. MC. Tram: 1, 2, 18.

Situated inside a restored 250-year-old windmill, this thoroughly charming pension has everything going for it, except location. Ten minutes by tram from the Hradčanská metro station, Větrník is fitted with heavy country furnishings. Unusually friendly proprietors make its restful atmosphere feel homey. Guests can enjoy a private walled garden and free use of an exclusive tennis court. Home-cooked meals are prepared on request.

8 Hostels

One of the least expensive ways to keep a roof over your head is by staying in a hostel, typically a multishare accommodation with anywhere from 2 to 50 beds in a room. Prague has several of these dormitory-style accommodations. Unfortunately, most are far from the center, necessitating both a metro and bus ride to reach them. Still, they're cheap, and you'll meet many other travelers.

Most hostels in Prague seem to be temporary affairs, popping up one year and disappearing the next. For the latest, contact the **AVE agency,** in the main train station (Hlavní nádraží (☎ **02/2422 3521;** fax 02/2422 3463). They can make reservations for you at most of the hostels in town, and are extremely convenient if you're arriving in Prague by train.

Hostel Sokol

Hellichova 1, Prague 1. ☎ **02/2451 0606,** ext. 397. Fax 02/561 85 64. 100 beds. 190 Kč ($7.04) per person. No credit cards. Open June–Sept. From Malostranská metro station, walk up Letenská, cross Malostranské náměstí and continue along Karmelitská. Turn left onto Hellichova and the hostel is one block ahead on your right.

Although this is one of the best-located hostels in Prague, Sokol does have its drawbacks. Rooms are packed with 10 to 12 beds each, they charge an extra 20 Kč if you return after 12:30am, and cleanliness is suspect. Located smack in the heart of Malá Strana, just a short walk from Charles Bridge, it's a great base for exploring—and for finding a more suitable place. The hostel is closed daily from 10am to 3pm.

The Strahov Hostels

Spartakiádní, Prague 6. 1,500 beds. 250–300 Kč ($9–$11) per person. No credit cards. Open June–Sept only. From Dejvická metro station, take bus 143, 149, or 217 to Strahov Stadium.

Located directly across the street from giant Strahov Stadium, the Strahov Hostels were built to house athletes for Eastern European Olympic-style games that were held annually before the fall of Communism. Today, these dozen concrete high-rises are students' homes throughout the school year, and budget tourist hotels during summer. Most rooms are doubles, none have private baths, and all are open 24 hours.

At least three different companies have contracted with the city to operate these summer hostels. Accommodations in each are identical, but services and prices vary slightly. ESTEC Hostel is the best known, probably because they run the buildings located closest to the road, and are the first ones tourists see. Petros and Sakbuild hostels are immediately adjacent to one another, and should be compared for price before committing.

5 Prague Dining

by Dan Levine

The restaurant scene is quite dynamic. Despite the rapidly expanding number of good dining rooms, however, there is still no world-class restaurant in this city. Precious few Praguers—including those in the food industry—can name a favorite local chef, and none of the city's eateries have a culinary reputation that extends beyond the country's borders.

Many fantastic traditional dishes are part of the Bohemian culinary repertoire—crêpes sturdy garlic-laden soups, juicy roast meats, and sweet *paličinky* (crêpes) are tops. And few dishes anywhere are better than the sautéed chicken livers served at Quido, or the grilled eel with butter and lemon served at Na Rybárně. But Czech cooking has not been raised to an art. From restaurant to restaurant, preparations are rarely distinctive and almost never imaginative; the great majority of Prague's eateries offer almost identical menus of conservatively prepared roasts and grills. Even in the relatively vanguard kitchens of Parnas, rich slices of venison are played off against the standard stewed sour cherries, and inexplicable piles of fruit garnish many plates. Like everywhere else, presentations are largely two-dimensional, and there is little attempt at any kind of "fooditecture." As of yet, there are just not enough dedicated foodies in this city willing to put their money where their mouths are for top-of-the-line meals. The fine-dining market is not yet strong enough to support the opening of a world-class restaurant attractive to either top chefs or investors.

The quality of local game is among the best in the world. When available, order goose, duck, boar, rabbit, or venison, and you'll rarely be disappointed. It's hard to vouch for the health of the Czech Republic's lakes and rivers, but excellent-tasting freshwater fish such as trout, eel, and carp have long been a staple of local kitchens. The recent popularity of ocean fish is one of this landlocked city's most surprising gastronomical developments. Despite Prague's considerable distance from the sea, ocean fish can be quite acceptable. Most of the city's top restaurants offer fresh, ice-shipped seafood, and some even feature shell- and fin-fish almost exclusively.

As you might imagine, vegetarian restaurants in Prague are few and far between, but a few standouts are listed below.

As with almost every other sector of this nascent economy, the restaurant scene is slowly changing. The last five years have pushed local chefs toward change more than in the last fifty years combined.

Beware of Food Fraud

It's bad for the travel industry, bad for business, and a shame for the entire country, but visitors in Prague have to be on their guard when dining at Czech restaurants. Although overcharging in restaurants is less common now than it was a few years ago, many restaurateurs (and waiters) make a habit of cheating their patrons. Appetizers and other unordered foods are sometimes offered to trusting diners who only later discover that the small deviled egg or bowl of nuts cost as much as an entire meal. Sometimes when you order a main dish and ask to substitute boiled potatoes for french fries, the menu price inexplicably doubles. Here is the single rule you must **always** follow to avoid being ripped off: Know the price of everything before putting it in your mouth.

Credit cards are new to Czechs, and unscrupulous restaurateurs can easily add an extra zero or change a "1" to a "2." Avoid being ripped off by writing out in letters—anywhere on the charge slip—the total amount of your bill.

A growing number of places interpret traditional Czech cooking with a somewhat lighter hand but so far no local chef can claim to be the parent of a "New Bohemian" cuisine. The 1995 openings of La Provence, U Patrona, and Le Bistro de Marlene are being closely watched by would-be investors as they test these culinary waters.

SERVICE   Even at Prague's smartest eateries, service is sorely lacking. Poorly trained waitstaffs, having yet to master the art of unintrusive service, are almost universal. Waiters either interfere at inappropriate moments or (more commonly) are as absent as a cop when you need one. Poor service is a relic of Communism. Most waiters and waitresses are not accustomed to demanding patrons, and serve according to their own needs, not those of the client.

TAX & TIPPING   At most restaurants, menu prices include a value-added tax (VAT). When they don't, it must say so on the menu. In addition to tax, it's common for some restaurants to levy a small cover charge, usually about 10 Kč (37¢).

RESERVATIONS   Especially during the summer months, reservations are mandatory for top eateries, and should be made as far in advance as possible. Lunchtime tables are easier to come by, so if you're only in town for a couple of days, and just have to eat at The Blue Duckling, an afternoon meal might be your best bet.

DINING CUSTOMS   Few restaurants employ hosts to greet patrons at the door and seat them. If there is no host, just choose any available table. Many restaurants only offer large tables, seating six or more diners. In these establishments, it is expected that unrelated parties will share the same table. The custom is said to have begun during the Austrian monarchy, which banned intimate private tables and forced patrons to dine together with strangers. This allowed informers to eavesdrop on any possible revolutionary plans and report them to the Crown. This regulation turned out to be helpful for the Communist secret police as well. It's customary to ask "Je tu volno?" ("Is this spot free?") before joining a large table.

TIPS FOR TRAVELERS ON A BUDGET   It's a good idea to avoid imported foods, which are always much more expensive and less fresh than locally produced items. You can also save money by looking for fixed-price menus, two-for-one specials, and coupons in the local English-language newspapers. And, as mentioned in the "Beware of Food Fraud" box, don't eat anything without first determining its price. Some restaurants gouge customers by charging exorbitant amounts for nuts or other seemingly free pre-meal snacks. For very cheap meals, try the places discussed in the "Inexpensive Meals on the Run" section.

1 Best Bets

- **Best Spot for a Romantic Dinner:** An extremely seductive baroque palace atmosphere, discrete service, and sumptuous surroundings make the **Opera Grill** (☎ 02/26 55 08) a must for both lovers and intimate friends.
- **Best Spot for a Business Lunch:** With attentive service, good food, and pleasant surroundings, the upscale **Vinárna V Zátiší** (☎ 02/2422 8977) is a perfect place to conduct business. Tables are spaced for privacy, and there's enough room to spread out papers and sign a contract.
- **Best Spot for a Celebration: Avalon** (☎ 02/53 02 76) has a friendly and fun atmosphere—it's not at all stuffy. And it's a practical place to gather a group, with several large tables. Plus this American eatery is one of the few places in town where everyone in your party will get served at the same time.
- **Best Decor: The Blue Duckling** (☎ 02/2451 0217) is one of the few places in Prague where the decor is as sumptuous as the food. This beautifully decorated restaurant, with top-quality wall murals, is a festival for the eyes, as well as the palate.
- **Best View:** From **Nebozízek** (☎ 02/53 79 05), perched in the middle of Petřín Hill, the city of Prague looks like a storybook wonderland. The view from here is so utterly fantastic that it might keep you mind off the restaurant's very mediocre food.
- **Best Wine List:** Sure, you have to part with a mint to dine at **U Malířů** (☎ 02/2451 0269). But, if you want an extensive wine list, you'll have to come here. Vintages from every growing region in France are sold, along with some special reserve wines from Moravia.
- **Best Value:** By any standard, **Vinárna U Maltézských Rytířů** (☎ 02/53 63 57)—Knights of Malta—is a very good restaurant, and a meal like the one served here would cost double or triple the price in the West. The restaurant does a great job at controlling costs without cutting portions; even their wines are exceedingly well priced.
- **Best for Kids:** Nobody will mind if children make a mess enjoying nachos and other fun finger foods at **Red Hot & Blues** (☎ 02/231 46 39).
- **Best American Cuisine: Avalon** (☎ 02/53 02 76) serves overstuffed sandwiches, grilled chicken, burgers, potato skins, and buffalo wings in an inviting environment that's as authentic as the food.
- **Best Continental Cuisine:** For years, **Parnas** (☎ 02/2422 7614 or 02/2422 9248) has been serving some of Prague's finest food. Good chefs are recruited from throughout Europe to create menus that would be respected in any of the world's major cities.
- **Best Czech Cuisine:** Packed with in-the-know locals, it's no secret that **Quido** (☎ 02/27 09 50) serves some of the city's best meals including fantastic grilled chicken livers and pig's knees. Squeamish? Try anything that comes off the gas-fired lava grill and you won't be disappointed at this excellent restaurant in Vinohrady.
- **Best French Cuisine:** Opened in 1995, **Le Bistro de Marlene** (☎ 02/29 10 77) was immediately hailed as the best country French restaurant in Prague. Traditional

know-how combine with fresh local ingredients to make this fine restaurant one of the city's most important newcomers.

- **Best Seafood:** One of Prague's most respected fish houses, **Na Rybárně** (☎ 02/29 97 95) has been wowing knowledgeable Praguers with the freshest local fish for almost a dozen years. Few meals are better than this restaurant's eel in butter.
- **Best Pizza:** It's still not as good as Naples, but **Pizzeria Rugantino** (☎ 02/231 81 72) near Old Town Square serves good crispy pies, topped with your choice of a dozen delicacies. Good calzones are available too.
- **Best Late-Night Dining:** The **Radost F/X Café** (☎ 02/25 12 10) serves its inexpensive vegetarian fare until 5am daily. There's always something going on at this lively restaurant, and after you eat, you can descend into the nightclub below.
- **Best Outdoor Dining:** The patio at **Kampa Park** (☎ 02/53 48 00) overlooks Charles Bridge and across the water to Old Town; it's the best in Prague. The view often justifies the high prices and sometimes uneven food.
- **Best People-Watching:** Interesting-looking people seem to fill the trendy and stylish **Radost F/X Café** (☎ 02/25 12 10), which is above the coolest club in Prague. If you're young and hip, you'll want to be seen here.
- **Best Afternoon Tea:** What's best about the **Cafe Evropa** (☎ 02/2422 8117) is not the tea and pastry but the surroundings. Here, you'll be able to linger in unparalleled art nouveau surroundings—built in 1906.
- **Best Brunch:** At **Parnas** (☎ 02/2422 7614 or 02/2422 9248), brunch is an all-you-can-eat affair that includes elaborate dishes like smoked salmon puff pastries and mushroom quiche. Champagne and mimosas are bottomless.
- **Best for Pre-Theater Dinner:** Located adjacent to the National Theater, and within walking distance to most everything else in Old Town, the fine **Klásterní Vinárna** (☎ 02/29 05 96) serves all the Czech staples in an extraordinarily beautiful environment. The waitstaff will seat you promptly, and understand if you tell them you need to be out the door by 7:45pm.
- **Best Fast Food:** Located on the same square as McDonald's and Kentucky Fried Chicken, **Krone** (no phone), a Czech buffet, tops those chains with delicious ready-to-eat meals that run the gamut from rotisserie chicken to grilled trout. Take-away boxes are available for food to go.
- **Best Picnic Fare:** To get everything you need for a fantastic picnic, head to Wenceslas Square and visit **Obchod Čerstvých Uzenin** (at number 36) for cold cuts and the **Krone Bakery** (at number 21) for bread. Go around the corner to **Fruits de France** (Jindrišská 9) for imported cheeses and gourmet produce, then head for the hills—Petřín Hill, that is—to spread your blanket.

2 Restaurants by Cuisine

AMERICAN

Ambiente (Vinohrady, *M*)
Avalon Bar & Grill (Malá Strana, *M*)
Buffalo Bill's (New Town, *I*)
Jáma (New Town, *I*)
Jo's Bar (Malá Strana, *I*)
Red Hot & Blues (Old Town & Josefov, *I*)

BELGIAN

Au Saint Esprit (Old Town & Josefov, *E*)

CAFE/TEAROOM

Cafe Evropa (New Town)
Café Milena (Staré Město)
Dobrá Cajovna (New Town)
Dolce Vita (Josefov)

Key to abbreviations: *I*=Inexpensive; *M*=Moderate; *E*=Expensive; *VE*=Very Expensive

The Globe (Elsewhere in Prague)
Rudolfinum Kavárna (Staré Město)
Velryba (Staré Město)

CONTINENTAL

Cerberus (New Town, *E*)
Circle Line Brasserie (Malá
  Strana, *E*)
Kampa Park (Malá Strana, *E*)
Nebozízek (Hradčany, *M*)
Opera Grill (Old Town
  & Josefov, *E*)
Peklo (Hradčany, *E*)
Reykjavik (Old Town & Josefov, *M*)
U Patrona (Malá Strana, *E*)
Vinárna V Zátiší (Old Town &
  Josefov, *E*)

CZECH

Cerberus (New Town, *E*)
Gany's (New Town, *I*)
Hogo Fogo (Old Town & Josefov, *I*)
Jáma (New Town, *I*)
Klásterní Vinárna (New Town, *M*)
Klub Architektů (Old Town &
  Josefov, *I*)
Krone (New Town, *I*)
Na Zvonařce (Vinohrady, *I*)
Nebozízek (Hradčany, *M*)
Obchod Čerstvých Uzenin (New
  Town, *I*)
Quido (Vinohrady, *M*)
Restaurant U Čížků (New
  Town, *M*)
U Dlouhé (Old Town & Josefov, *I*)
U Modré Kachničky (Malá
  Strana, *E*)
U Patrona (Malá Strana, *E*)
U Radnice (Old Town & Josefov, *I*)
Vinárna U Maltézských Rytířů (Malá
  Strana, *M*)

DELI

Cornucopia (New Town)
Obchod Čerstvých Uzenin (New
  Town)

FAST FOOD/BURGERS

Harvey's (New Town)

FRENCH

Au Saint Esprit (Old Town &
  Josefov, *E*)
La Provance (Old Town
  & Josefov, *M*)
Le Bistro de Marlene (Vyšehrad, *M*)
U Malířů (Malá Strana, *E*)

HEALTH CONSCIOUS

Bona Vita (Old Town & Josefov, *I*)

INDIAN

Govinda Vegetarian Club (New
  Town, *I*)

INDONESIAN

Saté Grill (Hradčany, *I*)

INTERNATIONAL

Gany's (New Town, *I*)
Parnas (Old Town & Josefov, *E*)
Restaurant Adria (New Town, *M*)

ITALIAN

Bella Napoli (New Town, *M*)
Il Ritrovo (Vinohrady, *M*)
Segafredo (New Town, *M*)

LEBANESE

Fakhreldine (New Town, *E*)
Queenz Grill Bar (Old Town &
  Josefov, *I*)

MEXICAN

Jo's Bar (Malá Strana, *I*)

PIZZA

Pizzeria Kmotra (New Town, *I*)
Pizzeria Rugantino (Old Town &
  Josefov, *I*)

SANDWICHES

U Bakaláře (Old Town & Josefov)

SEAFOOD

Circle Line Brasserie (Malá
  Strana, *E*)
Na Rybárně (New Town, *M*)
Reykjavik (Old Town &
  Josefov, *M*)

VEGETARIAN

Country Life (New Town, *I*)
Govinda Vegetarian Club (New
Town, *I*)
Radost F/X Café (Vinohrady, *I*)

YUGOSLAV

Dolly Bell (Vyšehrad, *M*)
Zlatá Ulička (Old Town
& Josefov, *I*)

3 Staré Město (Old Town) & Josefov

EXPENSIVE

Au Saint Esprit

Elišky Krásnohorské 5, Prague 1. ☎ **02/231 00 39.** Reservations recommended. Main courses 300–400 Kč ($11.11–$14.80); Prix-fixe dinner 1,200 Kč ($44). AE, MC, V. Mon–Fri 11:30am–2pm and 7–10:30pm, Sat 7–10:30pm. Metro: Staroměstská. BELGIAN/FRENCH.

Architecturally, Au Saint Esprit mimics an upscale Western-style eatery better than any other restaurant in town. The single large contemporary dining room features crisp white walls and a polished light blond floor topped with fashionable furnishings. The upbeat bistro interior appeals to both international business types and tourists staying at the nearby Inter-Continental Hotel. Image is important at Au Saint Esprit, one of the few restaurants in Prague that will turn away prospective diners who are not dressed for success. The elegant Belgian-French menu changes with the seasons; entrees may include monkfish in a creamy tomato sauce, mint-scented lamb chops, and rabbit with baby vegetables. There's something nouvelle for everybody, plus a daily plat du jour, and a four-course, prix-fixe menu every evening.

Opera Grill

Karoliny Světlé 35, Prague 1. ☎ **02/26 55 08.** Reservations recommended. Main courses 250–350 Kč ($9.25–$13). AE, MC, V. Daily 7pm–2am. Metro: Staroměstská. CONTINENTAL.

An intimate 25-seater, Opera Grill feels both romantic and clubby, catering to couples and friends in search of a quiet meal in beautiful surroundings. A firm knock on a discrete door summons the maitre d' who then whisks you away to a small attractive dining room furnished with flowing drapery, overstuffed armchairs, and elegantly laid tables. A short list of continental dishes, presented on a hand-lettered menu, includes steaks, game, and seafood, as well as fish and pasta. While the food is good—not great—it's the thoroughly enchanting Old World atmosphere that makes me highly recommend Opera Grill.

✪ Parnas

Smetanovo nábřeží 2, Prague 1. ☎ **02/2422 7614** or 2422 9248. Reservations recommended. Main courses 350–550 Kč ($13–$20.40); Sunday brunch 450 Kč ($16.70). AE, DC, MC, V. Daily noon–3pm and 5:30–11pm, brunch Sun 11am–3:30pm. Metro: Národní třída. INTERNATIONAL.

One of the few Czech restaurants that would still be considered superior outside eastern Europe, Parnas can always be counted on for very good food served with studied precision by highly trained career waiters. Located on the embankment facing the Vltava, the restaurant is adjacent to the National Theater in a historical building where the composer Bedrich Smetana once lived. The lofty dining room is elegant with green marble pillars, inlaid wood paneling, and a museum-quality mosaic over the bar entitled *The Absinthe Drinkers.* A piano-based trio is almost always entertaining. Although they need to ignore the ceaseless automobile traffic outside, the luckiest diners have window seats, with great views of distant Prague Castle.

Little on the menu is either traditional or plain. Appetizers include cold North Sea shrimp with fresh kiwi, venison pâté with blue cheese, and a piping hot onion, leek, and mushroom tart. Spinach tagliatelle—a house specialty—is tossed with salmon and cream, garlic and herbs, or tomato and olives. Salmon with dill (poached to order and served either hot or cold) and prawns in a hot garlic sauce are the best of almost a dozen seafood main dishes. Roast duck is stuffed with untraditionally fresh vegetables, and braised rabbit is served with a stock reduction few babushkas know. The chefs only slack when it comes to meatless main courses; the vegetables au gratin and cottage cheese dishes seem like they're from a different restaurant entirely. The Sunday jazz brunch is the best in town, including an all-you-can eat buffet and free-flowing mimosas.

Vinárna V Zátiší

Liliová 1, Prague 1. ☎ **02/2422 8977.** Reservations recommended. Main courses 300–500 Kč ($11.11–$18.50); Sunday brunch 350 Kč ($13). AE, DC, MC, V. Mon–Sat noon–3pm and 5:30pm–11pm, Sun 11am–2pm and 5:30–11pm. Metro: Národní třída. CONTINENTAL.

Owned by the same group that runs the restaurant Parnas, Vinárna V Zátiší's self-consciously elegant dining room is designed to appeal to Prague's business crowd at both lunch and dinner. The chefs here are some of the best in Prague; they cook what is essentially the same food as Parnas at distinctly lower prices. Fitted with French furnishings from the upscale shop across the street, the restaurant feels both quiet and special, and not as staid as U Modré Kachničky (The Blue Duckling) or U Malířů (At the Painter's). The menu changes often, but almost always contains homemade pasta, fresh fish, rabbit, and roast duck. Lamb in puff pastry is an excellent starter, and the vegetarian lasagna is some of the best in the city. An excellent Sunday brunch includes an all-you-can eat buffet and all-you-can-drink sparkling wine and mimosas.

MODERATE

La Provance

Štupartská 9, Prague 1. ☎ **02/232 48 01.** Reservations recommended. Main courses 150–300 Kč ($5.55–$11.11). AE, MC, V. Daily noon–11:30pm. Metro: náměstí Republiky. FRENCH.

Opened in 1995, La Provance is the first of a new breed of Prague restaurants—a colorful, ultra-stylish international eatery. Located below Banana Cafe, a popular bar that has become a mainstay of the city's trendies, the restaurant serves its version of French Provençal cooking to a good-looking but uncritical crowd.

La Provance serves some adventurous dishes, albeit with mixed results. Escargots, served by the half-dozen in drawn butter, are more novel than tasty, as are any of their pâtés. Sliced grilled duck breast served over a garden salad is a much better appetizer. Main courses run the gamut from mediocre grilled scampi and bouillabaisse to very good coq au vin, and a roasted half-duck served with brussels sprouts and potatoes au gratin.

La Provance is loud and fun. And because service is slow, you'll have plenty of time to appreciate the eclectic French country decor, pillow-covered benches, and warm lighting.

Reykjavik

Karlova 20, Prague 1. ☎ **02/2422 9251.** Reservations not necessary. Main courses 150–250 Kč ($5.55–$9.25). AE, MC, V. Daily 11am–11pm. Metro: Staroměstská. SEAFOOD/CONTINENTAL.

Everyone who visits Prague passes Reykjavik restaurant, located on the main pedestrian street between Old Town Square and Charles Bridge. Because of its location, the restaurant does good business, especially in the summer when they put almost two

Old Town Dining

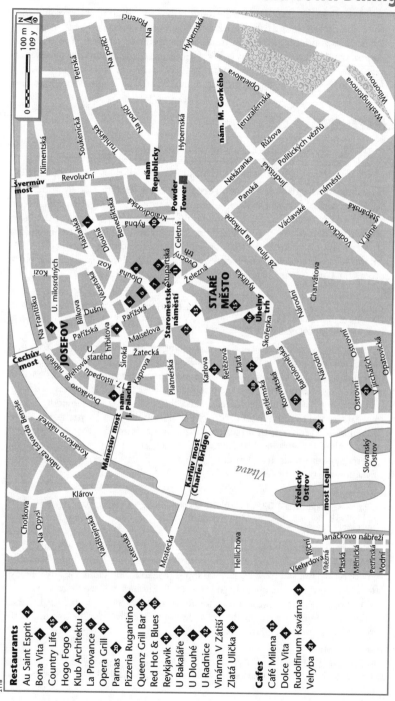

Restaurants
Au Saint Esprit ❷
Bona Vita ❼
Country Life ⓯
Hogo Fogo ❺
Klub Architektu ⓱
La Provance ❾
Opera Grill ⓳
Parnas ⓴
Pizzeria Rugantino ❻
Queenz Grill Bar ⓰
Red Hot & Blues ⓾
Reykjavík ⓮
U Bakaláře ⓫
U Dlouhé ❶
U Radnice ❹
Vinárna V Zátiší ⓲
Zlatá Ulička ❽

Cafes
Café Milena ⓭
Dolce Vita ❹
Rudolfinum Kavárna ❸
Velryba ㉑

89

dozen tables on the street. Despite the tourists, Reykjavik is surprisingly recommendable. The kitchen stresses fish in general, and salmon in particular—both frozen Icelandic filets and fresh Norwegian steaks are competently prepared. You'll find no surprises with other menu items either. Grilled meats and poultry are paired with vegetables and potatoes and are good, if not particularly memorable. For those not looking to be wowed, Reykjavik provides an honest meal at fair prices for such a central location.

INEXPENSIVE

Bona Vita

Dlouhá 4, Prague 1. ☎ **02/231 13 76.** Reservations not accepted. 45–50 Kč ($1.70–$1.85). No credit cards. Mon–Fri 8am–10pm. Metro: Staroměstská. HEALTH-CONSCIOUS CAFETERIA.

This unusual cafeteria-style restaurant, opened as a showplace for a locally made packaged soy product, is meant to demonstrate all the wonderful things that can be done with dried soy meat. The chewy mixed results include soy with curry, stir-fried soy, soy with chili, soy burgers and other somewhat inventive yet strange-tasting dishes. You can also order chicken, steak, or sandwiches. The dining room is clean and bright, with mirrored walls and blond wood furnishings. Bona Vita is just one block from Old Town Square, behind and to the left of the Jan Hus statue.

ⓢ U Dlouhé

Dlouhá 35, Prague 1. ☎ **02/231 61 25.** Reservations recommended on weekends. Main courses 90–160 Kč ($3.33–$5.93). AE, MC, V. Mon–Sat 11am–11pm, Sun 11am–10pm. Metro: náměstí Republiky. CZECH.

Looking for very good, authentic Czech cooking without all the tourists? Your best bet is Dlouhé, a very large Old Town restaurant that serves all the Bohemian "hits" in a traditional pub-like atmosphere. The long cloth-covered tables are designed to be shared by several parties, but the restaurant is large enough so sharing is usually not necessary. The menu offers excellent straightforward Czech soul food from various parts of the country. Several different combination plates let you taste a bit of Bohemia or Moravia with mixtures of roast duck, smoked meats, sausages and knedliky; most cost under 150 Kč ($6). Service is also traditional—slow, and not necessarily with a smile. It's all washed down with half-liters of beer, which keep coming automatically until you say *"ne."*

Hogo Fogo

Salvátorská 4, Prague 1. ☎ **02/231 70 23.** Reservations not accepted. Main courses 40–75 Kč ($1.48–$2.78). AE, MC, V. Mon–Fri noon–midnight, Sat–Sun noon–2am. Metro: Staroměstská. CZECH.

It's not hard to determine exactly what attracts Hogo Fogo's loyal following of Americans and Czechs in their twenties. The bare basement dining room is unremarkable, service is sluggish, and most of the food is just tolerable. But, located just two blocks from Old Town Square, Hogo Fogo is one of the cheapest full-service restaurants in Old Town. There are some menu standouts, such as the lentil soup and fried cheese, and the rock music is good. Half liters of beer are just 30 Kč ($1.20), and diners are encouraged to sit all day if they wish.

Klub Architektů

Betlémské nám. 5a, Prague 1. ☎ **02/2440 1214.** Reservations recommended. Main courses 60–100 Kč ($2.22–$3.70). No credit cards. Mon–Sat 11:30am–midnight. Metro: Národní třída. CZECH.

This hard-to-find restaurant, located in a dimly lit, labyrinthine, 12th-century cellar, combines medieval tranquility with big-city chic. The architect owners have designed an excellent space. Soft rock music bounces off centuries-old whitewashed vaulted ceilings. Contemporary furnishings and exposed ducts complete an environment that appeals to in-the-know young Czechs. Less distinctive is the food, which, for the most part, is strictly functional. Few dishes are great—cheese-stuffed chicken is a standout. The restaurant is located under Bethlehem Church; go through the church's front gates, and turn right. Make a reservation, then be prepared to wait.

$ Pizzeria Rugantino

Dušní 4, Prague 1. ☎ **02/231 81 72.** Reservations not accepted. Pizzas 80–140 Kč ($2.96–$5.19). No credit cards. Mon–Sat 11am–11pm, Sun 6–11pm. Metro: Staroměstská. PIZZA.

One of the best restaurants to open in Prague in 1995, Pizzeria Rugantino serves very good Neapolitan-style pies baked in a beautiful wood-fired exhibition oven situated in the front of the restaurant. The well-designed twin dining rooms are filled with wood tables and bench seating designed for eating rather than lingering. The restaurant is large, but not large enough to accommodate the dinnertime crowds who have discovered this fine food at reasonable prices so close to Old Town Square. The best of some two dozen pizza offerings are cheese, potato, garlic, and rosemary; and tomato, cheese, and artichokes. Calzones and salads are also available.

Red Hot & Blues

Jakubská 12, Prague 1. ☎ **02/231 46 39.** Reservations not necessary. Main courses 90–250 Kč ($3.33–$9.25). AE, MC, V. Daily 9am–11pm. Metro: náměstí Republiky. REGIONAL AMERICAN.

A popular American ex-pat hangout at its inception, Red Hot & Blues has evolved into a Czech-oriented regional American theme restaurant serving decent shrimp Creole, étouffée, burgers, and nachos. Bourbon Street it's not, but gastronomical authenticity is not what this populist restaurant strives for. Paintings and posters cover the walls of two simple dining rooms—the front one is smaller and holds the bar, while the rear room accommodates a dozen wood-topped iron tables and the live jazz combo that regularly performs. An adjacent ceilingless atrium opens during warmer months. Red Hot & Blues is at its blistering best on Sundays, when they serve a good à la carte brunch that includes French toast and Creole omelettes.

$ U Radnice

U Radnice 10, Prague 1. ☎ **02/2422 8136.** Reservations not accepted. Main courses 70–150 Kč ($2.59–$5.55). No credit cards. Daily 11am–11pm. Metro: Staroměstská. CZECH.

This established restaurant is one of the last proletariat holdouts near Old Town Square where you can get a traditional goulash for under 50 Kč ($2), and roast duck for under 150 Kč ($6). Other typical Czech meals, including grilled venison, pork, and beef, are served with the requisite dumplings and half-liters of Staropramen beer. Free pretzels are offered at long, cloth-topped wooden tables that are meant to be shared with other customers. There are three parts to U Radnice; make sure you sit in the dining room, rather than the pub or the bar.

✪ Zlatá Ulička

Masná 9, Prague 1. ☎ **02/232 08 84.** Reservations are not necessary. Main courses 110–200 Kč ($4.07–$7.40). No credit cards. Daily 10am–midnight. Metro: náměstí Republiky. YUGOSLAV.

Hidden in the backstreets of Staré Město near Kastel sv. Jakuba (St. James' Church), and named after the Hradčany street of colorful 16th-century cottages, pint-sized Zlatá Ulička is one of central Prague's most unique finds. The restaurant's low-kitsch interior, designed by an architect from Sarajevo, suggests a surreal Renaissance-era courtyard, surrounded by faux yellow and blue cottage facades complete with shingle roofs. Stereo speakers sing from birdcages, a ladder climbs to nowhere, and several gold plaques, inscribed with wistful Serbian-language poems, are embedded in the restaurant's floor (". . . maybe tomorrow the ships will come"). On the menu, many dishes served here seem similar to those available at any number of Czech restaurants around town. On the plate, however, diners discover the food's Yugoslavian qualities—savory spices that are almost completely absent in Bohemia. Whole trout is pan-fried in olive oil with garlic and parsley, while a medley of piquant spices enliven giant homemade hamburgers. The very traditional Yugoslavian shish kabob alternates marinated veal and vegetables.

4 Nové Město (New Town)

EXPENSIVE

Cerberus

Soukenická 19, Prague 1. ☎ **02/231 09 85.** Reservations recommended on weekends. Main courses 120–350 Kč ($4.44–$13). AE, MC, V. Daily noon–4pm and 5pm–midnight. Metro: náměstí Republiky. CZECH/CONTINENTAL.

It's hard to imagine exactly what the interior designer had in mind when he put together this restaurant's hodgepodge of styles. A long and narrow booth-lined dining room is colored crimson and cardinal, like an upscale International House of Pancakes. More tables and chairs are located at the end of the dining hall in a bright, leafy gastrodome that's topped by a glass skylight. And although the restaurant is named for the three-headed dog of Greek mythology, Cerberus is devoid of Athenian accents in either dining room or the kitchen.

The menu, which is presented on a paper scroll, is just as eclectic as the decor. Recommendable starters include rosemary-marinated chicken breasts served with a peppery tomato sauce, and chilled shrimp—sweet small shrimp from the North Sea—served traditionally with lemon on a bed of iceberg lettuce. Pasta, one of the restaurant's best values, is all homemade, and tossed with bacon and mushrooms, basil-tomato sauce, or garlic, green peas, and butter. Main dishes are all à la carte, and run the gamut from poached salmon to stewed rabbit to duck with tomatoes, thyme, and cognac. Several excellent vegetarian meals are also served, including cauliflower soufflé and potato/vegetable au gratin. At the meal's end, the staff will even provide you with a Cuban cigar, if you ask.

✪ Fakhreldine

Klimentská 48, Prague 1. ☎ **02/232 79 70.** Main courses 250–350 Kč ($9.25–$13). AE, DC, MC, V. Daily noon–midnight. Metro: Florenc. LEBANESE.

Fakhreldine is exceptional because it is one of Prague's only top-of-the-line non-European restaurants. This very upscale eatery is the only other branch of London's most famous Lebanese restaurant, and the quality here rivals its English parent in both flavor and atmosphere. The chandeliered dining room is uncluttered and elegant, staffed by professionally dressed waiters who are both well-trained and attentive. And although the restaurant aims itself squarely at Prague's well-heeled Middle Eastern community, plenty of Westerners come here too. Diplomats are common, tourists rare.

A long list of entrees includes char-grilled lamb, marinated veal, and steaks. A better strategy, however, is to avoid main courses entirely, and make a meal out of the arm's length–list of appetizers. The beautifully presented starters are the tastiest treats, and include raw lamb, grilled spicy Armenian sausages, babaganush, Lebanese cream cheese, hummus, and plenty of homemade Arabic bread. Three kinds of baklava and cardamom-scented coffee round out the meal.

MODERATE

Bella Napoli

V jámě 8, Prague 1. ☎ **02/2422 7315.** Reservations recommended on weekends. Main courses 130–220 Kč ($4.81–$8.15). No credit cards. Daily noon–3pm and 6pm–midnight. Metro: Můstek. SOUTHERN ITALIAN.

The best thing about Bella Napoli is the antipasti bar, a table of cold appetizers that on any given night might include roasted peppers, calamari rings, marinated mushrooms, or grilled eggplant. First courses include a wide range of pasta dishes, including a particularly good tortellini gorgonzola, but the quality tends to be inconsistent. The best main courses are made with local beef, cheese, and red sauces. The restaurant's single small dining room feels warm and comfortable, and is a nice place to relax with friends. And although nothing in Bella Napoli can match even a mediocre restaurant in Naples, this remains one of Prague's best southern Italian restaurants.

Klásterní Vinárna

Národní třída 8, Prague 1. ☎ **02/29 05 96.** Reservations not necessary. Main courses 90–250 Kč ($3.33–$9.25). AE, MC. Daily 11:30am–4:30pm and 5pm–midnight. Metro: Národní třída. CZECH.

The perfect pre- or post-theater restaurant, Klásterní Vinárna is located in a former 17th-century Ursuline convent, just steps from the National Theater. The main dining room is both large and romantic, an effect achieved by wooden partitions, antique wall coverings, well-spaced tables, and an attentive yet unobtrusive waitstaff. A second dining area, in a smaller anteroom containing a short wooden bar, is more crowded and less desirable.

A traditional Czech kitchen prepares all the standards admirably, including appetizers like Prague ham (served with the traditional horseradish) and caviar (served with butter and toast). Main dishes, like baked chicken breast with peaches, roast pork with ham and melted cheese, and large beefsteaks, are equally authentic and consistently good. Even trout and salmon are smothered Bohemian style, with butter sauce or another caloric but savory gravy. The restaurant's mixed vegetables swimming in curry gravy is an edible but misguided vegetarian dish.

✪ Na Rybárně

Gorazdova 17, Prague 2. ☎ **02/29 97 95.** Reservations recommended. Main courses 130–220 Kč ($4.81–$8.15). AE, DC, MC, V. Daily noon–midnight. Metro: Karlovo náměstí. SEAFOOD.

One of Prague's oldest fish restaurants, Na Rybárně specializes in local freshwater offerings like trout, carp, and eel. Meals here are almost always great. The fish is prepared simply, usually grilled with lemon and butter. Typical Czech meat dishes are also available. The atmosphere is informal—somewhere between restaurant and pub. The best tables are located in the back room, where famous visitors, including musician Paul Simon and members of the Rolling Stones, have autographed the white walls. President Václav Havel was a familiar face here a few years ago, when he lived around the corner. The restaurant remains popular with knowledgeable Czechs (and a few tourists) who know where to go for a top-quality meal.

Restaurant Adria

Národní třída 40, Prague 1. ☎ **02/2422 8065.** Reservations not necessary. Main courses 100–250 Kč ($3.70–$9.25); fixed-price menu 200 Kč ($8). AE, MC, V. Daily 11:30am–midnight. Metro: Můstek. INTERNATIONAL.

The best thing about Restaurant Adria is its awesome second-floor terrace overlooking Národní, topped by a colossal statue of wrestling titans and buzzing with diners.

Prague Dining

Restaurants
Ambiente ❸❹
Avalon Bar & Grill ❷
Bella Napoli ❷❽
Le Bistro de Marlene ❸❽
Buffalo Bill's ❷❻
Cerberus ❶❸
Circle Line Brasserie ❷
Cornucopia ❸⓿
Dolly Bell ❸❽
Fakhreldine ❶❶
Gany's ❶❽
Govinda Vegetarian Club ❶❷
Harvey's ❷❸
Il Ritrovo ❸❻
Jáma ❷❾
Jo's Bar ❸
Kampa Park ❼
Klásterní Vinárna ❷⓿
Krone ❷❹
Na Rybárně ❸❷
Na Zvonařce ❸❼
Nebozízek ❾
Obchod Čerstvých Uzenin ❷❺
Peklo ❶
Pizzeria Kmotra ❷❶
Quido ❸❸
Radost F/X Café ❸❺
Restaurant Adria ❷❷
Restaurant U Čížků ❸❶
Saté Grill ❶
Segafredo ❶❻
U Malířů ❻
U Modré Kachničky ❽
U Patrona ❺
Vinárna U Maltézských
    Rytířů ❹

Cafes/Tearooms
Cafe Evropa ❷❹
Dobrá Čajovna ❷❼
The Globe ❶⓿

Late-Night Bites
Masarykovo Nonstop ❶❺
Národní Gyro Stand ❶❾
Snack-Bar Agnes ❶❹
U Zlatého Stromu ❶❼

2119

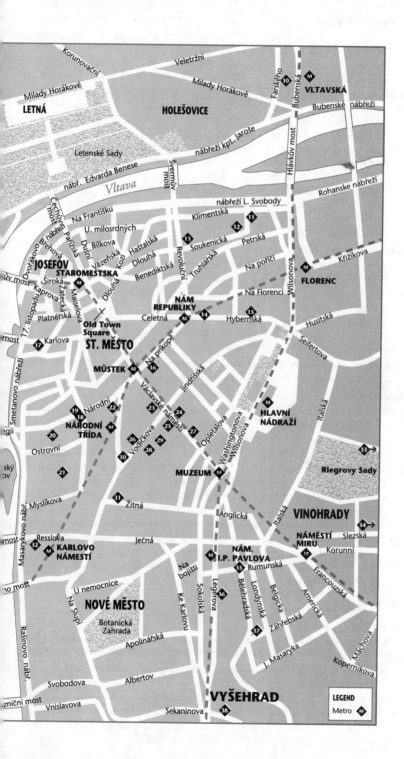

LETNÁ

Korunovační

Milady Horákové

HOLEŠOVICE

Milady Horákové

Veletržní

Farského

VLTAVSKÁ

Bubenská

10 Ⓜ

Bubenské nábřeží

Letenské Sady

Švermův most

nábř. Edvarda Benese

Vltava

Čechův most

Dvořákovo nábř.

Přehová

Pařížská

17. listopadu

Kaprova

Žatecká

most

Na Františku

nábřeží kpt. Jaroše

Hlávkův most

Rohanske nábřeží

nábřeží L. Svobody

Klimentská

12

11

U. milosrdných

Bílkova

Dušní

Vězeňská

Haštalská

13

Soukenická

Petrská

Kozí

Dlouhá

Revoluční

Benediktská

Truhlářská

Na poříčí

Křižíkova

JOSEFOV

STAROMESTSKÁ Ⓜ

Široká

Maiselova

Dlouhá

NÁM
REPUBLIKY

Celetná

14 Ⓜ

Hybernská

Na Florenci

Wilsonova

FLORENC

15

Platnéřská

Old Town
Square

Husitská

Seifertova

most

17

Karlova

ST. MĚSTO

Na příkopě

MŮSTEK Ⓜ

16

Jindřišská

Smetanovo nábřeží

egii

Národní

19

18

22

23

Václavské náměstí

24

25

27

Opletalova

Washingtonova

Wilsonova

Ⓜ

HLAVNÍ
NÁDRAŽÍ

Italská

NÁRODNÍ
TŘÍDA Ⓜ

26

Vodičkova

29

28

Ⓜ

20

Ostrovní

30

33 →

sický
ov

21

MUZEUM Ⓜ

Riegrovy Sady

Myslíkova

31

Žitná

Anglická

Italská

VINOHRADY

Masarykovo nábř.

Ječná

NÁMĚSTÍ
MIRU

34 →

most

32

Ⓜ

Resslova

KARLOVO
NÁMĚSTÍ

NÁM.
I.P. PAVLOVA

Rumunská

Slezská

Korunní

no most

U nemocnice

Ⓜ

35

Legerova

Bělehradská

Londýnská

Belgická

Americká

Francouzská

Na
bojišti

36

Sokolská

Ke Karlovu

NOVÉ MĚSTO

Rašínovo nábř.

Botanická
Zahrada

Apolinářská

Záhřebská

37

J. Masaryka

Kopernikova

Machova

Svobodova

Albertov

zniční most

Vnislavova

VYŠEHRAD

38

Sekaninova

LEGEND

Metro Ⓜ

95

There's no better place to lunch near Wenceslas Square on a warm afternoon. Both the food and service at Adria are good, but not exceptional. The same can be said for the bright interior dining room, which features wraparound windows, an open kitchen, and an exposed full bar. The restaurant's considerable menu is a veritable tour of Czech and continental cookery. Many foods, both hot and cold, can be chosen by sight from a glass case in the dining room. Tried and true appetizers include chilled smoked trout filets and surprisingly greaseless fried mushrooms. The plethora of pasta, topped with a variety of seafood, meat, and cheese sauces, are respectable by Prague standards. The restaurant does its best work with fish, which is grilled and sold by weight, and traditional Czech dishes, including roast pork with dumplings and cabbage. If you're in the mood for the limited offerings of the fixed-price menu, it represents a very good value. Set meals include soup of the day, a choice of goulash with dumplings, roasted pork with cabbage, venison, or deep-fried chicken breast, and dessert.

❂ Restaurant U Čížků

Karlovo nám. 34, Prague 2. ☎ **02/29 88 91.** Reservations recommended. Main courses 150–300 Kč ($5.55–$11.11). AE, MC, V. Daily noon–10pm. Metro: Karlovo náměstí. CZECH.

For the quintessential classical Czech meal, you can do no better than this slightly out-of-the-way traditional restaurant serving some of the best dumpling-based dinners around. The restaurant's dark, timbered dining room complements the hearty meals served in giant portions. The smoked pork, juicy duck, and cream-topped beef dishes are the best of their kind. And you can sample several varieties of dumplings. Many German tourists have discovered U Čížků, and prices have risen because of it. Quality remains high, however, making this one of the best restaurants in Prague.

Segafredo

Na Příkopě 10, Prague 1. ☎ **02/2421 0716.** Reservations recommended. Main courses 180–250 Kč ($6.67–$9.25). AE, MC, V. Daily 11am–11pm. Metro: Můstek. ITALIAN.

Opened in 1994 by the same Scandinavian duo who own Kampa Park restaurant in Malá Strana, Segafredo is a stylish Italian restaurant serving good pastas and meats right in the heart of touristland. The restaurant is best in summer, when dozens of outdoor tables allow for lively alfresco dining. The two-part interior consists of a bright bar room in front, fitted with small cafe tables and oversized fashion posters, and a far less desirable windowless dining room in back. A plate of Italian charcuteries—salami and a variety of hams, nicely garnished with crudités—is relatively ordinary. Penne with salmon, thyme, and chili in a cream sauce is chunky and delicious, as is the grilled beef tenderloin in red wine sauce, and beef in mushroom sauce. Salads, nice-sized plates of designer greens, are especially good here. The service, however, is another story.

INEXPENSIVE

Buffalo Bill's

Vodičkova 9, Prague 1. ☎ **02/2421 5479.** Reservations recommended on weekends. Main courses 100–170 Kč ($3.70–$6.30). AE, MC. Daily noon–midnight. Metro: Můstek. AMERICAN.

This basement Czech/Mex is a theme restaurant serving Texas-sized platters of chicken wings, burritos, fajitas, ribs, and nachos that will win no awards at the Texas State Fair. Their guacamole begins life as frozen avocado purée, and the salsa has never seen a single jalapeño. Still, Buffalo Bill's is wildly popular with Czechs who don't know any better, American ex-pats who crave a little taste of home, and visitors who just can't stand the sight of another piece of fried pork.

Gany's

Národní třída 20, Prague 1. ☎ **02/29 74 72.** Reservations not accepted. Main courses 90–180 Kč ($3.33–$6.67). AE, DC, MC, V. Daily 8am–11pm. Metro: Můstek. CZECH/INTERNATIONAL.

You will almost certainly walk past Gany's on your wanderings around Prague; it's situated on a major thoroughfare, equidistant from Václavské náměstí and the National Theater. But, unless you're looking for it, you could easily pass by. Don't be discouraged by the disheveled entrance that leads up two flights of dingy stairs to the restaurant. Persevere past the seedy-looking Riviera Disco to a bona fide institution that is, both literally and figuratively, one of Prague's brightest restaurants. Grand, gracious Gany's is a successful amalgam of new and old. Its fabulous, understated art nouveau interior, complete with original globe chandeliers, has been perfectly restored and enlivened with trendy, period-style oil paintings.

Although food here is not spectacular by any means, meals are good, inexpensive, and plentiful. The restaurant's curious combination of cuisines means a choice of starters that includes smoked salmon, battered and fried asparagus, and ham au gratin with vegetables, and main dishes that encompass everything from trout with horse-radish to beans with garlic sauce. In between is a long list of chicken, beef, veal, and pork dishes, each drowned in a complementary, if not extraordinary, sauce. They serve post-curtain. There's also a well-appointed billiards parlor in the back.

✪ Govinda Vegetarian Club

Soukenická 27, Prague 1. No phone. Meals 45 Kč ($1.48). No credit cards. Mon–Fri 11am–5pm, Sat 8am–5pm. Metro: náměstí Republiky. INDIAN/VEGETARIAN.

Operated by the Hare Krishnas, Govinda serves Indian soul foods like curried lentils, vegetable stew, and crispy nan breads. Place your order at the counter, take your meal to one of a dozen wooden tables in the bright second-floor dining room, and return for free refills as often as you like. The bakery and tea shop downstairs sell excellent Indian desserts made with tropical fruits, nuts and spices—all at amazingly low prices.

A second (and even cheaper) Govinda is located at Na hrázi 5, Prague 8 (☎ **02/ 82 14 38**).

Jáma

V Jámě 7, Prague 1. ☎ **02/26 41 27.** Reservations not necessary. Main courses 80–150 Kč ($2.96–$5.55). No credit cards. Daily 11am–1am. Metro: Můstek. CZECH/AMERICAN.

When you've had one plate of roast pork too many, Jáma comes to the rescue with Czechified renditions of American comfort foods like potato skins, lasagna, and burritos. Some creations, like a greasy tuna sandwich served on a rock-hard roll, fail miserably. Others, like an American-style potato pancake, are well-spiced and delicious. Walk past several excellent pinball machines into a college-style rock and roll atmosphere that's popular with a good cross-section of locals and visitors who come here in groups and dig in for the evening. An occasional jazz band performs, and five beers on tap makes for interesting tastings.

Pizzeria Kmotra

V jirchářích 12, Prague 1. ☎ **02/2491 5809.** Reservations not accepted. Pizzas 70–130 Kč ($2.59–$4.81). No credit cards. Daily 11am–1am. Metro: Národní třída. PIZZA.

Of the dozens of Yugoslavian-owned pizza restaurants in Prague, Kmotra is tops, serving flavorful Neapolitan-style pies with a variety of traditional toppings. Pizzas the size of your head come out of a wood-fired oven and are served piping hot at one of a dozen wooden tables set in a medieval cellar. The dining room is perpetually packed, meaning the wait can be long at the height of the dinner hour. It's not uncommon to see a group of students sitting on the sidewalk out front, eating pizza that they had to order boxed to go.

5 Malá Strana

EXPENSIVE

Circle Line Brasserie

Malostranské nám. 12, Prague 1. ☎ 02/53 02 76. Reservations recommended. Main courses 180–300 Kč ($6.67–$11.11). AE, MC, V. Daily 11am–1am. Metro: Malostranská. SEAFOOD.

This cellar restaurant, located below the American-style eatery Avalon, primarily serves fresh fish in an upbeat basement dining room. Oysters, shrimp, crab, and lobster are served either on their own or as a shellfish medley that arrives on a giant platter of crushed ice. Large parties of locals are common here, and the food has gotten fresher since the restaurant's supplier started delivering from Belgium almost daily. A whimsical nautical theme, evoked by murals of cruise-ship lounges, almost makes up for the fact this restaurant is situated in a basement. During warm months, diners can eat alfresco, on the sidewalk overlooking the square's imposing Nicholas Church.

Kampa Park

Na Kampě 8b, Prague 1. ☎ 02/53 48 00. Reservations recommended. Main courses 200–400 Kč ($7.40–$14.80). AE, DC, MC, V. Daily 11:30am–11:30pm. Metro: Malostranská. CONTINENTAL.

In the summer, there is no prettier place for a meal than on the outdoor waterside patio at Kampa Park. The water of the Vltava practically laps at your feet, and you'll enjoy the most magnificent view of Charles Bridge and the Old Town skyline. Owned by an intelligent team of Scandinavian businessmen, the restaurant looks like a top European eatery. Vested waiters and well-composed plates make diners feel special. Culinarily speaking, however, the food has proved uneven. Sometimes meals here are superlative; fillet of venison in red wine sauce or fresh grilled salmon steak topped with a light creamy caper sauce can be sublime. Other times, however, mediocrity reigns. During the winter, dining is confined to two beautiful, candlelit dining rooms; I suggest reserving in advance a table in the smaller room, which has views.

U Malířů

Maltézské náměstí 11. ☎ 02/2451 0269. Reservations recommended. Main courses 1,200–1,700 Kč ($44–$63); Menu Gourmand 3,500 Kč ($130). AE, DC, MC, V. Daily 11:30am–2:30pm and 7–10pm. Metro: Malostranská. FRENCH.

When U Malířů opened in 1991 with a French chef in the kitchen and hand-painted murals in three small, elegant dining rooms, no other restaurant could even come close to the quality and beauty that was offered here. And nothing wowed Prague's restaurant-going public more than this restaurant's famously high prices—dinner here still costs two or three times more than a meal at Parnas, its closest competitor.

Is it worth it? U Malířů's Czech-born chef Jaromír Froulik is an excellent student, and he has mastered the traditional French menus that rotate here on a seasonal basis. Summer starters include herb-marinated salmon and goose-liver pâté, which is usually followed by a palate-cleansing dish of green-apple sherbet. Entrees include braised sole filets with mushrooms and filet of beef rolled in bacon with truffle sauce. While the food is good and the service excellent, only the high prices make the meal particularly memorable. Choose the Menu Gourmand for a particularly fun culinary experience—a fixed-price dinner of eight sample dishes that are representative of the entire menu. One of the city's best wine lists offers selections from most every growing region of France—at Parisian prices. An assortment of French cheese is available, along with a tempting selection of desserts prepared by dedicated pastry chefs.

The three small, elegant dining rooms feel utterly romantic. They're perfect for trysts, as most locals can be quite sure they won't bump into anyone they know.

✪ U Modré Kachničky (The Blue Duckling)

Nebovidská 6, Prague 1. ☎ **02/2451 0217.** Reservations recommended. Main courses 150–320 Kč ($5.55–$11.85). AE, MC, V. Daily noon–3:30pm and 6:30–11:30pm. Metro: Malostranská. CZECH.

Although The Blue Duckling has recently suffered from management trouble and several chef changes, the restaurant remains one of the top eateries in Prague, serving traditional country Czech food in inimitable surroundings. It's hard to complain about a restaurant that has everything: charm, intimacy, style, good service, and fine food. Each of the three small dining rooms has vaulted ceilings covered with contemporary frescoes, antique furnishings, Oriental carpets, and a profusion of upholstery patterns and colors that compete for the attentions of diners.

From pheasant soup to stag sausage, wild game is the house specialty; if it's hunted, it's probably on the menu. Cold starters include Russian malossol caviar, smoked salmon, goose liver with apples and red wine, and asparagus baked with ham and cheese. They are all excellent. Boar goulash is an interesting twist on the original, duck is smoked before being served with the traditional cabbage, and rabbit is cooked with a cream sauce and cranberries. Deer, beef, pork, and chicken are also available, as is the "hunter's pin," a skewered medley of the kitchen's most interesting meats. Carp, a popular Czech fish, is baked with anchovies, and the single vegetarian main dish, risotto, is made-to-order with mushrooms and cheese. Last, but not least, the traditional Czech *palačinky,* crêpes filled with fruit, nuts, and chocolate, are top of the line.

U Patrona

Dražického nám. 4, Prague 1. ☎ **02/53 15 12.** Reservations recommended. Main courses 250–350 Kč ($9.25–$13). AE, MC, V. Daily 11am–1pm and 5:30–11pm. Metro: Malostranská. CZECH/CONTINENTAL.

Johan de Batselier, the young Belgian wonderkid who heads the kitchen at U Patrona, just might be the very best chef in Prague. His delightful menus, which change monthly, are new interpretations of Bohemian grandmothers' cooking. Meat, fish, and game dishes are always represented. Beef tenderloin is topped with a sauce tinged with plum brandy, trout is steamed and served with fresh vegetables, and rabbit is infused with marjoram and other aromatic herbs. The little gem of a dining room seats no more than 30, and feels like it was designed for romantic evenings. Walls adorned with murals of 1920s-era *bon vivants* hark back to a time when this space was occupied by another eatery and patronized by notable Europeans. At this writing, U Patrona, which opened in 1995, had not yet garnered the loyal local following it will need to survive. If it's still open when you read this, success has visited, and so should you.

MODERATE

Avalon Bar & Grill

Malostranské nám. 12, Prague 1. ☎ **02/53 02 76.** Reservations not necessary. Main courses 120–250 Kč ($4.44–$9.25). AE, MC, V. Daily 11am–1am. Metro: Malostranská. AMERICAN.

A California-themed restaurant, Avalon is a fun eatery, where good American food is served in ultracontemporary surroundings. The dining room, which feels something like Los Angeles, is both authentic and unique (for Prague)—not just someone's idea

🍴 Family-Friendly Restaurants

Restaurant Adria *(see p. 93)*   One of the largest menus in Prague makes it very likely your child will find something acceptable to eat.

Red Hot & Blues *(see p. 91)*   Nachos, toasted sandwiches, and an American-oriented staff make this restaurant a good choice for U.S. kids and their families.

Bella Napoli *(see p. 93)*   When your child (or you) tire of Czech fare, this Italian savior steps in with decent food that's fun to eat.

of California kitsch. Enormously popular when it opened in 1994, the dining room has settled down somewhat and matured into one of the city's most important standbys. When debating over where to eat, locals can always count on this restaurant's overstuffed sandwiches, grilled chicken, burgers, potato skins, and buffalo wings. The fun food complements a celebratory atmosphere that is particularly conducive to large parties. Avalon recently began serving American-style brunches on Saturdays and Sundays from 11am to 4pm.

✪ Vinárna U Maltézských Rytírů (Knights of Malta)
Prokopská 10, Prague 1. ☎ **02/53 63 57.** Reservations recommended. Main courses 150–300 Kč ($5.55–$11.11). AE, MC. Daily 11:30am–11pm. Metro: Malostranská. CZECH.

When the Wine Tavern of the Knights of Malta opened in 1993, it was widely acclaimed as one of the best restaurants in Prague. A lot has changed in the last few years, but Knights of Malta isn't one of them. In terms of food, service, and location, this restaurant continues to be one of the city's best. And although prices have risen slightly, Knights of Malta still remains one of the city's best buys. The restaurant occupies the ground floor and cellar of a charming house that once functioned as a Knights-operated hospice. There are just four cloth-covered tables in the cozy whitewashed ground-floor dining room and another 10 or so in the cavernous candle-lit cellar below. Nadia Černiková, the restaurant's eternally cheerful co-owner and hostess, keeps a watchful eye on the front of the house, personally greeting and seating the majority of the restaurant's patrons. Many are loyal regulars. *Prague Post* editor-in-chief Alan Levy can often be spotted here, as well as many well-heeled ex-pat locals.

A short menu usually indicates intelligent preparations and fresh food, and the somewhat meager list here is no exception. Asparagus-filled turkey breast, salmon steak with herb butter, lamb cutlet with spinach, chateaubriand, and steak with caper sauce and almonds are five of the six available main courses. The sixth is vegetable au gratin, Prague's all-purpose vegetarian dish. With remarkable consistency, meats arrive perfectly grilled—seared on the outside and pink within; a great accompaniment are excellent potato croquettes that should be ordered with every meal. Nadia's homemade apple strudel—a not too sweet, nutty, fruit-packed pie—is a special dessert that's worth sticking around for.

INEXPENSIVE

Jo's Bar
Malostranské náměstí 7, Prague 1. No phone. Reservations not accepted. Main courses 100–150 Kč ($3.70–$5.55). No credit cards. Daily 11am–1am. Metro: Malostranská. MEXICAN/AMERICAN.

One of the first North American-owned restaurants in post-Communist Eastern Europe, Jo's was once Prague's chief hangout for expatriates. The restaurant/bar is still packed with foreigners in their twenties, but the majority are now tourists who have heard about this legendary place. Jo's great attraction has never been the restaurant's mediocre tacos, guacamole, and salsa; rather the beer and camaraderie with other English speakers draw the crowds. A planned 1996 expansion into the basement should breathe new life into this institution.

6 Hradčany

EXPENSIVE

Peklo

Strahovské nádvoří 1, Prague 1. ☎ **02/2451 0032.** Reservations recommended. Main courses 300–400 Kč ($11.11–$14.80). AE, DC, MC, V. Daily 6pm–2am. Tram: 22. CONTINENTAL.

Located in the ancient wine cellars of Strahov Monastery, Peklo (which means "hell") is a stunningly beautiful subterranean restaurant serving good continental food to well-heeled tourists and ex-pat businesspeople. Although sauces can sometimes be mild to the point of being a whisper, most meals are generally as flavorful as the presentations are thoughtful. Recommendable starters include a creamy tomato soup with shrimp and plump Greenland mussels in curry sauce. Sturgeon and vegetables baked in puff pastry and perfectly broiled steak are typical entrees. The wine list is impressive. The restaurant's selective hiring policy ensures one of the city's best looking waitstaffs. Peklo is expensive, but the prices are justified if you are staying in the neighborhood and don't want to descend into Old Town or Mála Strana. However, those coming from down below might question whether it's worth the trip.

MODERATE

Nebozízek

Petřínské sady 411, Prague 1. ☎ **02/53 79 05.** Reservations recommended. Main courses 80–200 Kč ($2.96–$7.40). AE, MC, V. Daily 11am–6pm and 7–11pm. Tram: 12 or 22 to Újezd, then funicular up Petřín Hill. CZECH/CONTINENTAL.

Getting to Nebozízek is half the fun. No, make that three quarters. Located in the middle of Petřín Hill, the restaurant is accessible by funicular, a kind of cable car on a track (see "Getting Around" in Chapter 3). Unlike the food, which is mediocre at best, the view overlooking the entire city of Prague is truly unmatched. In fact, dining above the storybook rooftops is so enchanting that dinner reservations are sometimes required days in advance. In the summer, the most coveted seats are on a trellised patio. In the winter, it's the window seats, of which there are precious few.

House-prepared appetizers, like roast beef and lobster tail salad, should be passed over in favor of the more trustworthy caviar. Similarly, main dishes, which are heavy on steak and pork, should be chosen carefully, with an eye toward simple preparations like pepper steak and roast pork. The garlic soup is exceptional.

INEXPENSIVE

Ⓢ Saté Grill

Pohořelec 3, Prague 1. No phone. Main courses 50–100 Kč ($1.85–$3.70). No credit cards. Daily 12:30–10pm. Tram: 22. INDONESIAN.

Begun as a take-out shop, Saté Grill has proved so popular that it has become a restaurant. Pork saté with peanut sauce is the centerpiece of a short Indonesian menu that also features Migoreng, a spicy noodle dish that some pundits think tastes a bit too close to the ramen that got you through college. Prices are extremely low for a restaurant so close to the castle, and service is unusually quick.

7 Vinohrady

MODERATE

Ambiente

Mánesova 59, Prague 2. ☎ **02/627 59 22.** Reservations recommended. Main courses 150–200 Kč ($5.55–$7.40). No credit cards. Mon–Fri 11am–11:30pm, Sat–Sun 4pm–11:30pm. Metro: Jiřího z Poděbrad. AMERICAN.

One of the most notable newcomers of 1995, Ambiente is a California-Czech restaurant serving some of the city's firmest pasta and tastiest ribs. Chicken wings baked in a spicy sweet marinade come with two dipping sauces. Steaks are marinated in oil with black pepper and served with sweet, spiced butter and a huge amount of sweet corn and french fries. The restaurant is comfortably lit and modern, perfect for sociable lunches and casual dinners. Walls are adorned with Californian memorabilia, and service comes with an American smile. Since Ambiente is located well outside the main tourist area, its customers and prices are Czech. Save room because the best dish is the last—a chocolate fondue served with sliced bananas or pineapples.

Il Ritrovo

Lublaňská 11, Prague 2. ☎ **02/29 65 29.** Reservations recommended on weekends. Main courses 120–250 Kč ($4.44–$9.25). No credit cards. Tues–Sun noon–3pm and 6pm–11:30pm. Metro: I. P. Pavlova. ITALIAN.

Once they get around to serving you, diners can sit back and enjoy one of the finest Italian meals in town. Good antipasti give way to about two dozen pasta choices, including excellent farfelle with pesto, and penne with smoked salmon. Pepper steak is the best of about a dozen second courses. The dining room is a bit low on atmosphere, despite a recent remodeling. But the uninspiring surroundings don't seem to bother most patrons, the majority of whom are Italian. There's a good list of Italian wines, and chocolate tartuffo and tiramisu for dessert.

✪ Quido

Kubelíkova 22, Prague 3. ☎ **02/27 09 50.** Reservations recommended. Main courses 130–250 Kč ($4.81–$9.25). AE, MC, V. Mon–Sat 11:30am–11pm. Metro: Jiřího z Poděbrad. CZECH.

Quido is one of the best restaurants in Prague. The large menu, which includes a long list of starters and over 25 entrees, is a veritable survey of Bohemian cooking. One of the best traditional appetizers is pork tongue—home smoked, sliced thin, and pleasantly arranged. The garlic soup is full of meat and potatoes, and the sautéed chicken livers are simply out of this world. The most successful main courses come from the restaurant's gas-fired lava grill. These include a cheese-filled hunter's steak, and chicken breast with pineapple, both of which are served with white cabbage and carrots. If you're looking for a particularly Czech experience, order the roasted pig's knee, over two pounds of meat served on a big wooden board with the customary sweet mustard, horseradish, and rye bread. It's a local delicacy.

INEXPENSIVE

Na Zvonařce

Šafaříkova 1, Prague 2. ☎ **02/691 13 11.** Reservations not necessary. Main courses 50–120 Kč ($1.85–$4.44). V. Mon–Fri 11am–11pm, Sat–Sun noon–11pm. Metro: I. P. Pavlova. CZECH.

Once a pub for bellmakers, then a dingy Communist-era restaurant, Na Zvonařce has blossomed into one of the best all-around Czech restaurants in Prague. There's a book-size menu, relatively good service, equally good food, and a terrific open-air patio overlooking the Nusle valley. And this real find is reasonably priced. Meals are strictly tried-and-true Czech favorites: roasted duck with dumplings and cabbage, pork tongue with potatoes . . .you get the idea. When it's available, however, Na Zvonařce makes one of the best grilled whole trouts in town. Beef in cream sauce with wheat dumplings also gets high marks, along with great Plzeň Urquell beer.

✪ Radost F/X Café

Bělehradská 120, Prague 2. ☎ **02/25 12 10.** Reservations not accepted. Main courses 55–120 Kč ($2.04–$4.44). MC, V. Daily 11am–5am. Metro: I. P. Pavlova. VEGETARIAN.

One of the only completely vegetarian restaurants in Prague, Radost is recommendable for good soup, like garlicky spinach and oniony lentil, and hearty sandwiches, such as tofu with stir-fried vegetables. There are some disappointments, including an anchovyless Greek salad and lackluster pizzas. But for the most part, Radost gets a rave. The restaurant is funky and stylish, looking more like a cafe than a serious dining establishment. Because it's located above a popular American-style dance club of the same name, Radost's clientele is almost exclusively young and non-Czech, and the dining room is usually a happening place to be.

Radost is also one of the few restaurants in the city that's open all night. Their fine Bloody Marys complement 4am breakfasts. On weekends, the restaurant serves the best downscale brunch in town.

8 Elsewhere in Prague

MODERATE

Dolly Bell

Neklanova 20, Prague 2. ☎ **02/29 88 15.** Reservations recommended. Main courses 100–250 Kč ($3.70–$9.25). AE, DC, MC, V. Daily 2pm–midnight. Metro: Vyšehrad. YUGOSLAV.

This unofficial Serbian embassy is the best Yugoslav restaurant in town, serving traditional meats and soups that look like Czech dishes, but are far more zesty. Like so many other restaurants in this city, food here is uneven. On a lucky day, you'll be delighted with a Balkan moussaka consisting of layers of potatoes and ground beef and topped with bechamel sauce. Flaky cheese and meat pies usually make excellent appetizers, while skewered meats and bean-based stews can usually be counted on when it comes to entrees. The single dining room feels elegant and is far from stifling. The main design statements are cluttered upside-down tables fixed to the ceiling above diners' heads. Most diners are usually well dressed and, in accordance with Yugoslav tradition, the restaurant doesn't usually fill up until about 10pm.

Le Bistro de Marlene

Plavecká 4, Prague 2. ☎ **02/29 10 77.** Reservations recommended. Main courses 150–350 Kč ($5.55–$13). No credit cards. Mon–Fri noon–2:30pm and 7:30–10pm, Sat 7:30–10pm. Metro: Vyšehrad. FRENCH.

It doesn't matter that Le Bistro de Marlene is hidden on a small residential street near Vyšehrad Castle. The restaurant is packed anyway, with locals and visitors in search of the finest French cuisine in town. The bistro atmosphere is made upbeat with mirrored walls, good music, plenty of plants, and a very friendly, very French staff. Chef Marlene Salomon has kept the menu short and simple, focusing on high-quality meats and produce. Many appetizers are recommendable, including flan aux champignons, a wonderful mushroom loaf served on a parsley sauce; terrine de lapin, a subtle rabbit terrine; and a salad with bacon, walnuts, and croutons, dressed in a pungent vinaigrette. Of entrées, roast leg of lamb is herb-infused and arrives perfectly pink.

A petit steak is topped with a sweet curry sauce, and a fresh fish dish is usually available nightly. Most everything comes with a side of vegetables, simply steamed, or baked in a gratin with layers of cheese.

9   Inexpensive Meals on the Run

It's well worth finding Ⓢ **U Bakaláře,** a small sandwich bar at Celetná 12, hidden inside a reconstructed building on the main street connecting Old Town Square and náměstí Republiky. Popular with Charles University students, the restaurant (☎ **02/2481 1870,** ext. 257) serves little toasties—inexpensive ready-to-eat open-face sandwiches (*chelbíčky*)—with toppingês that include sardines, cheese, salami spread, and tuna. Their spinach *palačinky* (crêpes) are particular good, as are the miniature fried vegetable patties. Order at the counter and take your meal to one of a half-dozen contemporary tables. Toasties cost 10 to 15 Kč (37¢–55¢); crepes 25 Kč (93¢). Open Monday to Friday from 9:30am to 7pm, Saturday and Sunday 12:30 to 7pm.

There are only a few counter seats at **Queenz Grill Bar,** a fast-food falafel restaurant, located in the middle of Havelská market at Havelská 12. In addition to yummy falafel, the Queenz sells decent gyros and salads. Food here is cheap and good, a much better bet than those horrible pizza-by-the-slice places that seem to be popping up everywhere. Lunches are best, as the restaurant routinely sells out early. Sandwiches are 40 to 70 Kč ($1.48–$2.59). Open daily 10am to 8:30pm.

In New Town, **Cornucopia,** Jungmannova 10 (☎ **02/2422 0950**) is a small American-style deli with great soups and decent sandwiches. It's particularly popular with American ex-pats during the midday lunch crunch. Ham, salami, vegetables, and a variety of meat and fish salads are the fillings for most sandwiches. Soups are exceptionally flavorful and meaty, and along with a roll make a light meal. Many locals come here just for the cheesecake, chocolate chip cookies, and other desserts. Breakfast options include eggs, bacon, pancakes, home fries, and french toast. Order at the counter, then take your meal to one of a half-dozen booths. Sandwiches are 50 to 70 Kč ($1.85–$2.59). Open Monday to Friday 10am to 10pm, Saturday and Sunday 11am to 10pm.

Don't miss the Czech delicatessen **Obchod Čerstvých Uzenin,** Václavské náměstí 36, on the ground floor of the Melantrich Building, from which Václav Havel addressed the throngs below during the 1989 Velvet Revolution. Vegetarians hurry past the meaty aromas wafting over the short line of patrons that often forms out the door. The front of the shop is a take-out deli offering dozens of kinds of cooked and smoked meat, sausage, and salami. In back a small restaurant serves goulash, cooked meats, and beer without side dishes—just a dollop of mustard and a slice of dense bread. You have to eat standing up, but the selection is extensive, you can't get it any fresher, and prices are pure Czech. There are no tourists here; expect to pay about 65 Kč ($2.41) for a plate of meat and a beer. Open Monday to Friday from 7:30am to 7pm, Saturday 8am to 6pm, Sunday 10am to 4:30pm.

Vegetarians will want to stop by **Country Life,** Melantrichova 15, a health food store-cum-take-out-restaurant run by the Seventh-Day Adventists that offers a strictly meatless menu served to go. Light snacks like bread with tofu spread, tomato, cucumber, and shredded cabbage are augmented by heavier offerings like vegetable salads, a zesty wheat bread pizza topped with red pepper, garlic, and onions, and vegetable burgers served on a multigrain buns with garlic-yogurt dressing. You can also pick up fresh bread or dried beans. The restaurant is located on the main street connecting Wenceslas Square with Old Town Square. Main courses are 30 to 70 Kč ($1.11–$2.59). Open Monday to Thursday from 9am to 6:30pm, Friday 9am to 3pm.

And if you're craving a burger, try **Harvey's,** Václavské nám. 18 (☎ **02/2423 7015**). As the sole Czech outpost of Canada's most popular hamburger chain, Harvey's not only sells burgers to rival McDonald's (located across the street), but serves healthful grilled chicken breast sandwiches and uses fresh vegetables that are unheard of at the U.S.-based chain. Burgers are 27 to 65 Kč ($1–$2.41). Open daily 7am to midnight.

At **Krone,** Václavské nám. 21, located on the ground floor of one of the city's largest department stores, this buffet-style eatery serves up all the most famous Czech specialties including roast duck, rotisserie chicken, goulash, dumplings, and croquettes. Take your meal to one of a half-dozen tables, or do like some locals and eat while standing at an appropriately tall table. Food here is surprisingly excellent. There's a terrific variety and, since it's all displayed under glass, you can see what's cooking before you order it. Main courses are 50 to 80 Kč ($1.85–$2.96). Open Monday to Saturday from 9am to 8pm, Sunday 10am to 7pm.

10   Cafes & Tearooms

Prague's reputation as a "Left Bank of the nineties" leads many to believe that there is a thriving cafe culture in the capital. Truth is, the city's coffeehouses and tearooms are only now catching up to the cliche. If you ask for "normal" coffee in a restaurant or cafe, you will receive a smallish cup of strong, muddy brew—the coffee grounds have been stirred directly into the boiling water and allowed to settle to the bottom of the cup. American-style filter-brewed coffee is virtually unknown, as is decaffeinated coffee. Most of the cafes listed below have espresso machines—and some employees actually know how to operate one.

NOVÉ MĚSTO (NEW TOWN)

Cafe Evropa
Václavské náměstí 25, Prague 1. ☎ **02/2422 8117.** Cappuccino 30 Kč ($1.11); pastries 30–100 Kč ($1.11–$3.70). AE, MC, V. Daily 7am–midnight. Metro: Můstek.

Spin through the etched-glass revolving door into the otherworldliness of Prague's finest art nouveau cafe. Built in 1906, the cafe is bedecked with period chandeliers and hand-carved woods, all made even more elegant by musicians, who entertain every afternoon. Drinks are relatively expensive and service is terrible. But compared to western European standards it's cheap, and few diners are in a mood to hurry. There's a 30 Kč ($1.11) cover charge after 3pm.

Dobrá Čajovna
Václavské náměstí 14, Prague 1. No phone. Small pot of tea 30 Kč ($1.11). No credit cards. Mon–Sat 10am–9pm, Sun 3–9pm. Metro: Můstek.

Inside the cafe's intimate, pillow-covered cavern, it's difficult to discern whether you're in Prague or Pakistan. Hidden at the end of a narrow passage, across Václavské náměstí from the Ambassador Hotel, Dobrá Čajovna is truly one of the city's greatest hidden finds. It's not for everyone, mind you. Most patrons sit on the floor, and the teahouse has a decidedly New Age bent. The front counter doubles as a health-and-spiritual gift shop.

STARÉ MĚSTO (OLD TOWN) & JOSEFOV

Café Milena
Staroměstské nám. 22, Prague 1. ☎ **02/26 08 43.** Light snacks and desserts 60–150 Kč ($2.22–$5.55). No credit cards. Daily 10am–10pm. Metro: Staroměstská.

Located on the second floor of a beautiful building directly across from Old Town Square's astronomical clock, this Viennese-style cafe operated by the Franz Kafka Society is named for Milena Jesenská, one of the famous writer's lovers. Decent light snacks and ice cream are served in comfortable surroundings. The luckiest patrons snare window seats, from which the clock's twelve apostles appear at almost eye level.

Dolce Vita

Široká 15, Prague 1. ☎ **02/232 9192.** Cappuccino 30 Kč ($1.20); pastries 30–100 Kč ($1.11–$3.70). No credit cards. Daily 10am–11pm. Metro: Staroměstská.

A half-block off Pařížská, in Prague's Jewish Quarter, is the city's finest Italian cafe. An excellent espresso machine operated by knowledgeable staff is the cafe's primary draw. But comfortable seating and light pastries and ice creams are the icings on this cake. The Dolce Vita is popular with Prague's modeling and well-to-do see-and-be-seen sets.

Rudolfinum Kavárna

Alšovo nábř. 12, Prague 1. ☎ **02/2489 3317.** Light snacks and desserts 30–90 Kč ($1.11–$3.33). No credit cards. Tues–Sun 10am–6pm. Metro: Staroměstská.

Located inside the Rudolfinum, which also contains one of Prague's most important concert halls, this beautiful cafe is one of the most elegant in town. High ceilings and ornate architecture contrast with relatively low-priced drinks and snacks. This hidden gem is definitely worth finding.

Velryba

Opatovická 24, Prague 1. ☎ **02/2491 2391.** Light meals 50–100 Kč ($1.85–$3.70). No credit cards. Daily 11am–2am. Metro: Národní třída.

Velryba was opened in July 1992 as a Czech literary cafe and quickly caught on with the city's intellectuals and theater types. Sort of down and dirty, the pub has become one of Prague's trendiest cafes. The "coolest" people sit in the back room. In addition to cafe drinks, Velryba serves well-priced pasta and light snacks.

ELSEWHERE IN PRAGUE

The Globe

Janovského 14, Prague 7. ☎ **6671 2610.** Sandwiches and desserts 60–100 Kč ($2.22–$3.70). No credit cards. Daily 10am–midnight. Metro: Vltavská.

Prague's only bookstore/coffeehouse is not only the best place in the city for used paperback literature and nonfiction, it's one of the best places for young American ex-pats to meet. The smart-looking barroom serves espresso-based drinks, sandwiches, salads, and desserts, and stocks a full bar.

What to See & Do in Prague

by John Mastrini

Prague's unique setting distinguishes it from most other major European cities. Where else will you find so many bastions, towers, domes, and spires in a relatively small, hilly area? In Prague, intricate buildings sit next to each other on finely-aged narrow streets. Grand palaces nestled on hills hover and reflect in the river below. The city's most enchanting sections remain relatively free of the blinding electric Technicolor world, although not always of scaffolding, thanks to incessant reconstruction.

Some folks have described Prague as "Baroque Disneyland," except the buildings are real, there's no all-day admission charge, and you will probably not find happy hostesses on Charles Bridge with well-trained smiles constantly welcoming you—at least not yet. No, the pleasures are sublime in this mystical city.

SUGGESTED ITINERARIES

The concept of an itinerary should be a loose one. Prague's most intriguing aspects are its architecture and atmosphere, best enjoyed slowly wandering through the city's heart. If you have the time and the energy, go to Charles Bridge at sunrise and then at sunset to view the grand architecture of Prague Castle and the Old Town skyline. You will see two completely different cities.

If You Have 1 Day

In order to digest enough of Prague's wonders, do what visiting kings and potentates do on a one-day visit: walk the Royal Route—but in reverse—downhill. From the top of the Hradčany Hill (tram 22 or a taxi is suggested for the ride up unless you're very fit), tour Prague Castle in the morning. The three key sights within the Castle grounds are the towering St. Vitus Cathedral, the Royal Palace, and St. George's Basilica, now an art gallery. Do not miss the tiny houses on the Golden Lane, also within the castle walls. Then begin your slow descent through the odd hill-bound architecture of Lesser Town (Malá Strana) for lunch. After lunch, stroll across Charles Bridge, on the way to the winding alleys of Old Town (Staré Město). You can happily get lost finding Old Town Square (Staroměstské náměstí), stopping at private galleries and cafes along the way. In the Old

Impressions

"Prague is a priceless asset which surely deserves to be spared from the worst excesses of modern development which have so ravaged the other cities of Europe. The challenge must be to find ways of ensuring . . . that it becomes once again the thriving prosperous heart of Europe, not merely a crumbling museum exhibit."

—Britain's Prince Charles to Prague's Leaders, May 7, 1991

Town Square, you can see a performance of the astronomical clock at the top of each hour, climb to the top of the Old Town Hall tower for a panoramic view of Prague, visit the Týn or St. Nicholas churches, explore the nearby Jewish Quarter, or continue on to the end of the Royal Route at the Powder Gate, which marks the edge of the Old Town walls. From Old Town it is a short walk to Wenceslas Square (Václavské náměstí), site of the mass demonstrations that led to the Velvet Revolution.

Along the route from Old Town you'll pass Mozart's Prague venue, the Estates' Theater, an exceptional place for putting yourself in a photograph from the past. Dinner and your evening entertainment are all probably within a 10-minute walk from anywhere in this area.

If You Have 2 Days

Day 1 Spend Day 1 as above.

Day 2 Explore the varied sights of Old Town, Lesser Town, and the Jewish Quarter (Josefov)—what you didn't have time for the day before. Just wander and browse. Throughout Old Town you'll find numerous shops and galleries offering the finest Bohemian crystal, porcelain, and modern artwork, as well as top fashion boutiques, cafes, and restaurants. While the shops aren't that much different than those in other European cities, the setting is. Nearby in Josefov you can visit the astonishing Old Jewish Cemetery, and the Ceremonial Hall, which displays heart-wrenching sketches drawn by the children held at the Terezín concentration camp.

From Old Town, it is just a short walk across Charles Bridge to Lesser Town. This once was the neighborhood for those who served the castle, with narrow houses squeezed between palaces and embassies. Visit the Waldstein Gardens, or get a low-angle view of the city and Charles Bridge from Kampa Park. The so-called Lennon Wall, a symbol of youthful defiance of the Communists depicting the late member of the Beatles, is near Kampa.

The dome of the Church of St. Nicholas (same saint, different church), with its gilded baroque interior, dominates the view from Lesser Town Square (Malostranské náměstí). As you head up Nerudova, the road leading to the castle, you will find dozens of small shops and galleries tucked into every narrow nook.

If You Have 3 Days

Days 1–2 Spend days 1 and 2 as above, except go lighter on touring Prague Castle to begin the first day (your ticket for Prague Castle is good for three days).

Day 3 After seeing what you held over from the first day at the Castle, spend the rest of the day on Hradčany Hill. Here you can visit the National Art Gallery at Šternberk Palace, the Military History Museum, the Strahov Monestary with its ornate libraries, and the Loreto Palace with its peculiar artwork. Or stroll over to Petřín Hill where kids will enjoy the view tower, observatory, and mirrored labyrinth. Try to work in a cruise on the Vltava or pilot your own rowboat ride in the evening.

What's Special About Prague

Architecture

- Charles Bridge, Prague's six-centuries-old, statue-lined, tower-guarded stone bridge, symbol of Czech heritage.
- Old Town Square, one of Europe's most attractive meeting places, combining Gothic, Renaissance, baroque, and rococo architecture.

Buildings

- Old Town Hall, dating from the 11th century, with its 14th-century tower, housing a massive astronomical clock.
- Powder Tower, the only tower remaining from Prague's medieval fortifications.
- The Estates' Theater, the 18th-century home of Mozart's opera *Don Giovanni*, recently restored to its neoclassical elegance and spectacular inside and out.

Places of Worship

- St. Vitus Cathedral, a massive 14th-century Gothic structure towering above the walls of Prague Castle, containing the tombs of St. Vitus and St. Wenceslas.
- Týn Church, with its dark twin 260-foot spires dominating the skyline above Old Town Square.
- Old New Synagogue, Europe's oldest remaining Jewish house of worship, and the heart of Prague's Jewish Quarter.

Castles

- Prague Castle, which started as a fortress in the 10th century and became one of the great European seats of power during Prague's golden age in the 14th century, dominating the west side of the Vltava River.
- Royal Palace, within the walls of Prague Castle, home of Bohemian kings and princes from the 9th to the 16th centuries.

Museums

- Šternberk Palace Art Museum, the most comprehensive of the Czech National Gallery members, with collections ranging from ancient Bohemian to Italian Renaissance to modern.
- National Museum, displaying the nation's archeological and historical past in a neo-Renaissance building at the top of Wenceslas Square.
- St. Agnes Convent, housing within its Gothic halls a gallery of 19th-century Czech art.

Parks and Gardens

- Vyšehrad, an ancient citadel from the last millennium, once the seat of Bohemian kings, now housing the National Cemetery, surrounded by well-groomed parks and spectacular city views.
- Letná Park, a tree-lined plain filled with walking trails and views back toward Old Town.
- Waldstein Palace Gardens, with delicate statue-lined paths surrounding Prague's first baroque palace.

If You Have 5 Days Or More

Days 1–3   Spend days 1 to 3 as above.
Beyond Day 3   Try touring one of the many other museums or galleries, or venture out of the city center. Visit the old southern citadel over the Vltava, Vyšehrad,

where you get a completely different view of the city you've explored the past three days. Here you can picnic and stroll among the paths winding throughout the large complex of churches, gardens, and cemeteries.

Beyond Prague's borders are easy day trips, such as an excursion to Karlštejn Castle, the most visited attraction outside of Prague. See Chapter 10 for details. For those with more time to discover Bohemia and even Moravia, visits to the historic towns of Karlovy Vary, Český Krumlov, Telč, České Budějovice, or the country's second city Brno, among others, reveal dozens of treasures laying outside golden Prague. See Chapters 11 and 12 for details on where to go.

1 Exploring Prague Castle (Pražský Hrad)

The huge hilltop complex that's known collectively as ✪ **Prague Castle** (Pražský Hrad), on Hradčanské náměstí, encompasses dozens of houses, towers, churches, courtyards, and monuments. (It is described in detail in Walking Tour 2 in Chapter 7, and there's a map on page 143.) A visit to the castle could easily take an entire day or more, depending on how thoroughly you explore it. Still, the top sights—St.Vitus Cathedral, the Royal Palace, and St. George's Basilica, plus the Golden Lane—can be seen in the space of a morning or afternoon.

You can also explore the castle complex at night, as it is generally lit until midnight. Some evenings, like New Year's Eve, it is lit later. The complex is always guarded and is said to be safe to wander at night, but keep to the lit areas of the courtyards just to be safe.

If you're feeling particularly fit, you can walk up to the castle, or you can take metro Line A to Malostranská or Hradčanská or Tram 22.

TICKETS & CASTLE INFORMATION   While you can wander the castle grounds for free, you need to buy an entrance ticket for St. Vitus Cathedral, the Royal Palace, and St. George's Basilica; tickets are valid for three days. Entrance to the three main attractions is 80 Kč ($2.96) for adults, 40 Kč ($1.48) for students without a tour guide; 120 Kč ($4.44) for adults, 80 Kč ($2.96) for students with an English-speaking guide. Open Tuesday to Sunday from 9am to 5pm (only until 4pm from November to March).

Tickets are sold at the **Prague Castle Information Center** (☎ 02/3337 3368), located in the second courtyard after passing through the main gate from Hradčanské náměstí. The information center also arranges tours in various languages and sells tickets for individual concerts and exhibitions held on the castle grounds.

You'll find a good selection of guidebooks, maps, and other related information in the entrance to the Royal Palace.

✪ ST. VITUS CATHEDRAL

St. Vitus Cathedral, named for a wealthy fourth-century Sicilian martyr, is not just the dominant part of the castle, it's also historically its most important section. Originally constructed in A.D. 926 as the court church of the Přemyslid princes, the church has long been the center of Prague's religious and political life. The key part of its Gothic construction took place in the 14th century under the direction of Mathias of Arras and Peter Parler of Gmuend. In the 18th and 19th centuries, subsequent baroque and neo-Gothic additions were made.

The **Golden Portal entrance** from the third courtyard is no longer used to enter the cathedral. However, take a look above the arch. The 1370 mosaic of *The Last Judgment* has been painstakingly restored with the help of computer-aided imagery provided by U.S. art researchers.

"I Don't Do Windows": The Czech Tradition of Defenestration

About 600 years before Prague's popular uprising brought down Communism, the Czech people began a long tradition of what might be considered a unique form of political protest.

In 1402, Jan Hus, a lecturer from Prague University, became the lead voice in a growing condemnation of the Catholic church. From a pulpit in Old Town's Bethlehem Chapel, Hus gained popular support for his claims that the omnipotent power of the mostly German dominated clergy had to be bridled. In 1414, he was invited to the Catholic ecclesiastical Council of Konstanz to explain his beliefs. Although the emperor had promised Hus safe conduct, when Hus arrived he was promptly arrested, and a year later he was burned at the stake. The Protestant Hussite supporters declared him a martyr and rallied their calls for change around his death.

On July 30, 1419, a group of radical Hussites stormed the New Town Hall on Charles Square and demanded the release of other arrested pro-reform Hussites. After town councilors rejected the demand, the Hussites tossed them out of third-story windows, killing several. This became known as the First "Defenestration," from the Latin for "out of the window." The incident sparked a 15-year battle known as the Hussite Wars, which ended in the defeat of the radical Protestants in 1434.

By the 17th century, the Austrian Catholics who came to power in Prague tolerated little dissent, but the Protestant Czechs continued to become more wealthy and began criticizing the Habsburg monarchy. This bubbled over again on May 23, 1618, when a group of Protestant nobles entered Prague Castle, seized two pro-Habsburg Czechs and their secretary, and tossed them out of the eastern window of the rear room of the Chancellery—the Second Defenestration. In the Garden on the Ramparts below the Ludwig Wing, two obelisks mark where they landed. This act led, in part, to the conflict known as the Thirty Years War, which ended again in victory in 1648 for the Catholics. The absolutist Habsburgs would remain in power for another 270 years, until the democratic Czechoslovak state was born.

Although Prague's 1989 overthrow of the totalitarian Communist regime gained the name "The Velvet Revolution" for its nonviolent nature, scattered calls for another defenestration (some serious, some as jokes) could be heard on the streets. Contemporary Czech politicians surely know to keep away from open windows.

As you enter the cathedral through the back entrance into the main aisle, you'll be dazzled by colored light seeping through the intricate stained-glass windows that tower to the Gothic ceiling above the high altar. The center windows, restored in the two years after World War II, depict the Holy Trinity with the Virgin Mary to the left, and St. Wenceslas kneeling to the right.

Of the massive Gothic cathedral's 21 chapels, the ✪ **Chapel of St. Wenceslas** stands out as one of the few indoor sights in Prague that every visitor really must see. Located midway toward the high altar on the right side, the chapel is encrusted with hundreds of pieces of jasper and amethyst, and decorated with paintings from the 14th to 16th centuries. It sits on top of the grave site of the patron saint of Bohemia, St. Wenceslas.

Just beyond this, the **Chapel of the Holy Rood** leads to the entrance to the underground **royal crypt.** Early this century, the crypt was reconstructed, and the remains of the kings and their relatives were replaced in new sarcophagi. The center sarcophagus is the final resting place of Charles IV, the favorite Bohemian king who died in 1378 and is the namesake of much of Prague. In the back row are Charles' four wives (all in one sarcophagus), and in front of them, is George of Poděbrady, the last Bohemian King who died in 1471.

CONTINUING THROUGH THE CASTLE COMPLEX

For more than 700 years, beginning in the 9th century, Bohemian kings and princes resided in **the Royal Palace,** located in the third courtyard of the castle grounds. Vaulted Vladislav Hall, the interior's centerpiece, was used for coronations and special occasions. Here Václav Havel was inaugurated president. The adjacent Diet was where the king met with his advisers and where the supreme court was held. And from a window in the Ludwig Wing, where the Bohemia Chancellery met, the second Defenestration took place; see the "I Don't Do Windows" box.

St. George's Basilica, adjacent to the Royal Palace, is the oldest Romanesque structure in Prague, dating from the 10th century. It was also the first convent in Bohemia. No longer serving a religious function, the building now houses a Czech art museum (see "Museums & Galleries" below). If you look carefully at the basilica's towers, you'll notice that they are slightly different from each other. The towers supposedly have an Adam-Eve motif: the wider south tower represents Adam, while the similar but more narrow north tower represents Eve, who is supposed to be in Adam's shadow.

Golden Lane (Zlatá ulička) is a picturesque street of tiny 16th-century houses built into the castle fortifications. Once home to castle sharpshooters, the houses now contain small shops, galleries, and refreshment bars. In 1917, Franz Kafka is said to have lived briefly at no. 22; however, the debate continues as to whether Kafka actually took up residence or just worked in a small office there.

Prague Castle Picture Gallery displays European and Bohemian masterpieces, but few are from the original Imperial collection, which was virtually destroyed during the Thirty Years' War. Of the works that have survived from the days of Emperors Rudolf II and Ferdinand III, the most celebrated is Hans von Aachen's *Portrait of a Girl* (1605–10), depicting the artist's daughter.

Like seemingly everything else in Prague, the castle is currently undergoing major changes. In order to make the building more accessible to the public, plans are underway to remodel and rebuild. These enhancements would be paid for by revenues from restaurants, coffeehouses, and even a hotel proposed for the castle site.

2 Other Top Sights

HRADČANY

✪ Strahov Monastery and Library (Strahovský klášter)

Strahovské nádvoří. ☎ **02/2451 1137.** Admission 30 Kč ($1.11) adults, 15 Kč (55¢) students. Tues–Sun 9am–noon and 1–5pm. Tram: 22 from Malostranská metro station.

The second oldest monastery in Prague, Strahov was founded high above Malá Strana in 1143 by Vladislav II. It is still home to Premonstratensian monks, a scholarly order closely related to the Jesuits. The monks' dormitories and refectory are off-limits to tourists. What draws visitors here are the monastery's ornate libraries, which hold over 125,000 volumes. Over the centuries, the monks have assembled one of the world's best collections of philosophical and theological texts, including many illuminated manuscripts and first editions.

The Philosophical Library's 46-foot-high ceiling is decorated with a 1794 fresco entitled *The Struggle of Mankind to Know Real Wisdom,* by A.F. Maulpertsch, a

Viennese master of rococo. Intricate woodwork frames the immense collection of books. Ancient wooden printing presses, downstairs in the Museum of Czech Literature, are also worth visiting.

The monastery also contains several altars and the remains of St. Norbert, a 10th-century German-born saint who founded the Premonstratensian order. His bones were brought here in 1627, when he became one of Bohemia's 10 patron saints. Paths leading through the monastery grounds take you to a breathtaking overlook of the city.

Loreto Palace (Loreta)

Loretánské náměstí 7. ☎ **02/2451 0789.** Admission 30 Kč ($1.11) adults, 20 Kč (74¢) students. Tues–Sun 9am–noon and 1–4:30pm. Tram: 22 from Malostranská.

Loreto Palace was named after the town of Loreto, Italy, where the dwelling of the Virgin Mary was said to have been brought by angels from Palestine in the 13th century. After the Roman Catholics defeated the Protestant Bohemians in 1620, the Loreto cult was chosen as the device for the re-Catholicization of Bohemia. The Loreto legend holds that a cottage in which the Virgin Mary lived had been miraculously transferred from Nazareth to Loreto, an Italian city near Ancona. The Loreto Palace is thought to be an imitation of this cottage, and more than 50 copies have been constructed throughout the Czech lands.

The Loreto's facade is decorated with 18th-century statues of the four writers of the Gospel—Matthew, Mark, Luke, and John—along with a lone female, St. Anne, the mother of the Virgin Mary. Inside the Church of the Nativity here are fully clothed remains of two Spanish saints, St. Felicissimus and St. Marcia. The wax masks on the skeletons' faces are particularly macabre.

Inside the Chapel of Our Lady of Sorrows is a painting of a bearded woman hanging on a cross. This is St. Starosta, or Vilgefortis, who, after taking a vow of virginity was forced to marry the king of Sicily. It is said that God, taking pity on the woman, gave her facial hair to make her undesirable, after which her pagan father had her crucified. Thus, Starosta went into history as the saint of unhappily married women. The painting was created in the 1700s. Also on display here is a portrait of St. Apolena (or Appollonia), a third-century deacon who had her teeth knocked out as part of a torture for refusing to renounce Christianity. She is often represented in art by a gold tooth or pincer. As the patron saint of dentists, Apolena is sometimes referred to as the "saint of toothaches."

MALÁ STRANA (LESSER TOWN)

✪ Church of St. Nicholas (Kostel Sv. Mikuláše)

Malostranské náměstí 1. Free admission. Metro: Line A to Malostranská.

This church, at Malostranské náměstí 1, is critically regarded as one of the best examples of high baroque north of the Alps. However, K.I. Dienzenhofer's original 1711 design did not have the massive dome that now dominates the Lesser Town skyline below Prague Castle. Dienzenhofer's son, Kryštof, added the 260-foot-high dome during additional work completed in 1752.

While Prague's smog has played havoc with the building's exterior, its gilded interior is stunning. Gold-capped marble-veneered columns frame altars packed with statuary and frescoes added through the centuries. A giant statue of the church's namesake looks down from the high altar, as midday sun strains through the domes lighting it and the frescoes with a mystical sheen.

Prague Attractions

Bertramka ⑮
Charles Bridge (Karlův most) ㉑
Charles Square (Karlovo náměstí) ㊵
Church of Our Lady Victorious ⑩
Church of St. Nicholas
  Mala Strana (Lesser Town) ⑨
  Old Town Square ㉔
Dancing Building ㊵
Dvořák Museum ㊸
The Estates' Theater ㉘
Havel's Market ㉗
House at the Black Mother of God ㉖
Jan Palach Square
  (náměstí Jana Palacha) ⑳
Kampa ⑬
Kinský Palace ㉕
The Labyrinth ⑭
Lennon Wall ⑫
Letná Park ⑯
Loreto Palace ⑥
Municipal House ㉚
Můstek Metro Station ㉞
Národní Memorial ㉳
National Military History Museum ⑦
National Museum ㊸
National Technical Museum ⑰
National Theater ㊴
New Jewish Cemetery ㊺
Old Jewish Cemetery ⑲
Old New Synagogue ⑲
Old Town Hall & Astronomical Clock ㉓
Old Town Square
  (Staroměstské náměstí) ㉖
Olšanské Cemetery ㊺
Petřín Tower and Petřín Hill ⑭
Powder Tower ㉝
Prague Castle ④
Prefabricated Apartment Buildings
  (Paneláky) ㊼
Royal Garden ①
St. Agnes Convent ⑱
St. Georges Convent at Prague Castle ②
St. Vitus Cathedral ③
Smetana Museum ㉒
State Jewish Museum ⑲
Štefánik Observatory ⑭
Šternberk Palace Art Museum ⑤
Strahov Monastery and Library ⑪
Týn Church ㉖
Vyšehrad ㊻
Waldstein Gardens ⑧
Wenceslas Square (Václavské náměstí) ㊲

Information
Castle Information Office ④
Čedok Office ㉟

Transportation/Mail
Florenc Bus Station ㉜
Main Post Office ㊱
Main Train Station ㊷
Masaryk Station ㉛

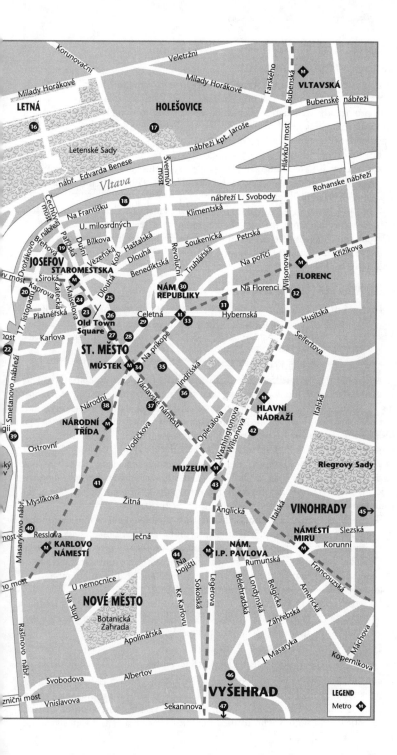

LETNÁ

Korunovační

Milady Horákové

Veletržní

Milady Horákové

Farského

Bubenská

VLTAVSKÁ

Bubenské nábřeží

16

Letenské Sady

HOLEŠOVICE

17

nábřeží kpt. Jaroše

Hlávkův most

nábř. Edvarda Beneše

Švermův most

Vltava

Rohanske nábřeží

nábřeží L. Svobody

18

Klimentská

Na Františku

U. milosrdných

Soukenická

Petrská

Křižíkova

Dušní

Bílkova

Haštalská

Na poříčí

Wilsonova

Pařížská

Vězeňská

Kozí

Dlouhá

Revoluční

Truhlářská

FLORENC

JOSEFOV

Benediktská

Na Florenci

19

STAROMESTSKA

Siroká

Žatecká

Maiselova

NÁM. 30
REPUBLIKY

32

Dvořákovo nábřeží

20

Kaprova

24

Dlouhá

Na Florenci

Husitská

17. listopadu

Platnéřská

23

25

Celetná

31

Hybernská

Seifertova

ost

22

Karlova

26

Old Town
Square

29

33

Na příkopě

Smetanovo nábřeží

27

28

ST. MĚSTO

MÚSTEK **34**

35

Jindřišská

HLAVNÍ
NÁDRAŽÍ

Italská

gii

Národní

38

37

Václavské náměstí

36

39

NÁRODNÍ
TŘÍDA

Vodičkova

Opletalova

Washingtonova

Wilsonova

42

ký

Ostrovní

v

MUZEUM

Riegrovy Sady

41

Myslíkova

Žitná

43

Masarykovo nábř.

Anglická

Italská

VINOHRADY

45

40

Resslova

Ječná

NÁM.

NÁMĚSTÍ
MIRU

Slezská

nost

KARLOVO
NÁMĚSTÍ

44

I.P. PAVLOVA

Korunní

Na
bojišti

Rumunská

Francouzská

U nemocnice

Legerova

Sokolská

Bělehradská

Londýnská

Belgická

Americká

no most

NOVÉ MĚSTO

Na Slupi

Ke Karlovu

Záhřebská

Máchova

Botanická
Zahrada

Apolinářská

I. Masaryka

Kopernikova

Rašínovo nábř.

Svobodova

Albertov

46

Vnislavova

VYŠEHRAD

zniční most

Sekaninova

47

LEGEND

Metro

CROSSING THE VLTAVA

✪ Charles Bridge (Karlův most)

Dating from the 14th century, Prague's most celebrated structure links Prague Castle to Staré Město. For most of its 600 years, the 1700-foot-long span has been a pedestrian promenade, although for centuries, walkers had to share the concourse with horse-drawn vehicles and trolleys. Today, the bridge is filled with folks walking among folksy artists and busking musicians.

The best times to stroll across the bridge are in early morning or around sunset, when the crowds have thinned and the shadows are more mysterious. But you'll be crisscrossing the bridge throughout the stay. The 30 statues lining the bridge are explained in detail in "Walking Tour 1" in Chapter 7.

Why has Charles Bridge stood for so long? One great yarn that has lived through the ages states that when the lovingly cut stones were being laid, the master builders would mix eggs into the mortar to strengthen the bond. One enterprising village, trying to impress the king, well, missed the point, sending carts full of hard boiled eggs to the capital.

STARÉ MĚSTO (OLD TOWN)

Old Town Hall (Staroměstská radnice) and Astronomical Clock (orloj)

Staroměstské náměstí. ☎ 02/2422 8456. Admission Town Hall tower 20 Kč (74¢) adults, 10 Kč (37¢) students and children. May–Oct, Tues–Sun 9am–6pm, Mon 11am–6pm; Nov–Apr, Tues–Sun 9am–5pm, Mon 11am–5pm. Metro: Line A to Staroměstská.

Crowds congregate hourly in front of Old Town Hall's Astronomical Clock (*orloj*) to watch the glockenspiel spectacle that occurs daily from 8am to 8pm. Originally constructed in 1410, the clock has long been an important symbol of Prague. According to legend, after the timepiece was remodeled at the end of the 15th century, clock artist Master Hanuš was blinded by the Municipal Council so he could not repeat his fine work elsewhere. In retribution, Hanuš threw himself into the clock mechanism and promptly died. The clock was out of kilter for almost a century.

It's not possible to determine the time of day from this timepiece; you have to look at the clock on the very top of Old Town Hall's tower for that. This astronomical clock, with all its hands and markings, is meant to mark the phases of the moon, the equinoxes, the season and day, and innumerable Christian holidays.

When the clock strikes the hour, viewers are treated to a kind of medieval morality play. Two doors slide open and the statues of the Twelve Apostles glide by, while the 15th-century conception of the "evils" of life—the skeleton of Death, a preening Vanity, a corrupt Turk, and an acquisitive Jew—shake and dance below. At the end of World War II, the horns and beard were removed from the moneybag-holding Jew, who is now politely referred to as "Greed."

It's worth climbing Town Hall Tower for an excellent view over the red rooftops of Staroměstské náměstí and the surrounding area, but be warned: The steps are narrow and steep and quite physically demanding.

The Estates' Theater (Stavovské divadlo)

Ovocný trh 1. ☎ 02/2421 5001. Metro: Line A or B to Můstek.

Completed in 1783 by the wealthy Count F.A. Nostitz, the neoclassical theater became an early symbol of the emerging high Czech culture—with the Greek theme *Patriae et Musis* (the Fatherland and Music) etched above its front columns. In 1799 the wealthy land barons who formed fiefdoms known as The Estates gave the theater its current name.

Wolfgang Amadeus Mozart staged the premier of *Don Giovanni* here in 1787 because he said the conservative patrons in Vienna did not appreciate him or his passionate and sometimes shocking work. They also wanted mostly German opera, but Praguers were quite happy to stage the performance in Italian. "Praguers understand me," Mozart was quoted as saying.

In 1834, the Czech playwright J.K. Tyl staged a comedy here called *Fidlovačka* in which the patriotic song "Kde domov můj?" ("Where is my home?") was a standout. It later became the Czech national anthem. In the heady days at the end of World War II in 1945, the Estates' Theater was renamed Tyl Theater, but when a total reconstruction of the building was completed in 1991, its previous name was reinstated.

Czech director Miloš Forman returned to his native country to film his Oscar-winning *Amadeus*, shooting the scenes of Mozart in Prague with perfect authenticity at the Estates' Theater.

The theater does not have daily tours, but tickets for performances—and the chance to sit in one of the many elegant private boxes—are usually available. Tour events are occasionally scheduled, and individual tours can be arranged through the city heritage group **Pražská vlastivěda** (☎ 02/2481 6184). Scheduled tours cost 15 Kč (55¢), plus the admission cost of the site. Private guides can be hired for 150 Kč ($5.55) per hour.

JOSEFOV

Within Josefov, you'll find a community that for centuries was forced to fend for itself, until the horrific purges under Nazi occupation in World War II. Although more than 118,000 Jews were recorded as living in the Czech lands of Bohemia and Moravia in 1939, only 30,000 survived to see the end of the Nazi occupation. Today, the Jewish community in the entire country numbers about 3,000 people, most of whom live in Prague.

Josefov's synagogues have been lovingly regarded as monuments to the survival of Judaism in Central Europe, and the Old Jewish Cemetery, with generation upon generation buried upon each other, is an odd relic of the cohesion of Prague's ghetto. Prague's Jewish Quarter is described in detail in "Walking Tour 4" in Chapter 7.

The Jewish Museum in Prague is now the name of the organization managing all the Jewish landmarks in Josefov. Ir provides guided package tours as part of a comprehensive admission price, with an English speaking guide. The package includes: the Ceremonial Hall, Old Jewish Cemetery, Old-New Synagogue, Pinkas Synagogue, Klaus Synagogue, and the Maisel Synagogue. During the high season from May to October, tours will leave on the hour, but there must be at least 10 people in a group. The packages costs 270 Kč ($10) for adults, 170 Kč ($6.30) for children ages 8 to 15.

The Maisel Synagogue now serves as the exhibition space for the Jewish Museum. In October 1994, the State Jewish Museum closed; the Torah covers, 100,000 books, and other exhibits once housed there were given to the Jewish community, who then proceeded to return many items to synagogues throughout the country. Most of Prague's ancient Judaica was destroyed by the Nazis during World War II. Ironically, those same Germans constructed a "exotic museum of an extinct race," thus salvaging thousands of objects, such as the valued Torah covers, books, and silver now displayed at the Maisel Synagogue.

✪ Old New Synagogue (Staronová synagóga)

Červená 2. ☎ 02/2781 0099. Admission 120 Kč ($4.44) adults, 70 Kč ($2.60) students. Sun–Fri 9:30am–6pm. Metro: Line A to Staroměstská.

> ### ❓ Did You Know?
>
> - Charles University, Central Europe's first post-secondary school, opened in Prague in 1348.
> - Albert Einstein was a professor of physics in Prague from 1911 to 1912.
> - The word *robot* was coined by Czech writer Karel Čapek, and comes from a Slavic root meaning *to work*.
> - Contact lenses were invented by a Czech scientist.
> - The word *dollar* came from the *Tolar* coins used during the Austrian empire; the coins were minted in the western Bohemian town of Jáchymov from silver mined nearby.

Originally called the New Synagogue, to distinguish it from an even older one that no longer exists, the Old New Synagogue, built around 1270, is the oldest Jewish house of worship in Europe. Worshipers have prayed continuously for more than 700 years, interrupted only between 1941 and 1945 because of the Nazi occupation. The synagogue is also one of Prague's largest Gothic buildings, built with vaulted ceilings and fitted with Renaissance-era columns.

✪ Old Jewish Cemetery (Starý židovský hřbitov)

U Starého hřbitova. ☎ 02/2481 0099. Admission 150 Kč ($5.55) adults, 100 Kč ($3.70) children. Sun–Fri 9:30am–6pm. Metro: Line A to Staroměstská.

One of Europe's oldest Jewish burial grounds, located just one block from the Old New Synagogue, dates from the mid-15th century. Because the local government of the time didn't allow Jews to bury their dead elsewhere, graves were dug deep enough to hold 12 bodies vertically, with each tombstone placed in front of the last. The result is one of the world's most crowded cemeteries: a one-block area filled with more than 20,000 graves. Among the most famous persons buried here are the celebrated Rabbi Loew (died 1609), who made the legendary Golem (a clay "monster" to protect Prague's Jews), and banker Markus Mordechai Maisel (died 1601), then the richest man in Prague and protector of the city's Jewish community during the reign of Rudolf II.

ELSEWHERE IN PRAGUE

✪ Vyšehrad

Soběslavová 1. ☎ 02/29 66 51. Tram: 17, 3 from Karlovo náměstí to Výtoň south of New Town.

The sprawling rocky hilltop complex is the cradle of the Bohemian state. From this spot, legend has it, Princess Libuše looked out over the Vltava valley toward the present day Prague Castle and predicted the founding of a great state and capital city. Vyšehard was the first seat of the first Czech kings in the Přemyslid dynasty before the dawn of this millennium.

This was also the first Royal Route. Before the kings could take their seat at the more modern Prague Castle, they first had to pay homage to their predecessors on Vyšehrad and then follow the route to Hradčany for the coronation.

Today, the fortifications remain on the rocky cliffs, blocking out the increasing noise and confusion below. Within the confines of the citadel, lush lawns and gardens are crisscrossed by dozens of paths, leading to historic buildings and cemeteries. Vyšehrad is still somewhat of a hidden treasure for picnics and romantic walks, and from here you'll see one of the most panoramic views of the city. All four corners of Prague can been seen from up here.

Vyšehrad Cemetery (Vyšehradský hřbitov) is the national cemetery within the ancient citadel on the east side of the Vltava. It's the final resting place of some 600 honored Czechs, including the composers Antonín Dvořák and Bedřich Smetana, and the art nouveau painter Alfons Mucha. The complex of churches and gardens is a pleasant getaway from the city crush.

3 Museums & Galleries

Prague's private galleries are the best places to see contemporary art. Many terrific eastern European artists, who have not yet gained acceptance into the renowned French and German art markets, are gravitating to Prague. Many fine art galleries in central Prague are within walking distance of Staroměstské náměstí. Although their primary interest is sales, most welcome window shoppers. See Chapter 8 for information on the city's top art galleries. As for public museums and galleries, note that many museums are closed on Mondays.

HRADČANY

✪ Šternberk Palace Art Museum of the National Gallery (Šternberský palác)

Hradčanské náměstí 15. ☎ **02/2751 0594.** Admission 50 Kč ($1.85) adults, 15 Kč (55¢) students and children. Tues–Sun 10am–6pm. Metro: Line A to Malostranská or Hradčanská.

The jewel in the National Gallery crown (also known as the European Art Museum), the gallery at Šternberk Palace adjacent to the main gate of Prague Castle displays a wide menu of European art throughout the ages. It features six centuries of everything from oils to sculptures. The permanent collection is divided chronologically into pre-19th-century art, 19th- and 20th-century art, and 20th-century French painting and sculpture. The collection includes a good selection of cubist paintings by Braque and Picasso, among others. Temporary exhibitions, such as Italian Renaissance bronzes, are always on show. The Veletržní Palace (see listing below) now houses most of the National Gallery's 20th-century art collection.

St. George's Convent at Prague Castle (Klášter sv. Jiřího na Pražském hradě)

Jiřské náměstí 33. ☎ **02/2451 0695.** Admission 50 Kč ($1.85), 15 Kč (55¢) students. Tues–Sun 10am–6pm. Metro: Line A to Malostranská or Hradčanská.

Dedicated to displaying old Czech art, the castle convent is especially packed with Gothic and baroque Bohemian iconography as well as portraits of patron saints. The most famous among their unique collection of Czech Gothic panel paintings are those by the Master of the Hohenfurth Altarpiece and the Master of Theodoricus. The collections are frequently arranged into special exhibitions usually revolving around a specific place, person, or time in history.

National Military History Museum

Schwarzenberg Palace, Hradčanské náměstí 2. ☎ **02/2020 4933.** Admission 30 Kč ($1.11) adults, 15 Kč (55¢) children. Open May–Oct Tues–Sun 10am–6pm. Metro: Line A to Malostranská or Hradčanská.

Adjacent to Prague Castle's main entrance and across from the Šternberk Palace Art Museum is the eye-catching Schwarzenberg Palace with its checkered parquet outer walls. Inside you'll find an extensive collection of ancient guns, ammunition, cannons, and military regalia from Bohemia's and Europe's war history. Uniforms, decorations, and explanations of major and minor battles from the first Bohemian armies until the founding of the Czechoslovak state in 1918 are on display.

STARÉ MĚSTO (OLD TOWN)

✪ Kinský Palace (Palác Kinských)

Staroměstské náměstí. ☎ 02/2481 0758. Admission 30 Kč ($1.11) adults, 10 Kč (37¢) students, free for children under 6. Tues–Sun 9am–6pm. Metro: Line A to Staroměstská.

The rococo Kinský Palace houses graphic works from the National Gallery collection, including works by Georges Braque, André Derain, and other modern masters. Pablo Picasso's 1907 *Self-Portrait* is housed within, and has virtually been adopted as the National Gallery's logo. Good-quality international exhibitions have included Max Ernst and Rembrandt retrospectives, as well as shows on functional art and crafts.

St. Agnes Convent (Klášter sv. Anežky České)

U milosrdných 17. ☎ 02/2481 0628. Admission 50 Kč($1.85) adults; 15 Kč (55¢) children; 60 Kč ($2.22) families. Tues–Sun 10am–6pm. Metro: Line A to Staroměstská.

A complex of early Gothic buildings and churches that date from the 13th century, the convent, tucked away in a corner of Staré Město, was once home to the Order of the Poor Clares. Established in 1234 by St. Agnes of Bohemia, sister of King Wenceslas I, the convent is now home to the National Gallery's collection of 19th- and 20th-century Czech art. The Blessed Agnes became St. Agnes when Pope John Paul II paid his first visit to Prague in 1990 for her canonization.

In addition to rooms of contemplative oils, the museum contains many bronze studies that preceded the casting of some of the city's greatest public monuments, including the equestrian statue of St. Wenceslas atop the National Theater. Downstairs, a Children's Workshop offers hands-on art activities for kids, most of which incorporate religious themes. The grounds surrounding the convent are pretty nice, too. The convent is located at the end of Anežka, off of Haštalské náměstí.

NOVÉ MĚSTO (NEW TOWN)

National Museum (Národní muzeum)

Václavské náměstí 68. ☎ 02/2423 0485. Admission 35 Kč ($1.30) adults, 10 Kč (37¢) students, free for children under 6, free for everyone on the first Mon of each month. Daily 10am–5pm, closed first Tues each month. Metro: Line A or C to Muzeum metro station.

The National Museum, which dominates upper Václavské náměstí, looks so much like an important government building that it even fooled the Communists, who fired upon it during their 1968 invasion. If you look closely you can still see shell marks.

The second-oldest museum in the Czech lands, it was opened in 1893. Built in neo-Renaissance style, the museum houses two floors of exhibits. On the first floor is an exhaustive collection of minerals, rocks, and meteorites from the Czech and Slovak Republics. Only 12,000 of the museum's collection of more than 200,000 rocks and gems are on display, all neatly arranged in old wooden cases.

The second-floor exhibits depict the ancient history of the Czech lands, as well as zoological and paleontological displays. Throughout the "prehistory" exhibit are cases of human bones, preserved in soil just as they were found. Nearby, a huge lifelike model of a woolly mammoth is mounted next to the bones of the real thing, and a half-dozen rooms are packed with more stuffed-and-mounted animals than you could shake a shotgun at.

ELSEWHERE IN PRAGUE

✪ Museum Of The City Of Prague (Muzeum hlavního města Prahy)

Švermovy sady 1554, near the main bus station. ☎ **02/236 2449**. Admission 20 Kč (70¢) adults, 10 Kč (35¢) students, free for children under 6. Tues–Sun 10am–6pm. Metro: Line B or C to Florenc.

Not just another warehouse of history, where unearthed artifacts unwanted by others are chronologically stashed, this delightfully upbeat museum encompasses Prague's illustrious past with pleasant brevity. Sure, the museum holds the expected displays of medieval weaponry and shop signs, but the best exhibit in this two-story Renaissance-style building is a miniature model of 18th-century Prague, painstakingly re-created in 1:480 scale. It's fascinating to see Staré Město as it used to be, and the Jewish Quarter before its 19th-century facelift. A reproduction of the original calendar face of the Old Town Hall astrological clock is also on display, as are a number of documents relating to Prague's Nazi occupation and the assassination of Nazi commander Reinhard Heydrich. The museum is located one block north of the Florenc metro station.

National Technical Museum (Národní technické muzeum)

Kostelní 42. Letná. ☎ **02/373 825**. Admission 30 Kč ($1.11) adult, 15 Kč (55¢) students. Tues–Sun 9am–5pm. Tram: 1, 8, 25, or 26 from Hradčanská metro to Letná Park.

The Czechs are justifiably proud of their long traditions in industry and technology. Before Communism, the country was one of the most advanced industrialized countries in the world. At the National Technical Museum it is clear why. The depository holds nearly one million articles, but it can only show about 40,000 at a time. The array of machines, vehicles, instruments, and the documents laying out their design are displayed in awesome detail. Visitors can see the harbingers of radio and television technology, the development of mechanization, and the golden age of Czech rail service during the Austrian Monarchy, where velvet-lined cars were standard.

Veletržní Palace (National Gallery)

Veletržní at Dukelských hrdinů. ☎ **02/2430-1015**. Admission 80 Kč ($2.96). Family pass 120 Kč ($4.44). Tues–Sun 10am–6pm, Thurs until 9pm. Metro: Line C to Vltavská or tram 17.

This 1925 constructionist palace, originally built for trade fairs, was recently remodeled and reopened in December 1995 to hold the bulk of the National Gallery's collection of 20th-century works by Czech and other European artists. Three atrium-lit concourses provide a comfortable setting for some catchy and some kitschy Czech sculpture and multi-media works. Unfortunately, the best cubist works from Braque and Picasso, Rodin bronzes, and many other primarily French pieces have been relegated to a poorly-lit section on the second floor. Other displays are devoted to peculiar works from Czech artists that demonstrate how creativity flowed even under the weight of the Iron Curtain. The first floor will feature temporary exhibits from traveling shows.

4 More to See & Do

CEMETERIES

New Jewish Cemetery (Nový židovský hřbitov)

Jana Želivského. Daily dawn–dusk. Metro: Line A to Želivského.

Although it's not as visually captivating, nor as historically important as Prague's Old Jewish Cemetery (see "Other Top Sights," above), the overgrown, ivy-enveloped New Jewish Cemetery is a popular attraction because the writer **Franz Kafka** is buried along one side of the cemetery. To find his grave, when you first enter the cemetery, turn immediately to your right. Go along the wall about 300 feet and look down in the first row of graves. There you will find the late Kafka's final resting place. If you don't have a yarmulke (Jewish skull cap) you must borrow one from the man in the small building at the entrance—he is quite happy to lend you one.

If you go this cemetery for Kafka, you will find yourself staying longer to roam. The ivy-covered cemetery is soothing and fascinating. And don't forget to return your yarmulke.

Olšanské Cemetery (Olšanské hřbitov)

Vinohradská. Daily dawn–dusk. Metro: Line A to Flora or Želivského.

Olšanské is the burial ground of some of the city's most prominent former residents, including the first Communist president, Klement Gottwald, and the anti-Soviet protester Jan Palach who burned himself to death after the 1968 invasion. Olšanské is located just on the other side of Jana Želivského street from the New Jewish Cemetery.

CHURCHES
STARÉ MĚSTO (OLD TOWN)
Church of St. Nicholas (Kostel Sv. Mikuláše)

Old Town Square at Pařížská. Admission free, except for occasional concerts. Tues–Sat 10am–5pm, Sun 10am–2pm, closed Mon. Metro: Line A to Staroměstská.

At the site of a former Gothic church started by German merchants, this St. Nicholas church was designed by the principal architect of Czech baroque, K.I. Dienzenhofer, in 1735. He is the same Dienzenhofer who designed the other St. Nicholas church in Prague in Lesser Town (see "Other Top Sights," above).

This St. Nicholas church is not nearly as ornate as the other, but has a more tumultuous history of management. The Catholic monastery was closed in 1787, and the church was handed over for use as a concert hall in 1865. The city's Russian Orthodox community began using it in 1871, but in 1920 management was handed to the Protestant Hussites. One notable piece inside the church is the 19th–century crystal-covered chandelier with glass brought from the town of Harrachov. Concerts are still held here; see the "Classical Concerts Around Town" box in Chapter 9.

Týn Church or the Church of Our Lady Before Týn (Kostel paní Marie před Týnem)

Staroměstské náměstí. Open only for mass Sun 11:30am and 1:30pm until reconstruction is complete. Metro: Line A to Staroměstská.

Huge double square towers with multiple black steeples make this church the most distinctive standout of Old Town Square. The church in its present configuration was completed mostly in the 1380s, and it became the main church of the Protestant Hussite movement in the 15th century (although the small Bethlehem Chapel in Old Town where Hus preached is the cradle of the Czech Protestant reformation).

Aside from the church's omnipresent lurch over the square and the peculiar way buildings were erected in front of it, the church is well known as the final resting place of the Danish astronomer Tyco de Brahe, who died while serving in the court of Austrian Emperor Ruldolf II in 1601. Brahe's tombstone bearing his effigy as an explorer of many worlds is located behind the church's main pulpit.

In 1995, the city of Prague cast a new lighting system upon the church's steeples, making it glow eerily in the night and earning it the name "The Batman Church" because it resembled the final scene of the original Tim Burton film *Batman*.

MALÁ STRANA (LESSER TOWN)
Church of Our Lady Victorious
Karmelitská 15. Donations requested, and fee for occasional concerts. Tues–Sat 10am–5pm, Sun 10am–2pm. Metro: Line A to Malostranská.

This 1613 early baroque home of the Carmelite Order is famous mostly throughout Italy and Latino countries for the wax statue of Jesus displayed on an altar to the right wing of the church. The **Bambini di Praga** (Baby of Prague) was presented to the Carmelites by the Habsburg patron Polyxena of Lobkowicz in 1628, and is revered as a valuable Catholic relic from Spain. Copies of the Bambini are sold frequently on the Lesser Town streets outside the church, angering some of the faithful.

HISTORIC BUILDINGS & MONUMENTS
STARÉ MĚSTO (OLD TOWN)
Powder Tower (Prašná brána, literally Powder Gate)
Náměstí Republiky. Metro: Line B to Náměstí Republiky.

Once part of Staré Město's system of fortifications, the Powder Tower was built in 1475 as one of the walled city's major gateways. The 140-foot-tall tower marks the beginning of the Royal Route, the traditional ³/₄-mile-long route along which medieval Bohemian monarchs paraded on their way to being crowned in Prague Castle's St. Vitus Cathedral. It also was the east gate to the Old Town on the road to Kutná Hora. The tower was acutely damaged during the Prussian invasion of Prague in 1737.

It got its name late in the 18th century, when the development of Nové Město rendered this protective tower obsolete; it was then used as a gunpowder storehouse. Early in this century, the tower served as the daily meeting place of Franz Kafka and his writer friend Max Brod. On the tower's west side, facing Old Town, you'll see a statue of King Přemysl Otakar II, under which is a bawdy relief depicting a young woman slapping a man who is grabbing her under her skirt.

The interior of the tower is usually open during summer months, but the renovations of the adjacent Municipal House has played havoc with the entrance and has closed it quite often. If the entrance is open when you visit, go in; you'll see the remains of the original construction on the first floor above the ground.

NOVÉ MĚSTO (NEW TOWN)
Můstek Metro Station
Václavské náměstí. Line A or B.

It's not the metro station itself, which is hardly 20 years old, that warrants an entry in this section. But descend to Můstek's lower escalators and you will see the illuminated stone remains of what was once a bridge that connected the fortifications of Prague's Old and New Towns. In Czech, *můstek* means "little bridge," but the ancient span is not the only medieval remains modern-day excavators discovered. Metro workers had to be inoculated when they also uncovered viable tuberculosis bacterium, which had lain here dormant, encased in horse excrement, since the Middle Ages.

Na příkopě, the pedestrian street above Můstek metro station, literally translates as "on the moat," a reminder that the street was built on top of a river that separated

Modern Memorials

One of the city's most photographed tourist attractions is the colorful, graffiti-filled **Lennon Wall**, located on Velkopřevorské náměstí. This quiet side street in Malá Strana's Kampa neighborhood near Charles Bridge is across from the French Embassy on the path leading from Kampa Park.

The wall is named after singer John Lennon, whose huge image is spray-painted on the wall's center. Following his death in 1980, Lennon became a hero of pacifism and counterculture throughout Eastern Europe, and this monument was born. During Communist rule, the wall, with pro-democracy and other slogans, was regularly whitewashed, only to be repainted by the faithful. When the new democratically elected government was installed in 1989, it is said that the French ambassador, whose stately offices are located directly across from the wall, phoned Prague's mayor and asked that the city government refrain from interfering with the monument. Today young locals and visitors continue to flock here, paying homage with flowers and candles.

Yet, it is relatively quieter at the **Národní Memorial**, Národní 16, under the arches midway between Václavské náměstí and the National Theater. This memorial marks the spot where hundreds of protesting Prague college students were seriously beaten by riot police on the brutal, icy night of November 17, 1989. (In January 1996, the building where the memorial stands had a fire; it is being reconstructed.)

Just five years later, only about 100 Czechs showed up to commemorate the fifth anniversary of the Velvet Revolution at the place that became the cradle of the rebellion. President Václav Havel laid flowers at the tiny monument, but all around him were examples of how things have changed.

A shiny new red Ferrari, with Czech plates, streaked past the group and screeched to a halt about a block further on. Throwing a blistering U-turn, it sped back. The driver, wearing designer sunglasses, stuck his head out to see that it was just a guy and some flowers. He disappointedly slid back into the car and peeled out back down Národní, as the police only shook their heads and said in awe, "What a car."

The street has itself become a monument to the country's new capitalism. Where armed police and dogs lined up outside the rotting *Maj* department store, tourists now flock to find bargains at the Tesco department store, formerly a K-Mart. Fashion boutiques, a plastic surgeon's private office, and sparkling new branches of private banks take spots once occupied by such "businesses" as the Castro grill at Cuban Culture Center.

It all obscures a small bronze monument whose peace-sign hands vaguely remind one of the night Czechoslovakia's bloodless revolution began. "We did not know what to expect as we marched, and we were afraid," says Hana Bláhová, a former agro-economics student, now 28, who escaped down a side street. But she, like most Czechs, says she doesn't have time to look back. She has started a small but profitable furniture factory with her husband. "The system has changed for the better, end of discussion," says Bláhová. "Now I am a businesswoman, something I didn't think would ever be possible."

the walls of Staré Město and Nové Město. In 1760, it was filled in. The street follows the line of the old fortifications all the way down to the Gothic Powder Tower at náměstí Republiky.

○ National Theater (Národní divadlo)
Národní 2. ☎ 02/2491 3437. Metro: Line B to Národní třída.

Lavishly constructed in the late Renaissance style of northern Italy, the gold-crowned National Theater, which overlooks the Vltava River, is one of Prague's most recognizable landmarks. Completed in 1881, the theater was built to nurture the Czech National Revival Movement—a drive to replace the dominant German culture with homegrown Czech works. To finance construction, small collection boxes with signs "For the prosperity of a dignified National Theater" were installed in public places.

Almost immediately upon completion, the building was wrecked by fire and rebuilt, opening in 1883 with the premiere of Bedřich Smetana's opera *Libuše*. The magnificent interior contains an allegorical sculpture about music, and busts of Czech theatrical personalities created by some of the country's best-known artists. The motto *"Národ sobě"* ("The Nation to Itself") is written above the stage. Smetana conducted the theater's orchestra here until 1874, when deafness forced him to relinquish his post.

The theater does not have daily tours, but tickets for performances are usually available, and tour events are occasionally scheduled. Individual tours can be arranged through the city heritage group **Pražská vlastivěda** (☎ 02/2481 6184).

SQUARES

○ Old Town Square (Staroměstské náměstí)
The most celebrated square in the city, Old Town Square is surrounded by baroque buildings and packed with colorful craftspeople, cafes, and entertainers. In ancient days, the site was a major crossroad on central European merchant routes. In its center stands a memorial to Jan Hus, the 15th-century martyr who crusaded against Prague's German-dominated religious and political establishment. Unveiled in 1915, on the 500th anniversary of Hus's execution, the monument's most compelling features are the asymmetry of its composition and the fluidity of the figures. Take metro Line A to Staroměstská. The square and Staré Město are described in more detail in "Walking Tour 3" in Chapter 7.

Jan Palach Square (náměstí Jana Palacha)
Officially dedicated in 1990, the square formerly known as Red Army Square is named for a 21-year-old philosophy student who set himself on fire on the National Museum steps to protest the 1968 Communist invasion. An estimated 800,000 Praguers attended his funeral march from Staroměstské náměstí to the Olšanské Cemetery, where he is buried (see "Cemeteries," above). To get to the square, take metro Line A to Staroměstská at the Old Town foot of Mánesův Bridge.

Charles University's philosophy department building is located on this square. On the lower left-hand corner of the building's facade is a memorial to the martyred student: a replica of Palach's death mask.

○ Wenceslas Square (Václavské náměstí)
One of the city's most historic squares, Wenceslas Square was once called the horse market (Koňský trh), and the often muddy swath between the buildings played host to the country's equine auctioneers. The top of the square, where the National Museum now stands, was once the outer wall of the New Town fortifications, bordering the Royal Vineyards. Trolleys streamed up and down the square until the early 1980s. Today the half-mile long boulevard is lined with cinemas, shops, hotels, restaurants, and entertainment venues, many of which are on the seedy side.

The square was given its present name in 1848. The giant equestrian statue of St. Wenceslas on horseback surrounded by four other saints, including his grandmother, St. Ludmila, and St. Adalbert, the 10th-century bishop of Prague, was completed by J.V. Myslbek in 1912. The statues' pedestal has become a popular platform for speakers. Actually, the square has thrice been the site of riots and revolutions—in 1848, 1968, and 1989. Take metro Line A or B to Můstek.

Charles Square (Karlovo náměstí)

Built by Charles IV in 1348, Charles Square once functioned as Prague's primary cattle market. New Town's Town Hall (Novoměstská radnice), which stands on the square's eastern side, was the sight of Prague's First Defenestration—a violent protest in which several Catholic councilors were thrown to their deaths from the building's windows, sparking the Hussite Wars in the 15th century. (See the "I Don't Do Windows: Prague's Tradition of Defenestration" box earlier in this chapter.)

Today, Charles Square is a lazy park in the center of the city, crisscrossed by tram lines and surrounded by buildings and shops. Take metro Line B to Karlovo náměstí.

UNIVERSITIES

Historically, education has always occupied an important place in Czech life. Professors at **Charles University**—the city's most prestigious and oldest university, founded in 1348—have been in the political and cultural vanguard, strongly influencing the everyday life of all citizens. During the last 50 years, the university has expanded into some of the city center's largest riverfront buildings, many of which are located between Karlův most (Charles Bridge) and Čechův most (Čech's Bridge).

VIEWS

Petřín Tower (Rozhledna)

A one-fifth scale copy of Paris' Eiffel Tower, Prague's Petřín Tower on top of Petřín Hill was constructed for the 1891 Prague Exhibition out of recycled railway track. The tower functioned as Prague's primary telecommunications tower until the Emir Hoffman tower opened (see below). Today the Eiffel replica exists solely as a tourist attraction. Those who climb the 195 feet to the top are treated to striking views, particularly at night. Admission is 20 Kč (74¢) for adults, 10 Kč (37¢) for students and children ages 6 to 15. Open daily April to October from 9:30am to 8pm, November to March Saturday and Sunday only from 9:30am to 5pm. Take tram 12 or 22 to Újezd, then ride the funicular to the top.

Emir Hoffman TV Tower

Towering above Prague, from atop a hill in Žižkov, the Emir Hoffman TV Tower is visible in the distance from most everywhere in the city. Conversely, most every place in the city is visible from the TV tower, which is why it's one of the best "high" places around.

Most everyone agrees that the white, 600-foot antenna-topped tower (completed in late 1989) is quite unsightly. It's not that nice inside either, but the vistas of central Prague and all its suburbs put the entire city and surroundings into solemn perspective. Unfortunately, landmarks are not well marked from the tower's observation cubicles, so bring a map.

Admission is 40 Kč ($1.48). Open daily 9am to 10pm. Take metro Line A to Jiřího z Poděbrad; the tower (☎ 02/27 61 63) is at Ondříčkova (Televizní Vysílač).

5 Parks & Gardens

The open-air **Havel's Market** (Havelský trh), located on Havelská ulice, a short street that runs perpendicular to the main route connecting Staroměstské náměstí with Václavské náměstí, is a great place to shop for picnic supplies. Here you'll find seasonal homegrown fruits and vegetables at inexpensive prices.

Vyšehrad (see "Other Top Sights" above) is my favorite place for a picnic.

HRADČANY

The ✪ **Royal Garden** (Královská zahrada) at Prague Castle, once the site of the sovereigns' vineyards, was founded in 1534. Dotted with lemon trees and surrounded by 16th-, 17th-, and 18th-century buildings, the park is consciously and conservatively laid out with abundant shrubbery and fountains. Enter from u Prašného mostu street, north of the castle complex.

The castle's ✪ **Garden on the Ramparts** (Zahrada na Valech), on the city-side ramparts below the castle, were re-opened again in spring 1995 after being thoroughly refurbished. Beyond the beautifully groomed lawns and sparse shrubbery there is a tranquil low-angle view of the castle above and the city below. Enter the garden from the southside of the castle complex, below Hradčanské náměstí. The park is open Tuesday through Sunday from 9am to 5pm.

MALÁ STRANA

Looming over Malá Strana, adjacent to Prague Castle, lush green **Petřín Hill** (Petřínské sady) is easily recognizable by the miniature replica of the Eiffel Tower that tops it. Gardens and orchards bloom throughout the spring and summer in the huge park. Throughout are a myriad of monuments, churches, a mirror maze, and an observatory (see "Especially for Kids," below). Hunger Wall, a lengthy, decaying 21-foot-high stone wall that runs up through Petřín to the grounds of Prague Castle, was commissioned by Charles IV in the 1360s as a medieval social project designed to provide jobs for Prague's starving poor. Take tram 12 or 22 to Újezd.

Located near the foot of Charles Bridge in Malá Strana, **Kampa** (Na Kampě) was named by Spanish soldiers who set up camp here after the Roman Catholics won the Battle of White Mountain in 1620. The park as it is today wasn't formed until the period of Nazi occupation, when the private gardens of three noble families were joined. It is fine place for an inner-city picnic, although the lawns are packed in the high tourism season.

Part of the excitement of **Waldstein** (or Wallenstein) **Gardens** (Valdštejnská zahrada) is its location, behind a 30-foot wall on the back streets of Malá Strana. Inside, elegant, leafy gravel paths, dotted by classical bronze statues and gurgling fountains, fan out in every direction. Laid out in the 17th century, the baroque park was the personal garden of General Albrecht Waldstein (or Wallenstein; 1581–1634), commander of the Roman Catholic armies during the Thirty Years' War. These gardens are the backyards of Waldstein's Palace—Prague's largest—which replaced 23 houses, three gardens, and the municipal brick kiln. The garden is open May through September daily, from 9am to 7pm.

ELSEWHERE IN PRAGUE

The flat plain above the upper western side of the Vltava is a densely tree-covered swath of land, maintained as a park since 1858. While **Letná Park** (Letenské sady) provides many quiet spaces for a picnic, a summer beer garden at the north end serves up cups of brew with a view. The garden is connected to two restaurants in a 19th-century neo-Renaissance chateau (Letenský zámeček) where you can get a pub-style meal or formal dinner.

The large art nouveau gazebo tucked into the center of the park, the Hanavský Pavilion, was built for the city's universal industrial fair in 1891. To get to Letná, Milady Horákové, take tram 1, 8, 25, or 26 from Hradčanská metro station.

6 Especially for Kids

ON PETŘÍN HILL

The kids will enjoy the funicular ride to the top of Petřín Hill, capped by a minia-ture replica of the Eiffel Tower. Once there, look for **The Labyrinth** (Bludiště), a maze of mirrors through which one walks. Like the tower replica, the Labyrinth was built for the 1891 Prague Exhibition, an expo that highlighted the beauty and accomplishments of Bohemia and Moravia.

Inside the Labyrinth is a gigantic painting/installation depicting the battle between Praguers and Swedes on the Charles Bridge in 1648, a commemoration of the fight-ing that ended the Thirty Years' War. In 1892, the building's other historical exhibits were replaced with mirrors, turning the Labyrinth into the funhouse we know today.

The Labyrinth is open daily April to August, from 10am to 7pm. Admission is 10 Kč (37¢) for adults, 5 Kč (18¢) for children.

Also in the park is the **Štefánik Observatory,** built in 1930 expressly for public star-gazing. Astronomers of all levels will find the observatory fascinating. Inside, a great number of magnifiers are displayed museum-style, plus there's a 90-year-old telescope for viewing the sun during the day, and stars and planets at night. The observatory is open Tuesday to Sunday from 11am to 11pm. Admission is 15 Kč (55¢) for adults, 10 Kč (37¢) for children.

The funicular departs from a small house in the park just above the middle of Újezd in Malá Strana; tram 12 or 22 will take you to Újezd.

ELSEWHERE IN PRAGUE

Budding astronomers can see how the sky would look if only you could see beyond the smog at the **Prague Planetarium,** located in Stromovka Park (☎ 02/371 746). There are four shows daily—at 2, 3, 4, and 5pm—under the dark dome, including one where highlighted constellations are set to music, and another that displays that night's sky. The shows are in Czech, but the sky is still the same. To reach the planetarium, take tram 5, 12, or 17 to Výstaviště and walk through the park to your left about 350 yards. Admission is 50 Kč ($1.85). Open Monday to Thursday from 9am to noon and 1 to 6pm, Friday 8am to noon, Saturday 9:30am to 5pm.

In the Vystaviště fairgrounds adjacent to Stromovka Park is **✪ Křižik's Fountain** (Křižíkova Fontana). A massive system of water spigots spout tall and delicate streams of color-lit water in a spectacular light show set to recorded classical and popular music. Small children are especially fascinated by this. There is also a little amuse-ment park on the fairgrounds. The water/music program (☎ 02/8729 204) runs April to October from 7 to 10pm. Admission is 10 Kč (37¢). Take tram 5, 12, or 17 to Výstaviště.

7 Special-Interest Sightseeing

FOR THE ARCHITECTURE BUFF

Prague's long history, combined with the good fortune of having avoided heavy war damage, makes it a wonderful city for architecture lovers. Along with the standard must-see castles and palaces comes a bountiful mixture of styles and periods. Buildings and monuments from the Middle Ages to the present day are interspersed with one another throughout the city.

The best examples of Romanesque architecture are parts of Prague Castle, including the Basilica of St. George.

In Staré Město you'll see the best examples of the three-century-long Gothic period: the Convent of St. Agnes, Na Františku; the Old New Synagogue, Pařížská třída; Old Town Hall and the Astronomical Clock, Staroměstské náměstí; Powder Tower, Celetná ulice; and Charles Bridge.

A few Renaissance buildings still stand, including Golden Lane, Malá Strana Town Hall, and Pinkas Synagogue, Široká ulice, in Staré Město.

Many of Prague's best-known structures are pure baroque and rococo, enduring styles that reigned throughout the 17th and 18th centuries. Buildings on Staroměstské náměstí and Nerudova street date from this period, as does St. Nicholas's Church, Malostranské náměstí, in Malá Strana, and the Loreto, Loretánské náměstí, in Hradčany.

Renaissance styles made a comeback in the late 19th century. Two neo-Renaissance buildings in particular—the National Theater, Národní třída, and the National Museum, Václavské náměstí—have endured as two of Prague's most identifiable landmarks.

Several excellent examples of whimsical art nouveau architecture include the Hotel Evropa, on Václavské náměstí, and the main railroad station, Wilsonova třída. But none is more flamboyant than the Municipal House (Obecní dům), built between 1906 and 1911. The building is Prague's outstanding monument to itself and its citizens, embellished inside and out with city-themed paintings and ornaments. Its interior is an extravaganza of murals, mosaics, sculptures, stained glass, and iron work. The building's most important salon, Smetana Hall, has a roof made of stained-glass windows. Iron and light fixtures curve above the main entrance. Unfortunately, at this writing, the Municipal House, náměstí Republiky 5, was closed for yet another round of reconstruction. It is expected to reopen in 1996 or early 1997. You can still see parts of the exterior.

Prague's finest cubist design has been embroiled in a property battle, but the House at the Black Mother of God (Dům U černé Matky Boží), at Celetná at Ovocný trh, is worth a look. Designed by J. Gočár and completed in 1912, this sharply-cut modernistic building is one of the few that blends nicely with its more classical surroundings on Czech Baker Street (Celetná). The building is named for the statuette of the Virgin Mary on its well-restored exterior. Most recently it has been used as a modern art gallery.

The city's most unappealing structures are the functional, socialist designs that were built from 1960 until the end of Communism. Central Prague examples include the main railroad station's entrance and departure hall; The Máj (now a British Tesco after K-Mart sold it in 1996) department store, Národní třída 26; the Kotva department store, náměstí Republiky; and the Hotel Inter-Continental, although it has recently added some newer, more aesthetic modern additions.

The worst of these are the prefabricated apartment buildings *(paneláky)* reached by taking metro line C to Chodov or Háje. The worst paneláks were built in the 1970s, when buildings grew really huge and dense, each 20 or more stories tall. This was the era of Chodov and Háje, suburbs south of the city center with more than 100,000 inhabitants. Today, half of Prague's residents live in paneláks.

One new post-revolution development—✪ **the Rašín Embankment Building,** Rašínovo nábřeží at Resslova—continues to fuel the debate about blending traditional architecture with progressive design. Known as the "Dancing Building," the Prague headquarters of a Dutch insurance company is scheduled to open here in 1996.

This curved twist of concrete and steel has never before been seen in Europe, or anywhere else. An elegant eight-story Ginger Rogers in her full-length gown embraces a svelt Fred Astaire dusting off his white tie and tails in a ballroom twirl above the Vltava. The staggered design of the pressed-in windows gives the structure motion when seen from afar. In fact, the only way to get the full effect is from across the river, or midway across the Jiráskův bridge.

Another twist is that the building right next to Fred and Ginger belongs to President Václav Havel. Until recently, he lived there in a modest apartment overlooking the river during his dissident days and first years as president. Apparently the president, who is quite the traditionalist, still does not object too much to the noise the new neighbors have created.

FOR MUSIC ENTHUSIASTS

Prague has more theaters and concert halls, per capita, than any other major city in the world. Between the opera houses, grand theaters, cathedrals, churches, palaces, conservatories, neighborhood cultural centers, and corner clubs, an astounding number of events occur each night (see Chapter 9 for details).

Beyond the performances, three sights pay tribute to the history of Prague's three most celebrated resident composers. Tickets for any of the concerts held at the Smetana, Dvořák, and Bertramka museums can be purchased at the museums themselves of through the Prague Information Service.

Bedřich Smetana Museum (Museum B. Smetany)

Novotného lavka 1. ☎ **02/2422 9075.** Admission 20 Kč (74¢) adults, 10 Kč (37¢) students and children. Tues–Sun 10am–5pm.

This museum, opened in 1936 (in what was the former Old Town waterworks) jutting out into the Vltava next to Charles Bridge, pays tribute to the deepest traditions of Czech classical music and its most patriotic composer, Bedřich Smetana. The exhibits contain scores of scores, diaries and manuscripts, and gifts presented to the composer while he was the pre-eminent man of Prague music in the middle of the 19th Century.

Concerts are usually held here at 8pm. Tickets cost 220 to 395 Kč ($8.15–$14.63).

Dvořák Museum (Muzeum A. Dvořáka)

Ke Karlovu 20, Praha 2. ☎ **02/29 82 14.** Admission 20 Kč (74¢) adults, 10 Kč (37¢) students and children. Tues–Sun 10am–5pm. Metro: Line C to I. P. Pavlova.

It's no accident that museum authorities chose this particular site to honor Antonín Dvořák, this country's best-loved composer. Built in 1712, the two-story rococo building, tucked away on a Nové Město side street, was Dvořák's home for 24 years until his death in 1901. In the 18th century, when the building was erected, this part of Prague was frontier land, and Czechs willing to open businesses so far from the center were called "Americans" for their pioneer spirit. This building came to be known as "America."

Established in 1932, the museum exhibits an extensive collection of memorabilia including the composer's piano, spectacles, a cap and gown he wore at Cambridge, photographs, and sculptures of the man, as well as his piano. Several rooms are furnished as they were around 1900.

Upstairs, a small and ornate recital hall hosts chamber music performances throughout the summer tourist season. Concerts are usually held at 8pm. Tickets cost 220 to 395 Kč ($8.15–$14.63).

✪ Bertramka (W. A. Mozart Museum)

Mozartova 169, Praha 5. ☎ **02/543 893.** Museum admission 50 Kč ($1.85) adults, 30 Kč ($1.11) students. Daily 9:30am–6pm. Tram: 2, 6, 7, 9, 14, or 16 from Anděl metro station.

Mozart loved Prague, and when he visited, the composer often stayed here with the family who owned this villa, the Dušeks. Now a museum, the villa contains displays that include his written work and his harpsichord. There's also a lock of Mozart's hair, encased in a cube of glass. Much of the Bertramka villa was destroyed by fire in the 1870s, but Mozart's rooms, where he finished composing the opera *Don Giovanni,* have miraculously remained untouched.

Chamber concerts are often held here. Tickets cost 280 Kč ($10.37) for adults, 180 Kč ($6.66) for children.

8 Organized Tours

ROW, ROW, ROW A BOAT

Many people rent rowboats and paddle boats on the Vltava, which is free from commercial boat traffic. The remarkably romantic—if not sparkling clean—river slowly snakes through the middle of town and gleams beneath the city's spires.

Rent-A-Boat, on Slovanský ostrov (Slavic Island), is the only company at this writing that offers lanterns for nighttime jaunts. This is an extremely romantic time to row; the amber lights of the city flicker above you. The docks are located at the bottom of the steps on the small island two blocks south of the National Theater; enter from just behind the National Theater. Rowboat rates are 40 Kč ($1.48) per hour during daylight for up to four people, 80 Kč ($2.96) with lanterns after dark. Paddle boats are 80 Kč ($2.96) per hour. Boats are available March through October (possibly in November if it's pleasant) from 10am to 11pm, weather permitting.

Located adjacent to Rent-A-Boat, **Půjčovna Romana Holana,** on Slovanský ostrov (Slavic Island), offers similar watercraft at cheaper rates, but only during the day. Rowboats cost 20 Kč (74¢) per hour, paddle boats 30 Kč ($1.11) per hour. You can rent boats from 10am till sunset March through September, weather permitting.

CRUISE SHIP TOURS

The Vltava gave Prague its reason to be, and although the quest for industrial development has caused unknown amounts of environmental damage, cruise ships are the only commercial vessels allowed to pass through the city. This is an enjoyable, low-impact way to view Prague. **Evropská vodní doprava** (☎ **02/231 0208** or **231 1915**), with a four-ship fleet, offers the most interesting sightseeing excursions, from April through October. Several tours, including some serving usually decent inexpensive meals, disembark from Čechův most at the northern turn of the Vltava and sail past

A Turn-of-the-Century Tram Ride Through Town

Prague has had a system of tram lines since horses used to pull cars in the mid-18th century. While the Communist-era tram cars are not very attractive, and the new futuristic designs are built for efficiency instead of charm, you would have to go back to the really old days to have fun in a Prague tram . . . and you can, thanks to the **Historic Tram Tour** (Elektrické dráhy DP), Patočkova 4, Praha 6 (☎/Fax 02/312 3349).

If you send a fax with details one day ahead, the city transport department will arrange a private tour using one of the turn-of-the-century wooden tram cars that actually travelled on regular lines through Prague. Up to 24 people can fit in one car, which sport wooden-planked floors, cast-iron conductors' levers, and the "ching-ching" of a proper tram bell. It costs 1,995 Kč ($73) per hour. Up to 60 people can fit into a double car for 2,310 Kč ($85) per hour. You can also order a cold smorgasbord with coffee, beer, champagne, a waiter to serve, and an accordion player if you wish.

And you can choose the route the tram takes. Hana and I suggest the following route: begin at Republic Square, slowly wind through to Wenceslas Square, along Vodičkova to Národní street, across the river through Lesser Town, and up to the castle as Tram 22 normally runs, ending at the western edge of the city, and then returning.

all of the key riverside sights. A daily lunch tour with smorgasbord and traditional Czech music leaves at 11:30am, travels to the south end of the city, and returns by 1:30pm. The price, including a meal, is 390 Kč for adults ($14.44), 180 Kč ($6.66) for children up to age 10. One-hour tours, without meals, sail to Charles Bridge and back, leaving at 2, 3, 4, and 5pm. It costs 150 Kč ($5.55) for adults, 75 Kč ($2.77) for children. A dinner cruise to the south end of town leaves at 7pm and returns by 9:30pm. Price including meal is 490 Kč ($18.15) for adults, 245 Kč ($9.07) for children. Throughout the year, groups can rent one of the ships for 1,500 Kč ($55.55) per hour, and 190 Kč ($7.03) per person for the smorgasbord.

BUS TOURS

Streets can often become gridlocked, making any tour by car or bus frustrating. But if you want to take a guided English-language bus tour, among the best are those given by **Welcome Touristic** (☎ 02/231 7598). Their 3¹/₂-hour "Grand City Tour" leaves twice daily at 9:30am and 2:30pm, April through October (only in the morning during the winter), from the company's bus stop at náměstí Republiky. The tour costs 590 Kč ($21.85) for adults, 390 Kč ($14.44) for children. A 2-hour tour leaves from the same spot at 11am, 1:30pm, and 3:30pm in the summer season, 1:30pm only in the winter; it costs 340 Kč ($12.60) for adults, 280 Kč ($10.37) for children. Group tours and night tours can be arranged individually, as well as bus tours outside of Prague.

WALKING TOURS

Sylvia Wittmann's tour company, **Wittman Tours** (☎ 02/25 12 35), offers daily walks around Prague's compact Jewish Quarter. A thousand years of history is discussed during the 2¹/₂-hour stroll. Tours led by an English-speaking guide depart daily, except Saturday, from Pařížská street at 10:30am. The tours include entrance fees to sights and cost 480 Kč ($18) for adults.

She also offers a bus tour to the concentration camp at Terezín that costs 950 Kč ($35.15) for adults. It leaves from the same spot on Pařížská. Call for tour times. See Chapter 10 for more on Terezín.

UP, UP & AWAY

You can also see Prague by air, thanks to **Prag Tourist Ballooning**, Na Balkáně 812, Praha 3 (☎ 02/684 5387). Up to four passengers per ride can float over Prague's Letná plain with a perfect view of the castle and Old Town, weather permitting. Rates are 4,000 Kč ($148) per hour, per person (half hours are possible). If you want a more pastoral setting, they will take you to the chateau at Konopiště; this costs 3,000 Kč ($111) per person, per hour. This includes insurance, but no champagne. Call at least a day before between 9am and 5pm to make reservations (English is spoken).

9 Outdoor & Indoor Activities, Plus Spectator Sports

OUTDOOR ACTIVITIES

CYCLING   Paul Radovsky of **Central European Adventure Tours**, pod útesy 8, Praha 5 (☎ 02/232 8879), will rent mountain or touring bikes and arrange whatever transport you need for them. But the best biking is outside of Prague, on the tertiary roads and paved paths in the provinces. Paul will suggest routes and provide maps.

GOLF   Czechs are rediscovering golf painfully on the tournament-caliber, brand new course with a world-class view at the **Praja Karlštejn Golf Club**, 30 minutes south of Prague. For details and directions, see "Tee Time" in Chapter 10.

JOGGING   Prague's sometimes thick smog makes jogging more like smoking, but on clear days—and there are many in the summer—the air is bearable. For the most scenic run, jog on the paths atop the Vyšehrad citadel; take tram 3 or 17 from Karlovo náměstí. The parks at Kampa or Letná are also good places to run. The paths that crisscross Petřín Hill offer a challenging uphill route.

If you want to run through Prague, stick to the traffic restricted walking zones. For an approximately 2-mile circuit, start at Můstek at the end of Wenceslas Square, run down Na Příkopě through the Powder Tower (Prašna brána) to Celetná street all the way to Old Town square and around the Hus monument, back to Železná street, past the Estates' Theatre on to Rytířská street, and back to Můstek. This route is virtually free of cars, but your feet will be pounding the bricks. Try running in early morning or late evening before the crowds block your way.

SWIMMING   Summer doesn't last long in Prague, and when it arrives, many city dwellers are only too happy to cool off in one of the city's many swimming pools. In addition to the Fitness Forum, in the Forum Hotel, listed under "Health & Fitness Clubs," the best place for tourists to swim is **Džbán Reservoir,** in the Šárka nature reserve, Prague 6. A natural lake in the ominous shadow of Communist-era panelák block housing, Džbán is fronted by a grassy "beach" that can—and often does—accommodate hundreds of bathers. Waterfront shops sell beer, snacks, and ice cream, and lockers and showers are available. In addition to two artificial swimming pools, the Šárka nature reserve also encompasses a rowboat-rental concession and a special section for nude swimming and sunbathing. To reach Šárka, take tram 20 or 26 from the Dejvická metro station.

TENNIS   You can play on the courts where Martina Navrátilová and Ivan Lendl trained. The **Czech Lawn Tennis Club** (ČLTK), Štvanice Island (☎ **02/232 4601**) offers daily court rental until sundown; rates are 250 Kč ($9.25) per hour per court. Although the name says lawn tennis, only clay courts remain. Buy tickets for court rental at the information booth in the stadium.

INDOOR ACTIVITIES

GOLF   You can play indoor golf at the **Erpet Golf Center,** Strakonická 510, Praha 5 (☎ **02/2451 1605**). Opened in 1994, the Erpet center has become a winter oasis in a golfing desert. Inside the renovated innards of a former Communist-era sports hall is a tropical setting of driving platforms, with pitching and putting greens on Astroturf and interactive video simulators. It's open daily from 8am to 11pm. Take Metro Line B to Smíchovské nádraží.

To use the driving range (into a net at the end with unlimited practice balls), as well as the putting range, the price in the early session (between 8am and 3pm) is 100 Kč ($3.70) per hour, with a discount for longer stays. From 3 to 11pm, the rate is 200 Kč ($7.40) per hour. You can rent one club for 100 Kč ($3.70), while a set of clubs is 400 Kč ($14.80).

The golf computer simulator with interactive video allowing you to play the great courses of the world costs an additional 150 Kč ($5.55) per hour in the morning per simulator where up to four can play, 300 Kč ($11.10) per hour in the evening. A training pro instructs for 150 Kč ($5.55) per hour. There is also a fitness and relaxation center (see below).

HEALTH & FITNESS CLUBS

Located on the 25th floor of the Forum Hotel, Kongresová 1, Praha 4, the **Fitness Forum** (☎ 02/6119 1326) has weight machines, free weights, exercise bikes, step machines, a small swimming pool, a sauna, and a solarium. The modern facility also offers tanning beds, squash courts, a whirlpool, and massages. It's open to non-guests. A one-day pass is 300 Kč ($11.10). Squash courts can be rented for 150 Kč ($5.55) per half-hour. Open Monday to Friday from 7am to 10pm, Saturday and Sunday 9am to 9pm. Take metro line C to Vyšehrad.

The **Erpet Golf Center** (Fitness Center), Strakonická 510, Praha 5 (☎ 02/2451 1605) has a fitness center, with modern machines, free weights, electronic rowers, and treadmills. There's also a relaxation center, with a dry sauna and a whirlpool that's usually open to the public and co-ed. Using the fitness center costs 50 Kč ($1.85) per hour from 8am to 2pm, 100 Kč ($3.70) per hour 2 to 11pm. Rates for the relaxation center are 150 Kč ($5.55) per hour from 8am to 2pm, 200 Kč ($7.40) for the evening. The Solarium costs 5 Kč (19¢) per minute. A massage is 150 Kč ($5.55) for part of the body, 280 Kč ($10.37) for the whole body. Open daily 8am to 11pm. Take Metro Line B to Smíchovské nádraží.

SPECTATOR SPORTS

For information on games, tickets, and times for the sports listed below, check the *Prague Post* sports section.

ICE HOCKEY   Although the Czech Republic's biggest star, Jaromír Jágr, has left his hometown of Kladno to earn millions of dollars as the All-Star forward for America's Pittsburgh Penguins, the **Sparta** hockey team still has more than its fair share of talent, and their rivals from elsewhere in the Czech first league always save a bit more for the Praguers. The team plays from mid-September through April at

HC Sparta ice rink (Sportovní hala), Za elektrárnou 49, Praha 7 (☎ **02/87 27 443**). Admission is 33 Kč ($1.22). Take Metro Line C to Holešovice and then tram 17 or 5 to Výstaviště.

SOCCER   Sparta, also the top local soccer team, has a fanatical following, and games always draw huge crowds to **Letná Stadium,** Praha 7. Brawls between opposing fans regularly erupt in the stands, especially when the arch rival crosstown Slavia team comes to play. Tickets for big matches often sell out long before game time, but seats are usually available right up to the last moment for lesser matches.

TENNIS   The Czech Open is played each August at the **Štvanice Island Stadium,** located near the Vltava metro station. Tickets can be purchased usually at the gate and cost 60 to 100 Kč ($2.22 to $3.70).

7

Strolling Around Prague

by John Mastrini

Except for the busy main streets, where you may have to dodge traffic, Prague is an ideal city for walking. Actually, walking is really the only way to explore Prague. Most of the oldest areas of the town are walking zones, with motor traffic restricted.

Wear very comfortable, preferably flat, shoes. The crevasses between the bricks in the street have been known to eat stiletto heels.

Below are recommended routes to take, but getting lost among these twisting narrow streets is not so bad. Let the turns take you where they may, as they will usually lead you to something wonderful.

WALKING TOUR 1
Charles Bridge & Malá Strana (Lesser Town)

Start: The Old Town Bridge Tower (Staroměstská mostecká věž)
Finish: Lesser Town Square (Malostranské náměstí)
Time: Allow about three to four hours.
Best times: Early morning or around sunset, when crowds are thinner and the shadows are most mysterious.
Worst time: Mid-afternoon, when the bridge is packed.

Dating from the 14th century, Charles Bridge is the city's most celebrated structure. As the primary link between Staré Město and the castle, it has always figured prominently in the city's commercial and military history. For most of its 600 years, the 1700-foot-long bridge span has been a pedestrian promenade, just as it is today.

The first sculpture, depicting St. John of Nepomuk, was placed on the bridge in 1683. It was such a hit that the church commissioned another 21 statues, which were created between 1698 and 1713. Since then the number has increased to 30. The location of the Charles Bridge statues, the most looked at sculptures in Prague, is shown on the accompanying map.

As you stand in the shadow of the massive tower on the Old Town side of the bridge, first turn to your right, where you'll find an 1848 statue in tribute to Charles IV, the man who commissioned the bridge's construction between Prague's oldest quarters. From here begin to walk toward the bridge entrance straight ahead, but first look up at:

Walking Tour—Charles Bridge & Malá Strana

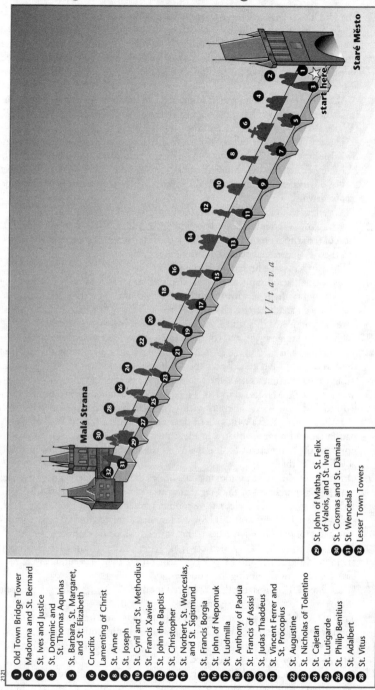

1. Old Town Bridge Tower
2. Madonna and St. Bernard
3. St. Ives and Justice
4. St. Dominic and St. Thomas Aquinas
5. St. Barbara, St. Margaret, and St. Elizabeth
6. Crucifix
7. Lamenting of Christ
8. St. Anne
9. St. Joseph
10. St. Cyril and St. Methodius
11. St. Francis Xavier
12. St. John the Baptist
13. St. Christopher
14. St. Norbert, St. Wenceslas, and St. Sigismund
15. St. Francis Borgia
16. St. John of Nepomuk
17. St. Ludmilla
18. St. Anthony of Padua
19. St. Francis of Assisi
20. St. Judas Thaddeus
21. St. Vincent Ferrer and St. Procopius
22. St. Augustine
23. St. Nicholas of Tolentino
24. St. Cajetan
25. St. Lutigarde
26. St. Philip Benitius
27. St. Adalbert
28. St. Vitus
29. St. John of Matha, St. Felix of Valois, and St. Ivan
30. St. Cosmas and St. Damian
31. St. Wenceslas
32. Lesser Town Towers

2121

137

1. **The Old Town Bridge Tower** (Staroměstská mostecká věž), a richly ornate 1357 design made for Charles IV by Peter Parler, the architect who drafted the Gothic plans for St. Vitus Cathedral. The original east side of the tower remains pristine, with intricate coats of arms of the Bohemian King and Holy Roman Empire. Shields also depict each of the territories under the auspices of the Bohemian crown at that time.

Above the eastside arch, seated to the right of the standing statue of St. Vitus, is Charles himself, while on the left is a statue of his ill-fated son, Wenceslas IV (Václav IV), who lost the crown of the Empire.

The tower's western side was severely damaged in a battle against invading Swedish armies in 1357. During the Thirty Years War, the heads of 12 anti-Habsburg Protestants were hung for public viewing from iron baskets on the tower.

The observation platform inside the tower has been recently reopened for more scenic viewing.

As you pass through the archway, the first statue on the right is of:

2. **The Madonna**, attending to a kneeling **St. Bernard**, flanked by cherubs. Like most of the statues on the bridge, this is a copy; the originals were removed to protect them from weather-related deterioration.

Directly across the bridge is a statue of:

3. **St. Ives,** the patron saint of lawyers, depicted promising to help a person who petitioned him. **Justice,** with a sword on his right, is also portrayed. If you see his outstretched hand holding a glass of beer, you will know that Prague's law students have just completed their finals.

Cross the bridge again, and continue to do so after you view each statue.

4. **St. Dominic** and **St. Thomas Aquinas** (1708) are shown receiving a rosary from the hands of the Madonna. Below the Madonna is a cloud-enshrouded globe and a dog with a torch in its jaws, the symbol of the Dominican order.

5. **St. Barbara**, **St. Margaret**, and **St. Elizabeth** were sculpted by two brothers who worked under the watchful eye of their father, Jan Brokoff, who signed the work as a whole. Franz Kafka writes about the finely sculpted hands of St. Barbara, the patron saint of miners, situated in the center of the monument. To art experts, however, the sculpture of St. Elizabeth (on the left) is the most artistically valuable figure in this group.

6. Originally produced for positioning on a bridge in Dresden, Germany, this bronze **crucifix** was purchased by the Prague magistrate and placed on Charles Bridge in 1657. The statue's gilded Hebrew inscription translates as "holy, holy, holy, God," and is believed to have been paid for with money extorted from an unknown Jew who had mocked a wooden crucifix that formerly stood on this site.

7. The **Lamenting of Christ** depicts Jesus lying in the Virgin Mary's lap with St. John in the center and Mary Magdalene on the right. Executions were regularly held on this site during the Middle Ages.

8. Created in 1707, this statue depicts Mary's mother, **St. Anne,** holding baby Jesus, while the child embraces the globe.

9. This statue of **St. Joseph** with Jesus dates from 1854, and was put here to replace another that was destroyed by gunfire six years earlier by anti-Habsburg rioters.

10. These two saints, **Cyril** and **Methodius,** are the Catholic missionaries credited with introducing Christianity to the Slavs.

11. **St. Francis Xavier,** the 18th-century co-founder of the Jesuit order, is depicted here carrying four pagan princes on his shoulders—an Indian, a Tartar, a Chinese, and a Moor—symbolizing the cultures targeted for proselytizing. This statue is widely regarded as one of the most outstanding Czech baroque sculptural works.

12. **St. John the Baptist** is depicted here with a cross and a shell, symbols of baptism.

13. **St. Christopher,** the patron saint of raftsmen, is shown here carrying baby Jesus on his shoulder. The statue stands on the site of the original bridge watch-house, which collapsed into the river along with several soldiers during the Great Flood of 1784.

14. The three saints portrayed here—**St. Norbert, St. Wenceslas,** and **St. Sigismund**—are patron saints of Bohemian provinces.

15. **St. Francis Borgia,** a Jesuit general, is depicted with two angels holding a painting of the Madonna. Look on the lower part of the sculpture's pedestal, where you'll see the three symbols of the life of the saint: a helmet, a ducal crown, and a cardinal's hat.

16. **St. John of Nepomuk** was thrown to his death in chains from this bridge, and this, the oldest sculpture on the span, was placed here to commemorate him. The bronze figure, sporting a gold-leaf halo, was completed in 1683. The bridge's sole bronze statue, St. John of Nepomuk is now green with age and worn from years of being touched for good luck.

17. This statue shows **St. Ludmilla** pointing to a Bible from which St. Wenceslas is learning to read. In her left hand, St. Ludmilla is holding the veil with which she was suffocated. The statue's relief depicts the murder of St. Wenceslas.

18. Dedicated in 1707, this statue of **St. Anthony of Padua** depicts the preacher with baby Jesus and a lily. The relief is designed around a motif inspired by the saint's life.

19. **St. Francis of Assisi,** the first Roman Catholic martyr to be incorporated into Bohemian liturgy, is shown here contemplatively, between two angels.

20. **St. Judas Thaddeus** is depicted here holding both the Gospel and the club with which he was fatally beaten.

21. **St. Vincent Ferrer** is depicted here boasting to **St. Procopius** of his many conversions: 8,000 Muslims and 25,000 Jews.

22. A 1974 copy of a 1708 work, the sculpture depicts church teacher **St. Augustine** holding a burning heart and walking on "heretical" books. On the pedestal there is the emblem of the Augustinians.

23. **St. Nicholas of Tolentino** is depicted handing out bread to the poor. Behind him is a house with a Madonna, a mangle, and a lantern on its top-floor balcony. Walk quickly. Legend holds that if the lantern goes out while you are passing by the statue, you will die within the year.

24. **St. Cajetan** stands here in front of a column of cherubs, while holding a sacred heart. Behind the statue of the saint, a triangle symbolizes the Holy Trinity.

25. Created in 1710 by 26-year-old M. B. Braun, this statue of **St. Lutigarde** is widely considered to be the most valuable sculpture on Charles Bridge. The sculpture portrays St. Lutigarde, a blind nun, seeing Christ on the cross, in order that she might kiss his wounds.

26. The only marble statue on the bridge is of **St. Philip Benitius,** the general of the Servite order. He is portrayed with a cross, a twig, and a book. The papal tiara is lying at his feet as a symbol of the saint's refusal of the papal see in 1268.

27. **St. Adalbert** (1709), the first bishop of Bohemia, is blessing the Czech lands after returning from Rome.

28. **St. Vitus,** attired as a Roman legionary, is standing on a rock between the lions to which he fell victim.

29. **St. John of Matha, St. Felix of Valois,** and **St. Ivan** were commissioned for the Trinitarian order, which rescued Christians from Turkish captivity. In the huge rock is a prison, in front of which there is a dog and a Turk with a cat-o'-nine-tails guarding the imprisoned Christians. With money for their freedom, St. John is standing on the summit of the rock. St. Ivan is seated on the left, and St. Felix is loosening the bonds of the prisoners.

30. This statue portrays **St. Cosmas** and **St. Damian,** the patron saints of physicians, who were known for dispensing free medical services to the poor. The saints, which were commissioned by the medical faculty in Prague, are attired in gowns and are holding containers of medicines.

31. This statue of **St. Wenceslas** was sculpted in 1858, on a commission by Prague's Klar Institute for the Blind.

Follow the brick path toward the archway at the end of the bridge but on your way look up at the:

32. **Lesser Town Towers** (Malostranské mostecké věže). The small tower on the left was built in the 12th century before Charles ever began construction on the bridge. It was originally a plain romanesque structure, but Renaissance accents were added in the 16th century. The taller tower was built in the 15th century and completed the connection of the archway from the smaller tower built in the early 1400s.

After passing through the tower, you now enter Mostecká street.

☕ **TAKE A BREAK**   At the first entrance on the left side of the street, at no. 3, is **Café U Mostecké věže,** a cool place to stop right after you get off the bridge. Hot and cold drinks with sweets and ice cream are served in the downstairs restaurant or in the backyard garden decked with rattan furniture. It's open 10am to 10pm daily, but the manager says that if the mood is right, he'll stay open until midnight.

Head back up Mostecká and take the first left to Lázeňská street. At no. 6, on the left, you'll find a graying former hotel and bath house:

33. **V lázních** (In the baths). This was a well-known stop for visitors to Prague in the 1800s. The pub and baths, which once hosted Chateaubriand, were operated on this spot from the earliest periods of Lesser Town.

Just up Lázeňská at no. 11, on the right side, is the hotel:

34. **U zlatého jednorožce** (At the Golden Unicorn). This was another favored stop for honored guests, including Beethoven. A plaque on the front bears the composer's face. The hotel was originally built into the heavy walls that once ringed Malá Strana. On the other side, at the curve of Lázeňská, you come to:

35. **The Church of Our Lady Below the Chain** (Kostel Panny Marie pod řetězem). One of the best romanesque designs built in Prague, this church was built for the Order of the Maltese Knights, replacing the oldest church in Malá Strana after it burned down in 1420. Remnants of the original can be seen inside the church courtyard.

Exiting the church back onto the street, go straight on Lázeňská about 20 steps to:

36. **Maltézské náměstí** (Maltese Square). On the first corner of the square to the left is one of the city's most posh French restaurants packed into a former pub, **U Malířů** or "At the Painters" (See the listing in Chapter 5).

☕ **TAKE A BREAK**   At no. 10 on the square is the **Restaurace Vinárna U vladaře** (at the Governor's), open 11am to 1am daily. You can sit out front on the terrace and order coffee and dessert, or a meal from a full Czech-style menu. Inside a more formal restaurant, on the left, serves Czech traditional food in a more

Walking Tour—Charles Bridge & Malá Strana

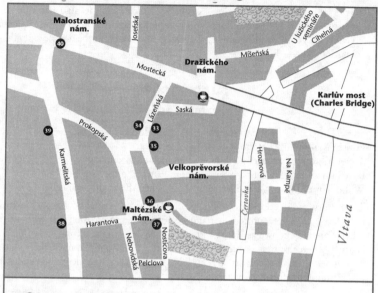

🔟 33 V lázních (In the Baths)

🔟 34 U zlatého jednorožce (At the Golden Unicorn)

🔟 35 The Church of Our Lady Below the Chain

🔟 36 Maltézské náměstí (Maltese Square)

🔟 37 Nostitz Palace

🔟 38 The Church of Our Lady Victorious

🔟 39 Vrtba Palace

🔟 40 Church of St. Nicholas (Kostel Sv. Mikuláše)

elegant setting. On the right, you'll find what used to be a horse stable, **The Konírna,** with vaulted ceilings, cozy heavy wooden furniture, and a full menu of hearty food.

Across Maltezské náměstí you will see a large palace, the:

37. **Nostitz Palace,** a grand 17th-century early baroque design attributed to Francesco Caratti. A Prague family who strongly supported the arts used to own it. The palace has been a center of attention for centuries. Its ornate halls once housed a famed private art collection. Chamber concerts can still be heard through its windows.

Crossing back though the little Maltese Square you will enter Harantova street on the way to Karmelitská. After crossing the street and walking another 150 yards, you will come to:

38. **The Church of Our Lady Victorious** (Kostel Panny Marie Vítězné). This is the home of the famed wax statue of the baby Jesus, the Bambini di Praga, seen as an important religious relic in Italian and Latino countries.

From the church entrance, continue up Karmelitská street to see a complex of houses on the left side at no. 25 collectively known as:

39. **Vrtba Palace.** In 1631, Sezima of Brtba seized a pair of Renaissance houses and then connected them in the middle to create his palace among the vineyards at the bottom of Petřín Hill. The lush terraced gardens surrounding this complex add to its beauty.

Proceed up Karmelitská where you will come finally to Malostranské náměstí. To the left around the uphill side of the square is the imposing dome of:

40. The Church of St. Nicholas (Kostel Sv. Mikuláše), the high-baroque gem designed by K.I. Dienzenhofer and completed by his son in 1752. Relax at your walk's end by sitting among the statues and taking in the marble and gilded interior.

WALKING TOUR 2
Prague Castle

Start: The castle's front entrance, located at Hradčanské náměstí.
Finish: Malostranská metro station.
Time: Allow approximately 2¹/₂ hours, not including rest stops.
Best Times: Tuesday through Sunday from 9am to 5pm.
Worst Times: Mondays and late afternoons, when the castle is closed.

The history and development of Prague Castle and the city of Prague are inextricably related; they grew up together and it's impossible to envision one without the other. Popularly known as "Hrad," Prague Castle dates to the second half of the 9th century when the first Czech royal family, the Přemyslids, moved their seat of government here. Settlements on both sides of the Vltava River developed under the protection of the fortified castle.

Begin your tour from the castle's front entrance, located at Hradčanské náměstí. Walk through the imposing rococo gateway, topped by the colossal Battling Giants statue, to the:

1. First Castle Courtyard (První hradní nádvoří). An informal changing of the guard ceremony occurs here daily on the hour. It only involves five guards, who do little more than some impressive heel-clicking and rifle-twirling. The guards wore rather drab khaki outfits until 1989, when Václav Havel asked his friend, costume designer Theodor Pištěk (who costumed the actors in the film *Amadeus*) to redress them. The guards' smart new blue outfits are reminiscent of those worn during the First Republic.

   Directly ahead is the:

2. Matthias Gateway (Matyásova brána). Built in 1614 as a freestanding gate, it was later incorporated into the castle itself. The gateway bears the coats of arms of the various lands ruled by Emperor Matthias. Once through the gateway, the stairway on the right leads to the state rooms of the president of the republic. They're not open to the public.

   The gateway leads into the Second Castle Courtyard (Druhé hradní nádvoří). Directly ahead, on the eastern side of the square, is the:

3. Holy Rood Chapel (kaple sv. Kríze), constructed in 1763, and redesigned in 1856. The chapel is noted for its high-altar sculpture and ceiling frescoes.

   On the western side of the courtyard is the opulent:

4. Spanish Hall (Španělsk; sál), which was originally constructed in the late 16th century. During restorations in 1993, officials at the castle discovered a series of 18th-century *trompe l'oeil* murals that lay hidden behind the mirrors that lined the hall's walls. The paintings were made to look as if the viewer were looking out of a window at detailed city scenery.

   Adjoining Spanish Hall is:

5. Rudolf Gallery, an official reception hall that once housed the art collections of Rudolf II. The last remodeling of this space—rococo-style stucco decorations—occurred in 1868.

Walking Tour—Prague Castle

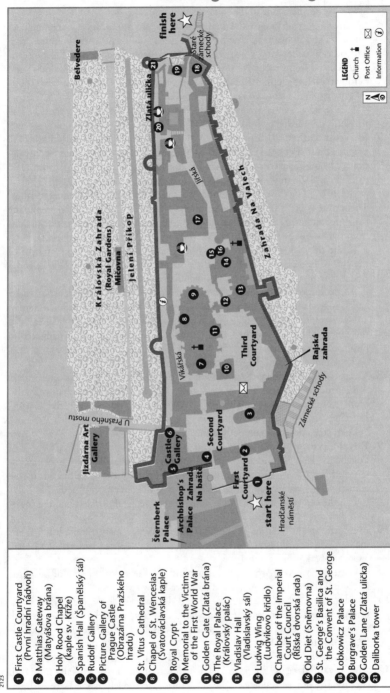

1 First Castle Courtyard (První hradní nádvoří)
2 Matthias Gateway (Matyášova brána)
3 Holy Rood Chapel (kaple sv. Kříže)
4 Spanish Hall (Španělský sál)
5 Rudolf Gallery
6 Picture Gallery of Prague Castle (Obrazárna Pražského hradu)
7 St. Vitus Cathedral
8 Chapel of St. Wenceslas (Svatováclavská kaple)
9 Royal Crypt
10 Memorial to the Victims of the First World War
11 Golden Gate (Zlatá brána)
12 The Royal Palace (Královský palác)
13 Vladislav Hall (Vladislavský sál)
14 Ludwig Wing (Ludvíkovo křídlo)
15 Chamber of the Imperial Court Council (Říšská dvorská rada)
16 Old Diet (Sněmovna)
17 St. George's Basilica and the Convent of St. George
18 Lobkowicz Palace
19 Burgrave's Palace
20 Golden Lane (Zlatá ulička)
21 Daliborka tower

2123

143

On the northern side of the square is the:

6. **Picture Gallery of Prague Castle** (Obrazárna Pražského hradu). Containing both European and Bohemian masterpieces, the gallery holds few works from the original Imperial collection, which was virtually destroyed during the Thirty Years' War. Of the works that have survived from the days of Emperors Rudolf II and Ferdinand III, the most celebrated is Hans von Aachen's *Portrait of a Girl* (1605–10), depicting the artist's daughter.

A covered passageway leads to the Third Castle Courtyard (Třetí hradní nádvoří), dominated by hulking:

7. **St. Vitus Cathedral.** Begun in 1334, under the watchful eye of Charles IV, Prague's most celebrated Gothic cathedral has undergone three serious reconstructions. The tower galleries date from 1562, the baroque onion roof was constructed in 1770, and the entire western part of the cathedral was begun in 1873.

Before entering the cathedral, notice the facade, decorated with statues of saints. The bronze doors are embellished with reliefs; those on the central door depict the construction history of the cathedral. The door on the left features representations from the lives of St. Adalbert (on the right) and St. Wenceslas (on the left).

Inside the cathedral's busy main body are several chapels, coats of arms of the city of Prague, a memorial to Bohemian casualties of World War I, and a Renaissance-era organ loft (with an organ dating from 1757).

According to legend, St. Vitus died in Rome but was then transported by angels to a small town in southern Italy. Since his remains were brought here in 1355, Vitus, the patron saint of Prague, has remained the most popular saint in the country. Nearly all of the Czech Republic's churches have altars dedicated to him.

The most celebrated chapel, located on your right, is the:

8. **Chapel of St. Wenceslas** (Svatováclavská kaple), built atop the saint's actual tomb. A multitude of polished semiprecious stones decorate the chapel's altar and walls. Stoneless spaces are filled in with 14th-century mural paintings depicting Christ's sufferings and the life of St. Wenceslas.

Below the church's main body is the:

9. **Royal Crypt,** which contains the sarcophagi of Kings Václav IV, George of Poděbrady, Rudolf II, and Charles IV and his four wives. The tomb was reconstructed early this century and the remains of the royalty were placed in new encasements. Charles' four wives are together in the same sarcophagus.

Exit the cathedral from the same door you entered and turn left into the courtyard past the:

10. **Memorial to the Victims of the First World War,** a marble monolith measuring over 35 feet tall. Just behind the memorial is an equestrian statue of St. George, a Gothic work produced in 1373.

Continue walking around the courtyard. In the southern wall of St. Vitus Cathedral you will see a ceremonial entrance known as the:

11. **Golden Gate** (Zlatá brána). The closed doorway is decorated with a 14th-century mosaic known as the *Last Judgment,* depicting a kneeling Charles IV with his wife Elizabeth of Pomerania. The doorway's 1950s-era decorative grille is designed with zodiac figures.

An archway in the Third Castle Courtyard connects St. Vitus Cathedral with:

12. **The Royal Palace** (Královský palác), which was, until the second half of the 16th century, the official residence of royalty. Inside, to the left, is the **Green Chamber (Zelená světnice),** where Charles IV presided over minor court sessions. A fresco of the court of Solomon is painted on the ceiling.

The Rolling Stones Light It Up

Are the lights flickering in Vladislav Hall? If they are, someone might be playing with the remote control that operates the chandeliers and spotlights. And that someone could be President Václav Havel.

He can control the lighting, thanks to the Rolling Stones. In summer 1995, the Stones played to a crowd of more than 100,000 people in their second concert in Prague since the Velvet Revolution. After they finished, the Stones gave Havel, who happens to be a big fan, a bright gift. They paid $32,000 for an overhaul of the lighting in four of the castle's ornate grand halls, including the Spanish Hall and Vladislav Hall. The Stones sent their director and lighting designer from their record-breaking "Voodoo Lounge" tour to manage the project.

The result? Well, it's a somewhat more dignified spectacle than the raucous light show that was part of the mythical "Voodooland" on stage. Mick Jagger, Keith Richards, Charlie Watts, and Ron Wood presented Havel with a remote control to operate the chandeliers and spotlights, now strategically casting their beams on baroque statues and tapestries.

The adjacent room is:

13. **Vladislav Hall** (Vladislavský sál), a ceremonial room that has held coronation banquets, political assemblies, and knightly tournaments. Since 1934, elections of the president of the republic have taken place here. In addition to the historical and political associations, it's worth visiting this hall to view the exquisite 40-foot-tall twisted-rib vaulted ceiling.

At the end of Vladislav Hall is a door giving access to the:

14. **Ludwig Wing** (Ludvíkovo křídlo), built in 1509. Here you'll find two rooms of the Chancellery of Bohemia (Česká kancelář), once the administrative body of the Land of the Crown of Bohemia. When the king was absent, Bohemia's nobles summoned assemblies here. On May 23, 1618, two hated governors, together with their secretary, were thrown out of the eastern window of the rear room. This act, known as the Second Defenestration, marked the beginning of the Thirty Years' War (see "I Don't Do Windows: The Czech Tradition of Defenestration" box in Chapter 6).

A spiral staircase leads to the:

15. **Chamber of the Imperial Court Council** (Říšská dvorská rada), which met here during the reign of Rudolf II. From this room the 27 rebellious squires and burghers who fomented the defenestration were sentenced to death and consequently executed on June 21, 1621, in Staroměstské náměstí. All the portraits on the walls of the chamber are of Habsburgs. The eastern part of Vladislav Hall opens onto a terrace from which there is a lovely view of the castle gardens and the city of Prague.

Also located in the palace is the:

16. **Old Diet** (Sněmovna), where the Provincial Court once assembled. It's interesting to notice the arrangement of the Diet's 19th-century furniture, which is all centered around the royal throne. To the sovereign's right is the chair of the archbishop; behind him are benches for the prelates. Along the walls are seats for the federal officials; opposite the throne is a bench for the representatives of the Estates. By the window on the right is a gallery for the representatives of the royal towns. Portraits of the Habsburgs adorn the walls.

Stairs lead down to St. George's Square (náměstí U Svatého Jiří), a courtyard at the eastern end of St. Vitus Cathedral. The square is dominated by:

17. **St. George's Basilica and the Convent of St. George,** founded in 973 by Benedictine Nuns. In 1967, the convent's premises were acquired by the National Gallery, which now uses the buildings to warehouse and display their collections of Bohemian art from Gothic to baroque periods. See Chapter 6 for complete information.

Leave the basilica and continue walking through the castle compound on Jiřská Street, the exit at the southeastern corner of St. George's Square. About 200 feet ahead on your right is the entrance to the:

18. **Lobkowicz Palace,** a 16th-century manor that now houses the Permanent History Exhibition of the National Museum, a gallery devoted exclusively to the history of the Czech lands.

Opposite Lobkowicz Palace is:

19. **Burgrave's Palace,** now the House of Czech Children, a 16th-century building used for cultural programs and exhibitions aimed toward children.

Walk up the steps located to the left of Burgrave's Palace to:

20. **Golden Lane** (Zlatá ulička), a picturesque street of 16th-century houses built into the castle fortifications. Once home to castle sharpshooters, this charm-filled lane now contains small shops, galleries, and refreshment bars. Franz Kafka supposedly lived or worked at no. 22 for a brief time in 1917.

☕ **TAKE A BREAK** At the top of Golden Lane is the **Espresso Bonal,** serving pizza, sandwiches, and cakes, plus coffee, wine, and spirits. There are several cozy tables in the back, but the place is often packed in the high season. Open daily 9:30am to 6pm.

Back toward St. George's Basilica is the **Café Gallery,** serving the same type of menu. It's a less cozy setting but has better prices. Open 9am to 6pm.

If the weather is nice, you can try the **Cafeteria** in the courtyard between St. Vitus and St. George's. At this terrace garden with white tables under trees, you can enjoy light fare and hot Czech food. Open 10am to 6pm.

Turn right on Golden Lane and walk to the end, where stands:

21. **Daliborka Tower,** part of the castle's late Gothic fortifications dating from 1496. The tower's name comes from Squire Dalibor of Kozojedy, who in 1498 became the first unlucky soul to be imprisoned here.

Turn right at Daliborka Tower, then left, and go through the passageway and down the old castle steps (Staré zámecké schody) to the Malostranská station on line A of Prague's metro.

WALKING TOUR 3
Staré Město (Old Town)

Start: Municipal House (Obecní dům), náměstí Republiky.
Finish: Havelský trh (Havel's Market)
Time: Allow approximately one hour, not including any breaks or museum visits.
Best Times: Sunday through Thursday from 9am to 5pm and Friday from 9am to 2pm, when the museums are open.
Worst Times: Friday afternoons and Mondays, when the museums are closed, and after 6pm, when the market is closed.

Walking Tour—Staré Město (Old Town)

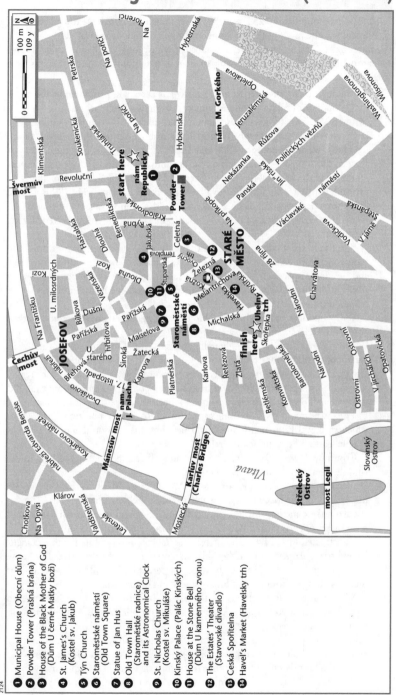

1. Municipal House (Obecní dům)
2. Powder Tower (Prašná brána)
3. House of the Black Mother of God (Dům U černé Matky boží)
4. St. James's Church (Kostel sv. Jakub)
5. Týn Church
6. Staroměstské náměstí (Old Town Square)
7. Statue of Jan Hus
8. Old Town Hall (Staroměstské radnice) and its Astronomical Clock
9. St. Nicholas Church (Kostel sv. Mikuláše)
10. Kinský Palace (Palác Kinských)
11. House at the Stone Bell (Dům U kamenného zvonu)
12. The Estates' Theater (Stavovské divadlo)
13. Česká Spořitelna
14. Havel's Market (Havelsky trh)

147

Staré Město, founded in 1234, was the first of Prague's original five towns. Its establishment was the result of Prague's growing importance along central European trade routes. Staré Město's ancient streets, most of which meander haphazardly around Staroměstské náměstí, are lined with many stately buildings, churches, shops, and theaters.

Although this tour is far from exhaustive, it takes you past some of the area's most important buildings and monuments. Begin your tour at the:

1. **Municipal House** (Obecní dům), náměstí Republiky 5, at the metro station. One of Prague's most photographed cultural and historical monuments, the Municipal House was built between 1906 and 1911 with money raised by the citizens of Prague. From the beginning, this ornate art nouveau building has held an important place in the national psyche as a Czech cultural symbol—the document granting independence to Czechoslovakia was signed here in 1918. The Prague Symphony performs in Smetana Hall, the building's most important room. It is named for Bedřich Smetana (1824–84), a popular composer and fervent Czech nationalist.

But times are changing. Today, the Municipal House also contains Café Nouveau and Brasserie Mozart, two large restaurants owned by North Americans and Swedes, respectively. The building's subterranean beer halls are also foreign run. Unfortunately, the building is closed for a massive restoration and won't reopen until mid-1996 or early 1997.

With your back to the Municipal House, turn right on náměstí Republiky, then right onto Celetná, under the arch of the:

2. **Powder Tower** (Prašná brána, literally Powder Gate). Once part of Staré Město's system of fortifications, the Powder Tower was built in 1475 as one of the walled city's major gateways. After New Town was incorporated into the City of Prague, the walls that separated Old Town from the new section became obsolete. So did the Powder Tower, which was recommissioned as a gunpowder storehouse.

The tower marks the beginning of the **Royal Route,** the traditional path along which medieval Bohemian monarchs paraded on their way to being crowned in Prague Castle's St. Vitus Cathedral.

Continue down Celetná (named after *calt,* a bread that was baked here in the Middle Ages) to the corner of Ovocný to the:

3. **House of the Black Mother of God** (Dům U černé Matky boží), Celetná 19, important not for its contents, but for its cubist architectural style. Cubism, an angular artistic movement, was confined to painting and sculpture in France and most of Europe. As an architectural style, cubism is exclusive to Bohemia.

Constructed in 1921, this house features tall columns, sculpted with rectangular and triangular shapes on either side of an ornate wrought-iron gate. The house is named for the Virgin Mary emblem on the corner of the building's second floor that was salvaged from the last building to stand on this site.

With your back to the House of the Black Mother of God, cross Celetná into Templová, walk two short blocks, and turn left onto Jakubská. At the corner, on your right, you'll see:

4. **St. James's Church** (Kostel sv. Jakub), Prague's second longest, containing 21 altars. Enter the church and look up, just inside the church's front door. The withered object dangling from above is the shriveled arm of a 16th-century thief.

Return to Celetná and continue walking about 300 feet. On the right side, below the towering spires is:

5. **Týn Church,** one of the largest and prettiest of Prague's many churches. Famous for its twin spires that loom over nearby Staroměstské náměstí, the church was closely connected to the 14th-century Hussite movement of religious reform. After the reformers were crushed by the Roman Catholics, many of the church's Hussite symbols were removed, including statues, insignia, and the tower bells that were once known by Hussite nicknames. Note the tomb of the Danish astronomer Tycho de Brahe (d. 1601), located close to the church's high altar.

Exit the church and continue a few more steps along Celetná, which opens up into:

6. **Staroměstské náměstí** (Old Town Square). Surrounded by baroque buildings, and packed with colorful craftsmen, cafes, and entertainers, Staroměstské náměstí looks just like an old European square is supposed to look. At any hour, it feels more like an amusement park than a city.

This square has not been just a center of tourist interest, but a focal point of Czech history and politics. It has always been a meeting place for commerce since the city's inception—from the simple bartering of the Middle Ages to the discussions of privatization deals by businesspeople in the 1990s.

The square has also seen its share of political protest and punishment. Protestant Hussites rioted here in the 1400s. In the 1620s, the Catholic Habsburg rulers beheaded 27 Protestants in the Square, and hung some of the heads in baskets above Charles Bridge. A small white cross has been imbedded in the square near the Old Town Hall for each of the beheaded.

This century, the square has witnessed a whirlwind of political change. In 1918, the Czechs celebrated the founding of the new sovereign Republic of Czechoslovakia here. But then in 1939, the Nazis celebrated their occupation of the country here. The Soviets then celebrated kicking the Nazis out of Prague here in 1945, only to have their tanks roll through again in their own invasion in 1968. In 1948, Klement Gottwald led a celebration in honor of the Communist's seizing the government. No wonder the Czechs chose nearby Wenceslas Square to celebrate the return of their government in 1989.

To begin your trip around the square, walk straight toward the massive black stone monument in the center of the square. Here you will find the statue of:

7. **Jan Hus,** a fiery 15th-century preacher who challenged the Roman Catholic hierarchy and was burned at the stake for it. The statue's pedestal has been used as a soap box by many a populist politician trying to gain points by associating himself with the ill-fated Protestant (see Chapter 1, "A Look at the Past").

The struggle between the supporters of Hus, known as Hussites, set the stage for the religious wars that tore Bohemia apart in the 15th and 17th centuries. The Hussite church still lives today in the Protestant following known as The Czech Brethren, but since Communism, its numbers have dwindled. Membership in the Catholic church has also declined.

From here, turn over your left shoulder and walk toward the clock tower. Try to time your walk so you can pass the:

8. **Old Town Hall** (Staroměstká radnice) and its **Astronomical Clock** at the top of the hour. While it's an understated show, each hour a mechanical parade of saints and sinners perform for the crowd watching below (see Chapter 6 for details). If you have time and your knees are up to it, try making the steep and narrow walk up to the top of the tower for a picturesque view of Old Town's red roofs.

Walking past the right side of the clock tower toward the northwest corner of the square you will find:

9. St. Nicholas Church (Kostel sv. Mikuláše), a 1735 design of Prague's baroque master architect K.I. Dienzenhofer. The three-towered edifice is not as beautiful nor as ornate inside as his design of the St. Nicholas Church in Lesser Town, but the crystal fixtures are worth a look. From the front of the church, walk behind the back of the Hus monument through the square to the broad palace with the reddish roof and balcony in front. This is:

10. Kinský Palace (Palác Kinských). From the rococo balcony jutting from this stuccoed facade, Communist leader Klement Gottwald declared the proletariat takeover of the Czechoslovak government in February 1945. The building was designed by the Italian architect Lurago for Count Goltz. It was later taken over by the Habsburg Prince Rudolf Kinský in 1768. It now houses a fine modern art collection in the Czech National Museum complex of palaces. (See "Museums and Galleries" in Chapter 6.) Next to this is the:

11. House at the Stone Bell (Dům U kamenného zvonu). The medieval gothic tower was built in the 14th century for the father of Charles IV, John of Luxembourg.

From here head back toward the Old Town Hall, but then about midway to the tower, turn left toward the square's south end and begin walking down Železná street. Continue down this car-restricted walking zone about 1,000 feet where, on the left, you'll see the pale green:

12. Estates' Theater (Stavovské divadlo). Mozart premiered his opera *Don Giovanni* in this late-18th-century grand hall. More recently, director Miloš Forman filmed the story of the composer's life here.

Make sure to walk down Rytířská street in front of the theater to get a full view of this beautifully restored building, which just reopened after the revolution.

From the front of the theater, walk about 10 steps back up Železná and take the first left on Havelská.

☕ **TAKE A BREAK**   At Havelská 27, you can stop for a tasty pizza, lasagna, gelato, or thick Italian espresso at the **Kogo Pizzeria and Café.** There are tightly packed tables inside, but if the weather is nice, sit outside in more comfortable seats in the archway.

Continue down Havelská. On the left you'll see:

13. Česká Spořitelna. The large neo-Renaissance building with statue inlays is, ironically, again the largest Czech savings bank after serving as the museum to the late Communist president Klement Gottwald. The building was completed in 1894 as a bank, but after the 1948 coup, was seized by the government and turned into a depository for Communist propaganda. After the 1989 revolution, the building was returned to the bank, which restored the intricate friezes and frescoes depicting its own propaganda from the days of early Czech capitalism. It's worth peeking inside.

Your next destination is the street market that overtakes the remainder of Havelská street. Simply continue on to:

14. Havel's Market (Havelský trh), the most popular central Prague market, a virtual outdoor mall of vegetables, fruits, drinks, soaps, toiletries, artwork, and leather goods. Prices here are generally lower than in most shops. Have fun browsing.

The nearest metro is Můstek, Line A or B.

WALKING TOUR 4
Josefov (The Jewish Quarter)

Start: The Lesser Square (Malé náměstí)
Finish: Dolce Vita cafe
Time: Allow approximately two hours, not including rest stops or museum visits.
Best Times: Sunday through Friday from 9am to 5pm, when the cemetery and sights are open.
Worst Time: Saturday, the holy day, when everything is closed.

Josefov, Prague's noted Jewish ghetto, is located entirely within Staré Město. It was once surrounded by a wall, before the wall was almost all destroyed to make way for 19th-century structures. Prague is considered one of Europe's great Jewish cities: Jews have been here since the end of the 10th century, and by 1708 more Jews lived here than anywhere else in Europe.

Today, the Prague Jewish community numbers less than 3,000 people. In 1992, the Jewish community elected Rabbi Karol Sidon as their new leader, and he has led a very public fight against anti-Semitism as reported incidents of attacks against Jews and Jewish property have increased. In addition, the government has recently tried to return property confiscated by the Nazis and then the Communists to Jewish citizens. However, many claims are still unresolved.

This tour may seem short, but the sights are gripping, so budget your time loosely. It starts at:

1. **Malé náměstí.** Literally the "lesser square," this small piazza adjacent to Staroměstské náměstí has as much history as its larger companion. Excavations have proven that Malé náměstí was a prime piece of real estate as far back as the 12th century. Archeologists have turned up bits of pottery, evidence of medieval pathways, and human bones that date from the late 1100s, when real estate developers committed the medieval equivalent of paving over a cemetery to build a shopping mall.

   From Malé náměstí, turn right, onto U radnice. One block ahead, in the courtyard across from the Magistrate building and tucked against St. Nicholas church, you will see the:

2. **Franz Kafka Exhibition,** a tribute to the famous writer whose themes at times reflect the life of a Jew in Prague. The small exhibit, on the very site of the building where Kafka was born, re-creates the history of his life and world through words, pictures, and a huge array of Franz Kafka paraphernalia. The photos and book collection are worth a stop. Unfortunately, it's not as interesting as it sounds; it's more of a souvenir shop than an in-depth look at the writer. Don't get too enthusiastic about the building itself either; only the gray doorway remains from Kafka's day. The exhibit is open Friday and Saturday from 10am to 6pm. Entrance for all is 10 Kčs (37¢).

   An unflattering cast-iron bust of Kafka, unveiled in 1965, sits just to the right of the exhibition entrance, at the corner of Maiselova and U radnice. Walk straight, onto:

3. **Maiselova Street,** one of the two main streets of the old, walled Jewish quarter, founded in 1254. As elsewhere in Europe, Prague's Jews were forced into ghettos following a formal Roman Catholic decision that "the Jews" killed Jesus. By the 16th century, Prague's 10,000 isolated Jews comprised 10% of the city's population.

The ban on Jews living outside the ghetto was lifted in 1848. Eighty percent of the ghetto's Jews moved to other parts of the city, and living conditions on this street, and those that surround it, seriously deteriorated. The authorities responded by razing the entire neighborhood, including numerous old medieval houses and synagogues. The majority of the buildings here now date from the end of the 19th century; several on this street sport stunning art nouveau facades.

About halfway down the street on your right, you'll see the:

4. **Maisel Synagogue** (Maiselova Synagóga), a neo-Gothic style temple built on a plot of land donated by Markus Mordechi Maisel, a wealthy inhabitant of Prague's old Jewish town. Though it was later rebuilt, the original synagogue was destroyed by fire in 1689. During the Nazi occupation of Prague, the synagogue was used to store furniture seized from the homes of deported Jews. Today, the building holds no religious services; it's home to the Jewish Museum's collection of silver ceremonial objects, books, and Torah covers confiscated from Bohemian synagogues by the Nazis during World War II.

Continue walking down Maiselova Street and turn left onto Široká. Walk past the former entrance to the Old Jewish Cemetery (Starý židovský hřbitov), through which you can catch a first glimpse of its shadowy headstones, to:

5. **Pinkas Synagogue** (Pinkasova Synagóga), Prague's second-oldest Jewish house of worship. After World War II the walls of the Pinkas Synagogue were painted with the names of more than 77,000 Czech Jews who perished in Nazi concentration camps. The names were subsequently erased by Czechoslovakia's Communist government; officials claimed the memorial was suffering from "moisture due to flooding." Funds were raised to restore and maintain the painted commemoration.

Backtrack up Široká Street and turn left onto Maiselova Street. The pink rococo building on the right-hand side of the street at Maiselova 18 is the:

6. **Jewish Community Center,** an information and cultural center for locals and tourists. It once was the Jewish Town Hall. Activities and events of interest to Prague's Jewish community are posted here, and the staff provides visitors with information about Jewish cultural activities and tours. Also inside is one of Prague's only truly Kosher restaurants, which, unfortunately, is closed to the public.

On the wall of the Community Center that faces the Old New Synagogue you'll see a clock with a Hebrew-inscribed face. It turns left, counter to what is considered by most to be "clockwise."

Continue walking one block along Maiselova and turn left onto U Starého hřbitova to the:

7. **Old Jewish Cemetery,** Europe's oldest Jewish burial ground, with the oldest grave dated 1439. Because the local government of the time didn't allow Jews to bury their dead elsewhere, as many as 12 bodies were placed vertically, with each new tombstone placed in front of the last. Hence, the crowded little cemetery contains more than 20,000 graves.

Like other Jewish cemeteries around the world, many of the tombstones here have small rocks and stones on them—a tradition said to date from the days when Jews were wandering in the desert. Passersby, it is believed, would add rocks to grave sites so as not to lose the deceased to the shifting sands. Along with stones, visitors often also leave small notes of prayer on top of tombstones.

Buried here is Rabbi Löw, who made from the mud of the Vltava River the legendary Golem, a clay "monster" to protect Prague's Jews. Golem was a one-eyed or three-eyed monster, depending how you look at him. Legend has it that the Rabbi would keep Golem around to protect the residents from the danger of mean-spirited Catholics outside the walls of the Jewish ghetto.

Walking Tour—The Jewish Quarter

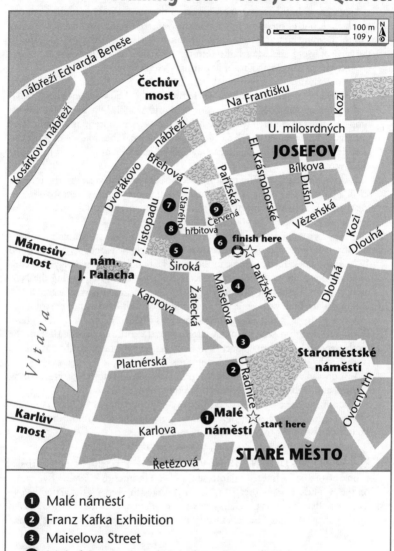

1. Malé náměstí
2. Franz Kafka Exhibition
3. Maiselova Street
4. Maisel Synagogue (Maiselova Synagóga)
5. Pinkas Synagogue (Pinkasova Synagóga)
6. Jewish Comunity Center
7. Old Jewish Cemetery
8. Ceremonial Hall
9. Old New Synagogue

Löw's grave, in the most remote corner of the cemetery opposite the Ceremonial Hall, is one of the most popular in the cemetery; you'll see that well-wishers
and the devout cram his tombstone with notes. Across the path from the rabbi is
the grave of Mordechai Maisel, the 16th-century mayor of Josefov whose name was
given to the nearby synagogue built during his term in office.

As you exit the cemetery you will pass the:

8. Ceremonial Hall. Inside the hall, where rites for the dead were once held, you'll
find a gripping reminder of the horrors of World War II. Displayed here are the
simple sketches of children who were held at the Terezín concentration camp west
of Prague. These drawings tell a shocking story of what the children experienced
as their parents and other relatives were packed up and sent to die, or just withered away.

Backtrack along U Starého hřbitova, cross Maiselova, and walk directly into the
small alley called Červená. You are now standing between two synagogues. On
the right is the High Synagogue (Vysoká synagóga), now an exhibition hall for the
Jewish State Museum. On your left is the:

9. Old New Synagogue. Originally called the New Synagogue to distinguish it from
an even older one that no longer exists, the Old New Synagogue, built around
1270, is the oldest Jewish temple in Europe. The building has been prayed in continuously for more than 700 years, except from 1941 to 1945, during the Nazi
occupation in World War II. The synagogue is also one of the largest Gothic buildings in Prague, built with vaulted ceilings and fitted with Renaissance-era columns.

Much of Josefov and Staré Město once was flooded regularly by the Vltava
River, until a 19th-century planning effort raised the entire area about 10 feet. The
Gothic-era Old New Synagogue, however, has preserved its original floor, which
is reached by going *down* a short set of stairs.

Visitors can attend services here. Men and women do still sit separately during
services, although that is not always rigorously enforced.

Continue to the end of the Červená alley and turn right onto Pařížská, or Paris
Street, Prague's most elegant thoroughfare, built around the turn of the century.
Follow Pařížská back to Staroměstské náměstí.

☕ **WINDING DOWN   Dolce Vita,** at Široká 15, a half-block off Pařížská,
is one of the city's finest Italian cafes. Its marble interior contains five tables
on the ground floor; another 10 tables on a verandah overlook the action below.
The cafe offers traditional Italian sandwiches, gelato, and espresso drinks, served
by an Italian-speaking Czech waitstaff. Patrons are encouraged to linger as long
as they'd like.

Prague Shopping 8

by Dan Levine

In no sector of the economy has the change from Communism to capitalism been more apparent than on the shopping front. Private retailers have only been allowed to operate here since the end of 1989, but many top international retailers have already arrived. Since most locals are still not wealthy enough to create a dynamic shopping scene in Prague, conventional wisdom holds that major retailers are here not for short-term profit, but for long-term investment. While the city's shops are still not abundant enough to get a serious shopper's pulse racing, Prague's retail environment is quickly becoming more diversified. Because Prague's shopping scene still lags far behind western European capitals, this city offers plenty of wonderful bargains that are unmatched elsewhere. Craft and specialty shops abound, and good deals can often be found in street markets, art studios, and galleries. You can also buy lingerie at Palmers, scarves at Pavilon, jewelry at Royal Bijou, cosmetics at Lancôme, a snazzy purse at Belt, a coat at Aquascutum, and eyeglasses at Christian Dior. And you can now pay for it all with credit cards.

1 The Shopping Scene

SHOPPING AREAS Since Prague has no single great shopping street, you'll have to walk around to find what you're looking for. Pařížská, a major street radiating from Old Town Square, is the swankiest address in the city, and will almost certainly become this city's equivalent of New York's Fifth Avenue or Paris' Champs Elysée. Celetná, the street that connects Old Town Square with náměstí Republiky, is slightly more downscale, but is crammed with many more shops, most geared toward tourists. Shops that line the main route from Old Town Square to Charles Bridge are also great for browsing. For clothing, jewelry, garnets, and glass, stroll around Wenceslas Square and Na příkopě, the street connecting Wenceslas Square with náměstí Republiky.

Throughout Prague, you'll find artists and craftspeople selling their jewelry, prints, handcrafts, and other wares. They're concentrated on Charles Bridge and in Staroměstské náměstí (Old Town Square).

SPECIAL SHOPPING NOTES Alarmed by the growing trade in antiques that is carting off many of the country's cultural treasures, the Czech government now requires export permits for a large

---

Best Buys

Garnets are the official Czech national gem, and the ones that you can buy here are among the world's finest, as well as one of the country's top exports. Most garnets are mined near Teplice, about 39 miles northwest of Prague. There are at least five specific kinds of this reddish gem. Bohemian garnets are the Pyrope type, an amalgam of calcium and magnesium that's almost always deep red.

For garnets set in silver, expect to pay anywhere from 200 to 2,000 Kč ($7.40 to $74). For stones set in gold, be prepared to pay anywhere from 2,000 to 40,000 Kč ($74 to $1,480). Be warned that fake garnets are common, so purchase your stones from a reputable shop (listed below in "Garnets").

Fine **crystal** has been produced in the Bohemian countryside since the 14th century. In the 17th and 18th centuries, this crystal became the preferred glass of the world's ruling elite, and Bohemia blossomed with hundreds of small glass-producing communities. Bohemian factories are responsible for artistic advances in gilding, cutting, and coloring. To this day, quality remains high, and you can still purchase contemporary glass for prices that are much lower than in the West. Of the country's estimated 200 artists in glass, about a half-dozen have international reputations. In addition to hand-blown functional pieces, Prague's galleries contain plenty of unusual crystal sculpture. The Museum of Applied Arts often exhibits glass. See "Crystal & Glass" below, for a list of Prague's most prominent glass retailers.

Antiques, and antiquarian books and prints are widely available in Prague, sold by specialist *Antikvariáts*. These antique shops are located throughout the city, but you'll find many in Old Town and New Town. Although few books are in English, the occasional find makes browsing worthwhile. Several Antikvariáts are listed below.

---

range of objects, including glass and graphics over 50 years old, miniature art objects valued at more than 3,000 Kč ($110), and paintings valued at more than 30,000 Kč ($1,100). Most antique shops provide export permits; ask for one if necessary.

In supermarkets, customers are expected to bring their own bags. If you don't have one, ask for a *tašku;* it will cost a couple of crowns.

HOURS & TAXES Prague's centrally located shops rely on tourist business and keep fairly long hours. Most are open Monday through Friday from about 10am to 6pm, Saturday from 10am to 1pm, and sometimes much later. Many open on Sunday as well, though usually for a shorter time. Note that some small food shops that keep long hours charge up to 20% more for all their goods after 8pm or so.

Prices for goods in shops include the government's 22% value-added tax (VAT). While some European countries encourage tourists to part with their dollars by offering to refund the VAT, the Czech Republic offers no such program.

SHIPPING Many Czechs don't trust the post office when it comes to shipping valuable goods. If your package is larger than a bread box, contact **American Rainbow,** Nikoly Tesly 10, Prague 6 (☎ 02/311 92 39), an international shipping company that air freights goods worldwide. You can either bring your package to them, or they will pick them up at no additional charge.

DHL, náměstí Republiky (☎ 02/310 4111), is another reputable business shipping to the United States and the rest of the world. They charge 1,750 Kč ($65) for the first half-pound to Europe, and 2,250 Kč ($83) for the first half-pound to the United States.

2 Shopping A to Z

ANTIQUES

When you shop for antiques, note that the Czech government now requires export permits for a large range of objects, including glass and graphics more than 50 years old, miniature art objects valued at more than 3,000 Kč ($110), and paintings valued at more than 30,000 Kč ($1,100). Most antique shops provide export permits; ask for one if necessary.

Art Deco Galerie

Michalská 21, Prague 1. ☎ **02/26 13 67.** Metro: Můstek.

A light bright shop filled with colored perfume bottles and clothing from the 1920s and 1930s, this gallery is a fun place to see bygone fashions that still are the epitome of style. The best pieces are household items like art deco clocks, lamps, and even chandeliers. Open Monday to Friday, from 2 to 7pm.

Jiří Vandas

Pařížská 8, Prague 1. ☎ **02/231 32 85.** Metro: Staroměstská.

It's amazing how many different kinds of Czechoslovak and Czech coins, medals, and paper currency have been issued over the years. The shop's extensive holdings attest to the country's continuously changing politics and economics. Even if you're just browsing, ask to see the Order of the White Lion with Sword, First Class—the highest Czechoslovak state medal, awarded to heads of state. Only 12 have ever been made; theirs is priced at 390,000 Kč ($14,430).

Lukas Antiques

Národní 21, Prague 1. ☎ **02/2421 3338.** Metro: Můstek.

The shop's proprietors boast 25-plus years of experience collaborating with the Czech Association of Antique Dealers. Their two-room gallery looks more like a nobleman's living room than a store. Goods range from paintings by masters of the Renaissance, baroque, and romantic ages to rare jewelry, old glass, weapons, and porcelain. Most items date from the 18th and 19th centuries. A Louis XIV desk sells for 380,000 Kč ($14,060), and Napoleon's personal pocket watch is available for 12,000,000 Kč ($444,000). Open Monday to Thursday from 10am to 1pm and from 2pm to 6pm, Friday from 2pm to 6pm, and Saturday from 10am to 1pm and 2 to 4pm.

Pražské Starožitnictví

Mikulandská 8, Prague 1. ☎ **02/29 41 70.** Metro: Národní třída or Můstek.

One of the most respected dealers in antique jewelry and porcelain, this excellent shop specializes in top-quality items that are as fine as they are expensive. A little porcelain angel costs 18,000 Kč ($666) and an Empire Berlin cup with a painted miniature sells for 69,000 Kč ($2,553). A large selection of watches, rings, brooches, and bracelets sell for as much as 130,000 Kč ($4,810). Open Monday to Thursday from 9am to noon and 2 to 6pm, Friday from 2 to 6pm.

Retro Bazar

Senovážná 2, Prague 1. No phone. Metro: náměstí Republiky.

A small shop close to náměstí Republiky, Retro Bazar offers a well-chosen selection of paintings, jewelry, statues, and porcelain, including dishes with the famous blue-onion pattern. Old typewriters, bottles, and other antique utilitarian items are also sold. Open Monday to Friday from 10am to noon and 12:30pm to 5pm.

Vladimír Kůrka Antiques
Panská 1, Prague 1. ☎ **02/26 14 25.** Metro: Můstek.

Located in a former monastery, this fine antique shop specializes in colorful Moravian folk costumes, embroidered tablecloths, and antique textiles. Open Monday to Friday from 10am to 6pm, Saturday from 10am to 2pm.

Zlatá Koruna
Pařížská 8, Prague 1. ☎ **02/231 32 85.** Metro: Staroměstská.

Collectors of old coins and badges will have a field day in this cluttered shop that seems to sell everything from 2,500-year-old coins to Communist-era pins embossed with the image of Klement Gottwald. Open Monday to Friday from 10am to 7pm, Saturday from 10am to 6pm.

ART GALLERIES

A+G Flora
In the Lucerna Passage, Štěpánská 61, Prague 1. ☎ **02/2421 1514.** Metro: Můstek.

In addition to painting and wall hangings, A+G Flora specializes in original wearable art, including clothes, accessories, and jewelry. Well-priced pants and jackets are available off-the-shelf, or made-to-order. Open Monday to Friday from 9am to 5pm, Saturday from 9am to 1pm.

Central Europe Gallery and Publishing House
Husova 10 & 21, Prague 1. ☎ **02/2422 2068.** Metro: Národní třída or Můstek.

This excellent gallery promotes contemporary Czech and other Eastern European artists exclusively. Catalogs with English-language descriptions and color reproductions usually accompany well-planned exhibitions. Open Tuesday through Sunday from 10am to noon and 1 to 6pm.

Dílo
Galerie Platýz, Národní 37, Prague 1. No phone. Metro: Národní třída or Můstek.

A member of Czech Fund of Creative Arts, Dílo displays and sells works by contemporary Czech painters, sculptors, and graphic artists on a rotating basis. The gallery is located in one of Prague's oldest apartment houses. Open Monday to Friday from 10am to 6pm, Saturday from 9am to noon.

Galerie Peithner-Lichenfels
Michalská 12, Prague 1. ☎ **02/2422 7680.** Metro: Můstek.

Here you'll find contemporary Czech and Austrian pieces by major artists, including Anderle, Brauer, Čapek, Crepaz, Hoffmeister, Jíra, Kubin, Valter, and Wagner. Open daily from 10am to 7pm.

BOOKS

Bohemian Ventures
Nám. Jana Palacha 2, Prague 1. ☎ **02/231 95 16.** Metro: Staroměstská.

Located inside the lobby of Charles University's philosophy building, this small shop sells English-language books with an Eastern European slant. There's a good guide selection, and translations of the most famous Czech bards. Open Monday to Friday from 9am to 5pm.

The Globe

Janovského 14, Prague 7. ☎ **02/6671 2610.** Metro: Vltavská.

Opened in 1993, Prague's first English-language bookstore/coffeehouse stocks more than 10,000 titles. This is the best place in the city for used paperback literature and nonfiction. The smart looking barroom serves good espresso drinks, sandwiches, salads and desserts, and stocks a full bar. Open daily from 10am to midnight.

U Knihomola

Mánesova 79, Prague 2. ☎ **02/627 77 70.** Metro: Jiřího z Poděbrad.

The largest foreign-language bookshop in Prague is also the best. English, French, German and Czech titles are all available; their art and literature titles are particularly strong. Open Monday to Saturday from 9am to 1am, Sunday from 11am to 6pm.

COSMETICS & FRAGRANCES

If you need to stock up or refill your cosmetic or fragrance supplies, you can shop for name brands at signature stores. However, prices are more or less comparable with the West. The **Elizabeth Arden** store, at Rybná 2 (☎ 02/232 54 71) is open Monday to Friday 10am to 7pm, Saturday 10am to 2pm. Take the metro to Náměstí Republiky. The **Estée Lauder** store, at Železná 18 (☎ 02/2423 2023) is open Monday to Friday 10am to 7pm, Saturday 9am to 2pm. Take the metro to Můstek. Also by Můstek is the **Perfumerie Lancôme,** at Jungmannovo nám. 20 (☎ 02/2421 7189), open Monday to Friday 9am to 7pm, Saturday 9am to 1pm. **Nina Ricci** is at Pařížská 4 (☎ **02/2481 0905),** open Monday to Friday 10am to 6pm, Saturday 10am to 2pm. At **Christian Dior,** Pařížská 7 (☎ **02/232 7382** or **02/232 6229),** you can buy perfumes, cosmetics, and accessories by both Christian Dior and Christian Lacroix. Open Monday to Friday from 10am to 6pm, Saturday from 9am to noon.

CRYSTAL & GLASS

Cristallino

Celetná 12, Prague 1. ☎ **02/26 12 65.** Metro: náměstí Republiky.

Here you'll find a good selection of stemware and vases in traditional designs. The shop's central location belies its excellent prices. Open Monday to Sunday from 9am to 8pm.

Furalo

Václavské nám. 60. ☎ **02/2422 0177.** Metro: Můstek or Muzeum.

With one of the city's most eclectic collections of glass, Furalo seems to be a veritable survey of Czech glassmaking, including gilded, colored, classical and modern items from useful tableware to pointless dust-collectors. Open Monday to Sunday from 9am to 6pm.

Moser

Na příkopě 12, Prague 1. ☎ **02/2421 1293.** Metro: Můstek.

The Jewish Moser family opened Prague's most prestigious crystal shop in 1857, and continued to produce their own works until the Nazis forced them to flee during World War II. Prague's Communist government nationalized the firm, but managed to retain the company's exacting standards. Even if you're not buying, the inimitable old-world shop is definitely worth a browse. Open Monday to Friday from 9am to 7pm, Saturday from 9am to 6pm.

A second shop is located at Malé nám. 11, Prague 1.

Preciosa

Václavské nám. 20, Prague 1. ☎ **02/2421 9291.** Metro: Můstek or Muzeum.

Although it's squarely aimed at tourists, this centrally located glass shop sells a wide variety of interesting gift items including cut crystal figurines, glass jewelry, souvenir prisms, and even crystal chandeliers.

DEPARTMENT STORES

In early 1996, the British retailer Tesco bought what was the first U.S. owned K-Mart in Prague, located at Národní třída 26.

Bílá Labut'

Na Poříčí 23, Prague 1. ☎ **02/2481 1364.** Metro: náměstí Republiky.

The pinnacle of elegance in 1937, Bílá Labut' now lags behind its department store competitors when it comes to current fashion and store design. The store's large supermarket offers a large range of imported foods. Open Monday to Friday from 8am to 7pm, Saturday from 8am to 6pm.

Kotva

Náměstí Republiky 8, Prague 1. ☎ **02/2480 1111.** Metro: náměstí Republiky.

Prague's largest department store features four floors of goods, and a large supermarket in the basement. From bicycles to furnishings, linens, and stationery, everything you'd expect from a major department store can be found here, and then some. Open weekdays 8am to 8pm, weekends 8am to 6pm.

Krone

Václavské náměstí 21, Prague 1. ☎ **02/2423 0477.** Metro: Můstek.

The largest store on Wenceslas Square, Krone sells a wide variety of goods, including cosmetics, stationery, fashions, auto accessories, linens, electronics, and lighting. The store's best feature is the basement supermarket, which has a good selection at favorable prices. Open Monday to Friday 8am to 7pm, Saturday 8am to 6pm, Sunday 10am to 6pm.

Pavilon

Vinohradská 50, Prague 2. ☎ **02/257 633.** Metro: náměstí Míru.

At this four-tiered consumer paradise, fashion junkies can browse in stores from Lacoste to Diesel, have their hair done, buy some Timberlands, and bring home a hunk of bacon from the Belgian Butcher. The only thing this brand new galleria lacks is 14-year-old mall rats. Open Monday to Saturday from 9:30am to 9pm, Sunday from noon to 6pm.

FASHIONS

Adam

Na příkopě 18, Prague 1. ☎ **02/26 15 23.** Metro: Můstek.

Men and women can buy Italian suits and other conservative business clothes here. Shirts, tops, and underwear are also sold. Tailor-made suits cost about 10,000 Kč ($370), plus fabric. Open Monday to Friday from 10am to 6pm, Saturday from 9am to 1pm.

Ano Ano

Panská 9, Prague 1. ☎ **02/2421 0492.** Metro: Můstek.

Name-brand German-made men's and women's fashions are sold in elegant surroundings; designs are by Hugo Boss, Betty Barclay, Sabu, Esquire, and others. Open Monday to Friday from 10am to 6pm, Saturday from 10am to 1pm.

Art & Fashion Gallery
Maiselova 21, Prague 1. ☎ **231 95 29.** Metro: Staroměstská.

Handmade Czech designs emphasize uniquely decorated wearable silk items from colorful scarves to heavy kimono jackets. Open daily from 10am to 7pm.

Green Lion Shark Shop
Melantrichova 8, Prague 1. ☎ **02/2423 3067.** Metro: Můstek.

Green Lion has cornered the market in nightclub wear. Colorful shirts and micro-miniskirts, high-heeled sneakers and rubber-soled lace-up boots are all the clothes you'll need for a night on the town. Three small floors of fashion include everything Lycra, lurex, satin, polyester, and acrylic.

Nostalgie
Jilská 22, Prague 1. ☎ **02/266 256.** Metro: Můstek.

A showplace for leading Czech designers, this second-floor shop attracts wealthy trendies who are in the market for unique crushed velvet dresses, bulky jackets, and unusual ties. Open daily from 10am to 7pm.

Point
Londýnská 81, Prague 2. ☎ **02/25 74 43.** Metro: náměstí Míru.

It may not be politically correct in the United States, but in Prague there's no better way to fight winter than wrapping yourself in fur. Choose from mink, raccoon, and several types of fox. Leather coats, belts, bags, and gloves are also sold. Open Monday to Friday from 10am to 6pm.

Viva Diva
Karoliny Světlé 12, Prague 1. ☎ **02/2422 0591.** Metro: Národní třída.

This very sexy, trendy women's clothing shop specializes in designs by Kookaï. The bright large store on an Old Town backstreet is one of the prettiest shops in Prague. Open Monday to Friday from 10:30am to 7pm, Saturday from 11am to 5pm.

GARNETS

Amor
Václavské nám. 40, Prague 1. ☎ **02/26 75 89.** Metro: Můstek.

The modern pendants and brooches sold here are some of the most unusual designs in the city. All items are set in 14- or 18-karat gold, and range from 400 to about 5,000 Kč ($14.80 to $185). Open Monday to Saturday from 9am to 8pm.

Český Granát
Celetná 4, Prague 1. ☎ **02/26 74 10.** Metro: Můstek.

This centrally located shop has an excellent reputation for good-quality jewelry at reasonable prices. Among the mostly rather traditional and conservative earrings, pendants, and bracelets you can find some interesting and unusual designs. Most pieces are set in 24-karat gold or gold-plated silver. Open daily from 10am to 7pm.

Granát Turnov
Dlouhá 30, Prague 1. ☎ **02/231 5612.** Metro: náměstí Republiky.

Granát Turnov, the monopoly that controls the Czech Republic's garnet industry, is *the* place to visit if you're serious about shopping for garnets. Expect to pay between 650 and 1,000 Kč ($24 and $37) for a mid-priced ring or bracelet that incorporates one of these ruby-colored jewels. Open Monday to Friday 10am to 5pm, Saturday 10am to 1pm.

GIFTS/SOUVENIRS

Dřevěné Hračky
Karlova 26, Prague 1. No phone. Metro: Můstek.

This large shop specializes in unpainted, handmade wooden toys, including small jigsaw-cut pigs on wheels, and toddler-size rocking horses. Walk to the back of the shop for other handcrafted items, including ceramic mugs and candleholders. Open daily from 10am to 8:30pm.

Exclusive
Vodičkova 28, Prague 1. ☎ 2416 2586. Metro: Můstek or Muzeum.

Bohemian glass, porcelain, jewelry, and other specialty items can be packed and shipped directly from this store. Open Monday to Friday 9am to 6pm, Saturday 9am to 4pm.

Fotoantique
Pařížská 12, Prague 1. No phone. Metro: Staromětská.

Original photographs by the most famous Czech photographers are sold alongside old cameras, ferrotypes, and magazines and catalogs from the beginnings of photography. Open Tuesday to Friday from 10am to 6pm, Saturday 9am to 2pm.

Karlovarský Porcelán
Pařížská 2, Prague 1. ☎ 2481 1023. Metro: Staromětská.

Some of the best pieces from the 21,000 tons of decorative and domestic porcelain that are produced annually in Karlovy Vary are on display in this high-quality shop. Open Monday to Friday from 9am to 7pm, Saturday and Sunday 10am to 7pm.

Music Praha Center
Revoluční 14, Prague 1. ☎ 231 16 93. Metro: náměstí Republiky.

What better gift for the budding musician than an instrument from the land where "every Czech is a musician"? Most every kind of eastern European-made stringed instrument is sold. Open Monday to Friday from 9am to 6pm.

Spartaklub
Milady Horákové 10, Prague 7. ☎ 38 16 67. Metro: Hradčanská.

This store sells shirts, shorts, and other clothing sporting the name "Sparta Praha," the city's most popular soccer team. Open Monday to Thursday from 9am to 6pm, Friday 9am to 5pm, Saturday from 8:30am to noon.

HATS

Model
Václavské nám. 8, Prague 1. ☎ 2423 8896. Metro: Můstek.

Prague's best haberdasher sells every type of topper from mink to straw, at prices that are distinctly un-Western. In addition to the hundreds of handcrafted hats on display, the haberdashery can specially produce a topper according to your specifications in just three days. Both men's and women's hats are sold. Open Monday to Friday from 9am to 7pm, Saturday from 10am to 2pm.

JEWELRY

Dušák (Watchmaker and Goldsmith)
Na příkopě 17, Prague 1. ☎ 2421 3025. Metro: Můstek.

Located on one of Prague's busiest shopping streets, Dušák is regarded as one of Prague's best watch shops. Noted brands, including Omega, Swatch, Raymond Weil,

Pierre Balmain, Seiko, and Rado, are sold, and watches of all kinds are repaired. Open Monday to Friday from 9am to 7pm, Saturday from 9am to 5pm, Sunday 1 to 6pm.

L. Mádr
Prokopská 3, Prague 1. No phone. Metro: Malostranská.

This front office for some of the country's top jewelry artists accepts commissions for work with silver and stones. Expect to pay around 2,000 Kč ($74) for a pendant. Open Monday to Friday from 10am to 6pm.

Royal Bijou
Na Příkopě 12, Prague 1. ☎ **2421 0552.** Metro: Můstek.

Costume jewelry gained popularity in the 19th century when the glass factories of northern Bohemia began to produce high-quality faux stones that rivalled the real things. This excellent shop is a true gem, offering a huge variety of baubles for 50 to 3,000 Kč ($1.85 to $111). Open Monday to Saturday from 9:30am to 7pm, Sunday 10am to 7pm.

LINGERIE

Celestýn
Dlouhá 20, Prague 1. ☎ **232 48 77.** Metro: náměstí Republiky.

Undergarments and swimwear from Triumph and Gossard are sold along with perfumes. Open Monday to Friday from 10am to 7pm.

Palmers
Královodvorská 7, Prague 1. ☎ **231 69 15.** Metro: náměstí Republiky.

House-brand panties, bras, corsets, and other pretty underthings are displayed on racks and in drawers that pull out of most every wall. Open Monday to Friday from 9am to 6pm, Saturday from 10am to 5pm.

MARKETS

After the fall of Communism private enterprise was strongly encouraged by the government, and it has clearly caught on again. You will see people selling tourist-related items throughout the busiest parts of central Prague, including Staroměstské náměstí, Charles Bridge, and along the streets that connect the two.

Havel's Market (Havelský trh)
Havelská ulice, Prague 1. Metro: Line A to Můstek.

Located on a short street that runs perpendicular to Melantrichova, the main route connecting Staroměstské náměstí with Václavské náměstí, this open-air market (named well before a Havel became president) features dozens of private vendors selling seasonal homegrown fruits and vegetables. Other goods, including detergent, flowers, and cheese, are also for sale.

Designed primarily for locals, prices here are exceedingly low by western European standards. The market is a great place to pick up picnic supplies. However, there seem to be more tourists than housewives, and fruit and flower vendors are slowly being edged out by souvenir and trinket sellers. Open Monday to Friday from 8am to 6pm, Saturday from 8am to 1pm.

MUSIC

Crazy Music Shop Mikaček
Října 8, Prague 1. ☎ **2421 8911.** Metro: Národní třída or Můstek.

For a taste of Czech rock and pop, visit this hip shop, which also sells the latest Western releases. Open daily 10am to 7pm.

Popron

Jungmannova 30, Prague 1. ☎ **2421 1982.** Metro: Národní třída or Můstek.

Satisfying most musical tastes, Popron offers everything from classical to contemporary, on formats ranging from vinyl to compact disc. Open Monday to Saturday from 9:30am to 7pm, Sunday 10am to 6pm.

Supraphon

Jungmannova 20, Prague 1. ☎ **26 33 83.** Metro: Národní třída or Můstek.

This store specializes in classical music, offering local and international pressings on CD, tape, and vinyl. You can listen before you buy using the store's two turnables and CD players. Classical music CDs can sometimes be a very good deal, but not always. Prices range from 100 to 550 Kč ($3.70 to $20). There is a small selection of children's music, some contemporary pop. Open Monday to Saturday from 10am to 6pm.

PHOTOGRAPHY

Jan Pazdera

Vodičkova 28, pasáž ABC, Prague 1. ☎ **2421 6197.** Metro: Můstek or Muzeum.

If you need to get your camera fixed or are looking for cheap darkroom equipment, come here. The bulk of the store's selection is secondhand cameras, ranging from clunkers big enough to stick your head in the back to the pocket sized Rollei 35mm. This is one of the only places to buy old telescopes, microscopes, light meters, enlargers and more, all at prices unheard of in western Europe. Open Monday to Friday from 10am to 6pm, Saturday 10am to 1pm.

PUPPETS

Obchod loutkami

Nerudova 47, Prague 1. ☎ **53 00 65.** Metro: Malostranská.

This busy shop offers what is probably the widest selection of puppets, old and new, for sale anywhere in Prague. Many kinds of puppets are available, including hand, glove, rod, and marionettes. There aren't any ventriloquist dummies, however. Obchod loutkami isn't cheap, but their creations are expertly made and beautifully sculpted. Hundreds of characters from trolls to barmen are available. Open daily from 10am to 7pm.

Obchod U Šaška

Jilská 7, Prague 1. No phone. Metro: Můstek.

This small, cave-like store is one of the most original puppet shops in the city. High-quality, imaginatively designed clowns, ghouls, witches and other marionettes range in price from 500 Kč ($18.50) for a small Good Soldier Švejk to 12,000 Kč ($440) for a giant evil-looking devil. Open Monday to Friday from 9:30am to 9pm, Saturday and Sunday from 10:30am to 9:30pm.

SHOES

Bat'a

Václavské nám. 6, Prague 1. ☎ **2421 8133.** Metro: Můstek.

One of the most successful Czech retailers, Bat'a is known worldwide for quality footwear. The company left Czechoslovakia before the Nazis rolled in, and returned after the 1989 revolution. This six-story flagship shop on Wenceslas Square stocks the full line of Baťa goods, including travel bags, leather accessories, and sports outfits, and has recently given over a half-floor to clothing from The Gap. Open Monday to Friday from 8:30am to 7pm, Saturday from 10am to 6pm, Sunday from 11am to 5pm.

SPORTING GOODS

Arms Shop
Národní 38, Prague 1. ☎ **2421 2519.** Metro: Národní třída or Můstek.

Eastern European sporting and hunting weapons are sold here, along with some unique shooting accessories. Open Monday to Friday from 8am to 6pm, Saturday from 9am to noon.

Kastner Ohler
Václavské náměstí 66, Prague 1. ☎ **2422 5432.** Metro: Můstek or Muzeum.

From track suits to skis and in-line skates, this large sporting emporium is stocked with a wide variety of sporting essentials. Open Monday to Friday from 10am to 7pm, Saturday from 10am to 2pm.

WINES & BEER

Budvar and Becherovka are sold in shops all over Prague, but the cheapest places to buy these popular drinks are food markets like **Obchod Čerstvých Uzenin,** Václavské nám. 36 (no phone). Expect to pay about 250 Kč ($9.25) for a medium-size bottle of Becherovka, and 120 Kč ($4.40) for a six-pack of Budvar.

Dionýsos
Botičská 10, Prague 2. ☎ **29 53 42.** Metro: Karlovo náměstí.

So you want to bring home a vintage bottle of Moravian wine, or just educate yourself about these little-known labels? The friendly and knowledgeable staff at Dionýsos specialize in top-grade wines and love to talk about them (in English). Open Monday to Friday from 10am to 6pm.

9

Prague After Dark

by Dan Levine

Prague's nightlife has changed completely since the 1989 Velvet Revolution, and the results are decidedly mixed.

If you want to sample the great traditions of Czech classical music, you may be disappointed, or you might get lucky. Funding for the arts has been severely cut by the budget-obsessed government, and producers have frequently skimped around the edges of the once grand operas. Still, seeing *Don Giovanni* in the original Estates' Theater (Stavovské divadlo) where Mozart first premiered it, or actually seeing any production in one of the city's grand halls, is usually worth the price of admission. Ticket prices, while low by Western standards, have become prohibitively expensive for the average Czech, and foreigners will often be the majority at most of the major productions. Yet you'll find the exact reverse in the rock and jazz scene. The previous regime regarded rock and jazz as subversive and few venues existed. In the last five years, dozens of rock and jazz clubs have opened, and world-class bands are finally playing in Prague on their European tours. The bar, pub, and club scenes have also blossomed.

It is said that "every Czech is a musician," and from the numerous concerts and theater performances that are scheduled in Prague at any given time, this certainly seems to be true. The city bustles with so many activities that you might have a hard time choosing which performance to attend, especially during the summer.

Turn to the two English-language periodicals, the *Prague Post* and *Velvet*, for listings on cultural events and nightlife around the city. Both are available at most newsstands in Old Town and Mála Strana.

TICKETS   Very few of Prague's cultural events ever sell out very far in advance. If something important is scheduled, and you want to buy tickets before arriving, contact the Czech travel bureau **Čedok,** in the United States at 10 E. 40th St, New York, NY 10016 (☎ **212/689-9720**); in Britain, at 49 Southwark St., London SE1 1RU (☎ **0171/378-6009**).

Once in Prague, you can purchase tickets either at theater box offices, or from any one of the dozens of ticket agencies located throughout the city center. The largest ticket agencies handle most of the entertainment offerings and usually include a service charge.

You should ask how much this is before buying, as sometimes rates are hiked substantially. Large, centrally located ticket agencies include **Prague Tourist Center,** Rytířská 12, Prague 1 (☎ **02/2421 2209**), open daily from 9am to 7pm; **Bohemia Ticket International**, Na příkopě 16, Prague 1 (☎ **02/2421 5031**); and **Čedok**, Na příkopě 18, Prague 1 (☎ **02/2481 1870**). You can buy event tickets in person at these computerized outlets.

Ticketpro, Rytířská 31, Prague 1 (☎ **02/2481 4020**), Prague's computerized ticket service, sells seats by phone to most events around town. You can purchase tickets using your credit card (Visa, MasterCard, Diners Club, or American Express).

1 The Performing Arts

Citizens of Prague have a historical love for serious music. In the 19th century, operas were received with enthusiasm, and Prague was a much-loved stop on the symphony tour. Both Mozart and Vivaldi had close ties with Prague, and Beethoven, Chopin, Paganini, and many other composers also visited the city.

Today, even though government support for the arts is declining, there's still plenty of culture in the capital to absorb.

OPERA

Although Prague has a strong operatic tradition, no world-class opera is currently being staged here. But good stagings are regularly scheduled in three major venues. The **National Opera,** performing in the National Theater, is the country's best-loved company. Although not a particularly adventurous company, the well-regarded National Opera sometimes attracts internationally acclaimed soloists. Seasons tend to concentrate on Czech works, although foreign-composed operas are also scheduled. The National Theater (Národní divadlo) is at Národní 2, Prague 1 (Metro: Národní třída).

The **State Opera Company** (Státní opera), performing in the State Opera House, owes its existence to an acrimonious 1992 split with the National Opera. Just slightly more flamboyant than its rival, the State Opera stages grand productions of popular, time-honored works like *Rigoletto* and *Aïda* almost exclusively. The State Opera House is located at Wilsonova 4, Prague 2 (Metro: Muzeum).

The **Estates' Theater** is the most beautiful of Prague's concert halls. Although the theater has no resident company, it regularly stages operas by Mozart. Productions run the gamut from traditional to outlandish, and are rarely better than the surroundings. See "Landmark Theaters" below for details.

Even if you're not really fond of opera, buying a seat at any of the above theaters is a relatively cheap gamble. Prices range from about 100 to 500 Kč ($3.70 to $18.50), and are often available up to curtain time.

CLASSICAL MUSIC

This small capital supports three full orchestras, yet all three have experienced financial woes, leading to more conservative programming. Because they desperately need to attract audiences, the orchestras perform (almost too many) popular time-tested works and classical repertoire standards. There are far too few programs of contemporary masters such as Stravinsky, Bartók, and Shostakovich.

Of the city's three orchestras, the **Czech Philharmonic** is the only one that claims an international reputation, although it is not considered to be one of the world's first-rate orchestras. At this writing, the orchestra is without a conductor; musical director and chief conductor Gerd Albrecht resigned in January 1996. Despite acute monetary problems, the Philharmonic had improved under the demanding baton of German-born Albrecht, appointed after a tumultuous three postrevolution seasons as the first non-Czech conductor. Although many critics delighted in saying that Albrecht tightened the ensemble playing and imposed disciplined precision, the conductor had his detractors as well, including high government officials and orchestra members. In a hail of accusations and counter-accusations of Czech and German nationalism (mostly sparked by the press in both countries), Albrecht resigned, claiming he had lost his artistic freedom.

The **Prague Symphony Orchestra** envisions itself as a younger and fresher alternative to the Philharmonic. They take more risks and focus on more 20th-century music than the Philharmonic. Each season's programming usually includes a world premiere, often by a contemporary Czech composer. Unfortunately, the Prague Symphony Orchestra's primary concert hall, located in Obecní dům, is closed for restoration until 1997, so the ensemble is currently performing in the Rudolfinum, where they have no permanent rehearsal space. Adding insult to injury, the Orchestra's long-time musical director retired in 1995, leaving as his replacement three rotating guest conductors. While this orchestra has a reputation for a generally high standard of playing, concerts can be somewhat erratic. Problems with intonation and precise ensemble playing are not unheard of, especially with newer, less familiar pieces.

The **Prague Radio Symphony Orchestra,** the capital's third orchestra, spends the majority of its time recording, but does make regular concert appearances. A rival of the Prague Symphony Orchestra, the Radio Symphony compares favorably, playing programs of classical and contemporary works to generally positive reviews.

All three orchestras usually perform at the Rudolfinum, náměstí Jana Palacha, Prague 1; for information on all three, call 02/2489 3352. You can also get information at any of the ticket agencies listed above. Ticket prices range from 100 to 600 Kč ($3.70 to $22).

Although there is plenty of music year-round, the city's symphonies and orchestras all come to life during the ✪ **Prague Spring Festival,** a three-week-long series of classical music and dance performances that starts at the beginning of May (see "Prague Calendar of Events" in Chapter 2 for complete information). The country's top performers usually participate in the festival, which runs from May 12 to June 2. Tickets for concerts range from 250 to 2,000 Kč ($9.25 to $74), and are available in advance from Hellichova 18, Prague 1 (☎ 02/2451 0422).

DANCE

When it comes to high-quality dance, the **National Theater Ballet,** performing at the National Theater, is one of the only games in town. The troupe has seen most of its top talent go west since 1989, but they still put on a good show. Some critics have complained that Prague's top troupe has been performing virtually the same dances for many years and that they are in serious need of refocusing. The Ballet's choreographer Libor Vaculíc has responded with humorous and quirky stagings of off-the-wall ballets like *Some Like it Hot* and *Psycho.* But even these remain rigidly classical, as Vaculíc criticizes the modern French trend toward plotless abstract theater that, according to him, alienates the audience. The result is that the National Theater Ballet doesn't incorporate the innovations in dance that propel world-class troupes around the globe. But Vaculíc's works are popular. Audiences are buying tickets in droves, making this theater one of the most financially stable troupes in eastern Europe. Tickets are 70 to 550 Kč ($2.60 to $20); call 02/2491 2673 for

Classical Concerts Around Town

When strolling through Prague you will undoubtedly pick up or be handed lots of leaflets advertising concerts in the city's churches, museums, and other venues. These chamber recitals and choral concerts usually have programs featuring a classical and baroque repertoire, with an emphasis on pieces by Czech composers. Of course, quality varies, but tough competition means that any performance is usually very good. Tickets range in price from about 50 to 250 Kč ($1.85 to $9.25), and can be purchased at the churchs' entrances, or (sometimes) from a hotel concierge.

Because of its extravagant beauty, the **Chapel of Mirrors,** in the Klementinum, Karlova, Prague 1 (☎ **02/2422 9780**), is one of the best concert venues. Almost every evening a different classical concert highlights strings, winds, or the organ. The varied programs often rely on popular works by Handel, Bach, Beethoven, and, of course, Prague's beloved Mozart.

The Church of St. Nicholas (Kostel sv. Mikuláše), Staroměstské náměstí, Prague 1 (no phone), is one of the city's finest baroque gems, designed by K.I. Dienzenhofer. Chamber concerts and organ recitals are popular here, and the acoustics are terrific. There's lots to look at: rich stucco decoration, sculptures of saints, and the crown crystal chandelier.

House At The Stone Bell (Dům U kamenného zvonu), Staroměstské náměstí 13, Prague 1 (☎ **02/2481 0036**), located just across the square from St. Nicholas, regularly hosts chamber concerts and other small gigs, including operatic arias and duets that are often performed here by soloists of the National Theater and State Opera.

information. The National Theater (Národní divadlo) is at Národní 2, Prague 1 (Metro: Národní třída).

You can occasionally spot performances by the **Prague Chamber Ballet,** the National Theater Ballet's lesser competitor. Also, each year, it seems a new ballet troupe pops up somewhere, only to recede back into the shadows shortly thereafter. Modern dance is largely unknown in Prague, though traveling troupes sometimes pull into town. Check the *Prague Post* and the listings magazine *Velvet* for the latest events.

LANDMARK THEATERS & CONCERT HALLS

The Estates' Theater (Stavovské divadlo)
Ovocný trh 1, Prague 1. ☎ **02/2421 5001.** Metro: Line A or B to Můstek.

In a city full of spectacularly beautiful theaters, the massive, pale green Estates' ranks as one of the most awesome. Built in 1783, this is the only theater in the world that's still in its original condition from Mozart's day. The Estates' was home to the premiere of Mozart's *Don Giovanni*, which was conducted by the composer himself. The building, an example of the late baroque style, was reopened on the 200th anniversary of Mozart's death in 1991, after nearly nine years of reconstruction.

Simultaneous English translation, transmitted via headphone, is available for most plays staged here.

National Theater (Národní divadlo)
Národní 2, Prague 1. ☎ **02/2491 3437.** Metro: Národní třída.

Lavishly constructed in the late Renaissance style of northern Italy, the gold-crowned National Theater, which overlooks the Vltava River, is one of Prague's most recognizable landmarks. Completed in 1881, the theater was built to nurture the Czech National Revival—a grassroots movement to replace the dominant German culture with that of native Czechs. To finance construction, small collection boxes with signs "For the prosperity of a dignified National Theater" were installed in public places. Almost immediately upon completion, the building was wrecked by fire and rebuilt, opening in 1883 with the premiere of Bedřich Smetana's opera *Libuše*. The magnificent interior contains an allegorical sculpture about music, and busts of Czech theatrical personalities created by some of the country's best-known artists. Composer Bedřich Smetana conducted the theater's orchestra here until 1874, when deafness forced him to relinquish his post.

Rudolfinum
náměstí Jana Palacha, Prague 1. ☎ **02/2489 3111.** Metro: Staroměstská.

Named for Prince Rudolf, the beautifully restored Rudolfinum has been one of the city's premier concert venues since it opened in the 19th century. The Rudolfinum's aptly named Little Hall mostly presents chamber concerts, while the larger, more celebrated Dvořák Hall is home to the Czech Philharmonic Orchestra. Although acoustics here are not faultless, the grandeur and opulence of the hall makes a concert experience here worthwhile.

Smetana Hall (Smetanova síň)
In the Municipal House (Obecní dům), náměstí Republiky 5, Prague 1. No phone. Metro: náměstí Republiky.

Named for the popular composer and fervent Czech nationalist Bedřich Smetana (1824–84), Smetana Hall is located within one of the most distinctive art nouveau buildings in the world. Unfortunately, it's closed for restoration until 1997.

State Opera House (Státní opera)
Wilsonova 4, Prague 2. ☎ **02/2422 7693.** Metro: Muzeum.

Originally called the New German Theater, then the Smetana Theater, the State Opera was built in the 1880s for the purpose of staging Germanic music and drama. Based on a Viennese design, the Renaissance-style theater was painstakingly rebuilt after suffering serious damage during the bombing of Prague in 1945. Over the years, the auditorium has hosted many great names, including Richard Wagner, Richard Strauss, and Gustav Mahler, whose Seventh Symphony premiered here. In addition to being home to the State Opera, the house stages other music and dance events.

THEATER
Theater has a long tradition of importance in Czech life. Its enormous influence was reconfirmed during the revolutionary events of 1989, when theaters became the strategy rooms for the opposition.

Most of the city's theater offerings are in Czech, but a few English-language troupes usually sprout up each summer. The most stable of these is **Misery Loves Company** (☎ **02/25 13 11**), the city's only professional English-language company. Plays are usually scheduled in repertory, so up to four different productions can be scheduled in any single month. Check the listings in the local English-language publications for what's being staged.

There's an abundance of Czech language theater in the capital. Productions by local and translated authors are staged almost every night of the year. The most highly respected theaters include **Labyrinth Theater** (Divadlo Labyrint), Štefánikova 57, Prague 5 (☎ **02/545 027**); **Vinohrady Theater** (Divadlo na Vinohradech), náměstí Míru 7, Prague 2 (☎ **02/25 70 41**); and **Theater on the Balustrade** (Divadlo na zábradlí), Anenské nám. 5, Prague 1 (☎ **02/2422 1933**). Tickets, which usually cost between 50 and 300 Kč ($1.85 to $11.11), should be bought in advance.

BLACK LIGHT THEATER

Black light theater is popular in Prague, with performances on up to six stages at any one time. The concept is simple: Actors and props coated with luminescent paint cavort under black lights that only illuminate bright objects. The result? Pantomime shows that combine light comic entertainment, exceptional Houdini-esque visual tricks, and supposedly deep meaning. After the first five minutes, it all starts to get a bit old, but the largely European audiences are always enthusiastic in their response. If you want to be entertained this way, visit **Image Theatre,** Pařížská 4, Prague 1 (☎ **02/232 9191**), for my money, the best of the lot. The show at **Ta Fantastika,** Karlova 8, Prague 1 (☎ **02/2422 9078**) is also recommendable. Tickets for both range from 150 to 250 Kč ($5.55 to $9.25).

Laterna Magika, Národní třída 4, Prague 1 (☎ **02/2491 4129**), a performance art show based in the new wing of the National Theater, is a popular theater experience that came out of the 1958 Brussels Expo. The multimedia show, which combines live theater with film and dance, was once considered to be on the radical edge, but today is tame to the point of boring. At up to 400 Kč ($14.80) each, tickets are expensive and, amazingly, sometimes hard to come by.

PUPPET THEATER

Marionette theater is a centuries-old tradition in Bohemia. One of the most popular Czech cultural art forms, puppet theater is performed in most every town in the country, and many families have collections of traditional marionettes. Charles University is one of the only major schools in the world offering a degree in puppet-theater direction. Both the marionettes and their costumed operators are part of the action, which usually includes humor and song. Productions run the gamut from serious stagings of ancient Greek literary classics to whimsical interpretations of Czech folktales.

Built specifically for puppet productions, the **National Marionette Theater** (Národní divadlo marionet), Žatecká 1, Prague 1 (☎ **02/232 4565**), is the best of Prague's small handful of puppet theaters. For the last several years, the company has been performing Mozart's *Don Giovanni.* For adults, the best thing about this show is the soundtrack. The puppets provide comic relief from the opera, as if the producer assumed the experience of Mozart was too daunting for most travelers. It's recommendable only if you have kids under 14 in tow, whom you're trying to introduce to classical music. Arrive early as it's open seating, and the production is best viewed from the front rows. Performances are usually scheduled nightly. Tickets cost 250 to 400 Kč ($9.25 to $14.80), depending on the time of year. The box office is open Tuesday to Sunday from 10am to 8pm. Take the metro to Staroměstská.

2 The Club & Music Scene

Prague's club and music scene is limited but lively. Each summer, several top international names stop here on tours of Europe, but these events are relatively few and far between. Czech musicians and bands perform around town almost nightly, and quality ranges from abysmal to excellent. Rockers to look out for include Lucie Bíla, the first Czech to have a video aired on MTV Europe; Support Lesbians, a kind of postpunk quintet; and Kabát, a guitar-heavy quintet that is currently one of the Czech Republic's most popular bands.

ROCK & DANCE CLUBS

Alterna Komotovka

Seifertova 3, Prague 3. ☎ **02/627 8691.** Cover 10–60 Kč (32¢–$2.22). Metro: Hlavni nádraží.

This catacosmic club is the place to go when you want to dance to 70s classic rock and "underground" local bands. Local ex-pats only come here when they don't want to see anyone they know. Music starts at 10pm. Open Monday to Saturday from 6pm to 5am, Sunday from 6pm to midnight.

Arkadia

Slovanský dům, 3rd floor, Na Příkopě 22, Prague 1. No phone. Cover 30 Kč ($1.11). Metro: náměsti Republiky or Můstek.

Best in summer, when the giant outdoor terrace is open, this low-maintenance club hosts good angry rock bands alternating with DJ reggae nights. On weekends especially, this club has become the chief hangout for Prague's African community. Open daily from 8pm to 5am.

Belmondo Revival Club

Bubenská 1, Prague 7. ☎ **02/791 48 54.** Cover 40 Kč ($1.48). Metro: Vltavská.

The Doors and the Beatles are alive and well at this massive concert hall that hosts local and foreign acts on one of the largest stages in the city. The booze is cheap, and the crowd young. Concerts begin at 8pm.

Bunkr

Lodecká 2, Prague 1. ☎ **02/2481 0665.** Cover 20–70 Kč (74¢–$2.60). Metro: náměstí Republiky.

A long, deep basement that once was a 1950s Civil Guard bunker and nuclear shelter, club Bunkr opened in November 1991, followed a few months later by a like-named street-level cafe. Despised by its neighbors, the club features loud DJ nights and a plethora of live bands. Owner Richard Nemčok has honest credentials; he was jailed by the socialists and signed Charter 77. Packed with lots of young twentysomething European tourists, Bunkr is sometimes laughed at by knowledge-able locals. Still it's hard to argue with its success; Havel has been spotted here, and every time I'm here I have a lot of fun. Music usually starts at 9pm. Cafe open daily from 11am to 3am; club open daily from 6pm to 5am.

Club X

Národní třída 25, Prague 1. ☎ **02/2422 9095.** Cover free to 30 Kč ($1.11). Metro: Národní třída or Můstek.

This basement dance space, opened in fall 1995 by the literary Jama Review crew, is popular with ex-pat Americans and a smatering of Czechs. And although the club is sure to be filled with tourists during summer, the jury is still out whether this place has any legs. Divided into a dance area and a lounge, the roomy club has a great flow that keeps people mingling. But the sound system isn't great and the DJs are from the stone ages. Open Tuesday to Saturday from 10pm to 5am.

Lávka

Novotného lávka 1, Prague 1. ☎ **02/2421 4797.** Cover 30–70 Kčs ($1.11–$2.60). Metro: Staroměstská.

Straightforward dance hits attract one of Prague's best-looking young crowds. Because of its location, next to the Staré Město foot of Charles Bridge, Lávka also attracts a lot of less well-dressed tourists. The club is one of the nicest in town, offering a large bar, good dance floor, and fantastic outdoor seating during warmer months. Open 24 hours daily.

Malostranská Beseda
Malostranské náměstí 21, Prague 1. ☎ **02/53 90 24.** Cover 25–50 Kč (93¢–$1.85); free after 11pm. Metro: Malostranská.

This Beseda, or "meeting place," on Malá Strana's main square is located in a building that was once the area's town hall. Situated on the second floor of the arcaded side of the square, the club consists of little more than two smallish rooms; one holds the bar, the other a stage on which live bands perform most every night. Although this is not the warmest venue in the city, it's hard to beat when a good band is playing. Music usually begins at 8pm. Open daily from 7pm to 1am.

Music Park
Francouzská 4, Prague 2. ☎ **02/691 17 68.** Cover 50 Kč ($1.85). Metro: náměstí Míru.

This mall of a club has regressed to become the center of the Czech Eurotrash scene, complete with greasy guys and plenty of tightly dressed high-priced hookers. A great sound system belts out current pop hits, while colorful lights whirl overhead and under the transparent dance floor. Open Sunday to Thursday from 9pm to 5am, Friday and Saturday 9pm to 6am.

Radost F/X
Bělehradská 120, Prague 2. ☎ **02/25 12 10.** Cover 40–50 Kč ($1.48–$1.85). Metro: I. P. Pavlova.

Popular with a very mixed gay and model crowd, Radost is built in the American mold. A subterranean labyrinth of nooks and crannies has a pulsating techno-heavy dance floor with good sightlines for wallflowers. Radost is extremely stylish and self-consciously urban. It's a great place, but a boring shame that it's the only game in town.

Radost's vegetarian cafe of the same name, upstairs, is usually combined with a trip to the club, and listed separately in Chapter 5. Open daily from 9pm to 5am.

Rock Cafe
Národní 22, Prague 1. ☎ **02/2491 4416.** Cover 25–50 Kč (93¢–$1.85). Metro: Národní třída.

A tourist-heavy centrally located venue, Rock Cafe is a nightly headbanger's ball attracting some of the longest hair in town. Trippy Robert Crumb murals enliven the walls. Live bands perform several nights a week, after which disks spin until closing. Open Monday to Friday from 10am to 3am, Saturday to Sunday from noon to 3am.

Rock Klub Újezd
Újezd 18, Prague 1. ☎ **02/53 83 62.** Cover 30 Kč ($1.11). Tram: 12 or 22.

Under Communism, this multilevel house was called Borat, and was Prague's best "underground" club. After November 1989, this living room–size place went legit, becoming at once both more mainstream and less interesting. There's a snug dance floor and a snugger stage on which live bands perform three to four nights each week. The music usually kicks in about 9pm. Open Tuesday to Thursday and Sunday from 6pm to 2am, Friday to Saturday from 6pm to 6am.

Roxy
Dlouhá 33, Prague 1. ☎ **02/231 63 31.** Cover 30 Kč ($1.11), more for concerts. Metro: náměstí Republiky.

One of the city's most unusual venues, Roxy is a great subterranean theater with a wrap-around balcony overlooking a concrete dance floor. The club is ultra downscale, and extremely popular on Friday and Saturday nights. Persian rugs and lanterns soften the atmosphere, but don't improve the lousy acoustics. Acid jazz, funk, techno, ambient, and other dancable tunes attract an artsy crowd. Arrive after midnight. Open Tuesday to Saturday from 8pm to 6am.

Subway

Slovanský dům, 1st floor, Na Příkopě 22, Prague 1. No phone. Cover 40 Kč ($1.48). Metro: náměsti Republiky or Můstek.

Located in a building in which both the Gestapo and the Communists held political functions, this busy club features a jazz room in front, and a rock room in the back. Both spaces host live bands and DJs, though it's hard to see them through the smoke. There are two pool tables. Open daily from 9pm to 5am.

JAZZ

Once regarded as a subtle form of protest against the Communist government, jazz has strong roots in the Czech Republic. Despite the popularity of this American music, Prague's reputation as a lively jazz center seems better-known to foreigners than to those who live here. There are lots of excellent Czech jazz musicians, but few seem to inflame the passions of locals, who stay away from most clubs in droves. Relatively high prices are one reason why foreigners seem to make up the bulk of most audiences, but that doesn't explain why there's such high turnover even with budget-priced clubs. Few big-name musicians put Prague on their European tour schedules, but you can catch high-quality local bands almost every night of the week.

AghaRTA Jazz Centrum

Krakovská 5, Prague 1. ☎ 02/2421 2914. Cover 60–100 Kč ($2.22–$3.70). Metro: Muzeum.

Relatively high prices guarantee this small jazz room a predominantly foreign clientele. Upscale by Czech standards, the AghaRTA jazzery regularly features some of the best music in town, running the gamut from standard acoustic trios to Dixieland, funk, and fusion. Hot Line, the house band led by AghaRTA part-owner and drummer extraordinaire Michael Hejuna, regularly takes the stage with its keyboard-and-sax Crusaders-like sound. Bands usually begin at 9pm. Open Monday to Friday from 4pm to 1am, Saturday and Sunday 7pm to 1am.

Metropolitan Jazz Club

Jungmannova 14, Prague 1. ☎ 02/2421 6025. Cover 25 Kč (93¢). Metro: Národní třída.

There never seems to be anyone under 30 in this sophisticated jazz club, fitted with ceramic-topped tables and red velvet chairs. The small cellar club is home to a house trio that plays several nights a month, and Dixie and swing bands fill the rest of the calendar. Concerts begin at 9pm. Open Monday to Friday from 11am to 1am, Saturday to Sunday from 7pm to 1am.

Reduta Jazz Club

Národní 20, Prague 1. ☎ 02/2491 2246. Cover 80–100 Kč ($2.96–$3.70). Metro: Národní třída.

Reduta is a smoky subterranean jazz room that looks exactly like a jazz cellar is supposed to look. An adventurous booking policy means different bands play almost every night of the week. Music usually starts around 9:30pm. Open Monday to Saturday from 9pm to midnight.

U Staré Paní

Michalská 9, Prague 1. ☎ 02/264 920. Cover 150 Kč ($5.55). Metro: Můstek.

This unauthentically clean cellar is the newest jazz venue in town. The nation's best bands perform on a small stage that is wonderfully close to most every table. A great place for jazz lovers, the club is both visually pleasant and acoustically superior. Concerts begin at 9pm, and usually last until midnight. Open daily from 9pm to midnight.

Viola
Národní 7, Prague 1. ☎ **02/2422 0844.** Cover 45 Kč ($1.67). Metro: Národní třída.

A half-dozen concerts per month are scheduled in this intimate showroom. A good-size stage and tiered seating is designed for listening, not background music. Mercifully, no smoking is permitted here. Look for Allen Ginsberg's signature on the lounge wall. Box office open Monday through Saturday from 4 to 8:15pm. Concerts start at 8pm.

3 The Bar Scene

Things have finally started to heat up in Prague, where you now have a good selection of watering holes serving excellent beer and mixed drinks in eclectic surroundings. Some of the best places stay open very late.

Akropolis
Kubelíkova 27, Prague 3. ☎ **02/27 21 84.** Metro: Jiřího z Poděbrad.

Perhaps its location on a residential backstreet in Vinohrady makes Akropolis one of the hippest bars in Prague. The owners are members of the satirical comedy team Pražská pětka (the Prague five). Not that anyone cares, though; most people just come here to drink. Legend has it that this was the first place in Prague to serve absinthe, a popular green poison that is illegal in most civilized countries. Open Monday to Saturday from 4pm to 2am, Sunday from 4pm to midnight.

Chapeau Rouge/Banana Cafe
Jakubská 2, Prague 1. No phone. Metro: Staroměstská.

Hidden on a small Old Town backstreet, this loud and lively drinkery has twin bars, industrial metal wall sconces, plank floors, and a good sound system playing contemporary rock music. They sell four types of beer on tap, and feature regular drink specials. It's busy and fun—if you avoid the headache-inducing concoctions from the frozen drink machine. Open daily from noon to 5am.

Chez Marcel
Haštalská 12, Prague 1. ☎ **02/231 56 76.** Metro: Staroměstská.

This very stylish authentic French cafe looks like it was plucked straight out of Montmartre. Although casual light meals are served, the kitchen is extremely uneven, and you would be ill advised to come here just for food. Chez Marcel is best as a cafe and bar, and a great place for a well-made café au lait. It attracts a good mix of hipsters and suits around sunset, and starts to thin out at about 11pm. Open Monday to Friday from 8am to 1am, Friday and Saturday 9am to 1am.

The Derby
Dukelských hrdinů 20, Prague 7. ☎ **02/87 99 69.** Metro: Vltavská.

An American-owned bar/restaurant that serves great pizzas and sandwiches, The Derby is an ex-pat nightmare packed to the gills on Friday nights with people who consider that time the highlight of their week. Several beer options include Guinness on tap. Open daily from 11am to 2am.

Jo's Bar
Malostranské nám. 7, Prague 1. No phone. Metro: Malostranská.

A popular backpackers' spot, this ex-pat fixture is still fun after all these years. See Chapter 5, "Prague Dining," for more details. Open daily from 11am to 2am.

Kamýk

At Švermův Bridge. No phone. Metro: náměstí Republiky.

Permanently docked at the foot of Revoluční třida, this small tarp-covered boat is home to one of the liveliest drug scenes in the city. Looking more than just a little bit like a pirate ship, Kamýk is quite an eyeful—and a noseful if the wind is blowing in your direction. It's really smoking after 4pm. Open in the summer only from 10am to 4am.

#1 Original Whiskey Club

Dlouhá 31, Trída, Prague 1. ☎ **02/231 0560.** Metro: náměstí Republiky.

It has an English name, but you won't run into many native English speakers here. Located in a nondescript neighborhood, this place boasts 180 different kinds of whiskey from around the world and a first-class smoke shop within it called The Pipe. Beer, coffees, cappuccino, and simple desserts and sandwiches are also available. The music is British and American rock and pop, but where isn't it? This is a nice place to hang out, with a friendly young staff. On some nights, there's live music. Open daily 11am to midnight.

XT-3 Bar

Pod Plynojemem 3, Prague 8. ☎ **02/68 42 163.**

This trendy grunge bar attracts teens and twentysomethings who are too cool to hang out in the city center. There's lots of pot smoking, and the cots in back have seen more than a few make-out sessions. Open daily from 6pm to 2am.

GAY BARS & CLUBS

Prague is certainly no San Francisco, but there is a small active gay culture in the city. See "For Gay & Lesbian Travelers" in Chapter 2 for information.

Drake's

Petřínská 5, Prague 5. No phone. Cover 30 Kč ($1.11). Tram: 12 or 22.

The Prague outpost of this Amsterdam-based chain is a slightly sleazy basement where loud music competes with flashing video screens. Two dozen "video cabinets" are often shared by couples, and a strip show is presented most nights at 9pm. It's 99% men. Open 24 hours.

Euroclub

Opletalova 5, Prague 1. No phone. Cover 50 Kč ($1.85). Metro: Muzeum or Můstek.

An excellent space with good prices and a fun crowd, Euroclub is best known for its drag show featuring campy performers portraying everyone from pop stars to princesses from Czech folklore. Shows usually start at midnight. It's 75% men. Open daily from 11pm to 5am.

Mercury

Kolínská 11, Prague 3. ☎ **02/6731 0603.** Cover 25 Kč (93¢). Metro: Křižikova.

Perhaps the best gay club in town, Mercury is a contemporary disco and restaurant named for the former Queen frontman. Compact and ultramodern, the club packs up to 200 revelers on good nights. Drag shows are often scheduled on weekends. It's 75% men. Open daily from 7:30pm to 6am.

Riviera

Národní 22, Prague 1. ☎ **02/2491 2249.** Cover 25 Kč (93¢). Metro: Národní třída.

Known locally as "the train station," Prague's best gay dance club is usually jam-packed till the wee hours with a mostly male crowd enjoying a large, aquarium-decorated dance floor and an activity-filled side room. Open daily from 9pm to 6am.

4 Pubs

Pubs are as common in Prague as they are in London and Munich, and as important to Czechs as cafes are to the French. For hundreds of years, Prague's pubs have engaged in a war of pride, each vying to serve the best beer. Although each pub serves only one or two kinds of beer, the quality of the beer served is almost always high. And it's inexpensive; a half-liter almost never costs more than 30 Kč ($1.11) a glass.

For tips on pub etiquette and descriptions of the different beers available, please refer to the "*Není Pivo Jako Pivo:* There's No Beer Like Beer" section in Chapter 1.

Foreign-owned pubs are opening at a record pace in Prague, giving this scene a much-needed shot in the arm. While most Czech pubs can only be told apart from the brand of beer they serve and amount of smoke-related discoloration on the walls, foreign-owned pubs offer much greater variety. The Irish are finding their rightful place as the world's publicans, but Americans, French, and Germans are well represented here as well. Below is a rundown of the best.

James Joyce Pub
Liliová 10, Prague 1. ☎ **02/2424 8793.** Metro: Staroměstská.

Guinness and Kilkenny on tap at authentic Irish prices keep locals to a minimum. Lots of knickknacks make this popular bar pretty close to the real McCoy. Juicy burgers and weekend brunches are also available. Open Monday to Saturday from 10:30am to 1am, Sunday from noon to midnight.

John Bull Pub
Senovážná 8, Prague 1. ☎ **02/26 92 55.** Metro: náměstí Republiky.

Both British and Czech beers are served by the pint in a clean carpeted English pub environment. Standard British pub food, including roast beef with Yorkshire pudding, costs just a fraction of the price back home. Open daily from 11am to 11pm.

Molly Malone's
U Obecniho Dvora 4, Prague 1. ☎ **02/231 62 22.** Metro: Staroměstská.

Sporting one of the best interiors in Prague, this excellent Irish pub is the real McCoy with old-fashioned sewing-machine tables, green velvet drapes, a working fireplace, and turn-of-the-century skivvies hanging on a clothes line. There's plenty of boisterous laughter, Guinness on tap, and worn-out Pogues CDs. Pub meals are served daily from noon to 8pm. Open Sunday to Thursday from noon to 12:30am, Friday and Saturday from 2pm to 1:30am.

U Fleků
Křemencova 11. ☎ **02/2491 5118.** Metro: Národní třída.

Originally a brewery dating back to 1459, U Fleků is Prague's most famous beer hall, and one of the only pubs that still brews its own beer. It's a huge place with a myriad of timber-lined rooms and a large, loud courtyard where an oompah band performs. The ornately decorated medieval-style wood ceilings and courtyard columns are charming, but not very old. That doesn't seem to stop the tourists, most of whom come here by the busload. Because of this fact, U Fleků is avoided by disparaging locals who don't like its German atmosphere anyway. The pub's special d ark beer is excellent, however, and not available anywhere else; they brew only enough to service their own restaurant. Sausages, goulash, and other overcooked and overpriced traditional foods are served, and certainly not recommended. When a band performs in the garden a cover of 30 Kč ($1.11) is charged. Open daily from 9am to 11pm.

U Krále Jiřího

Liliová 10, Prague 1. ☎ 02/2424 8793. Metro: Staroměstská.

Located in the same complex as the James Joyce, this down and dirty cellar pub pours Platan beer for a mere 9 Kč (33¢) for a half-liter—the cheapest in Old Town. Frequented by drunken old Czech men and others in search of a bargain. Open daily from 10am to 1am.

U Malého Glena

Karmelitská 23, Prague 1. No phone. Metro: Malostranská.

Perhaps the best new bar of 1995, this cozy pub is owned by long-time ex-pat American called "Little Glen," which distinguishes him from "Big Glen" who owns Jo's Bar around the corner. Jazz is often performed in the pint-size cellar, one of the most intimate spaces in the city. Decent food—soups, salads, and focaccias—is served nightly until 1am. Open daily from 7:30am to 2am.

U Medviku (At the Little Bears)

na Pertýn at Narodní tridă. No phone. Metro: Narodní tridă.

This pub near the National Theater has Budvar on tap and serves typical Czech pub food, including *cmunda,* potato pancakes topped with sauerkraut and smoked meat. It's smokey inside, but it's easier to breath here than at most local pubs. Be sure to go to the right when you enter; if you don't you'll head into the restaurant, which serves the same food at close to twice the price. Open daily 11am to 11pm.

U Vejvodů

Jilská 4, Prague 1. ☎ 02/2421 0591. Metro: Staroměstská.

An excellent traditional 14th-century pub on a charming Old Town backstreet, U Vejvodů attracts a good mix of locals and visitors who come here for good Staropramen beer and decent Czech pub food. Open daily 11am to 11pm.

U Zlatého tygra (At the Golden Tiger)

Husova 17, Prague 1. ☎ 02/2422 9020. Metro: Staroměstská or Můstek.

One of the most famous Czech pubs, At the Golden Tiger is one of the favorite watering holes of both Václav Havel and writer Bohumil Hrabal. Particularly smoky, and not especially tourist friendly, this place is a one-stop education in Czech culture. Havel and President Bill Clinton joined Hrabal for a traditional Czech pub evening here during Clinton's visit to Prague in 1994. Open daily 3pm to 11pm.

5 More Entertainment

MOVIES

In the Czech Republic, foreign films are generally screened in the original language, with Czech subtitles. Mercifully, almost none are dubbed. Most first-run cinemas in the city center show Hollywood-style movies exclusively. A few others show Czech films, "smaller" American films and other international features.

A good portion of the city's major centrally located cinemas are on or near Václavské náměstí (Wenceslas Square). Tickets cost 30 to 50 Kč ($1.11 to $1.85). Almost every theater offers just two screenings daily; typically at 5:30 and 8pm. Check the local newspapers for listings.

Dlabačov, Bělohorská 24, Prague 6 (☎ 311 53 28), screens alternative films from September to February, before reverting to more mainstream features. Tickets cost from 20 to 25 Kč (74¢ to 93¢).

Ponrepo, Národní 40, Prague 1 (☎ 2422 7137), one of the city's newest film clubs, opened on January 3, 1993, to commemorate the 50th anniversary of the

National Film Archives, where it is located. Films are usually screened here twice daily. There is also a silent movie theater, where images are presented with live music every Monday at 7pm. Membership is required, and costs 120 Kč ($4.44) for adults, 80 Kč ($2.96) for students. Tickets are another 15 Kč (55¢).

CASINOS

Prague has many casinos, most offering blackjack, roulette, and slot machines. House rules are usually similar to Las Vegas, but there are often slight variations. **Casino Palais Savarin,** Na příkopé 10, Prague 1 (☎ **2422 1636**), occupying a former rococo palace, is the most beautiful gameroom in the city. It's open daily from 1pm to 4am (metro: Můstek). Other recommendable casinos include **Casino de France,** in the Hotel Hilton Atrium, Pobřežní 1, Prague 8 (☎ **2484 1111**), open daily from 2pm to 6am (metro: Florenc); and **Casino Admirál,** Vodičkova 30, Prague 1 (☎ **2416 2427**), open daily from 1pm to 5am (metro: Můstek).

LITERARY READINGS

You've heard all the hype that Prague is the "Left Bank of the '90s," but where are all those goatee-wearing bohemian writers and poets? Many come out of the wood-work weekly at the **Beefstew Readings,** held every Sunday from 6:30 to 9pm at Radost F/X, Bělehradská 120, Prague 2 (☎ **25 12 10**), a basement nightclub near the I. P. Pavlova metro station. Started in 1992 by a visiting American writer, the readings have become a kind of expatriate institution, attracting up to 100 poets, novelists, and songsters per week. Everyone is welcome and admission is free.

6 Only in Prague

Every night, when quiet descends on the city and moonlight reflects off the cobble-stones, Prague transforms into an enchanted fairy-tale city. Both Prague Castle and Týn Church are now lit until midnight. In the evening is a great time to walk through the castle courtyards, as the crowds are dispersed and there are wonderful views of the city lights twinkling below.

It's also worth wandering through Old Town and Malá Strana and finding pubs or restaurants located below ground, in vaulted basements that date as far back as the 12th century. Many buildings are so old that they have not one but two basements, one below the other. Don't be shy about descending into these ancient wonders.

Other nighttime stops might include the steps of the National Muzeum at the top of Wenceslas Square. There's also a great nighttime view (or daytime for that matter) from the pedestal located above the river Vltava on Letná hill. Take tram 17 to the first stop after crossing the Čechův Most (Cechs Bridge) on the Letná side of the river. The climb up the paths is dimly lit, so be careful, but once you're on the ped-estal (where a huge statue of Stalin once stood in the 1950s), you'll have a fantastic view of Prague's skyline.

Truly, one of the best things to do in Prague is to buy a bottle of wine and wile away the hours after sunset on Charles Bridge, hanging out next to some musicians.

7 Late-Night Bites

If you want to grab a bite after hours, several restaurants serve dinner after midnight, including Opera Grill, Jáma, Pizzeria Kmotra, Circle Line Brasserie, Avalon Bar & Grill, and Jo's Bar (see Chapter 5 for listings). But even these eateries are shut tight nightly by 2am. Radost F/X Café serves daily until 5am, and is often busy until closing.

Get Lost

Prague is popular—too popular, really—and you can find yourself in the middle of a special moment only to have it punctured by an umbrella or the loud voice of a tour guide from Ohio. So my advice to visitors trying to get a peek into the real life of Czechs is simple: get lost. Get really, really lost.

You won't stray too far, since "tourist Prague" encompasses a relatively small area. And you know the landmarks: the castle, the bridge, the river, the Old Town Square. So leave the map behind.

My favorite times to get lost in Prague were early morning and late at night. One foggy morning, I woke up early, grabbed a coffee in the breakfast room of my Communist-era hotel, and headed out. I'm not sure which direction I went—left, I think. I strolled several blocks into unfamiliar territory. I found a wonderful bookshop where I picked up a Czech version of Maurice Sendak's *Where the Wild Things Are*. Then I ducked into an old camera shop in search of film. The shop not only carried the latest in German and Japanese cameras, but fascinating, old eastern European cameras that looked to my American eyes like some discarded cosmonaut space garbage. Next, I discovered a little hut of a church that was dark and wonderful; two old Czech women dusted while I looked around. I'd love to tell you where these memorable places were, but you see, I was lost.

Another great way to get lost is to hop on a tram and let the driver take you where he's going. Get off when you see an intriguing neighborhood, or you're hungry, or you have to go to the bathroom. Or, if you're adventurous, follow someone. For 40 minutes, I trailed an old woman doing her shopping. Wow, did she get me lost! I followed her into a local food shop, not one of the big chains filled with processed foods and produce from Germany, but a little "czecha" shop. I bought some candy, which I still have—for me candy is the best kind of souvenir.

Late in the evening, as you wander aimlessly through Old Town, you'll half expect to see ghosts darting about. The lanterns along the uneven cobblestoned streets don't really help you navigate; instead, I'm convinced their function is to set a mysterious, quiet mood. That peacefulness is ocassionally interrupted by the sounds of late-night revellers. You may be tempted to join them for a *pivo* (beer).

Roaming the streets of Prague is like unraveling a big ball of twine. When you get lost, you're likely to find something special, some experience that will make you feel "of" the place for a short time, rather than feeling like you're just passing through.

So remember where you are. Now get lost.

—by Bill Boedeker

Other eateries that stay open late include **Snack-Bar Agnes,** Hybernská 1 (☎ 2421 9315). This is the best place in central Prague for traditional Czech food after midnight. Serving daily until 3am, Agnes offers a good selection of traditional meat dishes, each of which is freshly cooked to order. There are only a half-dozen tables here; the best ones are upstairs on the balcony. Main courses are 90 to 180 Kč ($3.33 to $6.66). Open daily 11am to 3am.

You can also try **U Zlatého Stromu,** Karlova 6 (☎ 2422 1385), a fine-looking labyrinth of dining rooms that descend to a particularly unpleasant disco. The restaurant serves a large Czech menu around the clock, and prices are extremely reasonable. Unfortunately, the food is mediocre at best. But if it's 4am and you just have to have some roast duck with dumplings, this is the only game in town. Main courses are 100 to 200 Kč ($3.70 to $7.40); credit cards are accepted. Open daily 24 hours.

Across from Reduta jazz club, the **Národní Gyro Stand,** on the corner of Národní třída and Na Perštýně, serves surprisingly good meat sandwiches, sliced to order from a rotating vertical skewer. Their plump pita sandwich is filled with lamb, shredded cabbage, cucumbers, and a few obligatory sliced peppers, then drenched in a garlicky cream sauce. Lousy sandwiches, cigarettes, and beer are also available. Gyros are 70 Kč ($2.60). Open daily 24 hours.

Every late-night clubber and cabbie knows **Masarykovo Nonstop,** Havlíčkova 2. This seedy train station snack bar is a gritty stand-up restaurant serving fried cheese with tartar sauce, a meaty goulash, and draught beer by the half-liter. There always seem to be plenty of old men with food in their beards picking fights with themselves. It's a unique experience. Meals are 17 to 30 Kč (63¢ to $1.11). Open daily 24 hours.

10

Day Trips from Prague

by Alan Crosby

Prague differs from nearby towns, where the tourist dollar has yet to renovate most crumbling facades and relieve storefront windows of their Communist-era dullness. While Prague has been blessed by spires, the surrounding area is dotted with some of Europe's most beautiful castles, such as the impressive Karlštejn, where you can play a round of golf or stay in a romantic inn. Also spectacular are the impregnable Český Šternberk, the hunting lodge of Konopiště, and the interior of Křivoklát. But my personal favorite is the castle in Orlík.

As much as these sites are a testament to the country's beauty, there are also monuments to reflect its suffering: Lidice, or the remains of what once was a small, sleepy village leveled by Nazi anger; and Terezín (*Theresienstadt* in German), the "model" Jewish ghetto, where a cruel trick duped the world and left thousands to die.

Worth exploring is the medieval mining town of Kutná Hora (with the macabre "Bone Church" a mile away in Sedlec). When you tire of touring castles, you can play a round of golf on a championship course in Karlštejn, get away to a romantic inn, or try the next generation of bungee jumping. You can also enjoy a glass of wine at the Renaissance Lobkovic Château, the center of wine-making in in Mělník.

Even if you don't have much time, try to spend at least a day or two outside of Prague to explore the countryside. Below I've listed the best easy day trips from the city.

1 Tips for Day Tripping

All of the destinations described in this chapter are easily accessible from Prague by car, train, or bus. Students should always show identification cards and ask for discounts. They are sometimes, but not always, available.

GETTING THERE

BY CAR　A liter of gasoline costs about 19 Kč (70¢), expensive by North American standards, but a little cheaper than western Europe. Gas stations are now plentiful in the Czech Republic.

Except for main highways, roads tend to be narrow and in need of repair. Add to this maniacal Czech drivers, and you may think

Day Trips from Prague

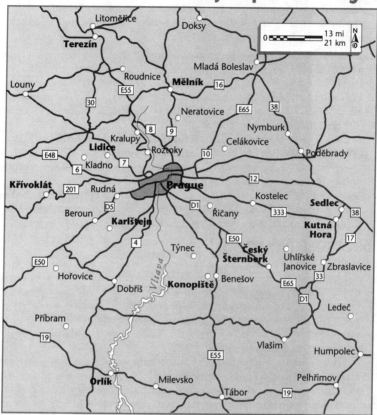

it's a better option to take the train. Especially at night, you should drive on major roads.

If you experience car trouble, major highways have some emergency telephones where you can call for assistance. There is also the **UAMK**, a 24-hour-a-day motor assistance club, which can provide service for a fee. They drive bright yellow pickup trucks and can be summoned on main highways by using the SOS emergency telephones located at the side of the road every kilometer or so. If you're not near one of these phones or on a road that does not have them, you can contact UAMK at ☎ **123** or ☎ **0123** outside of major towns. For details on car rentals, see Chapter 3.

BY TRAIN   Trains run by České dráhy (Czech Railways) provide a good and less expensive alternative, with the fare determined by how far you travel. Every 10 kilometers costs 4 Kč (15¢) in second class, 6 Kč (22¢) for first class (not usually available on short trips).

It's important to find out which Prague station your train departs from, since not all trains leave from the main station. Double check when you buy your tickets. Trains heading to destinations in the north, such as Terezin, usually depart from Nádraží Holešovice at the end of the red Metro line. Local trains to the southeast are commonly found at Smíchovské Nádraží on the yellow metro line. Most trains to west and south Bohemia and Moravia leave from Hlavní Nádraží (Main Station) in the center. Train stations in Prague are now better at providing information (even in several languages)—a far cry from when I first tried to take a train south to Jindřichův Hradec, but when I asked the information booth staff where to go, I ended up due east in Hradec Kralové.

BY BUS   Because trains often follow circuitous routes, bus transportation can be a better, although slightly more expensive option. A pretty good bus system operates in the Czech Republic. State-run ČSAD buses are still relatively inexpensive, surprisingly abundant, and offer terrific coverage of the country. Like the train, passengers are charged on a kilometer basis, with each kilometer working out to a cost of 50 hellers (half a crown) per kilometer.

Prague's main bus station, **Central Bus Station**—Florenc, Křižíkova 5, Praha 8 (☎ 02/2421 1060), is located above the Florenc metro stop (line C). Unfortunately, few employees speak English there, making it a bit tricky for non-Czech speakers to obtain schedule information. If you have some time before you depart Prague, your best bet for bus information and tickets is to visit **Čedok,** Na příkopě 18, or **Bohemia Tour,** Zlatnická 7 (☎ 02/232 3877). Neither agency charges an additional fee for their services, and both are open Monday through Friday from 9am to 5pm.

ORGANIZED DAY TOURS

In the wake of Čedok's demise as a state-run travel agency monopoly, several agencies have sprouted up around town offering services for guided tours both in, and outside Prague. Though most offer more or less the same services, it pays to shop around. I would recommend for the most part, however, going it alone. This gives you the freedom to change plans at the last minute to get in a little more of what you want, not what the tours provide. But if you decide to take a tour, the following agencies are the most reliable.

With a friendly, helpful staff, ✪ **Central European Adventures,** Jáchymova 4, Prague 1 (☎ 02/232 8879), is probably the most imaginative guided tour service in Prague. Several one-day guided (in English) adventure tours are offered in the Bohemian countryside from May to September; phone or stop by for complete information. Their bicycle tour around Karlštejn is fabulous and includes bus transportation from Prague and admission to Koněprusy Cave. The tour costs 650 Kč ($24), and departs from the Staroměstské náměstí 22 (Old Town Square) office Tuesday to Sunday at 8:30am. A canoe tour of a mild 10-mile stretch of the nearby Berounka River departs every Saturday and Sunday and includes life jackets and lunch. It costs 770 Kč ($28.50) per person. The company also offers guided countryside hikes tailored to suit your particular needs; the hikes include bus transportation from and to Prague and light refreshments. If you see a few people thinking about going on the same trip, band together. Groups of four people or more receive a 10% discount, enough for several Budvars at your favorite pub.

Martin Tour, Štěpánská 61, Prague 1 (☎/Fax 02/2421 2473), a less adventurous but just as reliable agency, has two tours worth investigating. The Karlštejn castle tour runs Tuesday to Sunday departing at 10am and includes a castle tour—nice because you don't have to wait around for hours until the next tour is available—and a typical Czech lunch at a nearby restaurant (diabetics, vegetarians, and babies can be accommodated). The second tour is one that very few other agencies offer: a tour of the Château Lobkovic at Mělník, including a tasting at the wine cellar and lunch at the château's restaurant.

The best tour offered by **Koala Leisure Tours,** Na Příkopě 33, Prague 1 (☎/fax 02/2422 2691), is a combination all-day tour of the castles Karlštejn and Konopiště that includes lunch. It's a good way to see two castles if you're pressed for time or don't want the hassle of negotiating the train and bus stations. However, the price tag is a little steep: 1,600 Kč ($59) for adults, 1,360 Kč ($50) for students, 800 Kč ($30) for children.

2 Karlštejn Castle

18 miles SW of Prague

By far the most popular destination in the Czech Republic after Prague, Karlštejn castle is an easy day trip for those interested in getting out of the city. Located 18 miles southwest of Prague, this medieval castle was built by Charles IV to safeguard the crown jewels of the Holy Roman Empire. It was constructed from 1348 to 1357. Today, it doesn't look like it has changed much. Although the castle has changed over the years, with such additions as late Gothic staircases and bridges, overzealous renovators removed these additions, restoring the castle to its original state.

As you approach the castle, little can prepare you for your first view: a spectacular, Disney-like castle perched high on a hill, surrounded by lush forests and vineyards. In its early days, the castle's beauty was enhanced by the King's jewels held within. These days, however, it is more spectacular from the outside than it is from the inside, since vandalism has forced several of its finest rooms to close.

ESSENTIALS

GETTING THERE The best way to get to Karlštejn is by train (there is no bus service). Most trains leave from Prague's Smíchov Station (at the Smichovské nádraží metro stop) hourly throughout the day and take about 45 minutes to reach Karlštejn. The one-way 2nd class fare is 14 Kč (52¢). It's a short, relaxing trip along the Berounka River. Look hard as you pass through Řevnice, Martina Navrátilová's birthplace, to see if a new prodigy is in the making and wait for your first glimpse of the majestic castle.

You can also drive along one of two routes, which both take 30 minutes. Here's the more scenic route: Leave Prague from the southwest along Highway 4 in the direction of Strakonice, and take the Karlštejn cutoff and follow the signs (and traffic!).

A trip to Karlštejn can easily be combined with a visit to Křívoklát—see below.

ORGANIZED TOURS The three tour operators listed in the "Organized Day Tours" section above offer tours of Karlštejn; see that section for details.

EXPLORING THE CASTLE

The walk up the hill to Karlštejn is, along with the view, one of the few features that make the trip worthwhile. Seeing hoards of tourists coming (an estimated 350,000 were expected in 1995), locals have discovered the value of fixing up the facades of their homes and opening small businesses, even if they have gone a little overboard on the number of outlets selling crystal. Restaurants have also improved tremendously since I first visited the castle almost six years ago. When you finally do reach the top, take some time to look out over the town and down the Well Tower. You also need to decide if the 90 Kč ($3.33) tour is worth the time and money.

If you have decided on taking the tour, be prepared: the **Holy Rood Chapel,** famous for the more than 2,000 precious and semiprecious inlaid gems that adorn its walls, is closed. So too is the **Chapel of St. Catherine,** King Karel IV's own private oratory. What is open are several rooms, most in the south palace. But the tour isn't a total waste of time. Both the **Audience Hall** and the **Imperial Bedroom** are impressive, despite being stripped of their original furnishings.

Admission to the castle is 90 Kč ($3.33) for adults, 45 Kč ($1.67) for children. Open May, June, and September from 9am to noon and 12:30pm to 6pm, July and

August 9am to noon and 12:30pm to 7pm, November and December 9am to noon and 1pm to 4pm.

In the end, Karlštejn is probably better viewed from a distance, so take time to browse in the stores, enjoy the fresh air, and sit out on one of the restaurant patios or down by the riverside. Buy a bottle of the locally grown Karlštejn wine, a vintage started by the king. This is what still makes the castle a worthwhile destination.

TEE TIME: KARLŠTEJN'S CHAMPIONSHIP GOLF COURSE

Golfers will take note of Karlštejn's newest addition, a championship, 6,370 meter par-72 golf course located on the hill just across the river from the castle. Completed in 1995, this North American-designed course at the Praha Karlštejn Golf Club is both very challenging and offers some very pretty castle views. At the elevated tee on the second hole, you'll hit toward the castle. It's a breathtaking place to lose a ball.

Karlštejn is one of the few courses in the Czech Republic that really challenges a golfer's ability; be prepared to walk uphill between holes. But it's a little expensive, especially for equipment such as golf balls and club rentals. The course is open daily from 8am to sundown. Reservations for weekends should be made one week prior; call 0311/947 16 or 947 17. Greens fees are 900 Kč ($33) for 18 holes Monday to Thursday; 1,200 Kč ($44) Friday to Sunday. Motorized cart rentals cost 100 Kč ($3.70) per hour, while a pull cart is 100 Kč ($3.70) per round. Club rental is 500 Kč ($18.50) per round. The golf pro charges 450 Kč ($16.66) per half-hour lesson.

To get here by car from Prague, take highway 116 south of Prague through the castle town of Karlštejn. Once you cross the river and a set of train tracks, stay on the road, which will veer right and go up a hill. You'll see the golf course on the left and an entrance soon after.

If you've taken the train here, you can walk to the course through town, but be warned that it's quite an uphill hike. I'd suggest taking a taxi, which should cost 30 to 50 Kč ($1.11 to $1.85).

WHERE TO DINE

The ✪ **Restaurace Blanky z Valois,** right on the main street heading up to the castle, tries for a Provençal feel. While this small and cozy restaurant doesn't exactly take you to France, the covered patio (where all but two of the eight or so tables are located) can be very romantic, especially during an afternoon or evening rain shower. The food is a cut above the standard fare served elsewhere in town, with wild game such as rabbit, boar, and venison the specialty. Main courses are 150 to 260 Kč ($5.55 to $9.63); some credit cards are accepted. A large wine list includes French and Italian vintages, but, I suggest sampling Karlštejn's own. This light dry wine is surprisingly good considering it's not from Moravia, and it costs less than half the price of the imports.

Also on the main street, the **Hotel Restaurace Koruna** is usually very busy, especially the terrace tables. The restaurant serves large portions; all of the usual Czech cuisine suspects are on the menu. The real bonus at this eatery is the staff: they are used to accommodating families or groups, and allow them to spread out over one of the large tables. Main courses are 49 to 100 Kč ($1.81 to $3.70); some credit cards are accepted.

At first glance there's not much difference between **Restaurace U Janů** and the Koruna across the road. And there isn't. But prices here are a little lower, and the terrace, shaded by trees, is a little nicer. The menu is basic Czech. Try one of the venison specials as a nice change from the usual meat and dumpling meals. Main courses

A Romantic Getaway: The Hotel Mlýn

If the air and noise of Prague start to grate on your nerves, or a quiet, romantic overnight trip to a castle in the country sounds like the perfect getaway, hide out for an evening at the ✪ **Hotel Mlýn** (Mill Hotel), 267 27 Karlštejn (☎ **0311/94 194,** fax 0311/94219).

On the river's edge on the bank opposite the castle, the Mlýn is exactly what its name says—a mill. Recently converted into a hotel, this reasonably-priced country inn takes you away from the hustle-and-bustle of traveling. Its 15 rooms are a little on the small side, but quaint and nicely decorated with rustic furniture. At the outdoor patio bar and very good restaurant, you can relax and enjoy the soothing sounds of the river, and forget what a disappointment the castle tour was. The breakfast is nothing special, so opt out and save the money for some better fare in town. Rates are 560 Kč ($21) single; 820 Kč ($30) double; 1,500 Kč ($56) suite. Breakfast costs an extra 280 Kč ($10). Some credit cards are accepted. To get to the hotel, take the bridge across the river that leads to the railway station and turn left at the first street. If you cross the railway tracks, you've gone too far.

are 35 to 115 Kč ($1.30 to $4.30); some credit cards are accepted. On weekends, live music adds a nice touch.

If you want a pleasant alternative to heavy sauces and dumplings, try the **Ů Smévavého Buldoka** (Smiling Bulldog), on the main road leading up to the castle. This is also a good place to stop for a quick bite if you don't have the time for a full sit-down meal. The barbecue you see out front is their "kitchen," so be prepared for meat—from hot dogs to pork chops. Main courses are 30 to 129 Kč ($1.11 to $4.78); no credit cards are accepted.

3 Křivoklát

27 miles W of Prague

Less crowded, and much less touristy than its neighbor upstream at Karlštejn, Křivoklát is the perfect destination for a lazy afternoon of touring. A royal castle mentioned as early as the 11th century, Křivoklát is set in the tranquil Berounka River Valley, west of Prague and along the river from Karlštejn. The fortress was rebuilt several times over the years, but still retains its Gothic style. The royal family was one of Křivoklát's frequent visitors, and during the Hussite Uprising, King Zigmund of Luxembourg hid his jewels here. The area surrounding the fortress is protected by UNESCO as a biosphere preservation area, making it an interesting place for a nature walk.

Křivoklát is near Karlštejn, so consider visiting both in one day if you either drive or take the train. The contrast between the bustling Karlštejn and the sleepy Křivoklát is startling.

ESSENTIALS

GETTING THERE   This is one of the nicer train rides in the Czech Republic, even though you have to change trains in Beroun. The train winds its way along the Berounka river through some wooded areas near Prague. Trains run regularly from Prague's Smíchov station to the town of Beroun, where you must change to go on to Křivoklát. The trip takes 1³/₄ hour; the one-way second-class fare is 28 Kč ($1.04).

If you're driving, leave Prague on the E50 expressway heading west toward Plzeň and exit at the Křívoklát cutoff. From there follow highway 116 as it snakes its way along the Berounka, and turn left on highway 201 which eventually winds its way around to Křívoklát. It's a 45-minute trip.

ORGANIZED TOURS   Koala Leisure Tours offers a combination tour of Karlštejn and Křívoklát; see the "Organized Day Tours" section above for details.

EXPLORING THE CASTLE

This is one of the castle tours I like most; it's almost a reverse of Karlštejn. Outside, Křívoklát pales in comparison to Karlštejn's beauty. But venture in, and Křívoklát blows its Berounka river rival out of the water. Take time to study the intricate carvings at the altar in the **Royal Chapel.** They're not exactly angelic. Actually, the angels are holding torture toys; Křívoklát was once a prison for political criminals. The **Kings Hall,** a whopping 80 feet long, is the second largest secular hallway in the country after Prague's Vladislav Hall. In the **Knights Hall** you will find a collection of fabulous late Gothic art. And the **Furstenberg Picture Gallery** is one of the country's largest castle libraries with some 53,000 volumes on its shelves. Take that, Karlštejn!

Admission is 90 Kč ($3.33) for adults, 45 Kč ($1.67) for children. Open June to August from 9am to 5pm Tuesday through Sunday; May and September, same days but closes at 4pm; October to December same days, but closes at 3pm. The tour runs about a half hour, and information in English is available.

WHERE TO DINE

Since Křívoklát is less touristy than Karlštejn, there aren't many restaurants here. In fact, the only place you'll see is the **Hotel Sykora** in town (don't ask me why they call it a hotel, since it doesn't have any rooms), which is best used as a watering hole. You're better off to wait and eat once back in Prague, or down the road in Karlštejn.

4 Kutná Hora

45 miles E of Prague

A medieval town that grew fantastically rich from the silver deposits beneath it, Kutná Hora is probably the second most popular day trip from Prague. Small enough to be seen in a single day at a brisk pace, the town's ancient heart is quite decayed, making it hard to believe that this was once the second most important city in Bohemia. But the town center is also mercifully free of the ugly Communist-era functionalist-style buildings that plague many of the country's small towns. Kutná Hora's main draws are the exquisite St. Barbara's Cathedral, and the macabre Bone Church (Kostnice), filled with human bones assembled in bizarre sculptures.

ESSENTIALS

GETTING THERE   The 50-minute drive from Prague is relatively easy. Take Vinohradská ulice, which runs due east from behind the National Museum at the top of Wenceslas Square straight to Kutná Hora. Once out of the city, the road turns into Highway 333.

If you don't have a car, Kutná Hora is best reached by bus, which departs from the terminal at Prague's Želivského metro station, and takes about an hour.

VISITOR INFORMATION   The **Culture and Information Center** (Kulturní a Informační Středisko), located on Paláckého náměstí, provides the most comprehensive information service in town. Check to see if anything special such as a recital or

Attractions
Barborská street ❷
Hrádek/District Museum of Mining
(Okresní Muzeum) ❹
Italian Court (Vlašský Dvur) ❺
Jesuit College ❸
St. Barbara's Cathedral ❶
St. James' Church (Kostel sv. Jakub) ❻

Dining
Restaurace Harmonica ❼
Ů Morového Sloupu ❽

exhibition is in town. The office is open Monday through Friday from 9am to 6pm, and on weekends between 10am and 4pm.

Across the square, the **Čedok** office, open weekdays from 8am to 4pm, can sometimes be helpful. The town has also posted very useful signs just about everywhere to help visitors get where they are going.

EXPLORING KUTNÁ HORA

The town's main attraction is the enormous **St. Barbara's Cathedral** (Chrám Sv. Barbora) at the southwestern edge of the town. In 1380, Peter Parler began construction of the cathedral. Yet the task was so great that it took several more great Gothic masters, including Matthias Rejsek and Benedikt Rejt, close to 200 years to complete the project. From the outside, the cathedral's soaring arches, dozens of spires, and intricate designs raise expectations that the interior will be just as impressive—you won't be disappointed.

Upon entering the cathedral (you have to enter from the side, not the front), you'll see several richly decorated frescoes full of symbols denoting the town's two main industries of mining and minting. The ceiling vaulting, with floral patterns and coats of arms, has made many a jaw drop. Admission is 20 Kč (74¢) for adults, 10 Kč (37¢) for children. Open Tuesday through Sunday from 9am to noon and 1pm to 5pm.

When you leave the cathedral, head down the statue-lined **Barborská street,** where you will pass the early **Baroque Jesuit College** built in the late 17th century by Domenico Orsi.

The "Bone" Church in Sedlec

A visit to Kutná Hora isn't complete without a trip to **Kostnice,** the "bone church." It's located a mile down the road in Sedlec; those who don't want to walk can board a local bus on Masarykova street. The fare is 6 Kč (22¢).

From the outside, Kostnice looks like most other Gothic churches. But from the moment you enter the front door, you know this is no ordinary church—all of the decorations in the church are made from human bones. Really! František Rint, the church's interior decorator, created crosses of bone, columns of bone, chalices of bone, and even a coat of arms in bone for the Schwarzenberg family who owned the church.

The obvious questions are where did the bones come from, and why were they used for decorations? The first question is easier to answer: The bones came from victims of the 14th-century plague and the 15th-century Hussite wars; both events left thousands of dead, who were buried in mass graves on the church's site. As the area developed, the bones were uncovered, and this was an idea the local monks came up with to put the bones to use.

Admission is 20 Kč (74¢) for adults, 10 Kč (37¢) for children. Open July and August daily from 9am to noon and 1 to 5pm; the rest of the year, Tuesday through Sunday from 9am to noon and 1 to 4pm.

Further down the road you will come upon **Hrádek,** a 15th-century castle that now houses the **District Museum of Mining (Okresní Muzeum).** If you take the tour of Hrádek, you'll actually see very little of the building. Instead, you'll tour one of the town's mine shafts. The tour begins in a small room filled with artifacts from the town's mining and minting industries. After a brief speech (guided tours are in Czech only so ask for a foreign language handout with details) it's time to don hardhats and work coats to tour the mine shaft. After a small hike of about 300 yards, you will descend into a narrow corridor of rock and dampness. *Two warnings:* the mine can be a little claustrophobic (what mine isn't?), and *never* take your hard hat off (low, jagged ceilings can quickly bring about premature balding). Children love this half-hour tour; you spend about 15 minutes in the mines. Admission is 50 Kč ($1.85) for adults, 25 Kč (93¢) for children. Open Tuesday through Sunday from 9am to noon and 1pm to 5pm.

Once back above ground, go down the hill to **St. James' Church** (Kostel sv. Jakub) and the **Italian Court** (Vlašský Dvur). Even though the door is usually closed at St. James', it's worth trying to open it; perhaps you'll glimpse the baroque paintings on the walls. It's more likely that you'll just have to admire the church from the outside and then head on to the Italian Court.

Constructed in 1300 as a royal mint (what better way for a town to become rich than to print money?), the Italian Court derives its name from its original occupants who were brought in from Florence to mint coins. The building houses a museum of coins made here between the 14th and 18th centuries, including the Czech *groschen,* the currency of choice in the Middle Ages. Another reason to take the tour is to see the ornate chapels, which are impressive for their attention to detail. Admission is 30 Kč ($1.11) for adults, 20 Kč (74¢) for children. Open April to September, daily 9am to 5pm; October to March, Tuesday through Sunday 10am to 4pm.

WHERE TO DINE

A nice terrace and quick service make the small **Restaurace Harmonica,** Komenského náměstí (to the rear of St James' church), a great place to eat before heading down the road to the bone church. The salads are fresh and the soups are hot and hearty, something that is not all too common in this town. Main courses are 50 to 90 Kč ($1.85 to $3.33); no credit cards are accepted. Open daily 11am to 10pm.

Ů **Morového Sloupu,** Šultyšova 3 (one block west of Palackého náměstí), is located in a 15th-century building that the owner has just completely renovated. Try to sit in the first room when you walk in; this is a pleasant dining room with dim lighting. In the second room, a decidedly modern look sterilizes whatever ambience there once was. The food on both sides is the same, however, with large portions of tasty pork steaks, schnitzels, and fish served. Main courses are 60 to 140 Kč ($2.22 to $5.19); credit cards are accepted. Open daily from 11am to 11pm.

5 Konopiště

30 miles S of Prague

A 17th-century castle-cum-hunting lodge built by the Habsburgs, Konopiště was the Club Med of its time. Here emperors and archdukes would relax amid the well-stocked hunting grounds that surround the castle. In 1887 the castle became the property of the Archduke Franz Ferdinand, who often went hunting, until that fateful day in Sarajevo when he became the prey.

If you're driving, you can see both Konopiště and Český Šternberk in one day (see directions on p. 192).

ESSENTIALS

GETTING THERE   If you're driving, leave Prague on the D1 expressway heading south and exit at the Benešov cutoff. From there, turn right at the signs for Konopiště. It's a 45-minute trip. Note that the parking lot just outside the castle is your best bet (20 Kč/74¢). There aren't any closer lots, and police are vigilant about ticketing or booting cars parked at the side of the road.

If you don't have a car, the bus is the next best option to reach Konopiště. Several buses run daily from Prague's Florenc station and let you off about a half-mile from the castle. The one-hour trip costs 30 Kč ($1.11).

It's a little trickier to get here by train since the closest train station is in nearby Benešov. The trip takes 50 minutes and costs 20 Kč (74¢) for a one-way second-class fare. From there you'll have to catch a local bus (fare is 6 Kč/22¢) to the castle.

EXPLORING THE CASTLE AND HUNTING GROUNDS

Since hunting on the grounds is no longer an option, Tour 1 at Konopiště will have to suffice. You'll know what I mean as soon as you begin the tour: hundreds of antlers, bears, wild boars, and birds of prey jump off of the walls, catching unsuspecting sweaters and dazzling children. The main hall is a testament to the Archduke, who reportedly bagged some 300,000 animals—that translates to an incredible 20 animals a day, every day for 40 years! Only 1% of his total hunting collection is on display at the castle, and it still ranks as one of the largest hunting collections in Europe. Tour 1 also takes you through the castle's parlors, which have been restored with great attention to detail. Of note are the hand-crafted wooden Italian cabinets with wonderfully detailed inlays, and the collection of Meissen porcelain. Admission for Tour I is 80 Kč ($2.96) for adults, 40 Kč ($1.48) for children.

Tour II (for which tickets must be purchased separately) takes visitors through the weapons room, the chapel, and the party room where only men were allowed to let their hair down. Admission is 80 Kč ($2.96) for adults, 40 Kč ($1.48) for children.

The third tour takes you through Ferdinand's private rooms. But for some reason this tour costs nearly three times what the other two tours cost; admission is 200 Kč ($5.40) for all. While the third tour is interesting, I don't think it's worth the money and it may be a little too much. Unless you're a diehard fan of castle rooms, your time is probably better spent roaming the grounds.

After exploring the castle's interior, wander around the manicured gardens where quails, pheasants, and peacocks roam freely. Children enjoy the moat, home to two bears who wander in circles for hours at a time. Down below the castle is a large pond where some people go swimming, although the water quality is questionable; I'd advise against swimming. Several large open areas beg for a blanket, some sandwiches, and a nice bottle of red Frankovka wine. Picnicking is not forbidden, but stock up before coming since there is no place to get groceries near the castle.

The castle is open May to August, Tuesday through Sunday from 9am to noon and 1 to 5pm; September, Tuesday through Sunday 9am to noon and 1 to 4pm. The castle grounds are open 24 hours daily.

WHERE TO DINE

Located on the castle grounds, **Stará Myslivna** is a straightforward Czech restaurant; its interior resembles a hunting lodge. The soups here are first rate, and the Czech specialty *svičkova na smetaně* (pork tenderloin in a cream sauce) is welcome on a cold day. When the sun is out, sit on the nice terrace around the corner, which usually only offers two meals: pork cutlets and chicken. Both will be cooking on the grill in front of you. Don't bother asking for side orders; they only serve what's on the grill. Main courses are 90 to 130 Kč ($3.33–$4.81); no credit cards are accepted.

6 Český Šternberk

30 miles SE of Prague

About 10 miles east of Benešov lies the menacing Český Šternberk, once one of Bohemia's most powerful fortifications. The structure was built in the first half of the 13th century during the reign of King Wenceslas I, in a Gothic style. Yet the Habsburgs put in some baroque additions and improved its defenses, leaving few Gothic elements in their wake.

ESSENTIALS

GETTING THERE   If you're driving, leave Prague on the D1 expressway heading south and exit at the Český Šternberk cut off. From there follow highway 111. It's a 55-minute drive. From Konopiště, take highway 112 to highway 111. It's a 25-minute drive.

Several buses run daily to and from the castle, but not from the main Florenc station. Instead, you must take the red Metro line (the "C" line) south to the Roztyly stops. You can buy tickets at the Florenc station, or from the bus driver at Roztyly. The bus takes about 1³/₄ hour.

EXPLORING THE FORTRESS

This impressive fortress stands atop a hill, rising above the Sázava River. It's worth taking the 1-hour tour of Český Šternberk. The enormous main hall and several smaller salons with fine baroque detailing, elaborate chandeliers, and period art are a testament to the wealth of the Šternberk family.

After the tour, enjoy the grounds and relax among the trees and babbling streams that surround the fortress before heading out. Admission is 70 Kč ($2.60) for adults, 40 Kč ($1.48) for children. Open July and August, Tuesday through Sunday from 9am to 6pm; in May, June, and September, open Tuesday through Sunday from 9am to 5pm.

WHERE TO DINE

Inside the castle, the **Vinarna Český Šternberk** serves standard Czech meat-and-potatoes–type meals, although its prices are higher than the quality of food and service deserve. Main courses are 60 to 110 Kč ($2.22 to $4.07); no credit cards are accepted.

7 Mělník

20 miles N of Prague

Bohemia is not known as a wine-making region—this is beer country. Except, that is, for the town of Mělník, about 20 miles north of Prague where the Vltava and Labe (Elbe) rivers meet. While it's not quite the Loire valley, Mělník has a decidedly French bent, as the vineyards are stocked with vines that originated in the Burgundy region.

The center of Mělník winemaking is the **Renaissance Lobkovic Château,** owned since 1739 by the family of the same name (except for a 40-year Communist-imposed interruption). The confluence of the rivers provides a stunning backdrop to the château, where another French pasttime—sitting on a terrace with a glass of Ludmilla, Mělník's finest, as the afternoon sun slowly fades—can reach an art form.

ESSENTIALS

GETTING THERE   If you're driving, from the north end of Prague, follow highway 9, which leads straight into Mělník. It's a 30-minute trip.

Buses leave for Mělník from both Florenc and Holešovice stations in Prague every hour or so. The trip takes about 45 minutes.

ORGANIZED TOURS   **Martin Tour** offers a day trip to Mělník; see the "Organized Day Tours" section above for details.

TOURING THE CHÂTEAU & TASTING WINE

Mělník's main attraction is the **Renaissance Lobkovic Château,** which only recently opened to the public. The château is a melange of styles from its Renaissance balconies and *sgrafitti* to its Gothic touches and baroque southern building. The tour showcases the Lobkovics' fine taste; in the living quarters, you'll see a barrage of baroque furniture and 17th- and 18th-century paintings. A second tour lets you into the 13th-century wine cellar, where wine-tastings regularly occur. (Ask at the gift shop for times of tastings.)

The château tour is 5 Kč (19¢), the wine cellar tour 20 Kč (74¢), and wine-tastings are 60 to 125 Kč ($2.22 to $4.63). Open daily 10am to 6pm.

WHERE TO DINE

Inside the château are two restaurants: a pricey vinárna and a more realistically priced restaurant, both with stunning views of the river. But I prefer the ground-floor restaurant, **Zámecká Restaurace,** since the food in the vinárna is not worth the additional money; instead, with my savings I buy an extra bottle of Ludmilla wine. Main courses are 60 to 120 Kč ($2.22 to $4.44); no credit cards are accepted.

8 Terezín (Theresienstadt)

30 miles NW of Prague

Noticing that northwest Bohemia was susceptible to Prussian attacks, Joseph II, the son of Maria Teresa, decided to build ✪ Terezín to ward off further offensives. Two fortresses were built, but the Prussian army bypassed the area during the last Austro-Prussian conflict, and in 1866 attacked Prague anyway. That spelled the end of Terezín's fortress charter, which was repealed in 1888. More than 50 years later, Terezín's fortifications were just what occupying Nazi forces needed.

When people around the world talk of Nazi atrocities in the World War II, the name Terezín (Theresienstadt in German) rarely comes up. There were no gas chambers, mass machine-gun executions, or medical testing rooms here. Terezín was not used to exterminate the Jews, gays, Gypsies, and political prisoners it held. The occupying Nazi forces used it as a transit camp. About 140,000 people passed though Terezín's gates; more than half ended up at the death camps of Auschwitz and Treblinka.

Instead, Terezín will live in infamy for the cruel trick the SS chief Heinrich Himmler played on the world within the walls of this concentration camp north of Prague. On June 23, 1944, three foreign observers—two from the Red Cross—came to Terezín to find out if the rumors of Nazi atrocities were true. They left under the impression that all was well, duped by a carefully planned "beautification" of the camp. Every detail of the visit had been planned by the Germans. The observers saw children studying at staged schools that didn't exist and store shelves, which had been specially set up, stocked with goods. So the observers wouldn't think the camp was overcrowded, the Nazis transported some 7,500 of the camp's sick and elderly prisoners to Auschwitz. Children even ran up to an SS commandant just as the observers passed; the commandant handed the children cans of sardines to shouts of "What? Only sardines again?" The trick worked so well that the Nazis made a film of the camp while it was still "self-governing" called "A Town Presented to the Jews from the Fuehrer."

Terezín was liberated by Russian forces on May 10, 1945, eight days after Berlin had fallen to the Allies. Today, the Terezín Camp exists as a memorial to the dead, and a monument to human depravity.

ESSENTIALS

GETTING THERE   If you're driving, Terezín lies directly on the main highway that leads north out of Prague and takes you eventually to Berlin via Dresden. It's a 45-minute drive.

Six buses leave daily from Florenc Bus Station (metro line C). The ride takes about an hour.

VISITOR INFORMATION   An information office, at no. 179 on the main square Náměstí Čs. Armady, is open Monday to Friday from 9am to 5pm (☎ **0416/ 922 27**). If it's closed, try the Museum of the Ghetto and the Minor fortress; both have shops that stock materials in several languages.

ORGANIZED TOURS   To arrange a guide at Terezín, contact the Town Information Center on Náměstí Čs. Armady 84 (☎ 0416/92 369). Expect to pay about 50 to 100 Kč ($1.85–$3.70)per person depending on the length of the tour.

Prague-based **Wittman Tours** (☎ **02/25 12 35**) offers a bus tour to Terezín that costs 950 Kč ($35.15) for adults. Call for tour times. See "Organized Tours" in Chapter 6.

SEEING TEREZÍN

The larger of the two fortresses is aptly named the **Main Fortress** (Hlavní Pevnost). Once inside, you'll immediately be struck by its drab plain streets. Just off the main square lies the **Museum of the Ghetto,** which chronicles in great detail the rise of Nazism and life in the camp. Several exhibitions use video, pictures, paintings, and writings. Admission is 50 Kč ($1.85) for adults, 25 Kč (93¢) for children. A ticket to enter both the Major and Minor Fortresses is 80 Kč ($2.96) for adults, 40 Kč ($1.48) for children. The Major Fortress is open daily 9am to 6pm.

The **Minor Fortress** is about a 10-minute walk from the Major Fortress over the Ohře River. Just in front of the fortress' main entrance is the **National Cemetery** (Národní Hřbítov), where the bodies exhumed from the mass graves were buried. As you enter the main gate, the sign above—*Arbeit Macht Frei* ("Work Sets One Free")— sets a gloomy tone. Here you can walk through the prison barracks, execution grounds, workshops, and isolation cells.

WHERE TO DINE

It's understandable that there are few places to eat in Terezín. Indeed, you may not want to stay here much longer than you have to. However, you'll find a small stand in the main parking lot where you can buy snacks and drinks. Inside the Major Fortress at Komenského 152 near the museum is a decent, inexpensive restaurant with standard Czech fare.

9 Lidice

20 miles NW of Prague

Two places in central Europe symbolize revenge more than almost anywhere else in the world: Dresden and Lidice. In 1942, when Czech paratroopers stationed in Britain assassinated the highest ranking officer in the Czech lands, SS Obergruppenfuhrer Reinhard Heydrich, the Nazis chose to focus their anger on this tiny village. As Hitler's main leader in the newly claimed Nazi protectorate of Bohemia and Moravia, Heydrich had ruthlessly and systematically exterminated Jews and intellectuals, while coddling "ordinary" Czechs. The assassination of such a high ranking official would be dealt with severely. Why did Hitler choose Lidice? No one knows for sure, but this tiny town northwest of Prague was rumored to have accommodated the assassins, and someone had to pay.

When you get to Lidice, you will only see a wooden cross and a green field where the town once stood. The Gestapo leveled the town, and murdered its men. Women and children were taken to concentration camps, with less than half returning alive. In all, 348 of Lidice's 500 residents were killed. But in 1948, the Czech government,

Impressions

"The most brutal thing was that they wanted to show a Terezín where there were nice healthy people. Each person was given a specific role to play. It was arranged before hand down to the last detail who would sit where and what they would say. Those people looking bad were not to appear at all. They (the Nazis) prepared Terezín so there weren't people looking ill, old, emaciated, or too many of them. They created the illusion of a self-governing normal town where . . . people lived relatively decently."
—Anita Frankova, survivor of Terezín

buffeted morally and financially by international outrage at this war crime, created a new town built on neighboring land. Today that town is beginning to get a little run down, which often makes visitors feel even more melancholy.

ESSENTIALS

GETTING THERE   If you're driving, take highway 7 from the west side of Prague past the airport and head west onto highway 551. It's a 20-minute drive.

Buses depart for Lidice at the bus stops across the street from the Diplomat Hotel near the Dejvice metro station (last stop on the green "A" line). Buses to Kladno don't stop in Lidice so make sure you're on the right bus by confirming it with the driver. The bus takes about 25 minutes.

LEARNING ABOUT LIDICE

The **Lidice Memorial Museum** is a sobering monument to the towns' martyred residents. In the museum are pictures of those killed with descriptions of their fate. A 20-minute English-language documentary can be seen upon request; otherwise a Czech version is usually running. There's also a 10-minute cassette you can listen to as you walk around. Admission is 20 Kč (74¢). Open daily 8am to 5pm.

Visitors are welcome to wander the field where the village once stood. Memorials in the "old" Lidice include a wooden cross marking the spot where the executed men were buried in a mass grave and Lidice's old and new cemeteries (the old one was desecrated by the Nazis who were looking for gold from the teeth of the dead).

10 Orlík

44 miles S of Prague

Castles closer to Prague like Karlštejn and Konopiště get all of the oohs and ahhs, but in my opinion, ✪ **Orlík castle** is more deserving of the attention. Set among forests that line the Vltava river where it swells from the Orlík Dam, the castle never disappoints me when I visit. Originally built in the 13th century, the castle has burned down several times, only to rise like a phoenix from the ashes with new additions and extensions. Inherited by the Schwarzenberg family in 1719 when Maria Ernestina died, the castle was set high upon a hill, overlooking a once vibrant trade route. It stayed that way until 1962 when water trapped by the Orlík Dam down river flooded thousands of hectares of land, bringing the water level up to the castle's lower walls.

Returned to the Schwarzenberg family in 1992, the castle retains its splendor, while the surrounding area has become one of the most popular lake resorts in the Czech Republic.

ESSENTIALS

GETTING THERE   By car, this is an easy 1-hour drive from Prague. Take highway 4 heading southwest out of the city. About halfway there the highway narrows from four lanes to two. Turn right on highway 19 and then right again into Orlík.

The Prague-Písek bus from the Florenc station (as many as six each day) stops near Orlík. Doublecheck with the driver to make sure you're on the right bus. It's a 75-minute trip that costs 20 Kč (74¢) one way.

VISITOR INFORMATION   There's no real information center in this tiny town, but if you go to the castle gift shop, you can get some basic information.

Jumping into the Fourth Dimension

If you're looking for a cheap thrill or a holiday pick-me-up, Orlík could be the place for you. While most visitors come here for the tranquillity of the castle grounds, or for a peaceful nature walk and day at the beach, the area's newest attraction has a decidedly different flavor.

From high above the river on the Žďákovsky Bridge, fearless men and women, tethered to two cords, jump off of the 50-meter-high structure to reach the "fourth dimension." That's what the staff from Hoboe International Organization (HOE), a worldwide umbrella group for sports such as bungee jumping and mountain climbing, call this pastime. Started in April 1995, HOE says that 4D jumping is better than traditional bungee jumping because it allows you to fall farther before the two cords (each capable of bearing a 2,000 kilogram load, I was assured) that tether you start to break your fall. According to organizers, an average of 25 people a day take the plunge, from an 11-year-old to a 56-year-old British woman. There's even a yearly contest to see which jumper has the lowest pulse rate while jumping. Each jump costs 500 Kč ($18.50). Weather permitting, you can take the plunge July and August daily from 10am to 6pm, and in April to June, September, and October, Saturday and Sunday from 10am to 6pm.

EXPLORING THE CASTLE

Castle tours explain the history of the Schwarzenberg family and take visitors through a fine collection of artifacts celebrating victory over Napoleon at the Battle of Leipzig in 1815. Keep an eye out for the wooden, hand-carved ceiling that took over four years to complete. Admission is 80 Kč ($2.96) for adults, 40 Kč ($1.48) for children. Open June through August from Tuesday to Saturday from 9am to noon and 1 to 5pm; in May and September open Tuesday to Saturday 9am to noon and 1 to 4pm.

WHERE TO DINE

Behind the castle gift shop, the ✪ **Restaurace U Toryků** (at the Castle) surprises with its quality, though portions could be bigger. It hits its stride, though, on Saturdays and Sundays in the summer when they hold a great grill party with live music. You'll be dancing the polka in no time flat. Main courses are 80 to 150 Kč ($2.96 to $5.55); no credit cards are accepted. Open daily 10am to 10pm.

11

The Best of Bohemia

by Alan Crosby

The Czech Republic is comprised of two regions: Bohemia and Moravia. The bigger of the two, Bohemia is marked with the triumphs and tragedies of war. Caught between a rock (Germany) and a hard place (the Austrian Empire), Bohemia was almost always in the center of regional conflicts, both secular and religious. But the area also flourished, as witnessed by the wealth of castles that dot the countryside and spa towns that were once the playgrounds of the rich and famous.

Today Bohemia is trying to return to that prominence, leaving behind its reputation as a satellite in the former East Bloc and forging a familiar old role as the center of Europe. Indeed, talk to the people (or even worse, the politicians), and a look of pain rises with every mention of the East. "This is central Europe, we are west of Vienna!" is a common refrain. While the people may wish to put the past 40 or so years away like a pair of worn trousers, the fact is they can't. But this fails to diminish the splendor of Bohemia's gentle rolling hills and majestic towns.

1 Exploring Bohemia

Though Bohemia is historically undivided, there are clear-cut distinctions in the region's geography that make going from town to town easier if you "cut" Bohemia into sections. After exploring Prague and central Bohemia, decide which area you would like to see first and then plan accordingly.

WEST BOHEMIA

Home to the country's spa towns, west Bohemia is one of the few places where a full-blown tourist infrastructure is already in place. Its main towns—Karlovy Vary (Carlsbad), Mariánské Lázně (Marienbad), and to a lesser extent Plzeň—offer a wide array of accommodations, restaurants, and services to meet every visitor's needs—and means.

A relatively inexpensive network of trains and buses covers the region, allowing travel between towns and to and from Prague with a minimum of fuss and confusion. West Bohemia is generally rougher terrain, so only serious cyclists should consider seeing the entire area on two wheels.

What's Special About Bohemia

Spa towns
- Karlovy Vary and Mariánské Lázně, two excellent examples of what was once central Europe's resort area, with hot springs that provide everything from drinking samples to body treatments.

Beer
- Pilsner Urquell and Budvar, two of the world's best and most famous beers, come from Bohemia, from the city of Plzeň in the west and České Budějovice in the south, respectively.

Castles, castles, and castles
- Český Krumlov, Bohemia's second largest castle, one of the most celebrated in Europe.
- Kotnov castle in Tábor, with its stunning view over the town and a museum of the Middle Ages.
- Hluboká nad Vltavou, near České Budějovice, with its vaunted ceilings.

Churches
- St. Giles Cathedral, in Třeboň, with some of central Europe's most significant Gothic sculptures.
- St. Bartholomew church, in Plzeň, with the country's tallest steeple.

SOUTH BOHEMIA

Once the religious hotbed of the country, south Bohemia was a focal point of the Hussite wars that eventually ravaged many of its towns and villages. Though the days of war took their toll, the region still features fine examples of architecture from every era. Southern Bohemia is also home to the Czech Republic's second largest castle, Český Krumlov, a UNESCO protected site that dazzles visitors no matter how many times they visit.

I've found two approaches to be the best ways to explore south Bohemia. If coming by train or bus from Prague, make Tábor your first stop. It's on a main route so the arrangements are easy. Then head south hooking up with Třeboň, České Budějovice and Český Krumlov. If time is of the essence, you may want to set up camp in the area's main city, České Budějovice, and make several day trips since nothing is that far (Tábor, the farthest town, is 37 miles away). In fact, several people I know have taken advantage of relatively cheap taxis and hired drivers to take them to nearby Třeboň for as little as 500 Kč ($18.50). If you split the cost between a couple of passengers, taxis can prove to be one of the most effective ways to see the countryside without breaking the bank.

For those who have more time, consider arranging a bike tour. These days, with the possibility of attack from Austria far diminished, south Bohemia is a much quieter setting with a less rugged terrain than west Bohemia. Biking here is a much more feasible method of transportation. ✪ **Central European Adventures** can arrange superb tours that include bike rentals, guides (in English), transportation, even canoe trips of southern Bohemia at a fraction of what it would cost if you arranged the same trip from home. Contact them at Jáchymova 4 (☎ **02/232 8879**).

A NOTE ON LODGING   Anywhere in the Czech Republic you have the option of staying in hotels or pensions on the main square. It's a beautiful sight but be prepared for serious noise, particularly on weekends. Light sleepers may prefer to trade the view for a good night's sleep.

Pensions are also a less expensive option than hotels, and often the best pensions are friendlier and more tasteful.

You may find that service tends not to be up to Western standards in most places; be warned that desk staff can be surly and unhelpful, and hotels may be understaffed. I've listed the best options below.

2 Karlovy Vary (Carlsbad)

75 miles W of Prague

The discovery of Karlovy Vary (Carlsbad) by King Charles IV reads something like a 14th-century episode of the television show *The Beverly Hillbillies*. According to local lore, the King was out hunting for some food when up from the ground came some bubbling water (though discovered by his dogs and not an errant gun shot). Knowing a good thing when he saw it, Charles immediately set to work on building a small castle in the area, naming the town that evolved around it Karlovy Vary, which translates to Charles' Boiling Place. The first spa buildings were built in 1522, and before long, notables such as Albrecht of Wallenstein, Russian Czar Peter the Great, and later Bach, Beethoven, Freud, and Marx all came to Karlovy Vary as a holiday retreat.

After World War II, East Bloc travelers (following in the footsteps of Marx no doubt) discovered the town, and Karlovy Vary became a destination for the proletariat. On doctor's orders, most workers would enjoy regular stays of two or three weeks, letting the mineral waters ranging from 43.5 to 72° Celsius from the town's 12 spas heal their tired and broken bodies. Even now, most spa guests are there by doctor's prescription.

But most of the 40-plus years of Communist neglect—they even took out most of the social aspect of spa-going and turned it into a science—have been erased as a barrage of renovators are restoring almost all of the spa's former glory. Gone is the statue of Yuri Gregarin, the Russian cosmonaut. Gone are almost all of the fading, crumbling building facades that used to line both sides of the river. In their place now stand restored buildings, cherubs, charatids, and more in the center.

Today, nearly 100,000 people travel annually to the spa resort to sip, bathe, and frolic, though most enjoy the 13th spring, a hearty herb and mineral liqueur called Becherovka, more than the 12 non-alcoholic versions. Czechs will tell you that all have medical benefits.

SPECIAL EVENTS The **Karlovy Vary International Film Festival** is one of the few places to see and be seen. Each summer (usually at the beginning of July), the country's films stars, celebrities, and wealthy folks, supported by a cast of international stars, take part in one of Europe's biggest film festivals. Six venues screen more than 200 films, many world premieres, during the 8 to 10-day festival.

Another event that brings out Czech stars by the dozen, including Karel Gott, the Czech version of Tom Jones, is the **Miss Czech Republic contest**, held annually in April at the Grand Hotel Pupp. However, the 1996 event is scheduled to be held in Plzeň.

Karlovy Vary also plays host to several other events including a **jazz festival** and **beer Olympiad** in May, the **Dvořák singing contest** in June, the **Summer Music Festival** in August, and the **Dvořák autumn Music Festival** in September and October.

Best of Bohemia

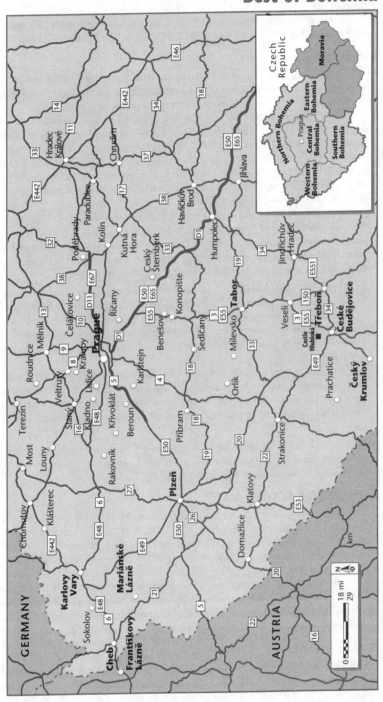

For more information on any of the festivals, contact **Kur-Info Vřídelní Kolonáda,** 360 01 Karlovy Vary (☎ **017/203 569** or **240 97**, fax 017/246 67).

ESSENTIALS

GETTING THERE   At all costs, avoid the train from Prague, which takes over four hours on a circuitous route. If you're arriving from another direction, Karlovy Vary's main train station is connected to the town center by bus no. 13.

Frequent express buses make the trip from Prague's Florenc station to Karlovy Vary's náměstí Dr. M. Horákové in about 2¹/₂ hours. Buses leave from platforms 21 or 22 five times daily at 7am, 9am, 9:40am, noon, and 4pm. Take a 10-minute walk or local bus no. 4 into Karlovy Vary's town center. Note that unlike Prague, you must have a ticket (4 Kč/15¢) to board local transportation. Tickets can be purchased at the main station stop, or, if you have no change, the kiosk across the street sells tickets during regular business hours.

The nearly two-hour drive from Prague to Karlovy Vary is easy. Take highway E48 from the western end of Prague and follow it straight through to Karlovy Vary. This two-lane highway widens in a few spots to let cars pass slow-moving vehicles on hills. However, be warned that this highway is a popular route for reckless drivers heading to and from the capital. Please take extra care when driving.

VISITOR INFORMATION   **Kuri-Info** is located inside the Vřídelní Kolonáda and is open Monday through Friday from 7am to 5pm, weekends from 9am to 3pm. It provides accommodation services, arranges guided tours and spa treatments, and sells tickets for some events. While there, be sure to pick up a copy of the *Cultural Calendar,* a comprehensive collection of events with a small map of the town center.

There are also two privately run **Info-Centrum** booths in Karlovy Vary: one in the train station and the other in a parking lot at the base of Jana Palácha ulice. Both give away free maps and a brochure of current cultural listings and events called *Promenáda.* Info-Centrum also books accommodations in private rooms and sells tours.

ORIENTATION   Karlovy Vary is shaped like a T, with the Teplá River running up the stem and the Ohře River at the top of the T. Most of the major streets here are pedestrian promenades lining both sides of the Teplá River.

EXPLORING KARLOVY VARY

The town's slow pace and pedestrian promenades, lined with turn-of-the-century art nouveau buildings, turn strolling into an art form. Nighttime walks take on an even more mystical presence as the sewers, river, and many major cracks in the roads emit steam from the hot springs running underneath. It feels like you could meet Vincent Price around every corner.

I suggest avoiding the new town, which happens to be conveniently left off most of the small tourist maps. If you're traveling here by train or bus, a good place to start your walking tour is the **Hotel Thermal** at the north end of the old town's center. The hotel, built in the 1960s, exemplifies how obtrusive Communist architecture can be. Nestled between the town's eastern hills and the Ohře river, the glass, steel, and concrete Thermal sticks out like a sore thumb amidst the rest of the town's 19th-century architecture. Nonetheless, you'll find three important places at the Thermal: its outdoor pool with mineral water, the only centrally located, outdoor public swimming pool; its upper terrace, which boasts a truly spectacular view of the town; and its theater, Karlovy Vary's largest, which holds many of the film festival's premier

Karlovy Vary

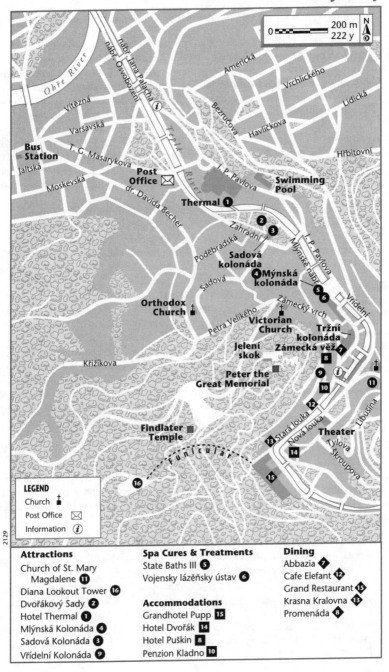

0 ——— 200 m
——— 222 y

N

Ohře River

nábř. Jana Palacha
nábř. Osvobození
Vítězná
Varšavská
Bus Station
Jaltská
T. G. Masarykova
Moskevská
dr. Davida Bechera

Americká
Vrchlického
Lidická
Bezručova
Havlíčkova
Hřbitovní

Post Office ✉
Thermal ❶
J. P. Pavlova
Swimming Pool
Teplá River

❷
Zahradní
❸
Poděbradská
J. P. Pavlova
Mlýnské nábř.
Sadová kolonáda
❹ **Mýnská kolonáda**
Sadová
❺
❻
Vřídelní

Orthodox Church †
Zámecký vrch
Petra Velikého
Victorian Church †
Tržní kolonáda
Zámecká věž ❼
Jelení skok
❽
Křižíkova
❾
ⓘ
❿ †
Peter the Great Memorial ⓫

⓬ Stará louka
Findlater Temple
⓭ Nová louka
Theater
⓮ Tylova
Škroupova
Libušina
⓯
Funicular
⓰

LEGEND
Church †
Post Office ✉
Information ⓘ

2129

Attractions
Church of St. Mary Magdalene ⓫
Diana Lookout Tower ⓰
Dvořákový Sady ❷
Hotel Thermal ❶
Mlýnská Kolonáda ❹
Sadová Kolonáda ❸
Vřídelní Kolonáda ❾

Spa Cures & Treatments
State Baths III ❺
Vojensky lázěňsky ústav ❻

Accommodations
Grandhotel Pupp ⓯
Hotel Dvořák ⓮
Hotel Puškin ❽
Penzion Kladno ❿

Dining
Abbazia ❼
Cafe Elefant ⓬
Grand Restaurant ⓯
Krasna Kralovna ⓭
Promenáda ❽

events. After seeing the Thermal, it's best to keep walking before you remember too much of it.

As you enter the heart of the town on the river's west side, the ornate white wrought-iron **Sadová Kolonáda** adorns a beautifully manicured park named **Dvořákový Sady.** Continue following the river, and about 100 meters later you will encounter the **Mlýnská Kolonáda.** This long, covered walkway houses several Karlovy Vary springs, which can be sampled 24 hours a day. Each spring has a plaque beside it telling which mineral elements are present and what temperature the water is. Bring your own cup, or buy one just about anywhere to sip the waters since most are too hot to just drink from your hands. When you hit the river bend, the majestic **Church of St. Mary Magdalene** sits perched atop a hill, overlooking the **Vřídlo,** the hottest spring in town. Built in 1736, the church is the work of Kilian Ignac Dientzenhofer, who also created two of Prague's more notable churches—both named St. Nicholas.

Housing Vřídlo, which blasts water some 50 feet into the air, is the glass building where the statue of Soviet astronaut Gregarin once stood. (Gregarin's statue has since made a safe landing at the Karlovy Vary airport.) Now called the **Vřídelní Kolonáda,** the structure, built in 1974, houses several hot springs. You can sample these free of charge. The building also holds the Kuri-Info information center, where visitors can find answers to almost all of their questions.

Heading away from the Vřídelní Kolonáda are Stará and Nova Louka streets, which line either side of the river. Along **Stará (Old) Louka** you'll find several fine cafes and glass and crystal shops. **Nova (New) Louka** is lined with many hotels and the historic town's main theater, currently under reconstruction.

Both streets lead to the **Grandhotel Pupp.** Both the main entrance and building of the Pupp are being renovated, as the hotel attempts to erase the effects of 40 years of Communism (the hotel used to be called the Moskva-Pupp). Regardless of capitalism or Communism, the Pupp remains what it always was: the Grand-dame of hotels in the area. Once catering to nobility from all over central Europe, the Pupp still houses one of the town's finest restaurants, the Grand, while its grounds are a favorite with the hiking crowd.

If you still have the energy, atop the hill behind the Pupp stands the **Diana Lookout Tower.** Footpaths lead to the tower through the forests and eventually spit you out at the base of the tower, as if to say, "Ha, the trip is only half over." The five-story climb up the tower tests your stamina, but the view of the town is more than worth it. Oh yes, for those who aren't up to the climb just to get to the tower, a cable car runs to the tower every 15 minutes or so.

SHOPPING FOR CRYSTAL AND PORCELAIN

Crystal and porcelain are Karlovy Vary's other claims to fame. Dozens of shops throughout town sell everything from plates to chandeliers.

Ludvík Moser founded his first glassware shop in 1857, and became one of this country's foremost names in glass. You can visit the **Moser Factory,** kapitána Jaroše 19 (☎ **017/41 61 11**), just west of the town center; take bus nos. 1, 10, or 16. It's open Monday through Friday only, from 7:30am to 3:30pm. The **Moser Store,** Stará Louka 40, is right in the heart of town, and is open Monday through Friday from 9am to 5pm.

WHERE TO STAY

Private rooms are the best places to stay in Karlovy Vary with regard to quality and price. Arrange your room through **Info-Centrum** (see "Visitor Information" above)

Spa Cures & Treatments

Most visitors to Karlovy Vary come for the specific reason of getting a spa treatment, a therapy that lasts one to three weeks. After consulting with a spa physician, guests are given a specific regimen of activities that may include mineral baths, massages, waxings, mud packs, electrotherapy, and pure oxygen inhalation. After spending the morning at a spa, or sanatorium, guests are usually directed to walk the paths of the town's surrounding forest.

The common denominator of all the cures is an ample daily dose of hot mineral water, which bubbles up from 12 different springs. This water definitely has a distinct odor and taste. You'll see people chugging down the water, but it doesn't necessarily taste very good. Some thermal springs actually taste and smell like rotten eggs. You may want to take a small sip at first.

You'll also notice that almost everyone in town seems to be carrying "the cup." This funny-looking cup is basically a mug with a built-in straw that runs through the handle. Young and old alike parade through town with their mugs, filling and refilling them at each new thermal water tap. You can buy these mugs everywhere for as little as 50 Kč ($1.85) or as much as 500 Kč ($18.50); they make a quirky souvenir. But be warned: none of the mugs can make the warmer hot springs taste any better!

The minimum spa treatment lasts one week and must be arranged in advance. A spa treatment package traditionally includes room, full board, and complete therapy regimen; the cost varies from about $40 to $100 per person per day, depending on season and facilities. Rates are highest from May through September, and lowest from November through February.

For information and reservations in the United States, contact **Čedok,** 10 E. 40th St., New York, NY 10016 (☎ **212/689-9720**). For information and reservations in Prague contact Čedok, Na příkopě 18. Many hotels also provide spa and health treatments, so ask when you book your room. Most hotels will happily arrange a treatment if they don't provide them directly.

Visitors to Karlovy Vary for just a day or two can experience the waters on an "outpatient" basis. The **State Baths III** (☎ **017/256 41**) welcomes day-trippers with mineral baths, massages, saunas, and a cold pool. They're open for men on Tuesday, Thursday, and Saturday, and for women on Monday, Wednesday, and Friday from 7:45am to 3pm. **Vojensky lázěňsky ústav,** Mlynské nábřeží 7 (☎ **017/222 06**), offers similar services, and costs about 750 Kč ($27.75) per day.

or **Čedok,** Karla IV č. 1 (☎ **017/261 10** or **267 05;** fax 017/278 35). The office is open Monday through Friday from 9am to 5pm and on Saturday from 9am to noon. Expect to pay about 500 Kč ($18.50) for a single and 750 Kč ($27.75) for a double.

The town's major spa hotels only accommodate those who are paying for complete treatment, unless, for some reason, their occupancy rates are particularly low. The hotels I've listed below accept guests for stays of any length.

EXPENSIVE

Grandhotel Pupp
Mírové náměstí 2, 360 91, Karlovy Vary. ☎ **017 209 111.** Fax 017/32 240 32. 270 rms and suites. MINIBAR TV TEL. From April 14–Nov 5 and Dec 28–Jan 4, 2,550 Kč ($94) single, 3,600–4200 Kč ($133–155) double, 5,350–16,900 Kč ($198–$626) suite; Jan 5–April 13 and

Nov 6–Dec 27, 1,850 Kč ($69) single, 2,550–2,990 Kč ($94–$110) double, 3,750–16,900 Kč ($138–$626) suite. AE, DC, MC, V.

Well known as one of Karlovy Vary's best hotels, Grandhotel Pupp, built in 1701, is also one of Europe's oldest. While the hotel's public areas are oozing with splendor and charm, the guest rooms are not as consistently enchanting. The best rooms tend to be those that face toward the town center and are located on the upper floors; these rooms have good views and sturdy wooden furniture.

Hotel Dvořák

Nova Louka 11, 360 21, Karlovy Vary. ☎ 017/241 45, fax 017/228 14. 79 rms and suites. MINIBAR TV TEL. 3,150 Kč ($117) single; 4,500 Kč ($167) double; 6,480 Kč ($240) suite. AE, DC, MC, V.

This hotel is within sight of the Grandhotel Pupp, but people who have stayed here say it's far beyond Karlovy Vary's vaunted hotel. If the Pupp has the history and elegance, they say, the Dvořák has the facilities, including a well-equipped fitness center. The rooms are spacious and well-appointed, and the staff is very attentive.

MODERATE

Hotel Puškin

Tržiště 37, 360 90 Karlovy Vary. ☎ 017/322 2646, fax 017/322 4134. 20 rms. TV TEL. May–Oct, 1,464 Kč ($54) single, 1,940–2,196 Kč ($72–$81) double, 3,093 Kč ($115) 4-person junior suite; Jan 3–April and Nov–Dec, 1,006 Kč ($37) single, 1,190–1,427 Kč ($44–$53) double, 1,647 Kč ($61) 4-person junior suite. No credit cards.

Named for the great Russian poet we know as Pushkin, this hotel occupies an intricately ornamented 19th-century building that has just been renovated. The hotel has a terrific location, close to the springs. The rooms are rather basic, but they are comfortable enough; ask for one that has a balcony facing St. Mary Magdalene church.

Penzion Kladno

Stará Louka č. 2, 360 01 Karlovy Vary. ☎ 017/251 95. 22 rms (3 with bath). TEL. 600 Kč ($22) single without bath; 750 Kč ($28) double without bath; 1,000 Kč ($37) double with bath. No credit cards.

Located just 150 feet from a hot spring, this basic hotel, in a beautiful 19th-century building, is very clean, well maintained, and quiet. Many rooms have balconies overlooking a major promenade.

WHERE TO DINE
EXPENSIVE

Grand Restaurant

In the Grand Hotel Pupp, Mírové náměstí 2. ☎ 017/221 21. Reservations recommended. Soups 70–85 Kč ($2.59–$3.15); main courses 290–590 Kč ($10.74–$21.85). AE, V. Daily noon–3pm, 6pm–10pm. CONTINENTAL.

It's no surprise that the Grandhotel Pupp has the nicest dining room in town, an elegant eatery with tall ceilings, huge mirrors, and glistening chandeliers. A large menu gives way to larger portions of salmon, chicken, veal, pork, turkey, and beef in a variety of heavy and heavier sauces. Even the trout with mushrooms is smothered in a butter sauce.

✪ Promenáda

Tržiště 31. ☎ 017/322 56 48. Reservations highly recommended. Soups 25–39 Kč (93¢–$1.45); main courses 180–289 Kč ($6.66–$10.70). AE, V. Daily noon–11pm. CZECH/CONTINENTAL.

This cozy, intimate spot may not be as elegant as the Grand restaurant in the Pupp, but for Karlovy Vary residents, it has become *the* place to dine. Located directly across from the Vřídelna Kolonáda, the Promenáda offers a wide selection of meals that come in generous portions. The daily menu usually includes well-prepared wild game, but most will tell you that the mixed grill for two or the chateaubriand, both flambéed at the table, are the chef's best dishes. The wine list features a large selection of wines from around Europe, but don't sell short the Czech wines on the menu, especially the white Ryslink and the red Frankovka. An order of crepes Suzette big enough to satisfy the sweet tooth of two diners rounds out a wonderful meal.

MODERATE

Abbazia

Vřídelní 51. ☎ **017/322 5648.** Reservations recommended. Main courses 99–300 Kč ($3.67–$11.11). AE, V. Daily noon–11pm. CZECH/CONTINENTAL.

From the outside, the Abbazia is easy to miss, but it's well worth finding. Located near the Vřídelní Kolonáda on the second floor, Abazzia has a wooden interior dominated by huge tables, making it one of the few places where large groups are always welcome. The rather large menu offers a wide assortment of Czech and international meals at reasonable prices. This is one of the few places in the Czech Republic where I would recommend the scampi; I usually order it as an appetizer to share with my dining partner(s).

As an added bonus, Ondřej Havelka and his Prague Syncopated Orchestra regularly stop by to play music from the 1920s and 1930s, complete with flappers dancing away. It's some of the best music you'll hear on either side of the Atlantic. Always check to see if he is in town, and don't miss him if he is.

Krásná Královna

Stará Louka 335. ☎ **017/255 08.** Reservations not needed. Soups 19–29 Kč (70¢–$1.07); main courses 89–299 Kč ($3.30–$11.07). No credit cards. Daily 10am–11pm. CZECH/CONTINENTAL.

In case you have not had your fill of meat, the recently refurbished Krásná Královna is a landlubber's paradise. This restaurant is one of the few in the Czech Republic that serves a proper, barbecued T-bone steak. Other menu favorites include the mixed grill for two, and the ever present Czech favorite roasted pork, cabbage, and dumplings. It also serves some of the coldest beer in Karlovy Vary, which always goes down well on the large patio by the river.

INEXPENSIVE

Cafe Elefant

Stará Louka 32. ☎ **017/234 06.** Cakes and desserts 20–50 Kč (74¢–$1.85). Daily 9am–10pm. DESSERTS.

A cafe in the true sense of the word, all you will find is coffee, tea, alcoholic and non-alcoholic drinks, desserts, and enough ambience to satisfy the hoards of Germans who flock to this landmark. The Elefant is widely known for its belle époque style that includes pink walls and mirrors and is famous for its freshly baked cakes. A large number of outdoor tables overlook the pedestrian promenade.

3 Mariánské Lázně (Marienbad)

29 miles SW of Karlovy Vary, 100 miles W of Prague

When Thomas Alva Edison visited Mariánské Lázně in the late 1800s, he proclaimed: "There is no more beautiful spa in all the world."

While the spa town of Mariánské Lázně now stands in the shadow of the Czech Republic's most famous spa town, Karlovy Vary, it was not always that way. First mentioned in 1528, the town's mineral waters gained prominence at the end of the 18th and beginning of the 19th centuries. Nestled among forested hills and packed with romantic and elegant pastel hotels and spa houses, the town, commonly known by its German name, Marienbad, has played host to such luminaries as Goethe (where his love for Ulrika von Levetzow took root), Mark Twain, composers Chopin, Strauss, and Wagner, as well as Freud and Kafka. England's King Edward VII found the spa resort so enchanting he visited nine times, and even commissioned the building of the country's first golf club.

SPECIAL EVENTS   One of the few places in central Europe not to claim Mozart as one of its sons, Mariánské Lázně has instead chosen to honor one of its frequent visitors, Chopin, with a yearly festival devoted entirely to the Polish composer and his works. The **Chopin Festival** usually runs for 8 to 10 days near the end of August. Musicians and directors from all over the world gather to play and listen to concerts and recitals. In addition, several local art galleries hold special exhibitions. Ticket prices range from 70 to 200 Kč ($2.60 to $7.40).

Each June, the town also plays host to a **classical music festival** with many of the Czech Republic's finest musicians, as well as those from around the world. For more information or ticket reservations for either event, contact **Infocentrum KaSS,** Dům Chopin, Hlavní 47, 353 01, Mariánské Lázně (☎ **02/0165/2427,** fax 0165/5892).

Patriotic Americans can show up on **July 4th** for a little down-home fun, including a parade and other flag-waving special events commemorating the town's liberation by U.S. soldiers in World War II.

In mid-August, the sports-minded traveler can see some of Europe's top golfers at the **Czech Open,** one of the newest events on the European PGA golf tour. Past participants have included Seve Ballesteros and Bernhard Langer.

ESSENTIALS

GETTING THERE   The express train from Prague takes just over 3 hours. Mariánské Lázně train station, Nádražní náměstí 292 (☎ **02/0165/5321**), is located south of the town center; take bus no. 5 into town. The one-way fare costs 136 Kč ($5) first class, 96 Kč ($3.55) second class.

The bus from Prague takes about 3 hours and costs about 65 Kč ($2.40). The Mariánské Lázně bus station is situated adjacent to the train station on Nádražní náměstí; take bus no. 5 into town.

Driving from Prague, take the E50 highway through Plzeň to Stříbo—about 22km past Plzeň—and head northwest on highway 21. The clearly marked route can take up to 2 hours.

VISITOR INFORMATION   Just across from the Hotel Bohemia, **City Service,** at Hlavní třída 1 (☎ /fax **02/0165/4218** or 3816), on the town's main street, is the best place for information. In addition to dispensing advice, the staff sells maps and arrange accommodations in hotels and private homes. Open Monday through Friday from 7am to 7pm, and on Saturday and Sunday from 9am to 6pm.

ORIENTATION   Mariánské Lázně is laid out around **Hlavní třída,** the main street. A plethora of hotels, restaurants, travel agencies, and stores front this street.

Lázeňské Colonnade, a long, covered block beginning at the northern end of Hlavní třída, contains six of the resort's eight major springs.

TAKING THE WATERS AT MARIÁNSKÉ LÁZNÊ

When walking through the town, it's almost impossible to miss the **Lázeňské Colonnade,** located just off Skalníkovy sady. From Hlavní třída, walk east on Vrchlického ulice. Recently restored to its former glory, the eye-catching cast-iron and glass colonnade is adorned with ceiling frescoes and Corinthian columns. Built in 1889, the colonnade connects a half-dozen major springs in the town center; this is the focal point of those partaking in the ritual. Bring a cup to fill, or, if you want to fit in with the thousands of guests who are serious about their spa water, buy one of the porcelain mugs with a built-in straw that are offered just about everywhere. Do keep in mind that the waters are used to treat internal disorders so the minerals may act to cleanse the body thoroughly. You can wander the colonnade any time; water is distributed daily from 6am to noon and 4 to 6pm.

For a relaxing mineral bubble bath or massage, make reservations through the **State Spa Office,** Masarykova 22 (☎ 02/0165/2170). Also ask at your hotel since most provide, spa treaments and massages or can arrange them. Treatments cost anywhere from 300 Kč ($11) and up.

LEARNING ABOUT THE CITY'S PAST

There's not much town history, since Mariánské Lázně only officially came into existence in 1808. But engaging brevity is what makes the two-story **City Museum (Muzeum Hlavního Města),** Goetheovo náměstí 11 (☎ 02/0165/2740), recommendable. Chronologically arranged displays include photos and documents of famous visitors. Goethe slept here, in the upstairs rooms in 1823, when he was 74 years old. If you ask nicely, the museum guards will play an English-language tape that describes the contents of each of the museum's rooms. You can also request to see the museum's English-language film about the town. Admission is 20 Kč (74¢). Open Tuesday through Sunday from 9am to 4pm.

HIKING OR PLAYING GOLF

If the thought of a spa treatment fails to appeal, relaxation can be found in Mariánské Lázně through one of the simpler things in life: a walk in the woods. The surrounding **Slavkovský les (Slavkov Forest)** has about 70 kilometers of marked footpaths and trails through the gentle hills that abound in the area.

If you're a die-hard golfer, or just looking for a little exercise, the **Mariánské Lázně Golf Club,** a 6,195-meter yard par-72 championship course, lies on the edge of town. The club takes pay-as-you-play golfers, with a fully equipped pro shop that rents clubs. Greens fees are 900 Kč ($33), club rental 300 Kč ($11).

WHERE TO STAY

The main strip along Hlavní třída is lined with hotels, many with rooms facing the Colonnade. If you feel comfortable about doing this, I suggest walking the street and shopping around for a room; most hotels charge from 2,000 to 3,500 Kč ($55–$110) for a double in high season (May through September). Off-season prices can fall by as much as half.

For private accommodations, try Paláckého ulice, which runs south of the main spa area.

EXPENSIVE

Hotel Golf

Zádub 55, 353 01 Mariánské Lázně. ☎ **0165/2651.** Fax 2655. 96 rms. MINIBAR TV TEL. 2,400 Kč ($89) single; 2,900 Kč ($107) double; 4,800 Kč ($178) suite. Rates include breakfast. AE, DC, MC, V.

One of the more luxurious hotels in town, the Hotel Golf is not actually in town, but across the street from the golf course about 2 miles away on the road leading to Karlovy Vary. This hotel is busy, so reservations are recommended. An English-speaking staff delivers on their pledge to cater to every wish. The rooms are bright and spacious, with an excellent restaurant and terrace on the first floor. Not surprisingly, given the hotel's name, staff can help arrange a quick 18 holes across the street. The hotel plans to open its own spa center in 1996 to pamper guests a little more.

Hotel Villa Butterfly

Hlavní třída 72, 353 01 Mariánské Lázně. ☎ **0165/6201.** Fax 0165/6210. 26 rms. MINIBAR TV TEL. 3,977 Kč ($147) single; 4,255 Kč ($158) double; 5,550–7,400 Kč ($206–$274) suite. Rates include breakfast. AE, DC, MC, V.

One of the newest hotels on the main street, the Villa Butterfly has rather ordinary rooms that are comfortable and spotlessly clean. An English-speaking staff and a good selection of foreign language newspapers at the reception are an added bonus that few hotels here provide.

MODERATE

Hotel Bohemia

Hlavní třída 100, 35301 Mariánské Lázně. ☎ **0165/2705.** Fax 0165/5346. 77 rms. MINIBAR TV TEL. 1,700 Kč ($63) single; 2,200 Kč ($81) double; 3,000 Kč ($111) suite. AE, DC, MC, V.

In the middle of the action on Hlavní, the Bohemia also has several rooms with balconies that look out to the Colonnade. Though not as upscale as the other hotels listed, the Bohemia is still very comfortable. Rooms tend to be plain with little flair.

Hotel Excelsior

Hlavní třída 121, 35301 Mariánské Lázně. ☎ **0165/2705.** Fax 0165/5346. 64 rms. MINIBAR TV TEL. 2,390 Kč ($89) single; 2,990 Kč ($111) double; and from 3,990 Kč ($148) suite. AE, DC, MC, V.

Across from Nové lázně (the New Bath), the Excelsior has benefitted inside and out from a post-Communist face-lift. Several rooms have balconies that overlook the park which leads up to the Colonnade. The hotel staff is also more attentive than those at other hotels in town.

Hotel Palace

Hlavní třída 67, 35301 Mariánské Lázně. ☎ **0165/2222.** Fax 0165/4262. 40 rms, 5 suites. MINIBAR TV TEL. May–Sept, 2,550 Kč ($94) single, 3,400 Kč ($126) double, 5,100 Kč ($189) suite; Apr and Oct, 2,040 Kč ($76) single, 2,720 Kč ($101) double, 3,400 Kč ($126) suite; Nov–March, 1,190 Kč ($44) single, 1,870 Kč ($69) double, 2,550 Kč ($94) suite. AE, DC, MC, V.

One of the top hotels in town, the 1920s-era Palace is a beautiful art nouveau-style hotel located just 300 feet from the spa colonnade. The extremely comfortable rooms contain direct-dial telephones. In addition to a good Bohemian restaurant, the hotel contains a cafe, wine room, and snack bar.

Hotel Zvon

Hlavní třída 68, 35301 Mariánské Lázně. ☎ **0165/2015.** Fax 0165/3245. 79 rms. MINIBAR TV TEL. 2,100 Kč ($78) single; 2,800 Kč ($104) double; 4,000 Kč ($148) 3-room suite. AE, DC, MC, V.

Next door to the Palace, the newly renovated Zvon lacks a bit of the panache that its smaller neighbor has, but still ranks as one of the town's nicer hotels.

INEXPENSIVE

Hotel Cristal Palace

Hlavní třída 61, 35344 Mariánské Lázně. ☎ **0165/2056** or 2057. Fax 0165/2058. 94 rms (4 with bath). 500 Kč ($18.50) single without bath; 1,000 Kč ($33) double without bath, 1,500 Kč ($48.35) double with bath; 1,300 Kč ($43.65) triple without bath. AE, DC, MC, V.

Neither "cristal" nor a palace, this decent hotel enjoys an enviable location just a few minutes south of the town center. Rooms are outfitted with 1950s-style furnishings and double doors to screen out hallway noise. The hotel contains a restaurant, cafe, wine room, and brasserie.

✪ Hotel Koliba

Dusíkova 592, 35301 Mariánské Lázně. ☎ **0165/5169**. Fax 0165/763 10. 10 rms. MINIBAR TV TEL. 1,050 Kč ($39) single; 1,600 Kč ($59) double.

Away from the main strip, but still only a 7-minute walk from the Colonnade, the Koliba is a rustic hunting lodge set in the hills on Dusíkova, the road that leads to the golf course and Karlovy Vary. Rooms are very comfortable. The hotel provides a wide array of spa and health treatments, which cost extra.

WHERE TO DINE
MODERATE

✪ Hotel Koliba Restaurant

Dusíkova 592. ☎ **0165/5169**. Reservations recommended. Soups 10–40 Kč (37¢–$1.48); main courses 120–400 Kč ($4.44–$14.81). No credit cards. Daily 11am–11pm. CZECH.

Like the hotel built into it, the Koliba restaurant is a shrine to the outdoors. The dining room is well-appointed with a hearty rustic atmosphere, which goes perfectly with the restaurant's strength: wild game. Check the daily menu to see what's new, or choose from the wide assortment of *specialty na roštu* (specialties from the grill), including wild boar and venison. The Koliba also has an excellent selection of Moravian wines that can be ordered with your meal, or at its wine bar, which also has dancing from 7pm to midnight (except Mondays).

Hotel Palace Restaurant

Hlavní třída 67. ☎ **0165/2222**. Reservations not needed. Soups 10–40 Kč (37¢–$1.48); main courses 140–320 Kč ($5.19–$11.85). AE, DC, MC, V. Daily 7am–11pm. CZECH/INTERNATIONAL.

The restaurant's mirror- and glass-packed neoclassical dining room is one of the prettiest in town, with a good view of the Colonnade. Bow-tied waiters serve traditional Bohemian specialties like succulent roast duck, boiled trout, and chateaubriand. Most everything comes with dumplings and sauerkraut. During good weather, the best tables are outside on a small street-front porch or on the second-floor terrace.

INEXPENSIVE

Churchill Club Restaurant

Hlavní třída 121. No phone. Reservations not needed. Main courses 110–150 Kč ($4.07–$5.56). No credit cards. Daily 11am–11pm. CZECH.

A lively bar atmosphere makes the Churchill one of the few fun places to be after dark in this quiet town. Don't let the name fool you—the food here is traditional Czech, not British, with few surprises, which is both good and bad. A large selection of beers also sets the Churchill apart from other restaurants along the main strip.

Classic Cafe/Restaurant
Hlavní třída. No phone. Reservations not needed. Salads 51–95 Kč ($1.89–$3.52); main courses 50–130 Kč ($1.85–$4.81). AE, MC, V. Daily 10am–11pm. CZECH.

A nice place to stop for a light bite to eat, the Classic offers a large assortment of good fresh salads. The open and airy cafe/restaurant has one of the friendliest staffs in town. It also brews a mean espresso.

4 Plzeň (Pilsen)

55 miles SW of Prague

Some 400 years ago, a group of men formed Plzeň's first beer-drinking guild, and today, beer is probably the only reason you will want to stop at this otherwise industrial town. Unfortunately for the town, its prosperity and architecture were ravaged during World War II, leaving few buildings untouched. The main square, náměstí Republiky, is worth a look, but after that, there's not much to see.

SPECIAL EVENTS If you're an American, or speak English, being in Plzeň in May is quite an experience. May 8 marks when General George S. Patton was forced to halt his advance after liberating the area, thanks to an Allied agreement to stop. The Russians were allowed to free Prague, becoming its successor superpower as agreed. Forty years of Communist oppression, however, means that the town now celebrates May 8 or **Liberation Day** with a vengeance. You will be fêted and praised into the wee hours of the night, as the city's people give thanks to the forces that ended Nazi occupation.

Anxious to capitalize on its beer heritage, and always happy to celebrate, Plzeň has started its own Octoberfest, called **Pivní slavností.**

For more information on festivities for the two events, contact the City Information Center Plzeň, náměstí Republiky 41, 301 16 Plzeň (☎ **019/7236 535,** fax 019/ 7224 473).

ESSENTIALS

GETTING THERE It's more comfortable taking the train to Plzeň than the bus. A fast train from Prague whisks travelers to Plzeň in just under 2 hours, about the same time the bus takes. Trains between the two cities are just as plentiful and fit most every schedule. The one-way train fare costs 88 Kč ($3.25) first class, 64 Kč ($2.37) second class. To get from the train station to town, walk out the main entrance and take Americká street across the river and turn right onto Jungmannova street, which leads to the main square.

The bus from Prague also takes about 2 hours, but tends to be cramped. If you do take the bus, head back into town along Husova to get to the square.

Unfortunately, the government's highway building scheme has not been finished, so about half of the drive between Prague and Plzeň is on narrow two-lane roads. Leave Prague to the west on the E50 highway. The trip takes about just over an hour, unless you get stuck behind an old Trabant or truck.

VISITOR INFORMATION Realizing it has to be as tourist-friendly as possible, the **City Information Center Plzeň,** náměstí Republiky 41, 301 16 Plzeň (☎ **019/ 7236 535,** fax 019/7224 473), is packed with literature to answer travelers' questions.

ORIENTATION Plzeň's old core is centered around náměstí Republiky. All of the sites, including the brewery, are no more than a 10-minute walk from here.

PLZEŇ'S CLAIM TO FAME

Founded in 1295 by Přemysl King Václav II, Plzeň was, and remains, western Bohemia's administrative center. King Václav's real gift to the town, however, was not making it an administrative nerve center, but granting it brewing rights. As a result, more than 200 microbreweries popped up in almost every street corner basement. Realizing the brews they were drinking had become mostly plonk by the late 1830s, rebellious beer drinkers demanded quality, forcing the brewers to try harder. "Give us what we want in Plzeň, good and cheap beer!" became the battle cry. Before long, in 1842, the brewers combined their expertise to produce a superior brew through what became known as the Pilsner brewing method. If you don't believe it's the best method, look in your refrigerator at home. Most likely, the best beer in there has written somewhere on its label "Pilsner brewed."

TOURING THE BEER SHRINES

Widely regarded as one of the best beers the world over, **Plzeňské Pivovary** (Pilsener Breweries), at U Prazdroje 7, will interest anyone who wants to learn more about the brewing process. The brewery actually is comprised of several different breweries, pumping out brands like Pilsner Urquell and Gambrinus, the most widely consumed beer in the Czech Republic. The 1-hour tour of the factory (which has barely changed since its creation) includes a 15-minute film and visits to the fermentation cellars and brewing rooms. There's only one tour a day at 12:30pm Monday through Saturday. It costs 30 Kč ($1.11) weekdays, 50 Kč ($1.85) Saturdays; the price includes a dozen beer-oriented postcards and some freshly brewed beer.

If you didn't get your fill of beer facts at the brewery, the **Pivovarské Muzeum** (Beer Museum) is one block away on Veleslavínova street. Inside this former 15th-century house you'll learn everything there is to know about beer, but were afraid to ask. In the first room, once a 19th-century pub, the guard winds up an old German polyphone music box from 1887 that plays the sweet, though somewhat scratchy, strains of Strauss' *Blue Danube*. Subsequent rooms display a wide collection of pub artifacts, brewing equipment, and mugs. Most displays have English captions, but ask for a more detailed museum description in English when you enter. Admission is 20 Kč (74¢). It's open Tuesday through Sunday from 10am to 6pm.

EXPLORING PLZEŇ

Safely full of more knowledge than you may want about the brewing process, proceed to the main square to see what's hopping (sorry, I couldn't resist). Dominating the center of the square is the **Gothic Cathedral of St. Bartholomew,** with the tallest steeple in the Czech Republic at 333 feet. Inside the church, a beautiful marble Madonna graces the main altar.

You'll see an Italian flair in the first four floors of the 16th-century **Town Hall** and in the *sgraffito* adorning its facade. Later on, more floors were added, as well as a tower, gables, and brass flags, making the building appear as though another had fallen on top of it. In front of the town hall, a **memorial** built in 1681 commemorates victims of the plague.

Just west of the square on Sady pětatřicátníku lies the shattered dreams of the 2,000 or so Jews who once called Plzeň home. The **Great Synagogue,** the third largest in the world, was built in the late 19th century. But sadly, its doors remain locked, with the building in need of urgent repairs.

WHERE TO STAY

For private rooms that are usually outside of the town center but a little cheaper, try **Čedok** at Sedláčkova 12 (☎ **019/366 48**), open Monday through Friday from 9am to noon and 1 to 5pm (until 6pm in summer), Saturday 9am to noon. Expect to pay about 300 to 400 Kč ($11 to $15) for a double room with a shower and WC.

Hotel Continental

Zbrojnická 8, 305 34 Plzeň. ☎ **019/352 92.** Fax 019/221 746. 42 rooms. TV TEL. 1,030 Kč ($38) single (with shower, but without WC), 1,500 Kč ($56) (with bath and WC); 1,530 Kč ($57) double (with shower, but without WC), 2,200 Kč ($81) double (with bath and WC). AE, MC, V.

Located about one block from the old town square, the modern Continental is considered by locals to be one of the best in town. Velvet-covered furniture and blue-tiled bathrooms greet guests in spacious, comfortable rooms. Downstairs the casino stays open late if you're feeling lucky, or just thirsty.

Hotel Slovan

Smetanovy sadý 1, 305 28 Plzeň. ☎ **019/227 256.** Fax 019/226 841. 110 rms. TV. 680 Kč ($25) single; 1,060 Kč ($39) double. AE, MC, V.

An elegant turn-of-the-century staircase graces the entrance foyer to this venerable hotel. But after that, the rooms fall into the same 1970s-modern decor that, hard as it is to believe, was once in fashion. Nonetheless, the rooms are clean and comfortable, and the square is only about two blocks north.

WHERE TO DINE

Pivnice Prazdroj

1, U Prazdroje (just outside the brewery gates). No phone. Reservations not needed. Soups 10–30 Kč (37¢–$1.11); main courses 40–90 Kč ($1.48–$3.33). No credit cards. Mon–Fri 10am–10pm, Sat–Sun 11am–9pm. CZECH.

Unlike the Na Spilce, this is not a tourist-oriented pub; mostly brewery workers frequent this eatery, just outside the brewery gates. Literally in the same building that houses the brewery's management, the pub has remained true to those who supply it with beverages by cooking hearty basic Czech meals.

Restaurace Na Spilce

U Prazdroje (just inside the brewery gates). No phone. Reservations not needed. Main courses 70–150 Kč ($2.59–$5.56). No credit cards. Daily 11am–10pm. CZECH.

Just inside the brewery gates, Restaurace Na Spilce looks like a 600-seat tourist trap, but the food is quite good and reasonably priced. Standard *řízký* (schnitzels), goulash, and *svíčková na smetaně* (pork tenderloin in a cream sauce) are hearty, and complement the beer that flows in a never-ending stream from the brewery.

5 Cheb (Eger) & Františkovy Lázně

105 miles W of Prague, 25 miles SW of Karlovy Vary

Like Plzeň, few people who travel through Cheb actually stop and take a look around. From the outside, that's understandable, but it's too bad, since the center of Cheb is one of the more architecturally interesting places in west Bohemia. Its history is fascinating as well.

A former stronghold for the Holy Roman Empire on its eastern flank, Eger, as it was then known, became part of Bohemia in 1322. Cheb stayed under Bohemian rule until it was handed to Germany as part of the 1938 Munich Pact. Soon after the end of the World War II, it returned to Czech hands, whereupon most of the area's native Germans, known as Sudeten Germans, were expelled for their open encouragement of the invading Nazi army. This bilingual, bicultural heritage can be seen in the town's main square, which could be mistaken for being on either side of the border, if it weren't for the Czech writing on windows. These days, the Germans have returned, but only for a few hours at a time, many for the town's thriving sex trade and cheap alcohol. Don't be surprised to see women around almost every corner looking to ply their trade. Still, Cheb is worth exploring for its melange of styles in the buildings, the eery Jewish quarter Špalíček, and the enormous, Romanesque Chebsky Hrad (Cheb Castle).

Only about 20 minutes up the road from Cheb is the smallest of the three major Bohemian spa towns, **Františkovy Lázně.** Though it pales in comparison to Karlovy Vary and Marianské Lázně, Františkovy Lázně has taken great strides in the past few years to try and erase the decline it experienced under Communism. There's not much to see save for the **Spa Museum,** which holds an interesting display of bathing artifacts, but it's a much quieter and cleaner place to spend the night than Cheb. I've listed places to stay and dine in both Cheb and Františkovy Lázně.

To get to Františkovy Lázně from Cheb by car, take highway E49. The trip takes about 20 minutes. You can also take a taxi; just agree with the driver before you get in that the fare won't be more than 100 Kč ($3.70).

ESSENTIALS

GETTING THERE   Cheb is located on the E48, one of the main highways leading to Germany. If you're driving from Prague take the same route as you would to Karlovy Vary, which eventually beings you to Cheb. The drive takes about 2½ hours.

Express trains from Prague usually stop in Cheb, as do several trains daily from Karlovy Vary. Cheb is on a main train route of the Czech Republic, so it's easy to catch many international connections here. The train takes 3½ hours and costs 151 Kč ($5.60) one way in first class, 106 Kč ($3.92) second class.

Cheb is a long bus ride from Prague, and I suggest avoiding taking the bus if possible. It's more manageable to take the bus from Karlovy Vary to Cheb.

ORIENTATION   At the center of the old town lies the triangular náměstí Krále Jiřího z Poděbrad. Most of the main sights visitors will want to see lie either directly on the square, or on one of the many streets leading off of it.

VISITOR INFORMATION   You'll find maps, guidebooks, lodging, and even a currency exchange (at a fairly steep price so only use it if desperate) at the **Informacní Centrum Goetz & Hanzlík,** náměstí Přemysla Otakara II 2 (☎ **0166/594 80,** fax 0166/592 91).

EXPLORING CHEB

The main square, **náměstí Krále Jiřího z Poděbrad,** attracts most of the attention, and is a good place to begin a tour of the old town. Though it has been overrun with touristy shops and cafes that serve uniformly mediocre German fare, the square still shines with Gothic burgher houses and the baroque **old town hall (stará radnice).** At its south end, the **statue Kašna Roland,** built in 1591 and a former symbol of capital punishment, reminds people of the strength justice can wield. At the other end of the square stands the **Kašna Herkules,** a monument to the town's former strength and power. Next to it stands a cluster of 11 timber houses, called **Špalíček.** These houses used to be owned by Jews in the early 14th century, but a fervently anti-Semitic clergy in the area incited such hatred against the Jews that they were forced up Židská ulice (Jews Street) and into an alleyway called ulička Zavražděných (Murderer's Lane), where they were unceremoniously slaughtered in 1350.

Across from Špalíček is the **Cheb Museum,** where another murder took place almost 300 years later—that of Albrecht von Wallenstein in 1634. On the upper level a display vividly depicts the assassination. The museum's first floor displays many 20th-century paintings from which one can trace the town's slow demise.

Admission is 20 Kč (74¢). Open Tuesday through Sunday from 9am to noon and 1pm to 5pm.

The old town of Cheb is also packed with several churches. The most interesting church is **St. Nicholas,** just around the corner from the museum. It's a hodgepodge of architecural styles: its Romanesque heritage is reflected in the tower windows, while a Gothic portal added later and baroque interior round out the renovations over the years.

TOURING CHEB CASTLE

A better example of Romanesque architecture can be found in the northeast part of the old town, where the **Cheb Castle** stands. Overlooking the Elbe River, the castle, built in the late 12th century, is one of central Europe's largest Romanesque structures.

The castle's main draws are its **chapel of Sts. Erhard and Ursala** and the **Černá věž** (Black Tower). The two-tiered, early Gothic chapel has a dark somber first floor where the proletariat would congregate, while the emperor and his family went to the much cheerier and brighter second floor with its Gothic windows. Unfortunately, there are no tours of the castle, and the English text provided at the entrance does little to inform visitors. Admission is 20 Kč (74¢). Open June through August, Tuesday to Sunday from 9am to noon and 1pm to 6pm; May and September, Tuesday to Sunday from 9am to noon and 1pm to 5pm; April and October, Tuesday to Sunday from 9am to noon and 1pm to 4pm.

Across the courtyard from the chapel stands the **Černá věž** (Black Tower). From its 60-foot-high lookout, you'll see the best views of the town. The tower seems dusty and smeared with pollution, but its color is not from the emissions of the Trabats and Škodas that drive through the streets. Rather the tower is black because the blocks it is made from are actually lava rocks taken from the nearby Komorni Hurka volcano (which is now dormant).

WHERE TO STAY
IN CHEB

Hotel Hvězda (Hotel Star)
náměstí Krále Jiřího z Poděbrad 3, 350 01 Cheb. ☎ **0166/225 49.** Fax 0166/225 46. 44 rooms. TV TEL. 800 Kč ($30) single; 1,000 Kč ($37) double. AE, MC, V.

Overlooking the rather noisy main square, the Hvězda is a lone star in the Cheb hotel universe. Small but clean rooms make it bearable, and the staff does try to make your stay comfortable. If you can't stay in Františkovy Lázně, and you don't want to drive further, this is really the only hotel I would recommend staying at in town.

IN FRANTIŠKOVY LÁZNĚ

Hotel Tří Lilie (The Three Lilies Hotel)
Jiráskova 17, 351 01 Františkovy Lázně. ☎ **0166/942 350.** Fax 0166/942 970. 32 rooms. TV TEL. 2,430 Kč ($90) single; 2,970 Kč ($110) double; 4,140 Kč ($153). AE, MC, V.

In 1808, Geothe stayed here and he knew what he was doing. The Three Lilies is worth the extra money since it's the only luxury hotel in the area. Cheb needs a nice hotel like this. You can relax here; at night, you can block out noise in the spotless, spacious, well-appointed rooms. The staff are very attentive and can arrange spa treatments, massages, and other health services. On the main floor there is a nice, if not pricey, bar and restaurant.

Interhotel Slovan

Národní Třída 5, 351 01 Františkovy Lázně. ☎ **0166/942 841.** Fax 0166/942 843. 25 rooms.
TV TEL. 650–750 Kč ($24–$28) single; 1,100–1,600 Kč ($41–$59) double. AE, MC, V.

This hotel is not as elegant as the Three Lillies just down the main street, but it's a
nice place nonetheless. Rooms are a little plain and small, but for the money, they're
one of the best bets in town. The only drawback is a staff that at times forgets that
the customer is also paying for service.

WHERE TO DINE
In Cheb

Staročeská Restaurace

Kamenná 1, Cheb. No phone. Reservations not needed. Main courses 65–110 Kč ($2.41–$4.07).
No credit cards. Daily 10am–10pm. CZECH/CHINESE.

This restaurant serves much the same fare as all of the other restaurants on or around
the square, but what caught my eye were the few Chinese meals offered. The *Kuře
Kung-Pao* (Kung pao chicken) was a good spicy alternative to the sausages and meat
and dumplings most of the other diners were having.

In Františkovy Lázně

Restaurace Interhotel Slovan

Národní Třída 5, Františkovy Lázně. No phone. Main courses 85–220 Kč ($3.15–$8.15). No
credit cards. Daily 8am–10pm. CZECH.

As the prices show, this restaurant tries to appeal to every budget. Be prepared for
more heavy central European cuisine, with all four Czech food groups—meat,
potatoes, dumplings and cabbage—well represented. The fish tend to be a lighter
meal than the pork cutlet smothered in cheese and ham, but both proved to
be excellent choices. Oddly, the service at the restaurant is markedly better than
the hotel.

6 České Budějovice

92 miles S of Prague

This fortress town was born in 1265, when King Otakar II decided that the intersection point of the Vltava and the Malše rivers would be the site of a bastion to
protect the approaches to southern Bohemia. Although King Otakar was killed at the
battle of the Moravian Field in 1278, and the town was subsequently ravaged by the
rival Vítkovic family, the construction of České Budějovice continued, eventually
taking the shape originally envisaged.

In the 15th century, the Hussite revolution swept across southern Bohemia, with
one exception—České Budějovice, which, with its largely Catholic population,
remained true to the king. Passing the loyalty test with flying colors, České Budějovice
developed into one of Bohemia's wealthiest and most important towns, reaching its
pinnacle in the 16th century. This rise made České Budějovice an architecturally
stunning place. As the town prospered, older Gothic buildings took on a Renaissance
look. A new town hall was built and the flourishing old market (Masné Krámy) was
rebuilt. Towering above it all was a newly built 72-meter-tall turret, the Black Tower.
Unfortunately, the Thirty Years War (1618–1648) and a major fire in 1641 ravaged
most of the town, leaving few buildings unscathed. But the Habsburg empire came
to the town's rescue in the 18th century, building baroque-style edifices that stand
to this day.

Today, České Budějovice, the hometown of the original Budweiser brand beer, is now more a bastion for the beer drinker than a protector of Bohemia. But its slow pace, relaxed atmosphere, and interesting architecture make it a worthy stop, especially as a base for exploring southern Bohemia, or for those heading to Austria.

SPECIAL EVENTS   Each August, České Budějovice hosts the largest **International Agricultural show** in the country.

If you're passing through in the late fall or winter and want to see Czechs become emotional, head out to a match of the **Czech Extraliga hockey** league at the Winter Stadium (Zimní stadion) on ulice F.A. Gerstnera where the local team does battle. Arguably some of the best hockey in the world is played in the Czech Republic, which you can see for a fraction of the price (about 30 Kč/$1.11) you would pay to see players of a similar caliber in Western countries.

ESSENTIALS

GETTING THERE   If you're driving, leave Prague to the south via the main D1 expressway, and take the cutoff for highway E55, which runs straight to České Budějovice. The trip takes about 1¹/₂ hours.

Daily express trains from Prague make the trip to České Budějovice in about 2¹/₂ hours. The one way fare is 124 Kč ($4.59) first class, 88 Kč ($3.25) second class.

Several express buses run from Prague's Florenc station each day and take two hours.

You can take a taxi for 500 Kč ($18.50) each way to Třeboň.

ORIENTATION   České Budějovice's circular Staré Město (Old Town) centers around the Czech Republic's largest cobblestone square, called náměstí Přemysla Otakara II.

VISITOR INFORMATION   **Informacní Centrum Goetz & Hanzlík,** náměstí Přemysla Otakara II 2 (☎ **038/594 80,** fax 038/592 91) provides maps, guidebooks, currency exchange (at a fairly steep price so use only if you're really desperate), and finds lodging.

EXPLORING THE TOWN

You can comfortably see České Budějovice in a day; it's small enough. At its center is one of central Europe's largest squares, the cobblestone **náměstí Přemysla Otakara II**—it may be too large as many of the buildings tend to get lost with all of the open space. The square contains the ornate **Fountain of Sampson**, an 18th-century water well that was once the town's principal water supply, plus a mishmash of baroque and Renaissance buildings. On the square's southwest corner is the **town hall**, an elegant baroque structure built by Martinelli between 1727 and 1730. On top of the town hall, the larger-than-life statues by Dietrich represent the civic virtues: justice, bravery, wisdom, and diligence.

One block northwest of the square is the **Černá věž** (Black Tower), which can be seen from almost every point in the city. Consequently, its 360 steps are worth the climb to get a bird's-eye view of the city in all directions. The most famous symbol of České Budějovice, this 232-foot-tall 16th-century tower was built as a belfry for the adjacent **St. Nicholas Church.** This 13th-century church, one of the town's most important sights, was a bastion of Roman Catholicism during the 15th-century Hussite rebellion. The church's flamboyant white-and-cream 17th-century baroque interior shouldn't be missed.

TOURING A BEER SHRINE

On the town's northern edge sits a shrine to those who pray to the gods of the amber nectar. This is where **Budějovicky Budvar,** the original brewer of the Budweiser-brand beer, has its one and only factory. Established in 1895, Budvar draws on more than 700 years of the area's brewing tradition to produce one of the world's best beers. Please refer to the "When You Say Bud . . ." box in Chapter 1 for more about the brewer.

Four trolley-buses—nos. 2, 4, 6, and 8—stop by the brewery; this is how the brewery ensures that its workers and visitors reach the plant safely each day. The trolley costs 6 Kč (22¢) to the brewery. You can also hop a cab from the town square for about 50 Kč ($1.85).

Tours can be arranged by phoning ahead, but only for groups. If you're traveling alone or with only one or two other people, ask a hotel concierge at one of the bigger hotels (I suggest the Hotel Zvon) if they can put you in with an already scheduled group. Failing that, you may want to take a chance and head up to the brewery where, if a group has arrived, another person or two will not be noticed.

Once inside the brewery, the smell may cause flashbacks to some of the wilder frat parties you've attended. This is a traditional brew, and one of the points that will jump out at you right from the beginning is that not much has changed at the brewery over the past hundred years or so. The room where everything moves along conveyer belts and goes from dirty old bottles to boxed cartons is fascinating, if you haven't seen this before. For more information contact Budvar n.p., Karolíny Světlé 4, České Budějovice (☎ **038/770 5111**).

A SIDE TRIP TO A 141-ROOM CASTLE

Only 8 kilometers away from the city to the north lies the **castle Hluboká nad Vltavou.** The distance is short enough to make a pleasant bike trip from the city, or a quick stop either on the way to, or coming from Prague, Třeboň, or Tábor.

If you're driving to Hluboká from České Budějovice, take the E49 highway north and then the 105 just after leaving the outskirts of České Budějovice. For cyclists or those driving who prefer a slower, more scenic route, take the road that runs behind the brewery; it passes through the village of Obora.

Built in the 13th century, Hluboká has undergone many face-lifts over the years, but none that left as lasting an impression as those ordered by the Schwarzenberg family. As a sign of the region's growing wealth and importance in the mid-19th century, the Schwarzenbergs remodeled the 141-room castle in the neo-Gothic style of England's Windsor Castle. Robin Leach would be proud. No expense was spared to gain opulence. The Schwartzenbergs removed the impressive wooden ceiling from their residence at Český Krumlov and re-installed it in the large dining room. Other rooms are as equally garish in their appointments, making a guided tour worth the time, even though only about a third of the rooms are open to the public. To complete the experience, the **Alšova Jihočeská Galerie** (Art Gallery of South Bohemia) in the riding school at Hluboká houses the second largest art collection in Bohemia, including many interesting Gothic sculptures from the area.

WHERE TO STAY

Several agencies can locate reasonably priced private rooms. Expect to pay between 300 and 600 Kč ($11–$22) per person, in cash. **Nimbus Travel**, Žižkova 3 (☎ 038/570 85) or **Goetz & Hanzlík,** náměstí Přemysla Otakara II 2 (☎ **038/594 80,** fax 038/592 91), usually have a wide selection of conveniently located rooms.

Hotel Gomel

Míru třída 14, 370 01 České Budějovice. ☎ **038/731 1390.** 180 rooms. MINIBAR TV TEL. 1,240 Kč ($45.90) single; 1,990 Kč ($74) double; 2,930 Kč ($108) suite. Rates include breakfast. AE, DC, MC, V.

Not known for its ambience, the 18-floor Gomel has a straightforward approach where you'll get a comfortable, clean room with either a bath or shower en suite and few other frills. Views from the upper floors can't be beat. Located just off the main road entering the city from the north, the Gomel is hard to miss and only a few minutes walk from the historic old town.

Hotel U solné brány

Radniční ulice 11, 370 01 České Budějovice. ☎ **038/541 21,** fax 038/541 20. 11 rms. MINIBAR TV TEL. 690 Kč ($26) single; 1,420 Kč ($53) double; 1,990 Kč ($74) suite. Rates include breakfast. MC, V.

Conveniently located just off of the main square, U solné brány is one of the products of post-Communism: a bright, renovated hotel with friendly management. It almost feels like a pension. Most rooms have balconies making a cold Budvar from the minibar almost mandatory in the early evening or as a nightcap. The hotel does have a curious rate structure, though, which encourages singles over doubles (though the singles are much smaller). Try not to make as obvious a double take as I did when I heard the prices.

Hotel Zvon

Žižkovo náměstí, 37042 České Budějovice. ☎ **038/353 61.** 45 rms. TV TEL. 990 Kč ($37) single; 1,490 Kč ($55) double; 1,890 Kč ($70) suite. AE, V.

Location is everything to the city's most elegant hotel, which occupies several historic buildings directly on the town's main square. Many upper-floor rooms have been renovated, while others are relatively plain and functional. The views from those in front, however, can't be topped, and since the square is so big, noise is rarely a problem. Rooms facing the square on the upper floors aren't only brighter, they're larger and nicer, too. Try to avoid the smaller rooms, which are usually reserved for tour groups. There is no elevator, but if you don't mind the climb, stay on the fourth floor. Watch out for the staff, though, who tend to be surly and indifferent to guests' needs.

WHERE TO DINE

⑤ Masné Krámy (Meat Shops)

Krajinská 29. ☎ **038/326 52.** Main courses 90–180 Kč ($3.33–$6.67). No credit cards. Daily 10am–11pm. CZECH.

If you have pledged not to go to any "tourist traps," rationalize going to this one by reminding yourself that it's also a historical building. Located just northwest of náměstí Přemysla Otakara II, labyrinthine Masné Krámy occupies a series of drinking rooms on either side of a long hallway and is a must for any serious pub-goer. The inexpensive and filling food is pure Bohemia, including several pork, duck, and trout dishes. Come here for the boisterous and lively atmosphere.

Rybářsky Sál

In the Hotel Gomel, Míru třída 14. ☎ **038/289 49.** Main courses 90–240 Kč ($3.33–$8.89). AE, DC, MC, V. Mon–Thurs 6am–10pm, Fri–Sat 6am–11pm. CZECH/INTERNATIONAL.

Generally acknowledged by locals as some of the best food in town, the Rybářsky Sál is a popular restaurant known for four freshwater fish: carp, trout, perch, and pike. Chicken Kiev and other "turf" dishes are also served. The dining room is modern and minimally decorated with hanging fishnets. If the menu is not what you want, try the **Myslivecky Sál** in the same hotel for wild game and more meat-laden dishes at similar prices.

U paní Emy

Široká 25. No phone. Reservations not needed. Main courses 80–190 Kč ($2.96–$7). No credit cards. Daily 10am–3am. CZECH/INTERNATIONAL.

Usually crowded, U paní Emy has a good selection on the menu with reasonable prices for both food and beverages. The chicken and fish dishes are the most popular choices. The pan-fried trout tastes very light, not oily as most Czech restaurants tend to make it. A wine bar here stays open to the wee hours.

7 Český Krumlov

12 miles SW of České Budějovice

If you only have time on your visit to the Czech Republic for one excursion, seriously consider making it ✪ Český Krumlov. One of Bohemia's prettiest towns, Krumlov is a living gallery of elegant Renaissance-era buildings housing charming cafes, pubs, restaurants, shops, and galleries. In 1992 UNESCO named Český Krumlov a World Heritage Site for its historical importance and physical beauty.

Bustling since medieval times, the town, after centuries of embellishment, is exquisitely beautiful. In 1302 the Rožmberk family inherited the castle and moved in, using it as their main residence for nearly 300 years. You'll feel that time has stopped as you look from the Lazebnický bridge, with the waters of the Vltava below, snaking past the castle's gray stone. At night, with the castle light, the view becomes even more dramatic.

Few deigned to change the appearance of Český Krumlov over the years, not even the Schwarzenbergs, who had a flair for opulence. At the turn of the 19th century, several facades of houses in the town's outer section were built, as were inner courtyards. Thankfully, economic stagnation in the area during Communism meant little money for "development," so no glass and steel edifice like the Hotel Thermal in Karlovy Vary, juts out to spoil the town's architectural beauty. Instead, a medieval sense reigns supreme in Český Krumlov, now augmented by the many festivals and renovations that keep the town's spirit alive.

Consider yourself warned, however, that word has spread about this town. Summer season can be unbearable as thousands of tourists blanket its medieval streets. If possible, try to visit in the off-season when the crowds recede, prices decrease, and the town's charm can really shine. Who knows, you may even hear some Czech!

SPECIAL EVENTS   After being banned during Communism (a little too feudalistic for Gottwald), the **Slavnost pětilisté ruže** (Festival of the Five-Petalled Rose) has made a triumphant comeback. It's held each year at the summer solstice. Residents of Český Krumlov dress up in Renaissance costume and parade through the streets. Afterward, the streets become a stage with plays, chess games with people dressed as pieces, music, and even duels "to the death."

Český Krumlov also plays host to a 2-week **International Music Festival** every August, attracting performers from all over the world. Performances are held in nine spectacular venues. For information or ticket reservations contact the festival organizer, **Auviex,** Obrovského 10, 141 00, Prague 4 (☎ **02/767 275** or **769 443;** fax 02/2 768-881; in Český Krumlov 0337/4275 3350).

ESSENTIALS

GETTING THERE　From České Budějovice, it's about a 45-minute drive to Krumlov, depending on traffic. Take highway 3 leading from the south of České Budějovice and turn onto highway 159. The roads are clearly marked, with several signs directing traffic to the town. From Prague, it's a two-hour drive.

The only way to reach Český Krumlov by train from Prague is via České Budějovice, a slow ride that will deposit you at a station relatively far from the town center. It takes 3½ hours; the one way fare is 136 Kč ($5.03) first class, 96 Kč ($3.56) second class.

The nearly 3-hour bus ride from Prague usually involves a transfer in České Budějovice. The bus station in Český Krumlov is a 15-minute walk from the town's main square.

ORIENTATION　Surrounded by a circular sweep of the Vltava River, Český Krumlov is very easy to negotiate. The main square, náměstí Svornosti, is located at the very center of the Inner town. The bridge that spans the Vltava a few blocks away leads to a rocky hill and Latrán, above which is a castle known as the Český Krumlov Château.

VISITOR INFORMATION　Located right on the main square, the **Information Centrum,** náměstí Svornosti 1, 381 00 Český Krumlov (☎ / Fax **0337/5670**) provides a complete array of tourist services from booking accommodations to ticket reservations for events, as well as a phone and fax service. Open daily from 9am to 6pm.

Be warned that the municipal hall is located in the same building, it's crowded with weddings on weekends. If someone holds out a hat, throw some change into it, take a traditional shot of liquor from them, and *blahopřát* (congratulate) just about everyone in the room.

A WALKING TOUR OF ČESKÝ KRUMLOV

Bring a good pair of walking shoes, and be prepared to wear them out. Český Krumlov not only lends itself to hours of strolling, but its hills and alleyways demand it. No cars, thank goodness, are allowed in the historic town, and the cobblestones keep most other vehicles at bay. The town is split into two parts—the **Inner town** and **Latrán,** which houses the castle. Each are better tackled separately, rather than crisscrossing the bridges several times.

Begin your tour at the **Okresní Muzeum** (Regional Museum) at the top of Horní ulice. Once a Jesuit seminary, the three-story museum now contains artifacts and displays relating to Český Krumlov's 1,000-year history. The highlight of this mass of folk art, clothing, furniture, and statues is a giant model of the town that offers a bird's-eye view of the buildings. Admission is 20 Kč (74¢). Open Tuesday through Sunday from 10am to 12:30pm and 1 to 6pm.

Across the street from the museum is the **Hotel Růže** (Rose), which was once a Jesuit student house. Built in the late 16th century, the hotel and the prelature next to it show the development of architecture; Gothic, Renaissance, and rococo influences are all present. If you're not staying at the hotel, don't be afraid to walk around and even ask questions at the reception desk.

Continue down the street to the impressive late Gothic **St. Vitus Cathedral.** Be sure to climb the church tower, which offers one of the most spectacular views of both the Inner town and the castle across the river.

As you tumble down the street further, you will come to **náměstí Svornosti.** Few buildings show any character, making the main square of such an impressive town

Český Krumlov

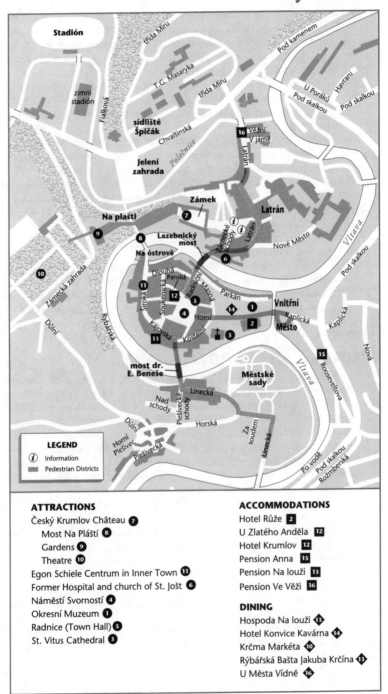

LEGEND
(i) Information
▬ Pedestrian Districts

ATTRACTIONS
Český Krumlov Château ❼
   Most Na Plášti ❽
   Gardens ❾
   Theatre ❿
Egon Schiele Centrum in Inner Town ⓫
Former Hospital and church of St. Jošt ❻
Náměstí Svornosti ❹
Okresní Muzeum ❶
Radnice (Town Hall) ❺
St. Vitus Cathedral ❸

ACCOMMODATIONS
Hotel Růže 🄬2
U Zlatého Anděla 🄬12
Hotel Krumlov 🄬12
Pension Anna 🄬15
Pension Na louži 🄬13
Pension Ve Věži 🄬16

DINING
Hospoda Na louži ⓭
Hotel Konvice Kavárna ⓮
Krčma Markéta ❿
Rýbářská Bašta Jakuba Krčína ⓭
U Města Vídně ⓰

a little disappointing. The **Radnice** (Town Hall) located at náměstí Svornosti 1 is one of the few exceptions. Its Gothic arcades and Renaissance vault inside are exceptionally beautiful in this otherwise rundown area. From the square, streets fan out in all directions. Take some time just to wander through the streets. You might want to grab a light snack before crossing the bridge.

As you cross the bridge and head toward the castle you will see immediately to your right the former **hospital and church of St. Jošt.** Founded at the beginning of the 14th century, it has since been turned into apartments. Feel free to snoop around, but don't enter the building.

One of Český Krumlov's most famous residents was the Austrian-born artist Egon Schiele. A bit of an eccentric who on more than one occasion raised the ire of the town's residents (many were distraught with his use of their young women as his nude models), Schiele's stay was cut short as residents' patience ran out. But the town readopted the artist in 1993, setting up the **Egon Schiele Foundation and the Egon Schiele Centrum** in Inner town, Široká 70-72, 381 01, Český Krumlov (☎ **0337/4232,** fax 0337/2820).

The center documents his life and work, housing a permanent selection of his paintings as well as exhibitions of other 20th-century artists. Admission depends on the exhibitions being displayed. Open daily 10am to 6pm.

For a different perspective on what the town looks like, take the stairs from the **Městské divadlo** (Town Theater) on Horní ulice down to the river front and rent a boat from **Maláček boat rentals.** Always willing to lend his advice, the affable Pepa Maláček will tell you what to watch out for, and where the best fishing is (even if you don't want him to!).

EXPLORING ČESKÝ KRUMLOV CHÂTEAU

Reputedly the second largest castle in Bohemia (after Prague Castle), **Český Krumlov Château** was constructed in the 13th century as part of a private estate. Throughout the ages, the castle has passed on to a variety of private owners, including the Rožmberk family, the largest landholders in Bohemia, and the Schwarzenbergs, the Bohemian equivalent of the TV show *Dynasty's* Carrington family.

From here you will begin the long climb up to the **castle**. Greeting visitors is a round 12th-century **tower**, with its Renaissance balcony. You'll pass over the moat, now occupied by two brown bears. Next is the **Dolní Hrad** (Lower Castle) and then the **Horní Hrad** (Upper Castle).

Perched high atop a rocky hill, the château is open to tourists from April to October only, exclusively by guided tour. Visits begin in the palace's rococo **Chapel of St. George**, continue through portrait-packed **Renaissance Hall,** and end with the **Royal Family Apartments,** outfitted with ornate furnishings that include Flemish wall tapestries and European paintings. Tours last 1 hour and depart frequently. Most are in Czech or German, however. If you want an English-language tour, arrange it ahead of time (☎ **0337/2075**).

The tour costs 90 Kč ($3.33) for adults, 45 Kč ($1.67) students. The castle hours are May through August, Tuesday to Sunday from 7:45am to noon and 12:45 to 4pm; September, Tuesday to Sunday from 8:45am to noon and 12:45 to 4pm; April and October, Tuesday to Sunday 8:45am to noon and 12:45 to 3pm. The last entrance is one hour before closing.

Once past the main castle building, one of the more stunning views of Český Krumlov can be seen from **Most Na Plášti,** a walkway that doubles as a belvedere to the Inner town. Even further up the hill lie the castle's riding school and gardens.

A Renaissance Pub Endures

Most visitors don't come this far up the castle during the day, let alone at night. That's their loss, for I have had what's been one of my finest dining experiences in the Czech Republic at **Krčma Markéta,** Latrán 67 (☎ 0337/3829).

To get here, walk all the way up the hill through the castle, past the Horní Hrad (Upper Castle) and past the Zámecké Divadlo (Castle Theater). Walk through the raised walkway and into the Zámecká Zahrada (Castle Garden) where you will eventually find this Renaissance pub.

When you go inside, you'll feel like you've left this century. There's no need for plates here, as meals are served on wooden blocks. Drinks come in pewter mugs. And at the center of it all stands the intimidating Robin Kratochvíl. Always sporting knee-high black leather boots, the 6′4″ cook laughs heartily all night as he wields a set of tongs big enough to turn a Volkswagen. Next to him (and almost the same size, I swear) is his dog, who knows how to con leftovers from even the stingiest table—and who guests love.

There's no menu here. Just go up to the spit and see what's roasting; usually there's a wide variety of meats, including succulent pork cutlets, rabbit, chickens, and pork knees, a Czech delicacy. When the plate comes, don't wait for the vegetables. Vegetarians need not apply.

Before the night is over, go up and talk to the affable cook. Robin is always willing to strike up a conversation (his English is weak but he's fluent in German). He tells tales that capture everyone's attention. Time seems to stand still. I know I didn't want to go home.

Krčma Markéta is open daily 6pm to 11pm. Reservations are recommended. Soup costs 15 Kč (56¢), and main courses are 60 to 130 Kč ($2.22–$4.81). No credit cards are accepted.

WHERE TO STAY

With the rise of free enterprise after the fall of Communism, many hotels have sprouted up, or are getting a "new" old look. "Pension" and "Zimmer Frei" signs line Horní and Rooseveltova streets, and offer some of the best values in town. For a comprehensive list of area hotels and help with bookings, call or write to the Infocentrum listed above in "Visitor Information."

MODERATE

Hotel Růže (Rose Hotel)
Horní 153, 38101 Český Krumlov. ☎ **0337/2245** or 5481. Fax 3381. 50 rms. MINIBAR TV TEL. May–Sept 1,260–1,350Kč ($47–$50) single; 1,980–2,070 Kč ($73–$77) double; 3,420–4,140 Kč ($127–$153) suite. Oct–April 940–1,080 Kč ($35–$40) single; 1,570–1,660 Kč ($58–$61) double; 2,750–3,320 Kč ($102–$123) suite. AE, MC, V.

Once a Jesuit seminary, this stunning Italian Renaissance structure has been turned into a well-appointed hotel. Comfortable in a big-city kind of way, the hotel is packed with amenities, and is one of the top places to stay in Český Krumlov. But for all of the splendor the building it holds, you may find the Růže a bit of a disappointment. Rooms are not period furnished, but look as though they were furnished from the floor of a Sears warehouse in the U.S. Midwest. While rooms are clean and spacious, the promise of a Renaissance stay dissipates quickly. For families or large groups, the larger suites, which have eight beds, provide good value.

INEXPENSIVE

Hotel Krumlov

náměstí Svorností 14, 38101 Český Krumlov. ☎ **0337/2040.** 33 rms (5 with full bath and WC, 4 with shower and WC). TV TEL. 490 Kč ($18) single without shower, 670 Kč ($25) single with shower only; 770 Kč ($29) double without shower, 1,100–1,250 Kč ($41–$46) double with bath and WC; 2,400 Kč ($89) suite with bath and WC. AE, DC, V.

Located on the town's main square, a few minutes' walk from Český Krumlov Château, Hotel Krumlov is an aging belle dating from 1309. Like so many others in the republic, there's nothing fancy here, just satisfactory rooms right in the heart of the city. The hotel's restaurant serves typical Bohemian fare daily from 7am to 11pm.

Hotel U Zlatého Anděla

náměstí Svorností 10, 38101 Český Krumlov. ☎ **0337/2473.** 4 rms. 1,000 Kč ($37). Rates include breakfast. No credit cards.

The publisher of Frommer's stayed here and preferred it to the Hotel Růže. He thought this hotel had a more comfortable and friendly atmosphere. The attractive rooms are also much less expensive, but those over the bar are noisy.

✪ Pension Anna

Rooseveltova 41, 38101 Český Krumlov. ☎ **0337/4418.** 8 rms. 1,000 Kč ($37) double; 1,200 Kč ($44) suite (with four beds). Rates include breakfast. No credit cards.

Along "pension alley," Anna is a very comfortable and rustic place to stay. What makes this pension a favorite among the others is the friendly management and homey feeling you get as you walk up to your room. Forget hotels—this is the kind of place where you can relax. The owners even let you buy drinks and snacks at the bar downstairs and take them to your room. The suites with four beds and a living room are great for families and group travelers.

Pension Na louži

Kájovská 66, 38101 Český Krumlov. ☎ / Fax **0337/5495.** 5 rms. 900 Kč ($33) single/double; 1,200 Kč triple ($44); 1,400 Kč ($52) suite. No credit cards.

Smack-dab in the heart of the Inner town, the small Na louži, decorated with early 20th- century wooden furniture, is oozing with charm. The only drawback is beds with foot boards that can be a little short for those over 6 feet tall.

✪ Pension Ve Věži (In the Tower)

Latrán 28, 38101 Český Krumlov. ☎ **0337/5287** or 4972. 4 rms (none with bath, common shower and WC for 2 rooms). May–Sept, 990 Kč ($37) double; 1,540 Kč ($57) quadruple. Oct–Apr, 770 Kč ($29) double, 1,320 Kč ($49) quad. Rates include breakfast. No credit cards.

A private pension located in a renovated medieval tower just a 5-minute walk from the castle, Ve Věži is one of the most magnificent places to stay in town. It's not the accommodations themselves that are so grand; none has a private bath, and all are sparsely decorated. Instead, what's wonderful is the ancient ambience that fills this place. Advance reservations are always recommended.

WHERE TO DINE

Hospoda Na louži

Kájovská 66, 381 01. No phone. Main courses 50–100 Kč ($1.85–$3.70). No credit cards. Daily 10am–10pm. CZECH.

The large wooden tables encourage you to get to know your neighbors in this locals-turned-touristy Inner town pub, located in a 15th-century house. Still, the atmosphere is fun and the food above average. If no table is available, stand and have a drink; tables turn over pretty quickly and the staff is accommodating. In the summer, the terrace seats only six so dash over if a seat becomes empty.

Kavárna
At the Hotel Konvice, Horní ul. 144. ☎ **0337/4180**. Reservations not necessary. Main courses 84–200 Kč ($3.11–$7.40). AE, MC, V. Daily 8am–10pm. CZECH.

If weather permits, eat outside overlooking the river at the Kavárna at the Hotel Konvice. Try the boned chicken breast smothered in cheese or any of the steaks and salads.

Rybařská Bašta Jakuba Krčína
Kájovská 54. ☎ **0337/671 83**. Reservations recommended. Main courses 120–300 Kč ($4.44–$11.11). AE, MC, V. Daily 7am–11pm. CZECH.

One of the town's most celebrated restaurants, this place specializes in freshwater fish from surrounding lakes. Trout, perch, pike, and eel are sautéed, grilled, baked, and fried in a variety of herbs and spices. Venison, rabbit, and other game are also available, along with the requisite roast beef and pork cutlet dinners.

U Města Vídně
Latrán 78. No phone. Reservations not necessary. Main courses 50–95 Kč ($1.85–$3.52). No credit cards. Daily 10am–10pm. CZECH.

This locals' kind of pub is not only a good restaurant but one of the best hangouts in town. Traditional meat-and-dumplings–style food is augmented by a few egg-based vegetarian dishes. Natives swear by the pub's locally brewed Českokrumlovské beer.

8 Třeboň

15 miles E of České Budějovice

Just a 30-minute bus ride east of České Budějovice (or a 500 Kč/$18.50 taxi ride one way), Třeboň is a diamond in the rough, a walled city that time, war, and disaster have failed to destroy. Surrounded by forests and ponds, the town slowly grew during the 12th and 13th centuries, until the mid-14th century when four of the Rožmberk brothers (also known as the Rosenbergs) took over, making Třeboň a home away from home (their official residence was down the road in Český Krumlov). Třeboň quickly flourished, attaining key brewing and salt customs rights. Adding to the town's coffers were more than 5,000 fish ponds built by fish masters Štěpánek Netolický and his successor Mikuláš Rathard.

Though war and fires in the 17th and 18th centuries razed most of the town's historical Renaissance architecture, a slow rebuilding process eventually restored nearly every square meter of the walled town to its original condition. Under Communism, Třeboň was awarded spa rights, which kept money flowing in and buildings in a state of good repair.

Some consider Třeboň to be the poorer sister to Český Krumlov, but I strongly disagree. Sure it's not the same, but Třeboň has not been completely overrun by tourists who trample everything in their wake. Instead, Třeboň exists with or without visitors. Many of my Czech friends stay here on a regular basis, but few of my foreign friends do. This alone makes me recommend Třeboň as the small town to stay in overnight when traveling in the region.

ESSENTIALS
GETTING THERE   Buses leave from the České Budějovice bus station every hour or so and cost about 100 Kč ($3.70).

By train, the town is a stop on the Prague-Tábor-Vienna route. Trains and buses also regularly leave for Třeboň from Jindřichův Hradec and Tábor. From Prague the train takes 1¹/₄ hours; the one way fare is 112 Kč ($4.15) first class, 80 Kč ($2.96) second class.

From Prague, take the E55 highway through Tabor and turn left onto highway 150 just past the town of Veselí nad Lužnicí. The trip takes at least 1¹/₂ hours. From České Budějovice, take E551 east to Třeboň. This last route is particularly good for bicyclists, as there are very few hills to climb and several nice villages along the way.

ORIENTATION   There are only three ways to penetrate Třeboň's old town walls, short of pole vaulting. To the east is the Hradecká brána (Castle gate); on the southern edge of town lies the Svinenská brána; and from the west is Budějovická brána. Once inside any of these gates, the six or so streets that comprise the old town can be easily navigated.

VISITOR INFORMATION   The **Informacní Středisko** can be found on Masarykovo náměstí in the heart of the old town, Masarykovo náměstí 102, 379 01 Třeboň (☎ **0333/2557** or 2695). Staff are excellent, helping in several languages (especially German) and providing maps, guidebooks, and information on tours and lodging.

EXPLORING TŘEBOŇ

Walk, hang out, and walk. City officials, quick to notice that helping tourists helps them, have placed signs guiding visitors to almost every nook and cranny of the center. Since the walled city is relatively small, there is no wrong place to begin a tour, but I prefer to start at the southern gate by the **Svinenská brána,** the oldest of the three, for reasons that will become immediately apparent. Just outside the gate and to the right stands the **Regent brewery,** founded in 1379. Locals will tell you that their brew is every bit as good as Budvar, and they're not lying. Upon entering the old town, continue straight through Žižkovo náměstí and you will arrive at **Masarykovo náměstí,** where beautifully colored Renaissance facades look as though they were built just yesterday.

To the left lies the entrance to Třeboň's showpiece, **Zámek Třeboň** (Třeboň Castle). The castle's history is similar to the town's history. The original Gothic castle was destroyed by fire and reconstructed several times, most recently in 1611. Rather ordinary looking from the outside, the castle has splendidly decorated rooms that show 16th-century furnishings at their best. Inside an exhibition on pond building fascinates most children. A large part of the castle now houses regional archives. Admission is 20 Kč (74¢). Open May through September, Tuesday to Sunday from 9am to noon and 1 to 5pm; on weekends and holidays only in April and October.

Walk out the castle gate and straight along Březanova street to the **Augustinian monastery** and the 14th-century **St. Giles church** next to it. Inside the church are replicas of some of the finest Gothic works in central Europe; the originals have been moved to the National Gallery in Prague.

To the south of the old town lies **Rybník Svět,** a large pond that locals flock to on hot afternoons. Several locations around the pond rent windsurfers, bikes, and other outdoor equipment to enjoy the surrounding areas. On the southeast shore of the pond is **Schwarzenberská hrobka** (Schwarzenberg Mausoleum). Built in 1877, this neo-Gothic chapel and crypt is the resting place for most members of the Schwarzenberg family.

WHERE TO STAY

Bilý Koníček (White Horse)

Masarykovo náměstí 97, 379 01 Třeboň. ☎ **0333/2818.** 10 rms. TEL. 490 Kč ($18) single, 690 Kč ($26) double; 920 Kč ($34) triple; 1,200 Kč ($45) suite. V.

Across the street from the Zlatá Hvězda, the Bilý Koníček (White Horse) has plain but tidy rooms. However, the rooms tend to be a little noisier here, because the one road cars use to go through town passes by. For the most part, though, the streets are pretty quiet.

Hotel Zlatá Hvězda

Masarykovo náměstí 107, 379 01, Třeboň, ☎ **0333/3365 8.** Fax. 2604. 38 double rooms, 2 single bed rooms, 2 suites. TV TEL. 1,430 Kč ($18.30) single, 1,530 Kč ($50) double; 2,000 Kč suite. Rates include all-you-can-eat buffet breakfast. AE, DC, MC, V.

Despite having rather Spartan rooms, the Zlatá Hvězda is nonetheless comfortable and its location on Masarykovo náměstí can't be beat. An added plus is that the friendly staff can help arrange brewery tours, fishing permits, horseback riding, bike rentals, and several other outdoor activities.

Pension Siesta

Hradební 26, 379 01 Třeboň. ☎ / Fax **0333/2324.** 7 rms. 360 Kč ($13) per person.

Just outside and to the right of the Hradecká brána lies the Pension Siesta, a small but quiet and clean alternative to the hotels on the square. What makes this pension special is Petr Matějů and his wife, who go out of their way to take care of their guests. The pension also has a pleasant terrace in front by the stream, where you can enjoy an afternoon drink and snack.

WHERE TO DINE

Bilý Koníček

Masarykovo náměstí 97, 379 01 Třeboň. ☎ **0333/2818.** Reservations not needed. Main courses 60–120 Kč ($2.22–$4.44). V. Daily 10am–11pm. CZECH.

Located in the hotel with the same name, Bily Koníček has a standard Czech menu of meat, dumplings, and potato dishes that are very reasonably priced. In the summer, its terrace is a great place to sit and cool off while grabbing a snack; the building's shadow keeps you out of the direct sun. The beer from just down the road is always fresh and cold.

Rybářská bašta

Hliník 750/2,379 01 Třeboň. ☎ **0333/3141.** Reservations not needed. Main courses 90–240 Kč ($3.33–$8.89). No credit cards. Daily 10:30am–midnight. CZECH.

With more than 5,000 ponds in the area, you know the fish served here will at least be fresh. This pond-side restaurant serves a wide selection of well-prepared fish dishes, especially carp. However, if you're dining later in the evening, the dance music begins to seep into your head and you may find yourself chewing to the beat.

9 Tábor

55 miles S of Prague, 37 miles N of České Budějovice

The center of the Hussite movement following religious leader Jan Hus' execution in Prague, Tábor was officially founded in 1420 and named by the Hussites after the biblical Mount Tábor. They had come to receive Christ upon his return to earth and forsook property as he had himself. The group of soldiers leading Tábor, some 15,000 in all, felt they had been commanded by God to break the temporal power of the Catholics at that time.

Legendary warrior Jan Žížka led the Táborites, as this sect of Hussites were known. Time and time again, Žížka rallied his troops to defeat the papal forces, until he was struck down in battle in 1424. For some 10 more years the Hussites battled on, but their loss at Lipany signaled the end of the uprising, and an agreement was reached with Emperor Sigmund of Luxembourg of the Holy Roman Empire. Later, the town submitted to the leadership of Bohemia's Jiří z Poděbrad (George of Poděbrad) and blossomed economically, creating the wealth needed to construct the Renaissance buildings now found in the historical old town.

SPECIAL EVENTS   Needless to say, things have quieted down since the days of Jan Žížka, except that is, in mid-August when the **Táborská Setkání** (Tábor Meeting) takes place. Each year, representatives from towns worldwide named after Mount Tábor congregate for some medieval fun—parades, music, and jousting. The four-day event even re-enacts the historical battle of Tábor, with brilliantly colored warriors fighting each other "to the death."

For more information on the Tábor Meeting and summer cultural events, contact **Infocentrum města Tábor,** Žižkovo náměstí 2, 390 01, Tábor (☎ / Fax **0361/ 254 658**).

ESSENTIALS

GETTING THERE   If you're driving, leave Prague by the D1 highway, and turn off at the E55 exit (signs Benešov, České Budějovice). Highway E55 runs straight into the city of Tábor. It's a one-hour drive.

Tábor is about 90 minutes by express train from Prague, or close to an hour from České Budějovice. The train station has a baggage check, and you can get to the center of town by taking bus nos. 11, 14, or 31. The one way fare in second class is 60 Kč ($2.22).

The bus trip to Tábor lasts about 1 1/2 hours from Prague. To get to the center, it's about a 20-minute walk; go through the park and then bear right at its farthest corner to walk along 9 Května Trida into town.

ORIENTATION   Outside of the historic town, there is little to see in Tábor besides factories and the ubiquitous *paneláks* (apartment buildings) that ring most every big Czech town and city.

Staré město (Old Town) is situated around Žížkovo náměstí, site of the town church and the Hussite museum. Medieval walls suround the entire Old Town core. The Kotnov castle, now one of the town's museums, is located at the southwest corner.

VISITOR INFORMATION   Next to the Hussite Museum, **Infocentrum města Tábor,** Žižkovo náměstí 2, 390 01, Tábor (☎ / Fax **0361/254 658**) is stocked with information of all types, from maps, film, and postcards to advice about lodging, restaurants, and the best place for ice cream. The center's staff have volumes of pamphlets, phone numbers, and good advice. Open May to September, Monday to Friday from 8:30am to 8pm, Saturday 9am to 12:30pm, Sunday 1pm to 6pm; October to April, Tuesday to Friday from 9am to 4pm.

EXPLORING TÁBOR

Most of the city's sights are located on or around **Žížkovo náměstí.** If you find that as you leave the square roads twist, turn and then end, the Táborites have caught you exactly as planned—the town was designed to hold off would-be attackers with its maze of streets.

On the square's west side is the **Museum of the Hussite Movement.** The late Gothic former Town Hall now chronicles the movement that put Tábor on the map and in the history books. In front of the building lie stone tables where Hussite ministers gave daily Communion. Leading from the museum's entrance, twisting and turning 650 meters underneath the square, is a labyrinth of **tunnels** dating back to the 15th century. After visiting the museum, take one of the guided tours that snake through the underground maze, which has housed everything from beer kegs to unruly women, imprisoned for such dastardly things as quarreling with men. The tunnels also doubled as a way to sneak under enemy guards if the town ever fell, allowing Hussite soldiers to launch an attack from behind. Admission to the Hussite Museum is 20 Kč (74¢), to the tunnels 16 Kč (59¢). Open year-round from 8:30am to 4pm. *Note:* There has been talk of closing the museum in the winter, so off-season guests should call the information center at 0361/254 658 to check.

When you emerge from the tunnels, you will be on the opposite side of the square, facing the **Church of Transfiguration of Our Lord,** with its vaulting, impressive stained-glass windows, and Gothic robbed wooden altar. Climb the tower for one of the best views of the town.

You can pay homage to the Hussite military mastermind Žížka at his **statue** stands next to the church. For a wondrous avenue of Renaissance buildings, stroll down **Pražská ulice** off the southeast corner of the square. From here you can turn down Divadelní and head along the Lužnice River toward **Kotnov Castle.** If your feet aren't up to the walk, you can take a more direct route to Kotnov by heading straight down Klokotská ulice, which runs away from the square next to the Hussite Museum.

A 14th-century castle that forms the southwest corner of the town wall, **Kotnov castle** is most recognizable for its round **tower,** where you can behold another great view of the town. Inside the castle is a well-organized collection on the Middle Ages, with old farming tools, armor, weapons, uniforms, and other artifacts. Admission is 20 Kč (74¢). Open Tuesday through Sunday from 8am to 4:30pm.

WHERE TO STAY

Tábor's lack of quality hotels gives one the perfect chance to "go local" and stay in a private pension. Expect to pay about $20 per person. The information center next to the Town Hall at Žižkovo náměstí 2 can provide a list of recommendations, or call and book a room for you.

The same service is also provided by a private tourist agency located on náměstí Františka Křižika (☎ **0361/234 01**), open daily from 10am to noon and 1 to 6pm.

Hotel Bohemia

Husovo náměstí 591, 390 01 Tábor. ☎ **0361/228 28.** 30 rms (21 with bath). TV TEL. 900 Kč ($33) single; 1,470 Kč ($54) double. No credit cards.

What a difference ownership makes! A perfect case study of how indifferent Communist management can ruin a place, the Bohemia has changed into private hands with incredible results. Once a drab, run-down train station hotel, the Bohemia has been spruced up right down to the staff, and is worth the walk if you can't find anything closer to the historic town.

Hotel Kapitál

9 května třída 617, 39001 Tábor, ☎ **0361/256 096.** Fax 252 411. 24 rms. TV TEL. 980 Kč ($36) single; 1,550 Kč ($57) double; 2,550 Kč ($94). MC, V.

Smaller and quieter than the Palcát, *das* recently-renovated Kapitál has a little more character than its bigger neighbor down the street. The rooms are big and the Kapitál seems to have a helpful staff, who also speak English. The restaurant serves large if unimaginative meals.

Hotel Palcát

9 května třída 2467, 39001 Tábor, ☎ **0361/229 01.** Fax 229 05. 68 rms. TV TEL. 1,040 Kč ($39) single; 1,600 Kč ($59) double; 2,560 Kč ($95) suite. AE, MC, V.

Since there are few quality hotels in Tábor, the Palcát, a modern but clean place, slips in as one of the town's finest. Though guests may be left cold from its Communist-era furnishings, the rooms are spacious, if not unforgettable. The higher floors have great views of the town, so working your way up makes your stay much more enjoyable.

WHERE TO DINE

Hotel Palcát

9 května 2467. ☎ **0361/229 01.** Reservations not needed. Soups 15–50 Kč (56¢–$1.85); main courses 50–150 Kč ($1.85–$5.56). Daily 11:30am–2:30pm and 4:30pm–11pm. CZECH.

Begrudgingly, I have to admit that the Palcát remains one of the better restaurants in town, although the decor looks as though it hasn't been changed since the 1960s. The soups served here are first-rate and the fish and beefsteak are fresh and tasty. Beware of the pizza—I swear it's Heinz ketchup (or a derivative thereof) moonlighting as sauce. For a nightcap, the bar/disco is open Tuesday through Saturday until 3am and is one of the few places rockin' in town.

Restaurace Beseda

Žížkovo náměstí. No phone. Reservations not needed. Main courses 68–89 Kč ($2.52–$3.30). No credit cards. Daily 10am–10pm. CZECH.

The only restaurant with a terrace on the square, Beseda is a good place to stop after slinking through the tunnels and climbing the tower at the Church of Trans-figuration of Our Lord. You've probably seen this menu in just about every town so far, but the food is above average, if not new. On hot summer days, the patio is great for people-watching while drinking a cold Budvar (13.5 Kč/50¢). Too bad no food is served al fresco, or this place would move up a notch.

Zlatý Drak (Golden Dragon)

Žížkovo náměstí. No phone. Reservations not needed. Soups 30–55 Kč ($1.11–$2.04); main courses 80–190 Kč ($2.96–$7.04). AE, MC, V. Daily 11:30am–2:30pm and 4:30pm–11pm. CHINESE.

I have always been wary of a Chinese restaurant that serves french fries, but the Golden Dragon can provide a nice change from heavy Czech cuisine. The chicken dishes tend to outshine their tougher beef counterparts.

12

The Best of Moravia

by Alan Crosby

Amalgamated with Bohemia more than 1,000 years ago, Moravia has managed to keep its rich culture and tradition despite always being lumped together with its wealthier, more densely populated cousin to the west. Because of this lack of wealth, Moravia saw far fewer castles built, far less attention paid to is capital Brno, and in turn, now gets far fewer tourists than Bohemia. So Brno isn't Prague.

Yet Moravia still has many features that make it a worthwhile destination, especially the smaller towns that show the real Moravian character with lively song and dance, and colorful traditional costumes that seem to have fallen by the wayside in Bohemia. Even the food is a little different. The bland goulash in Prague tends to become a little spicier in Moravian cuisine, owing to the Hungarian influence brought through neighboring Slovakia. And replacing beer as a staple beverage is wine, especially to the south where wine-making is taken as seriously as it is in most other European grape-growing regions. Many wine bars throughout Moravia serve the village's best straight from the cask.

Having seen its fair share of history, Moravia conjures up a different image than Bohemia: a sort of kinder, gentler, central Europe where material wealth is replaced by a rich folklore and more pastoral setting. Here too, castles and picture-perfect town squares exist. But the people and slower lifestyle set Moravia apart. There's a far greater tradition of song and dance, and with the country's finest vineyards, it's not very hard to find a local hangout with all three.

A NOTE ON LODGING   Anywhere in the Czech Republic you have the option of staying in hotels or pensions on the main square. It's a beautiful sight but be prepared for serious noise, particularly on weekends. Light sleepers may prefer to trade the view for a good night's sleep.

1 Brno: The Region's Capital

140 miles SE of Prague, 80 miles N of Vienna

An industrial city with an industrial-strength image as boring, Brno suffers a fate that many second cities around the world endure—no respect. But it's undeserved. In fact, Brno, the capital of Moravia, is a vibrant and interesting city with a panache all its own.

Since Brno came of age in the 19th century on the back of its textile industry, the city's architecture, for the most part, lacks the

What's Special About Moravia

Architecture
- Telč's massive town square, lined by Gothic and Renaissance houses that are centuries old.

Churches
- Catherine Rotunda, in Znojmo, one of the country's oldest romanesque structures.
- Cathedral of Saints Peter and Paul, in Brno, whose church bells strike 12 an hour early as a reminder of a city under siege.

Wine
- Vineyards of southern Moravia produce many of the country's finest vintages, such as Frankovka—a smooth, full-bodied red—or Ryzlink—a light, dry white—with the words Znojemské (from Znojmo) or Mikulov on the label.

Culture
- Colorful traditional costumes, decorated with intricate needlepoint, go hand in hand with lively song and dance, especially at town events in Telč and during the Znojmo wine festival in September.

Renaissance facades and meandering alleyways other towns have been blessed with. Indeed, the main square, náměstí Svobody, bears this out. But spend a day or two here, and the beauty of the old city center magically unfolds before your eyes. Empire and neoclassical buildings abound. Quirky sights like the Brno Dragon or the Wagon Wheel add character. Špilberk Castle and the Gothic cathedral of Saints Peter and Paul give historical perspective. And lush streets and parks make aimless wandering a pleasure. Besides, what do critics know? They probably pass by Telč without stopping, either.

SPECIAL EVENTS   Usually when the words "special events" and "Brno" are mentioned in the same sentence, the phrase "trade fair" is not too far behind. Many fairs held at Brno's BVV exhibition grounds are world-class displays of technology, industrial machinery, even well-groomed pets.

Brno celebrates music as well, hosting the **Janáček Music Festival** each June, and the **Brno International Music Festival** in September and October.

However, probably the single-most attended event in Brno occurs each August when the **Motorcycle Grand Prix** tour rolls into town to tackle the Masaryk Okruh (Masaryk Ring).

For information on all events and a list of fairs at the BVV fairgrounds contact **Informacní Služba,** Radnická 4-10 Brno (☎ **05/4221 1090**).

ESSENTIALS

GETTING THERE   Driving to Brno is a trade off. Take the E50—also named the D1—freeway that leads from the south of Prague all the way. The drive shouldn't take more than 2 hours. But the scenery is little more than one roadside stop after another.

Brno is the focal point for train travel in Moravia and most points east, making it an easy 3¹/₄-hour trip from Prague. Trains leave almost every hour; the majority go from Hlavní Nádraží (Main Station). The one way fare is 181 Kč ($6.70) first class, 126 Kč ($4.66) second class.

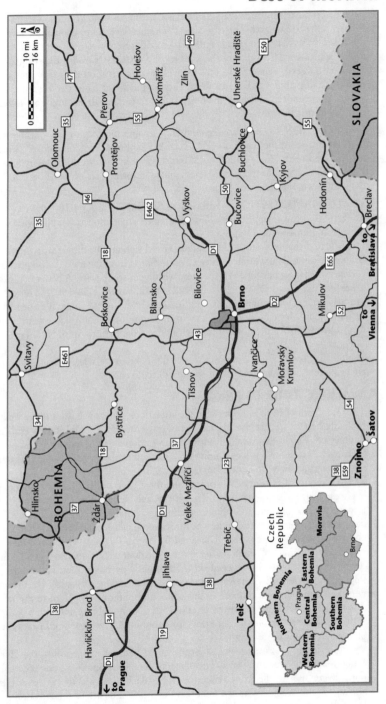

Nonstop buses run from Prague's Florence station to Brno as often as trains do, thanks to the free market. The trip takes 2¹/₂ hours. Several bus companies have set up their own services along the Prague-Brno corridor to compete with the inefficient former state-owned ČSAD. Probably the best deal is **Český Národní Express** (Czech National Express), where 59 Kč ($2.18) will get you a seat on the exact same type of bus ČSAD runs. CNE buses depart across the street from the Florence bus station at the underpass behind the McDonald's restaurant. Reservations are recommended during peak hours.

ORIENTATION   Brno is a large rambling city, but most sights are concentrated in its inner core. At the center of it all is **Náměstí Svobody** (Freedom Square), which is connected to the train station by Masarykova ulice. Just west of Masarykova is **Zelný trh** (Cabbage Market), the largest square in town. Cars cannot pass through the Old Town, but tram no. 4 does.

VISITOR INFORMATION   **Informacní Služba**, Radnická 4-10 Brno (☎ 05/ 4221 1090), provides a plethora of information on accommodations, plus what's on in Brno and how to see it.

You'll find the ubiquitous blue **Čedok Travel** sign at four different locations in Brno. The conveniently located office across the street from the train station provides currency exchange, but little else for those wishing to see the city. A better bet is the office at Masarykovo 37, Brno (☎ **05/4221 0942**, Fax 05/4221 1562). This office can help arrange accommodations both in hotels and private rooms. It's open May to September, Monday through Friday from 9am to 6pm, Saturday 9am to noon; from October to April, Monday through Friday from 9am to 5pm, Saturday 9am to noon.

Note that like Prague and some other cities, the antiquated telephone lines of Brno are being replaced. All phone numbers are subject to change.

A WALKING TOUR OF BRNO

The Old Town of Brno holds most of the attractions visitors will want to see, so it's probably best to start at the former seat of government, the **Old Town Hall** on Radnická 8. To get there, walk from the train station along Masarykovo and make a left at Orlí street, or if you're coming from náměstí Svobody, head toward the train station and turn right on either Panská or Orlí.

The oldest secular building in Brno, from the 13th century, the Old Town Hall is a hodgepodge of styles— Gothic, Renaissance, and baroque elements meld together to show the development of Brno through the ages. Almost everything in the building has a story or legend attached to it. The first one you will encounter is the front door and its crooked Gothic portal. Designed by Anton Pilgram, who lists Vienna's vaunted St. Stephen's Church on his resume, the door was completed in 1510. But town officials supposedly reneged on their original payment offer, and a furious Pilgram took revenge by bending the turret above the Statue of Justice. On the second floor a modest collection of armor, coins, and photos is displayed in the same room where town councilors met from the 13th century right up until 1935. Climb the stairs of the tower for an interesting, if not beautiful, city view; smokestacks and baroque buildings battle for attention.

Before leaving, examine two of Brno's most beloved attractions—the **Brno Dragon** and the **Wagon Wheel.** The "dragon" hanging from the ceiling is actually not a dragon, but an alligator given to the city by Archprince Matayáš in 1608. Here also stands the Wagon Wheel, a testament to Brno's industrious image. Local lore has it that a carpenter named Jiří Birek from nearby Lednice wagered with locals that

Brno

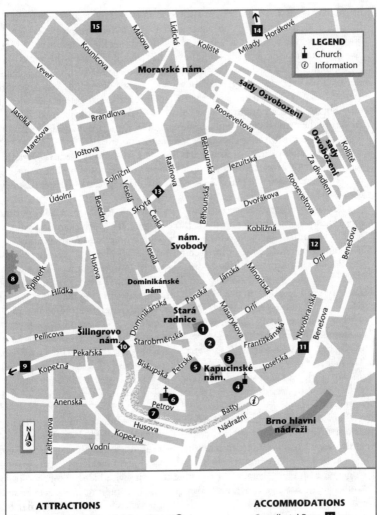

LEGEND
✝ Church
ⓘ Information

ATTRACTIONS

Cathedral of Saints Peter and Paul ➏

Denisovy sady ➐

Kapučínsky Klášter
(Capuchin Monastery) ➍

Kostel Náležení svatého Kříže ➍

Moravian Museum ➎

Old Town Hall ➊

Parnas fountain ➋

Redulta Divadlo ➌

Špilberk castle ➑

Zelný trh (Cabbage market) ➋

ACCOMMODATIONS

Grandhotel Brno 11

Holiday Inn 9

Hotel Astoria 12

Hotel Boby 14

Hotel Continental 15

Hotel Voronež 9

DINING

Modra Hvězda ➓

Pivnice Pegas 13

Zahradní restaurace ⓫

he could chop down a tree, fashion a wheel from it, and roll it the 40 kilometers to Brno all in a single day. Well, he managed to do it, but the townspeople, certain that one man could not do so much in one day, decided that Birek must have had some assistance from the devil. With this mindset, they refused to ever buy his works again.

Just south of the Old Town Hall is **Zelný trh** (Cabbage Market), a farmers' market since the 13th century. You can still buy a head or two of the leafy vegetable at the market today as entrepreneurs sell their wares under the gaze of the **Hercules,** depicted in the **Parnas Fountain** in the square's center. The fountain used to be a vital part of the market; quick-thinking fishermen let their carp swim and relax in the fountain until the fish were chosen for someone's dinner.

At the southern corner of **Zelný trh** lies the 17th-century **Reduta Divadlo,** a former home of Mozart. Another block closer to the train station, on Kapučínské náměstí is the Kostel Náležení svatého Kříže and the Kapučínsky Klášter (Capuchin Monastery).

The Capuchin Monastery is famous for its catacombs, which hold many of Brno's most famous citizens. Among those interred here are Moritz Grimm, who was responsible for rebuilding the cathedral in the 18th century, and Austrian army Colonel František Trenck, who, in intervening years lost his head to vandals. A unique ventilation system preserves the bodies, displayed in open coffins. This display is slightly morbid; skin and clothing are slowly decaying. Parents may want to look ahead or get a brochure to make sure children are up to seeing the coffins. Admission is 12 Kč (44¢). Open Tuesday through Saturday from 9am to noon and 2 to 4:30pm, Sunday 11 to 11:45am and 2 to 4:30pm.

Dominating **Zelný trh** at its southwest corner is the Moravian Museum, housed in the Dietrichstein Palace. Completed in 1620, the palace was used by Russian Marshal Kutuzov to prepare for the battle of Austerlitz. These days, the museum displays a wide array of stuffed birds and wild game, as well as art, coins, and temporary exhibitions. Admission is 16 Kč (59¢). It's open Tuesday through Sunday from 9am to 6pm.

From the museum, head up Petrská street to the Cathedral of Saints Peter and Paul. Perched on top of a hill overlooking the city, the cathedral was originally built in the late 11th and early 13th centuries. In 1743 it was rebuilt in a baroque style, only to be re-Gothicized just before World War I. This melding of styles gives the cathedral its unique character of a Gothic structure with baroque touches. Inside, Gothic arches rise high above, while Baroque designs complement spaces in between. The cathedral is open Monday through Wednesday and Friday and Saturday from 6:30am to 6pm, Thursday 6:30am to 7:30pm, Sunday 8:30am to 6pm.

Take a break at **Denisovy sady,** the park behind the cathedral, and prepare to climb the hill to get to **Špilberk Castle.** If you're not up for it, trams 6, 9, 14, and 17 go near the castle, but you'll still have a short but strenuous walk from there. The fare is 6 Kč (22¢). If you want to walk all the way, head along Biskupská, where interesting houses provide a nice foreground to the bustling city behind. Make a left on Starobrněnská to Husova and then on to Pellicova. At Pellicova 11 stands a fine example of František Uherka's cubist architectural vision.

But the real reason for this climb is Špilberk. If there's one building in the Czech Republic that's ready to be overrun by visitors, Špilberk is—and it's had practice. Built in the 13th century, the Hussites controlled the castle in the 15th century. The Prussians saw the castle's position as an excellent lookout when they occupied it in the early 17th century. And the Nazis turned it into a torture chamber during their stay, executing some 80,000 people deep inside the castle dungeons.

What Time Is It?

If you're touring the cathedral in the late morning, you may think you have switched time zones. Don't worry, the cathedral bells strike noon an hour early in remembrance of a quick-thinking bell ringer who, seeing the city was on the verge of attack by the Swedes during the Thirty Years War, found out that the army was planning to take the city by noon. If not successful by then, Swedish commander General Torstenson was said to have decided the attack would be called off, and the army would beat a hasty retreat. The bell ringer, sensing the town could not repel the Swedes, rang the cathedral bells an hour early at 11am, before the army could attack. True to his word, Torstenson packed up and went home.

Renovated in 1994, Špilberk can be conquered without a guide. Wander through the seemingly endless corridors beneath the bastions to get a feel for what those who perished here saw. It's open June to September, Tuesday through Sunday from 9am to 6pm; April and May, Tuesday through Sunday from 9am to 5pm; March and October, Tuesday through Sunday from 9am to 4pm.

SHOPPING   Once back in the city center, take some time for a quick meal and browse along the pedestrian shopping zone, which unfolds between náměstí Svobody and the train station. Prices for goods are often cheaper here than in Prague, so you may find a better price for the crystal vase or pair of earrings you were thinking of buying.

SOCCER   Sports fans can partake in a Sunday ritual as dear to Czechs as football is to Americans by taking the 20-minute walk north from the main square to Brno stadium, where first league **soccer team Boby Brno** plays its home games. Grab a beer and a sausage and cheer along with the Boby faithful. Tickets (about 30Kč/$1.11) are always plentiful and can be bought at the stadium on game day.

WHERE TO STAY

Note that even high-season prices often jump without warning for major trade fairs and the Motorcycle Grand Prix.

EXPENSIVE

Grandhotel Brno

Benešova 18-20, 657 83 Brno. ☎ **05/4232 1287**, Fax 05/4221 0345. 113 rms. MINIBAR TV TEL. 2,745 Kč ($102) single; 4,050 Kč ($150) double. AE, DC, MC, V.

Recently taken over by the Austrian hotel chain Austrotel, the Grandhotel Brno lives up to its name. Rooms are spacious and well-appointed, although some located at the front of the building get a little noisy due to the major street running past; ask for a room that has windows facing north, away from the commotion. The hotel, with elegant fixtures throughout, has two excellent restaurants, a nightclub, and a casino.

MODERATE

Holiday Inn

Křížovského 20, 603 00 Brno. ☎ 05/4312 2018. Fax 05/336 990. 205 rms. MINIBAR TV TEL. 1,650–2,200 Kč ($61–$81) standard single/double; 2,300–2,850 Kč ($85–$106) executive single/double; 3,200–3,750 Kč ($139) suite. AE, MC, V.

Yes, that's right. No surprises here. The Holiday Inn Brno, located directly on the fairgrounds, caters mainly to the trade fair crowd. Everything, from the rooms to the hotel restaurant and bars, looks eerily similar to other Holiday Inns around the world. Still, the beds are more comfortable than most, and rooms are spotless. Staff is very friendly and all speak at least some English.

Hotel Boby

Sportovní 2a, 602 00 Brno. ☎ **05/7272 118.** Fax 05/7272 103. 140 rms. MINIBAR TV TEL. 1,800–2,000 Kč ($67–$74) single; 2,400 Kč ($89) double; 3,650 Kč ($135) suite.

The Hotel Boby, or the Bob as many refer to it, is one of Brno's newest luxury hotels. Located just north of the city center, the Bob often attracts guests who never leave the hotel. Inside and on the surrounding grounds you will find a health center, a bowling alley, a shopping mall, tennis courts, squash courts, a swimming pool, a roller-skating rink, several bars and restaurants, even a car wash. Rooms are very comfortable. The walk from the center is a nice 25-minute stroll through long parks.

Hotel Continental

Kounicova 20, 662 21 Brno. ☎ **05/4121 2806.** Fax 05/4121 1203. 228 rms. TEL. 1,100 Kč ($41) single; 1,730 Kč ($64) double. AE, DC, MC, V.

This is another Communist-era hotel trying to make it in the free market. The comfortable and clean rooms are a little on the small side, and a little too modern for some tastes. The very helpful staff is quite approachable for advice on how to get to the sights. The Continental is located north of the city center.

Hotel Voroněž

Křížovského 47, 603 73 Brno. ☎ **05/4314 1111.** Fax 05/4321 2002. 500 rms. MINIBAR TV TEL. 1,100 Kč ($41) single; 1,600 Kč ($59) double. AE, MC, V.

Basically a Czech *panelák* (apartment) dressed up as a hotel, the Voroněž is trying hard to shed its Communist-era image—and furniture. It's located across the street from the fairgrounds. In many of the medium-sized rooms, modern, Naugahyde 1970s furnishings have been replaced with light pastel-and-wood beds, desks, and chairs, and these redone rooms now cut the mustard. Except during the busiest times, you can always find a room here.

INEXPENSIVE

Hotel Astoria

Novobranská 3, 662 21 Brno. ☎ **05/4232 1302.** Fax 05/4221 1428. 89 rms. TEL. 630 Kč ($23) single; 1,050 Kč ($39) double. AE, DC, MC, V.

The Astoria, formerly the Morava, has basic, small, nondescript rooms that are clean. It's very close to the city center and the train station.

WHERE TO DINE

Ⓢ Modrá Hvězda (Blue Star)

Šilingrovo náměstí 7. No phone. Reservations not needed. Soups 15–50 Kč (56¢–$1.85); main courses 70–150 Kč ($2.59–$5.56). Daily 11am–1am. CZECH.

Recommended to me by a friend who used to live in Brno, the Blue Star is one of the few moderately priced restaurants in town where you can get good-quality food well into the night. The mixed grill for two is excellent, served with fresh (not canned) vegetables.

Pivnice Pegas

Jakubská 4. No phone. Reservations not needed. Main courses 40–80 Kč ($1.48–$2.96). No credit cards. Daily 9am–midnight. CZECH.

Come here for a beer and a quick meal during the day, rather than a formal dinner at night. The Pegas is one of the few pubs in the city center where locals and tourists mix. Hearty goulash and dumplings are always a good choice, as is the fried cheese, though your arteries may not agree.

Zahradní Restaurace (Garden Restaurant)

Grandhotel Brno, Benešova 18-20. ☎ **05/4232 1287.** Reservations recommended. Main courses 120–300 Kč ($4.44–$11.11). AE, DC, MC, V. Daily 11:30am–10:30pm. CZECH/ INTERNATIONAL/CHINESE.

When you enter this restaurant, you'll expect to pay a lot more than you do. The setting is first-rate, with fountains and lots of plants. Background music doesn't intrude. This used to be one of eastern Europe's finest Chinese restaurants, and it still is, but with some Czech and international dishes thrown in for good measure. For a taste of local cuisine, try the Moravian plate piled with pork, duck, smoked meat, sauerkraut and two kinds of dumplings.

2 Telč

93 miles SE of Prague, 54 miles west of Brno

As you pass through towns on your way to Telč and approach its outskirts, you may be tempted to pass up another "small town with a nice square." Don't. Those who make the trip to Telč strike gold. Telč is one of the few towns in Europe that can boast of not being reconstructed since its original edifices were built. It now enjoys the honor of being a United Nations (UNESCO) World Heritage Site. Its uniformly built houses and castle give it an almost too perfect look, as though no one ever really lived here.

Due to its small size, Telč can be explored in a day for those traveling from Prague, or as a leg of a trip further afield. Those traveling by car to Brno or Vienna should stop on their way. Because of the town's beauty and tranquility, I recommend spending the night to admire the illuminated castle and square, especially if there is an evening recital or concert at the castle. You can also combine a stop here with a visit to Znojmo; see below.

SPECIAL EVENTS   Although no one special event occurs in Telč, the **Telčské Kulturní Léto** (Telč Cultural Summer) season of concerts, recitals, and fairs runs from the beginning of June to the end of September. For more information, contact the **Telč Informační Středisko,** náměstí Zachariaše z Hradce, 588 56 Telč (☎ **0618/962 233**; Fax 0618/962 557).

ESSENTIALS

GETTING THERE   Located about halfway between České Budějovice and Brno, Telč can be reached by taking highway 23. From Prague, take the D1 highway in the direction of Brno, and exit at Jihlava where you pick up highway 38 after going through the town. Then head west on highway 23. You can leave your car in the large parking lot near the town's north gate. It's a two hour drive from Prague.

Train connections to Telč are not great, so be patient. The town lies on the Tábor-Jindřichův Hradec line; you'll have to change at Kostelec u Jihlavy. Once you get there, you'll find about nine trains departing daily to Telč. The train station offers storage, though its hours are not the most dependable.

I recommend taking the more direct route by bus. Buses leave from Prague's Florenc bus station daily and take about 3 hours. The castle and town square are a 10-minute walk from the bus station. To get to town, exit through the station's back entrance, turn right on Tyršova, and then left on Rudnerova. Follow this street as it bears left, and turn right at the second small alleyway. This will guide you to the main square.

ORIENTATION   Telč's historic center is shaped like a trapezoid, and surrounded by lakes on three sides. At the center is a very large square named after the town's former owner, Zachariaše z Hradce.

VISITOR INFORMATION   Since UNESCO gave its backing to Telč in 1992, services for tourists have blossomed, and none more so than the information center on the main square. At the **Telč Informační Středisko,** náměstí Zachariaše z Hradce, 588 56 Telč (☎ **0618/962 233;** Fax 0618/962 557), you'll find a wealth of information concerning accommodations, cultural events, guided tours, even hunting; brochures are in Czech, German, and English. Staff are eager to arrange reservations. The small white Telč guide book that costs 40 Kč ($1.48) is invaluable, filled with minute details about almost every edifice in town.

EXPLORING TELČ

Start with a tour of **Telč château** at the northwest end of the main square. Zacharias of Neuhaus, whose name now graces the main square, was so enamored of the Renaissance-style rampant in Italy that in 1553 he commissioned Antonio Vlach, and later Baldassare Maggi de Ronio, to rebuild the château, originally a 14th-century Gothic structure. The castle's exterior, however, cannot prepare you for its interior, hall after hall of lavish rooms with spectacular ceilings.

Highlights inside the castle include the **Africa Hall,** with rhino heads, tiger skins, and other exotica from hunting expeditions that Karel Podstatky, a relative of the castle's last owner, accumulated in the early 1900s; the **Banquet Hall** where *sgrafitti* seems to mock those who overindulge; and the **Marble Hall of Knights,** with a wood ceiling decorated with bas-reliefs from 1570, plus a fine collection of armor. In the **Golden Hall,** where balls and ceremonies once took place, 30 octagonal coffers with mythological scenes stare down at you from the ceiling.

A 1-hour guided tour of the castle halls costs 60 Kč ($2.22). For those who wish to see the castle apartments, take the additional 45-minute tour, which also costs 60 Kč ($2.22). The castle is open May through August, Tuesday to Sunday from 9am to noon and 1 to 5pm; in April, September, and October, Tuesday to Sunday from 9am to noon and 1 to 4pm.

Next to the castle is the **church of St. James (Kostel sv. Jakub),** its walls adorned with late-15th-century paintings. Next to St. James is the baroque **Jesuit Church of the Name of Jesus.**

After strolling the castle grounds, head back to the main square, where a sea of soft pastel facades awaits. If you find yourself wondering how the entire square could be so uniform, you're not alone. After rebuilding the castle, Zacharias realized the rest of the place looked, well, out of place. To rectify the situation, he promptly rebuilt the facade of each building on the square, though Gothic columns belie what once was. Of particular note is the building referred to as **House 15,** where a round oriel and *sgrafitti* portaying the crucifixion, Saul and David, Christopher, and faith and justice, jut out onto the street corner. And watching over it all are the cherubs on the Marian column, built in 1718.

WHERE TO STAY

If you have not arranged lodging ahead of time, head straight to the information center in the main square, where the staff have a complete list of what's available. For hotels, expect to pay anywhere from 570 to 1,400 Kč ($21–$52) for a single, and 870 to 1,800 Kč ($32–$66) for a double.

Private accommodations are also available, and for the most part, these rooms are comparable to hotel rooms (if not better and less expensive), although there are far fewer amenities. Information center staff will call and arrange for you to meet the room's owner so you can check out the place. Several rooms located directly on the square are available. Expect to pay about 300 to 500 Kč ($11–$18) per night, per person. On slow days, owners will usually negotiate a better price.

Hotel Celerin

Náměstí Zachariaše z Hradce 43, 588 56 Telč. ☎ **0618/962 477.** 12 rms. No credit cards. 1,300–1,800 Kč ($48–$67) single or double. Rates include breakfast.

The most upscale hotel on the square, the Celerin has very comfortable, medium-sized rooms, some with a view of the square. The hotel's location is one of its strong points.

ⓢ Hotel Černy Orel (Black Owl Hotel)

Náměstí Zachariaše z Hradce 7, 588 56 Telč. ☎ **0618/962 221.** 30 rms. No credit cards. 570 Kč ($21) single; 870 Kč ($32) double.

Located on the main square overlooking the Marian column, the Black Owl is a favorite among visitors. The recently renovated rooms are spartan, but clean. Ask for a view of the square; the staff will usually accommodate this request if a room is available. A lively restaurant downstairs serves good Czech fare.

WHERE TO DINE

U Černého Orla (At the Black Owl)

Náměstí Zachariaše z Hradce 7. ☎ **0618/962 221.** Reservations not needed. Soups 10–20 Kč (37¢–74¢), main courses 50–100 Kč ($1.85–$3.70). No credit cards. Daily 7am–10pm. Closed Mon Oct–May. CZECH.

If it looks as though every tourist in town is trying to get in here, it's because they are. The Black Owl is worth the effort. This is one of the few restaurants in Telč that can be trusted to serve good food consistently. Crowd in at any free space, and enjoy a wide range of Czech meals. The trout is always fresh, and I have never heard a complaint about it or the *řízek* (pork schnitzel). The hearty soups are especially welcome on days when the sun isn't shining. When it is, get a table on the terrace out front—although the service, which is quick if you're sitting inside, usually slows down considerably.

3 Znojmo

119 miles SE of Prague, 40 miles S of Brno

Most travelers blow through Znojmo, the wine and pickle capital of the Czech Republic, at about 60 miles per hour, tired of getting caught behind trucks and buses that make the trip to Vienna a long 4-hour haul. But it wasn't always that way.

Znojmo was settled as far back as the 7th century, and the town gained prominence in the 9th century, when the Great Moravian Empire took control. In the 11th and 12th centuries, Prince Břetislav I constructed a fortress, and soon after, in 1226, the town was granted rights from the King—even before the Moravian capital of Brno. Znojmo's geographic position on the border made it a natural location as a trading center, and Czech kings always ensured the town was taken care of, using it as a lookout over the Austrian frontier. Unfortunately, the original town hall was destroyed during World War II, and the Communist-inspired sprawl that followed has taken away some of Znojmo's character. But the old center remains vibrant, and many religious buildings are still intact.

Why do the pickles taste so good? They are made from the best cucumbers the country has to offer. And when put into a spicy sauce, as they are in *Znojemské guláš*, they really taste great. These sweet and sour tasting pickles are also special because the town really plays them up. You'll get pickle fever too, I promise. When you do, and want to buy some, you'll notice just how many shops proudly display the Znojmo pickle.

And then there's the wine. If you're looking for the region's best vintages, look no further than Frankovka—a smooth, full-bodied red—or Ryzlink—a light, dry white—with Znojemské (from Znojmo) or Mikulov on the label. These superb wines are available almost everywhere; a liter bottle costs no more than $2 or $3 dollars. Wine bars often serve the best vintages straight from the cask; you can also fill up—both wine and fuel—at a gas station.

To best enjoy the town's wine and pickles, you should at least spend a few hours here, or stay overnight to sample some of the country's finest wines. Znojmo's location on the Prague-Vienna route makes it a natural place to stop. An added bonus is its proximity to Telč; you can see both in one day if you want.

SPECIAL EVENTS   In late August and early September, residents of Znojmo celebrate one of their most famous commodities at the **Znojmo Wine Festival.** Taste vintages, eat pickles, and listen to traditional Moravian music late into the usually tranquil night. For information contact **Informacní Středisko,** náměstí T.G. Masaryk 22, Znojmo, (☎ **0624/4369**).

ESSENTIALS

GETTING THERE   Znojmo is most easily reached by car, and is especially convenient for those heading to or from Vienna or Telč. Take the D1 highway from Prague and exit at highway 38 in the direction of Jihlava. As you enter the town you're already on the right highway, so just pass by the town center and follow the signs. From Prague the trip should take about 2¹/₂ hours.

Several trains leave Brno throughout the day, though some require a quick change in Hrušovany. The ride takes about 2 hours. From Prague, it's a 4-hour trip total; halfway, you must change in Jihlava.

You can also take one of three bus trips from Prague's Florenc station, but this 3-hour trip is more cramped and less fun. On the plus side, there's no transferring. From Brno, the trip is much quicker and less painful. Almost as many buses run between the two places as do trains.

ORIENTATION   Znojmo's main square is **náměstí T.G. Masaryk,** and pretty much all you will want to see is on or near it. **Zelenářská street,** which runs off of the square's northwest corner, leads to the castle and St. Nicholas Church.

VISITOR INFORMATION   Located in the center of the main square in Znojemská beseda, **Informacní Středisko,** náměstí T.G. Masaryk 22, Znojmo (☎ **0624/4369**), can help with accommodations, maps, and directions. Ask what's on in town, and they can book tickets for you on the spot. The office is open Monday through Friday from 8am to 8pm, Saturday 8am to noon.

A WALKING TOUR OF ZNOJMO

A walking tour of Znojmo takes about 2 or 3 hours. Begin at **Masaryk Square,** where the **Art House** (Dum umění) holds a small collection of coins, plus temporary exhibitions. The southern end of the square is one of the few historic areas that has not been maintained well; the dilapidated **Capuchin Monastery** (Kapučinsky klášter) and **Church of St. John the Baptist** show few signs that they were once focal points for the town.

Impossible to miss is the **Town Hall Tower,** the only remaining piece of what was once referred to as Moravia's prettiest town hall. The actual Town Hall met misfortune during World War II, but the late Gothic, 70-meter-high tower still stands guard. For 15 Kč (55¢), climb up to the lookout, which offers a picturesque view of the castle and the Dyje River below. Try not to let the nondescript department store that occupies the spot where the town hall once stood wreck the picture. Open May to September from 8:30am to 4pm daily, October to April from 9am to 3:30pm.

Directly north of the tower on Obrokova ulice is the entrance to the **Znojemské podzemí** (Znojmo Underground), where almost 30 kilometers of tunnels used to store everything from pickles to munitions are accessed. If there is a tour just leaving, or a few people waiting, arrange to join them since the tours (which are in Czech) are only given to groups of more than six people. Admission is 30 Kč ($1.11). Open May to September from 8:30am to 4pm, October to April 9am to 3:30pm.

Head back one-block west to Zelenářská ulice and follow it away from the square to Malá Mikulašská ulice, which leads to the Gothic **St. Nicholas Church** and behind it the two-level **St. Wenceslas Chapel.** The church is only supposed to be open for services and the occasional concert, but check the door just in case.

Further on you will come to the 11th-century **Rotunda Sv. Kateřiny,** one of the oldest and best examples of Romanesque architecture still standing in the Czech Republic. Inside you'll see painstakingly restored frescoes of the Přemyslid rulers dating back to the mid-12th century.

At the edge of the embankment lies the **Znojmo Castle,** which now houses the **Jihomoravské Muzeum** (South Moravian Museum). Admission is 15 Kč (55¢); if you take the tour, note that both sights are included in the tour price. Open Tuesday through Sunday from 9am to 4pm.

WHERE TO STAY

There's not much in the way of quality accommodations in Znojmo, which is probably one reason why so few people spend the night. If you choose to stay, your best option may prove to be the information center, which can arrange a private room. Expect to pay around 300 Kč ($11) per person.

Hotel Družba (Friendship Hotel)
Pražská 100, 669 02 Znojmo. ☎ **0624/756 21.** 60 rms. No credit cards. 680 Kč ($25) double.

Just off the road leading to Prague, the Družba is exactly what a Communist-era hotel was meant to be—adequate. The small but clean rooms are sparsely furnished with 1970s beds. En suite toilets and showers are a redeeming feature.

Hotel Dukla
Antonín Zápoteckého 5, Znojmo. ☎ **0624/763 20.** 110 rms. 765 Kč ($28) double. AE, DC, MC, V.

In the south part of Znojmo, the Dukla, which always has a free room, gets its name from the army, but is nicer than the barracks. Rooms are functional and clean.

WHERE TO DINE

Hotel Dukla Restaurace
Antonín Zápoteckého 5. ☎ **0624/763 20.** Soups 12–20 Kč (44¢–74¢), main courses 40–90 Kč ($1.48–$3.33). Daily 8am–11pm. CZECH.

The Painted Cellar of the Šatov Vineyard

Wine, art, and history aficionados unite! The painted cellar of Šatov, one of the region's most proliferate vineyards, awaits. But this isn't an ordinary tour of a vineyard, or just a historic place—it's both.

The town of Šatov lies just before the Austrian border, about 6 miles south of Znojmo. So close to the border, in fact, is Šatov, that it once was part of Austria. The town and its surrounding vineyards have long produced some of the country's finest Moravian wines. The town's excellent soil conditions and continental climate make it perfectly suited for grapes.

You'll find several cellars here, and during late autumn, Moravian hospitality opens the doors to just about anyone who knocks. Few, however, knock on the door of Josef Kučera, who can give a different sort of tour. Mr. Kučera, who once patrolled the border to ensure the vices of capitalism did not breach the country, will happily lead you down a hidden path for about a half-mile until you get to a small, unassuming house.

The house's cellar was most likely carved out in the late 19th century for reasons still a mystery today, but took on its current form when a one-armed man named Max Appeltauer took to the tunnels and began his work here in 1934. As you enter the cellar and descend about 20 yards, a musty odor envelops you, and you wonder how Appeltauer could have spent so much time here. But as you look around the 22-yard tunnel, you will be thankful he did. Not an artist by trade, Appeltauer set to carving and then painting into the sandstone walls an eclectic set of scenes portaying everything from Prague Castle to Snow White and the Seven Dwarves, as well as the Šatov coat of arms. Running off of the main tunnel are five smaller rooms, each depicting a separate theme and carved and painted to painstaking detail. It's almost as though Appeltauer was expecting one day to escape to his residence inside the cellar, celebrating his departure from life above ground. Indeed, celebrating had already taken place inside the dark cellar, as the inscription *"Vino, žena a zpěv, zahladí veškery hněv"* ("Wine, women, and song will remove all anger") indicates. Kučera will tell you that the cellar was at one time a popular place, where the masses gathered after Mass, girlfriends and all. Wives searching for their husbands would often enter, sending girlfriends scurrying into the sub-cellar. Local lore has it that Hitler visited the cellar when inspecting the military bunkers set up to defend his southern flank.

Appeltauer left the cellar for good in 1968, and died four years later, never realizing his next dream—to paint further into the cellar. Some cans of paint and a few jars still sit idly by at the point where he stopped, untouched after 25 years of waiting for the party that never came.

To get to Šatov by car or bike, take highway 59 out of Znojmo to the south, and turn right at the sign for Šatov. Buses and trains also run to the village from Znojmo on a regular basis.

Kučera will kindly give tours of the cellar for 5 Kč (18¢) a person, but he only speaks Czech, so you'll need to take along someone who can translate or at least communicate in rudimentary Czech. His wife says she will give tours in German if need be. Call at least one day in advance, so the Kučeras can arrange their schedule (☎ 0624/7178).

The restaurant's setting is a bit sterile, but you'll find hearty, basic Czech meals here. For a local flavor, try the tasty Znojemsky goulash, made with (what else?) Znojmo pickles.

Morava

Horní náměstí 17. No phone. Soups 15–25 Kč (56¢–93¢), main courses 70–225 Kč ($2.59–$8.33). No credit cards. Daily 10am–10pm. CZECH/INTERNATIONAL.

This small restaurant has a relatively big selection of meals, and, not surprisingly, a good choice of Moravian wines. Many items on the menu may look similar to those in other Czech restaurants, but the cooking has a south Moravian accent, so it's a pleasant surprise when meals like goulash come to the table with a little more spice. The Morava also has several pork dishes that are well-prepared with a nice blend of picante spices.

Appendix

A Czech Basic Phrases & Vocabulary

CZECH ALPHABET

There are 32 vowels and consonants in the Czech alphabet, and most of the consonants are pronounced about as they are in English. Accent marks over vowels lengthen the sound of the vowel, as does the *kroužek*, or little circle ("°"), which appears only over "o" and "u."

A, a f*a*ther	N, n *n*o
B, b *b*oy	Ň, ň Ta*ny*a
C, c get*s*	O, o *aw*ful
Č, č *ch*oice	P, p *p*en
D, d *d*ay	R, r slightly trilled *r*
Ď, ď *Di*or	Ř, ř slightly trilled *r* + *sh* as in cru*sh*
E, e n*e*ver	S, s *s*eat
F, f *f*ood	Š, š cru*sh*
G, g *g*oal	T, t *t*oo
H, h un*h*and	Ť, ť no*t* *y*et
Ch, ch Lo*ch* Lomond	U, u r*oo*m
I, i n*ee*d	V, v *v*ery
J, j *y*es	W, w *v*ague
K, k *k*ey	Y, y funn*y*
L, l *l*ord	Z, z *z*ebra
M, m *m*ama	Ž, ž a*z*ure, plea*s*ure

CZECH VOCABULARY

Everyday Expressions

English	Czech	Pronunciation
Hello	**Dobrý den**	*daw*-bree den
Good morning	**Dobré jitro**	*daw*-breh *yee*-traw
Good evening	**Dobrý večer**	*daw*-bree *veh*-chair
How are you?	**Jak se máte?**	*yahk* seh *mah*-teh
Very well	**Velmi dobře**	*vel*-mee *daw*-brsheh
Thank you	**Děkuji vam**	*dyek*-ooee vahm
You're welcome	**Prosím**	*praw*-seem
Please	**Prosím**	*praw*-seem
Yes	**Ano**	*ah*-no
No	**Ne**	neh
Excuse me	**Promiňte**	*praw*-min-teh

How much does it cost?	**Kolik to stojí?**	*kaw*-leek taw *staw*-ee
I don't understand.	**Nerozumím.**	*neh*-raw-zoo-meem
Just a moment.	**Moment, prosím.**	*maw*-ment, *praw*-seem
Good-bye	**Na shledanou**	*nah* skleh-dah-noh-oo

TRAVELING

Where is the . . . ?	**Kde je . . . ?**	*gde* yeh . . . ?
bus station	**autobusové nádrazí**	*ahoo*-taw-boos-oh-veh *nah*-drah-shee
train station	**nádrazí**	*nah*-drah-shee
airport	**letiště**	*leh*-tyish-tyeh
baggage check	**úschovna zavazadel**	*oo*-skohv-nah *zah*-vahz-ah-del
Where can I find a taxi?	**Kde najdu taxi?**	*gde nai*-doo *tahks*-eh
Where can I find a gas station?	**Kde najdu benzínovou pumpu?**	*gde nai*-doo *ben*-zeen-oh-voh *poomp*-oo
How much is gas?	**Kolik stojí benzín?**	*koh*-leek *stoh*-yee *ben*-zeen
Please fill the tank.	**Naplňte mi nádrž, prosím.**	*nah*-puln-teh mee *nah*-dursh, *praw*-seem.
How much is the fare?	**Kolik je jízdné?**	*koh*-leek yeh yeesd-neh
I am going to . . .	**Pojedu do . . .**	*poh*-yeh-doo doh . . .
One-way ticket	**Jízdenka**	*yeez*-den-kah
Round-trip ticket	**Zpáteční jízdenka**	*zpah*-tech-nee *jeez*-den-kah
Car-rental office	**Pujčovna aut**	*poo*-eech-awv-nah ah-oot

ACCOMMODATIONS

I'm looking for . . .	**Hledám . . .**	*hleh*-dahm . . .
a hotel	**hotel**	*haw*-tel
a youth hostel	**studentskou ubytovnu**	*stoo*-dent-skoh *oo*-beet-ohv-noo
I am staying . . .	**Z(u)stanu . . .**	zoo-stah-noo . . .
a few days	**několik dn(u)**	*nyeh*-koh-leek dnoo
two weeks	**dva týdny**	dvah tid-*neh*
a month	**jeden měsíc**	*yeh*-den *myeh*-seets
I have a reservation.	**Mám zamluvený nocleh.**	mahm *zah*-mloo-veh-ni *nawts*-leh.
My name is . . .	**Jmenují se . . .**	*meh*-noo-yee seh . . .
Do you have a room . . . ?	**Máte pokoj . . . ?**	*mah*-teh *poh*-koy . . . ?
for tonight	**na dnešek**	*nah* dneh-sheck
for three nights	**na tři dny**	*nah* trshee dnee
for a week	**na týden**	*nah* tee-den
I would like . . .	**Chci . . .**	khtsee . . .
a single	**jednol(u)žkový pokoj**	*jed*-noh-loosh-koh-vee *poh*-koy
a double	**dvojl(u)žkový pokoj**	*dvoy*-loosh-koh-vee *poh*-koy
I want a room . . .	**Chci pokoj . . .**	khtsee *poh*-koy . . .
with a bath	**s koupelnou**	*skoh*-pehl-noh
without a bath	**bez koupelny**	*behz* koh-pehl-nee
with a shower	**se sprchou**	*seh* spur-choh
without a shower	**bez sprchy**	*bez* sprech-eh
with a view	**s pohledem**	*spoh*-hlehd-ehm

How much is the room?	**Kolik stojí pokoj?**	*koh*-leek *stoh*-yee *paw*-koy?
with breakfast?	**se snídaní?**	*seh* snee-dan-nyee
May I see the room?	**Mohu vidět ten pokoj?**	*moh*-hoo *vee*-dyet ten *paw*-koy
The key	**Klíč**	kleech
The bill, please.	**Dejte mi učet, prosím.**	*day*-teh mee *oo*-cheht, *praw*-seem

GETTING AROUND

I'm looking for . . .	**Hledám . . .**	*hleh*-dahm . . .
a bank	**banku**	*bahnk*-oo
the church	**kostel**	*kaws*-tell
the city center	**centrum**	*tsent*-room
the museum	**muzeum**	*moo*-zeh-oom
a pharmacy	**lekarnu**	*lek*-ahr-noo
the park	**park**	pahrk
the theater	**divadlo**	*dee*-vahd-loh
the tourist office	**cestovní kancelář**	*tses*-tohv-nee *kahn*-teh-larsh
the embassy	**velvyslanectví**	*vehl*-vee-slahn-ets-tvee
Where is the nearest telephone?	**Kde je nejbližší telefon?**	gde yeh *nay*-bleesh-ee *tel*-oh-fohn
I would like to buy . . .	**Chci koupit . . .**	khtsee *koh*-peet . . .
a stamp	**známku**	*znahm*-koo
a postcard	**pohlednici**	*poh*-hlehd-nit-seh
a map	**mapu**	*mahp*-oo

SIGNS

No Trespassing	**Cizím vstup zakázán**	No Smoking	**Kouření zakázáno**
No Parking	**Neparkovat**	Arrivals	**Príjezd**
Entrance	**Vchod**	Departures	**Odjezd**
Exit	**Východ**	Toilets	**Toalety**
Information	**Informace**	Danger	**Pozor, nebezpecí**

NUMBERS

1	**jeden** (*yeh*-den)	16	**šestnáct** (*shest*-nahtst)
2	**dva** (dvah)	17	**sedmnáct** (*seh*-doom- nahtst)
3	**tři** (trshee)	18	**osmnáct** (*aw*-soom-nahtst)
4	**čtyři** (*chtee*-rshee)	19	**devatenáct** (*deh*-vah-teh-nahtst)
5	**pět** (pyet)	20	**dvacet** (*dvah*-tset)
6	**šest** (shest)	30	**třicet** (*trshee*-tset)
7	**sedm** (*seh*-duhm)	40	**čtyřicet** (*chti*-rshee-tset)
8	**osm** (*aw*-suhm)	50	**padesát** (*pah*-deh-saht)
9	**devět** (*deh*-vyet)	60	**šedesát** (*she*-deh-saht)
10	**deset** (*deh*-set)	70	**sedmdesát** (*seh*-duhm-deh-saht)
11	**jedenáct** (*yeh*-deh-nahtst)	80	**osmdesát** (*aw*-suhm-deh-saht)
12	**dvanáct** (*dvah*-nahtst)	90	**devadesát** (*deh*-vah-deh-saht)
13	**třináct** (*trshee*-nahtst)	100	**sto** (staw)
14	**čtrnáct** (*chtur*-nahtst)	500	**pět set** (*pyet* set)
15	**patnáct** (*paht*-nahtst)	1,000	**tisíc** (*tyee*-seets)

DINING

Restaurant	**Restaurace**	*rehs*-tow-rah-tseh
Breakfast	**Snídaně**	*snee*-dah-nyeh
Lunch	**Oběd**	*oh*-byed
Dinner	**Večeře**	*veh*-chair-sheh
A table for two, please. (Lit.: There are two of us.)	**Jsme dva.**	*ees*-meh dvah
Waiter	**Císník**	*cheess*-neek
Waitress	**Servírka**	ser-*veer*-ka
I would like . . .	**Chci . . .**	khtsee . . .
a menu	**jídelní lístek**	*yee*-del-nee *lees*-teck
a fork	**vidličku**	*veed*-leech-koo
a knife	**n(u)ž**	noosh
a spoon	**lžičku**	lu-*shich*-koo
a napkin	**ubrousek**	*oo*-broh-seck
a glass (of water)	**skleničku (vody)**	*sklehn*-ich-koo (vod-*deh*)
the check, please	**účet, prosím**	*oo*-cheht, *praw*-seem
Is the tip included?	**Je v tom zahrnuto spropitné?**	yeh *ftohm*-zah *hur*-noo-toh *sproh*-peet-neh?

B   Menu Terms

GENERAL

Soup	**Polévka**	*poh*-lehv-kah
Eggs	**Vejce**	*vayts*-eh
Meat	**Maso**	*mahs*-oh
Fish	**Ryba**	*ree*-bah
Vegetables	**Zelenina**	*zehl*-eh-nee-nah
Fruit	**Ovoce**	*oh*-voh-tseh
Desserts	**Moučníky**	*mohch*-nee-kee
Beverages	**Nápoje**	*nah*-poy-yeh
Salt	**S(u)l**	sool
Pepper	**Pepř**	*peh*-prsh
Mayonnaise	**Majonéza**	*mai*-o-neza
Mustard	**Hořčice**	*hohrsh*-chee-tseh
Vinegar	**Ocet**	*oh*-tseht
Oil	**Olej**	*oh*-lay
Sugar	**Cukr**	*tsoo*-ker
Tea	**čaj**	chye
Coffee	**Káva**	*kah*-vah
Bread	**Chléba**	*khlehb*-ah
Butter	**Máslo**	*mahs*-loh
Wine	**Víno**	*vee*-noh
Fried	**Smažený**	*smah*-sheh-nee
Roasted	**Pečený**	*pech*-eh-nee
Boiled	**Vařený**	*vah*-rsheh-nee
Grilled	**Grilovaný**	*gree*-loh-vah-nee

SOUP

Bramborová potato
čočková lentil
Gulášová goulash

Rajaská tomato
Slepicí chicken
Zeleninová vegetable

MEAT

Biftek steak
Guláš goulash
Hovězi beef
Játra liver
Jehněcí lamb
Kachna duck

Klobása sausage
Králík rabbit
Skopové mutton
Telecí veal
Telecí kotleta veal cutlet
Vepřové pork

FISH

Karp carp
Kaviár caviar
Rybí filé fish filet
Sled herring

štika pike
Treska cod
Úhoř eel
Ústřice oysters

EGGS

Míchaná vejce scrambled eggs
Smažená vejce fried eggs
Vařená vejce boiled eggs

Vejce na měkko soft-boiled eggs
Vejce se slaninou bacon and eggs
Vejce se šunkou ham and eggs

SALAD

Fazolový salát bean salad
Hlávkový salát mixed green salad

Okurkový salát cucumber salad
Salát z červené řepy beet salad

VEGETABLES

Brambory potatoes
Celer celery
Chřest asparagus
Cibule onions
Houby mushrooms

Květák cauliflower
Mrkev carrots
Paprika peppers
Rajská jablíčka tomatoes
Zelí cabbage

DESSERT

Koláč cake
Cukrovi cookies
čokoládová zmrzlina chocolate ice cream

Jablkový závin apple strudel
Palačinky pancakes
Vanilková zmrzlina vanilla ice cream

FRUIT

Citrón lemon
Hruška pears

Jablko apple
švestky plums

BEVERAGE

čaj tea
Káva coffee
Mléko milk
Víno wine

cervené red
bílé white
Voda water

Index*

*Unless specified, hotels, restaurants, and attractions are located in Prague. Abbreviations for other cities are as follows: ČB=České Budějovice; FL=Františkovy Lázně; KV=Karlovy Vary; ML=Mariánské Lázně.

FROMMER'S COMPLETE TRAVEL GUIDES
(Comprehensive guides to sightseeing, dining, and accommodations, with selections in all price ranges from deluxe to budget)

Acapulco/Ixtapa/Taxco, 2nd Ed.
Alaska, 4th Ed.
Arizona '96
Australia, 4th Ed.
Austria, 6th Ed.
Bahamas '96
Belgium/Holland/Luxembourg, 4th Ed.
Bermuda '96
Budapest & the Best of Hungary, 1st Ed.
California '96
Canada, 9th Ed.
Caribbean '96
Carolinas/Georgia, 3rd Ed.
Colorado, 3rd Ed.
Costa Rica, 1st Ed.
Cruises '95-'96
Delaware/Maryland, 2nd Ed.
England '96
Florida '96
France '96
Germany '96
Greece, 1st Ed.
Honolulu/Waikiki/Oahu, 4th Ed.
Ireland, 1st Ed.
Italy '96
Jamaica/Barbados, 2nd Ed.
Japan, 3rd Ed.
Maui, 1st Ed.
Mexico '96
Montana/Wyoming, 1st Ed.
Nepal, 3rd Ed.
New England '96
New Mexico, 3rd Ed.
New York State '94-'95
Nova Scotia/New Brunswick/Prince Edward Island, 1st Ed.
Portugal, 14th Ed.
Prague & the Best of the Czech Republic, 1st Ed.
Puerto Rico '95-'96
Puerto Vallarta/Manzanillo/Guadalajara, 3rd Ed.
Scandinavia, 16th Ed.
Scotland, 3rd Ed.
South Pacific, 5th Ed.
Spain, 16th Ed.
Switzerland, 7th Ed.
Thailand, 2nd Ed.
U.S.A., 4th Ed.
Utah, 1st Ed.
Virgin Islands, 3rd Ed.
Virginia, 3rd Ed.
Washington/Oregon, 6th Ed.
Yucatan '95-'96

FROMMER'S FRUGAL TRAVELER'S GUIDES
(Dream vacations at down-to-earth prices)

Australia on $45 '95-'96
Berlin from $50, 3rd Ed.
Caribbean from $60, 1st Ed.
Costa Rica/Guatemala/Belize on $35, 3rd Ed.
Eastern Europe on $30, 5th Ed.
England from $50, 21st Ed.
Europe from $50 '96
Greece from $45, 6th Ed.
Hawaii from $60, 30th Ed.
Ireland from $45, 16th Ed.
Israel from $45, 16th Ed.
London from $60 '96
Mexico from $35 '96
New York on $70 '94-'95
New Zealand from $45, 6th Ed.
Paris from $65 '96
South America on $40, 16th Ed.
Washington, D.C. from $50 '96

FROMMER'S COMPLETE CITY GUIDES
(Comprehensive guides to sightseeing, dining, and accommodations in all price ranges)

Amsterdam, 8th Ed.
Athens, 10th Ed.
Atlanta & the Summer Olympic Games '96
Bangkok, 2nd Ed.
Berlin, 3rd Ed.
Boston '96

Chicago '96
Denver/Boulder/Colorado Springs, 2nd Ed.
Disney World/Orlando '96
Dublin, 2nd Ed.
Hong Kong, 4th Ed.
Las Vegas '96
London '96
Los Angeles '96
Madrid/Costa del Sol, 2nd Ed.
Mexico City, 1st Ed.
Miami '95-'96
Minneapolis/St. Paul, 4th Ed.
Montreal/Quebec City, 8th Ed.
Nashville/Memphis, 2nd Ed.
New Orleans '96
New York City '96

Paris '96
Philadelphia, 8th Ed.
Rome, 10th Ed.
St. Louis/Kansas City, 2nd Ed.
San Antonio/Austin, 1st Ed.
San Diego, 4th Ed.
San Francisco '96
Santa Fe/Taos/Albuquerque '96
Seattle/Portland, 4th Ed.
Sydney, 4th Ed.
Tampa/St. Petersburg, 3rd Ed.
Tokyo, 4th Ed.
Toronto, 3rd Ed.
Vancouver/Victoria, 3rd Ed.
Washington, D.C. '96

FROMMER'S FAMILY GUIDES

(Guides to family-friendly hotels, restaurants, activities, and attractions)

California with Kids
Los Angeles with Kids
New York City with Kids

San Francisco with Kids
Washington, D.C. with Kids

FROMMER'S WALKING TOURS

(Memorable strolls through colorful and historic neighborhoods, accompanied by detailed directions and maps)

Berlin
Chicago
England's Favorite Cities
London, 2nd Ed.
Montreal/Quebec City
New York, 2nd Ed.

Paris, 2nd Ed.
San Francisco, 2nd Ed.
Spain's Favorite Cities
Tokyo
Venice
Washington, D.C., 2nd Ed.

FROMMER'S AMERICA ON WHEELS

(Guides for travelers who are exploring the USA by car, featuring a brand-new rating system for accommodations and full-color road maps)

Arizona and New Mexico
California and Nevada

Florida
Mid-Atlantic

FROMMER'S SPECIAL-INTEREST TITLES

Arthur Frommer's Branson!
Arthur Frommer's New World of Travel,
  5th Ed.
Frommer's America's 100 Best-Loved
  State Parks
Frommer's Caribbean Hideaways, 7th Ed.
Frommer's Complete Hostel Vacation Guide
  to England, Scotland & Wales

Frommer's National Park Guide, 29th Ed.
USA Sports Traveler's and TV Viewer's
  Golf Tournament Guide
USA Sports Minor League Baseball Book
USA Today Golf Atlas

FROMMER'S BEST BEACH VACATIONS

(The top places to sun, stroll, shop, stay, play, party, and swim, with each beach rated for beauty, swimming, sand, and amenities)

California
Carolinas/Georgia
Florida
Hawaii

Mid-Atlantic from New York to
    Washington, D.C.
New England

FROMMER'S BED & BREAKFAST GUIDES

(Selective guides with four-color photos and full description of the best inns in each region)

California
Caribbean
Great American Cities
Hawaii
Mid-Atlantic

New England
Pacific Northwest
Rockies
Southeast States
Southwest

FROMMER'S IRREVERENT GUIDES

(Wickedly honest guides for sophisticated travelers and those who want to be)

Amsterdam
Chicago
London

Manhattan
New Orleans
San Francisco

FROMMER'S DRIVING TOURS

(Four-color photos and detailed maps outlining spectacular scenic driving routes)

Australia
Austria
Britain
Florida
France
Germany
Ireland

Italy
Scandinavia
Scotland
Spain
Switzerland
U.S.A.

FROMMER'S BORN TO SHOP

(The ultimate travel guides for discriminating shoppers from cut-rate to couture)

Great Britain
Hong Kong

London
New York

FROMMER'S FOOD LOVER'S COMPANIONS

(Lavishly illustrated guides to regional specialties, restaurants, gourmet shops, markets, local wines, and more)

France
Italy